goats

infinite
typewriters

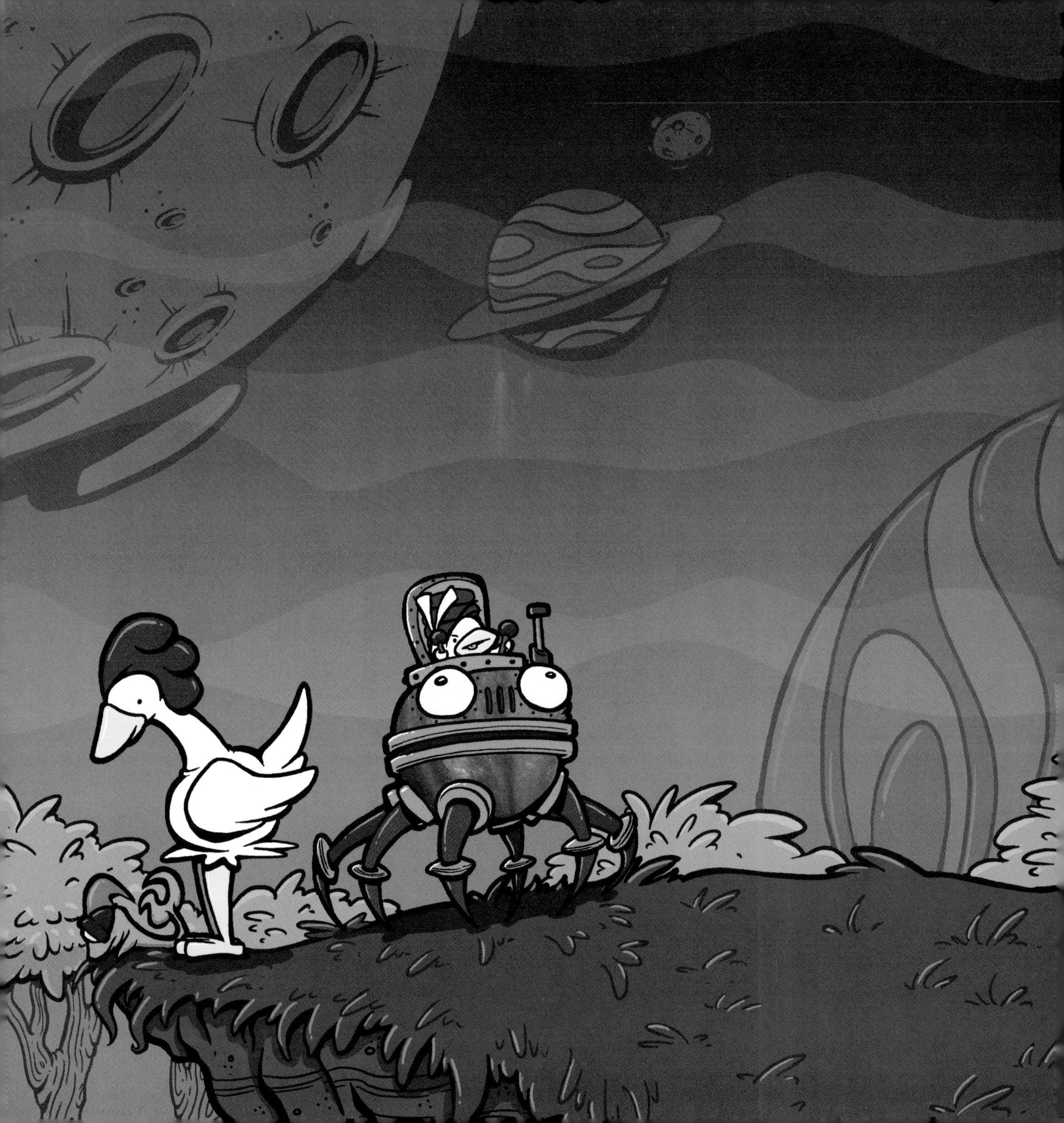

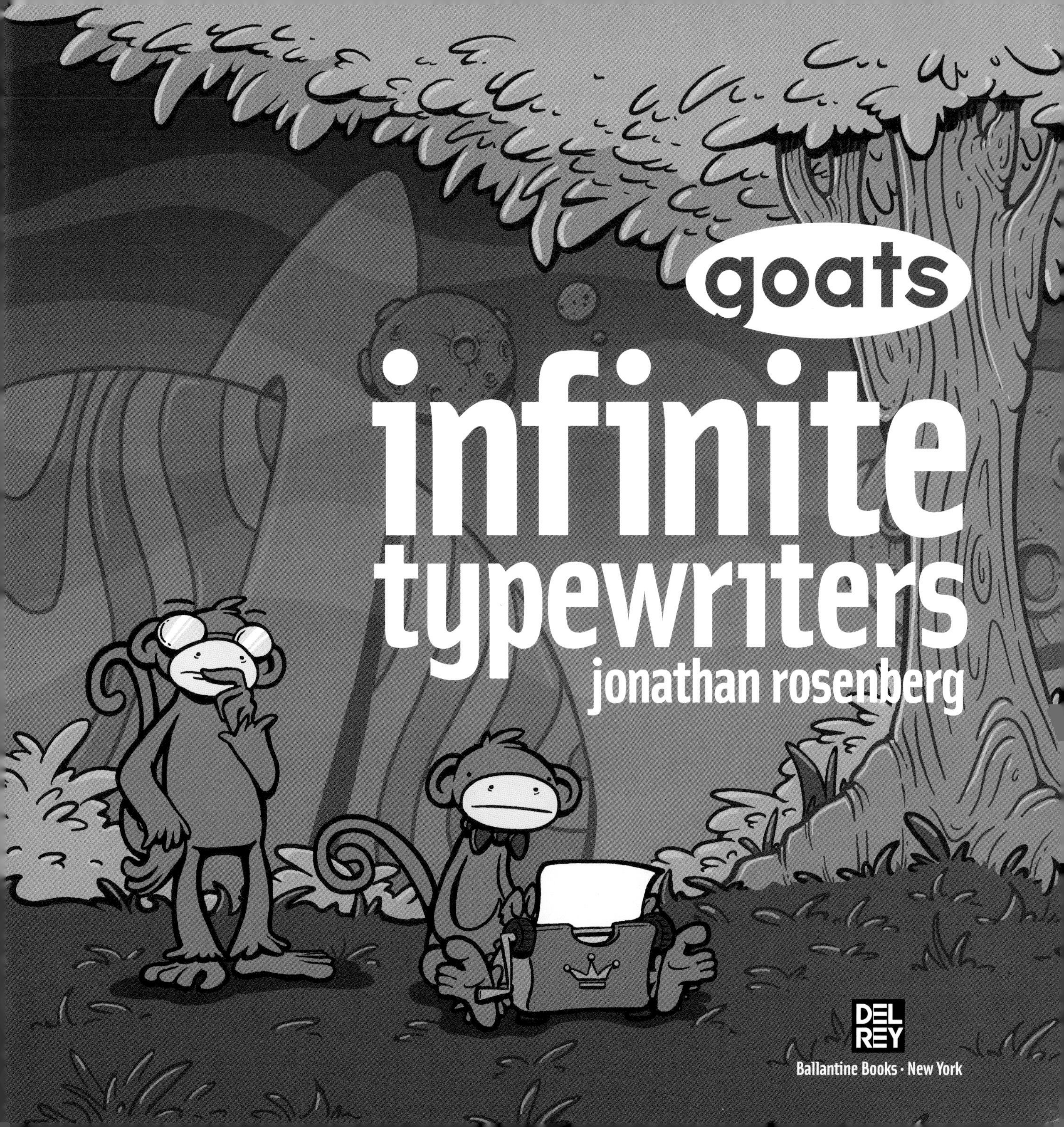

goats
infinite typewriters

jonathan rosenberg

DEL REY
Ballantine Books · New York

Goats: Infinite Typewriters is a work of fiction. All incidents and dialogue, and all characters with the exception of some well-known public figures, are products of the author's imagination and are not to be construed as real. Where real-life public figures appear, the situations, incidents, and dialogues concerning those persons are entirely fictional and are not intended to depict actual events or to change the entirely fictional nature of the work. In all other respects, any resemblance to persons living or dead is entirely coincidental.

A Del Rey Trade Paperback Original

Published in the United States by Del Rey, an imprint of The Random House Publishing Group, a division of Random House, Inc., New York.

Originally published on www.goats.com

ISBN 978-0-345-51092-1

www.goats.com
www.delreybooks.com

9 8 7 6 5 4 3 2 1

Designer: Amy Melnikoff Rosenberg

For Norah

With special thanks to: Phillip Karlsson, Lauren Karlsson, Rich Stevens, Meredith Gran, Jeffrey Rowland, Holly Post, John Allison, Andrew Bell, Jackie MacLeod, Steven Cloud, Ellie Jostad, Sam Brown, Mrs. Sam Brown, Chris Hastings, Carly Monardo, Rene Engström, Rick Marshall, Brian Warmoth, Gary Tyrell, M.C. Frontalot, Kurt Brunetto, Melissa Melville, Vincent LaBate, Dave Bort, Ferocious Jon Sung, Alfred Rutz, Ken Hauptman, Mark Skolnick, Lore Sjöberg, Stewart O'Nan, Charlie Stross, Wil Wheaton, Scott McCloud, Paul Southworth, Kris Straub, Dave Kellett, Brad Guigar, Scott Kurtz, Jerry Holkins, Mike Krahulik, Jeph Jacques, Darren Bleuel, Jeff Zugale, Kazu Kibuishi, Kean Soo, Jeff Lowrey, Rich Kempter, Simon Larsen, Erich Schoeneweiss, Dave Stevenson, Dallas Middaugh, Tricia Narwani, Nick Harris, Sylvie Rabineau, and Judy Hansen. Special huge thanks to Mom, Dad, Seth, Amy, and Norah, for all your love and support.

Foreword

I honestly can't stand *Goats*.

Is it the vile, satanic poultry? Not really. I've sort of come to terms with it.

Is it the author's unctuous political screeds? No. Actually, I agree on virtually all counts.

Is it the lemon, then? The desolate, glowing lemon?

Perhaps it's the way *Goats: The Comic Strip* teaches us all a little about ourselves.

There are literally thousands of crimes or near crimes I could catalog, but I guess the rest of this book is full of comics.

No, it's that when Jon Rosenberg toils for our amusement, he hits the mark unerringly — and he doesn't have the simple decency to make it look difficult.

Tycho Brahe
Seattle, Washington

goats

infinite
typewriters

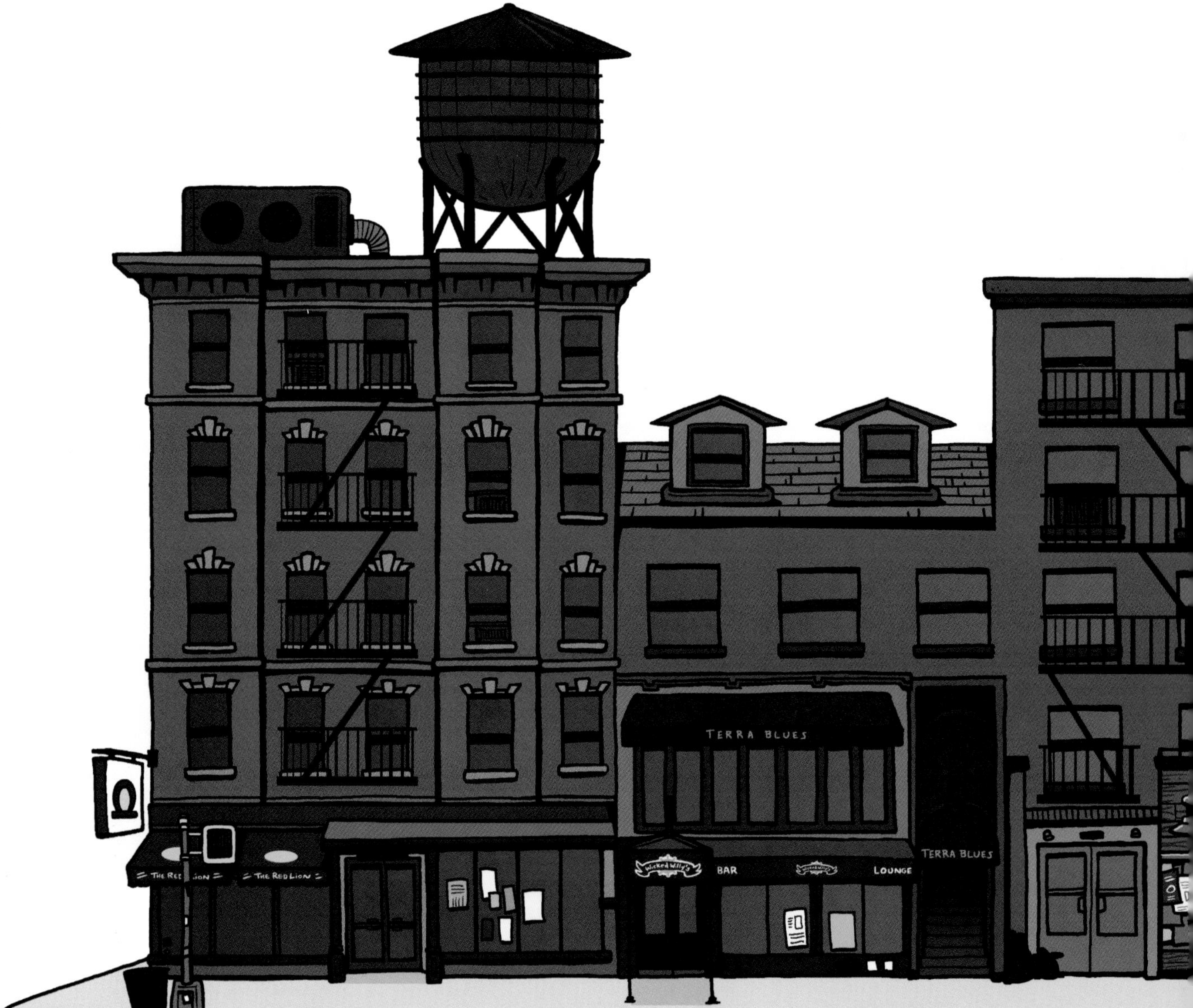

TERRA BLUES
THE RED LION
THE RED LION
Wicked Willy's
BAR
LOUNGE
TERRA BLUES

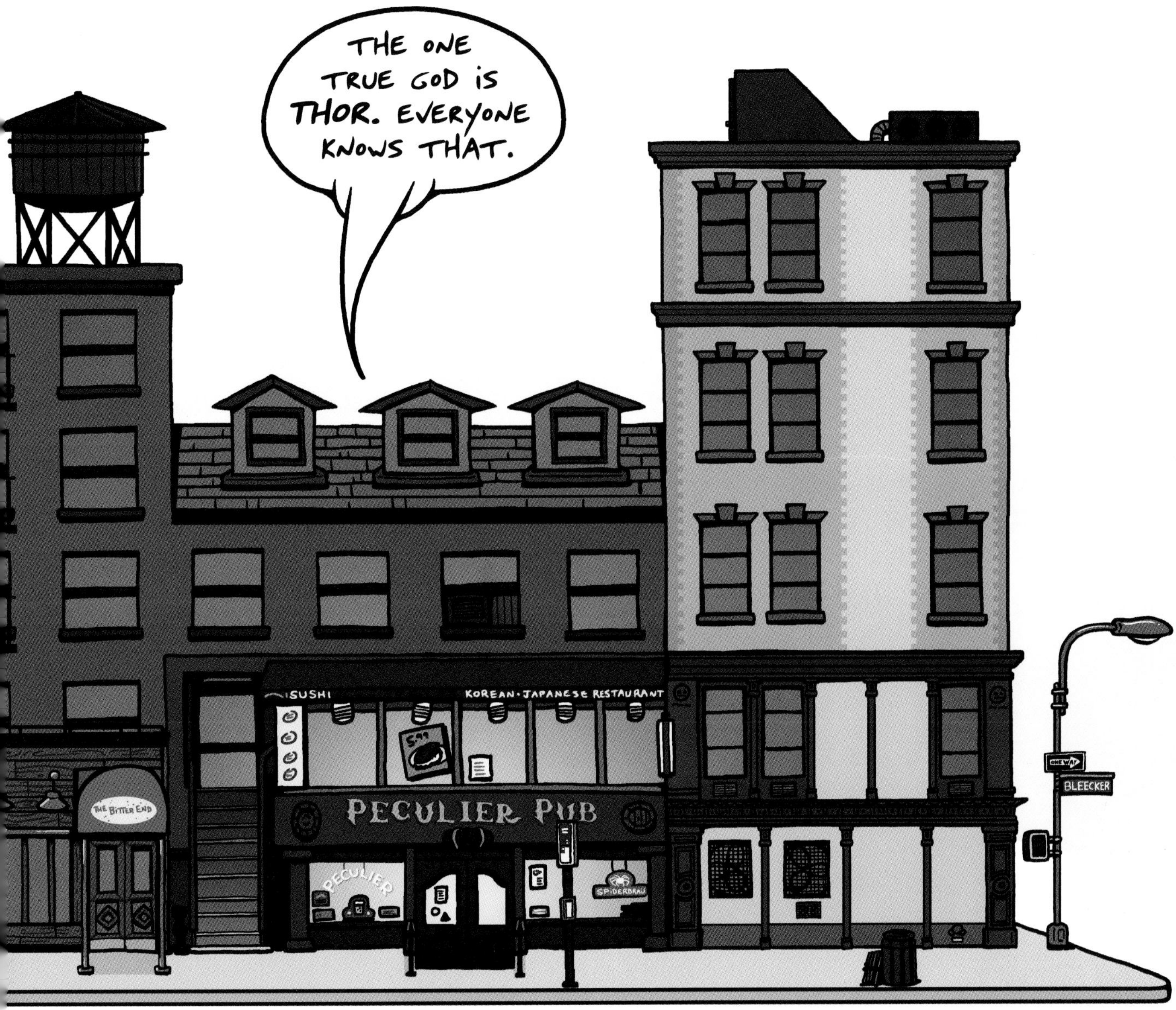
THE ONE TRUE GOD is THOR. EVERYONE KNOWS THAT.
THE BITTER END
SUSHI
KOREAN·JAPANESE RESTAURANT
PECULIER PUB
PECULIER
SPIDERBRAU
ONE WAY
BLEECKER

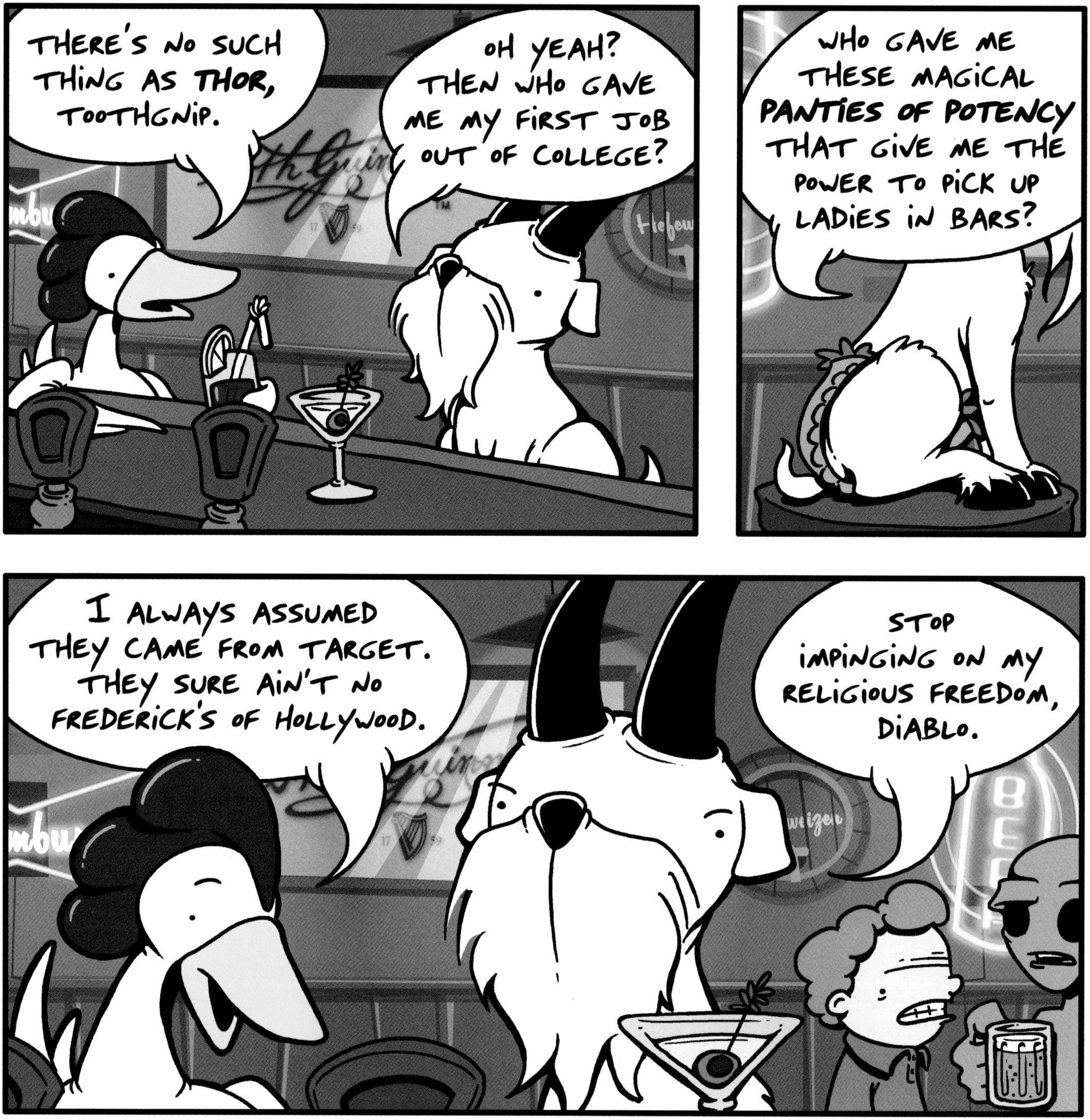
THERE'S NO SUCH THING AS THOR, TOOTHGNIP.
OH YEAH? THEN WHO GAVE ME MY FIRST JOB OUT OF COLLEGE?
WHO GAVE ME THESE MAGICAL PANTIES OF POTENCY THAT GIVE ME THE POWER TO PICK UP LADIES IN BARS?
I ALWAYS ASSUMED THEY CAME FROM TARGET. THEY SURE AIN'T NO FREDERICK'S OF HOLLYWOOD.
STOP IMPINGING ON MY RELIGIOUS FREEDOM, DIABLO.

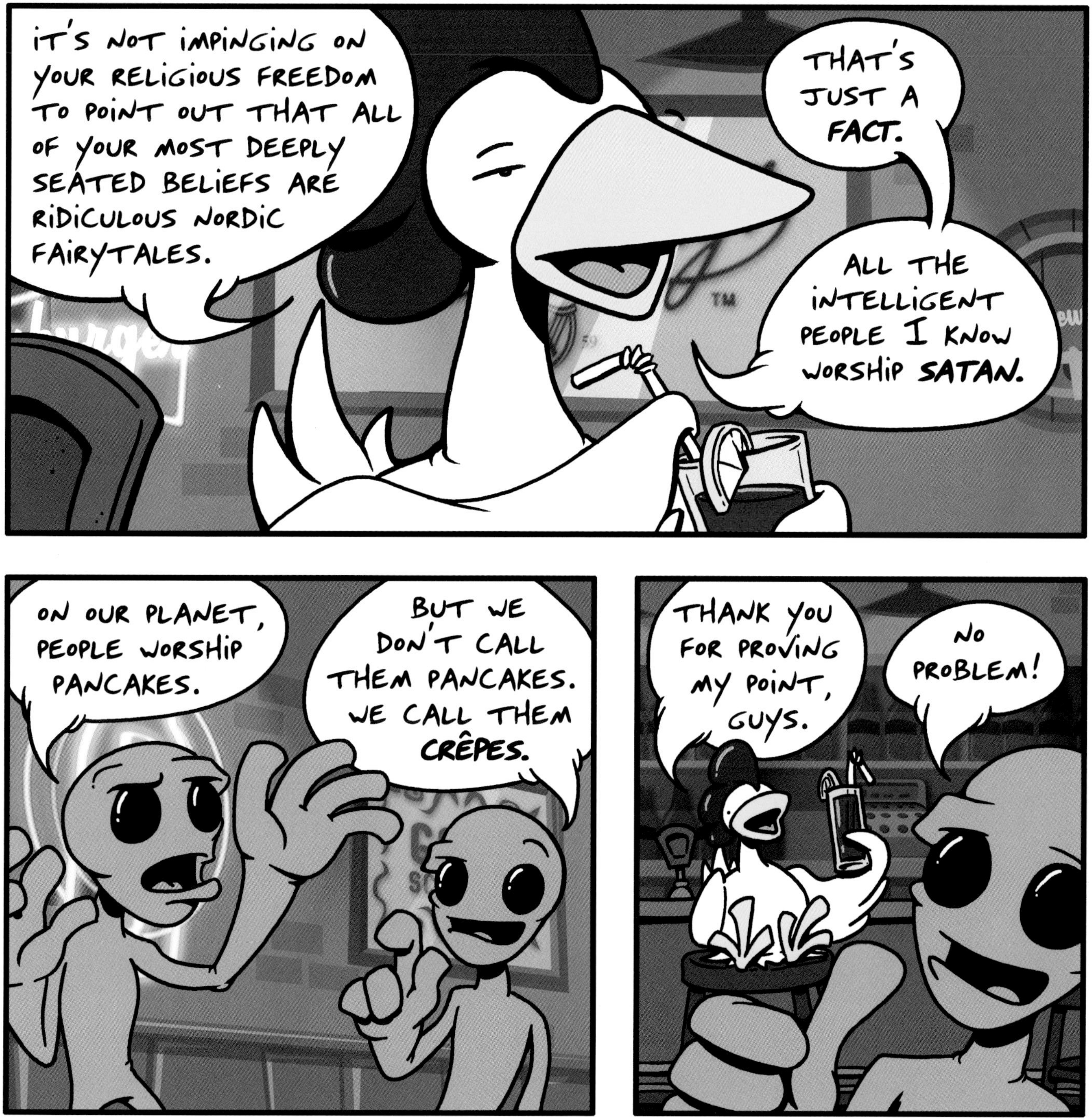
IT'S NOT IMPINGING ON YOUR RELIGIOUS FREEDOM TO POINT OUT THAT ALL OF YOUR MOST DEEPLY SEATED BELIEFS ARE RIDICULOUS NORDIC FAIRYTALES.
THAT'S JUST A **FACT.**
ALL THE INTELLIGENT PEOPLE I KNOW WORSHIP **SATAN.**
ON OUR PLANET, PEOPLE WORSHIP PANCAKES.
BUT WE DON'T CALL THEM PANCAKES. WE CALL THEM **CRÊPES.**
THANK YOU FOR PROVING MY POINT, GUYS.
NO PROBLEM!

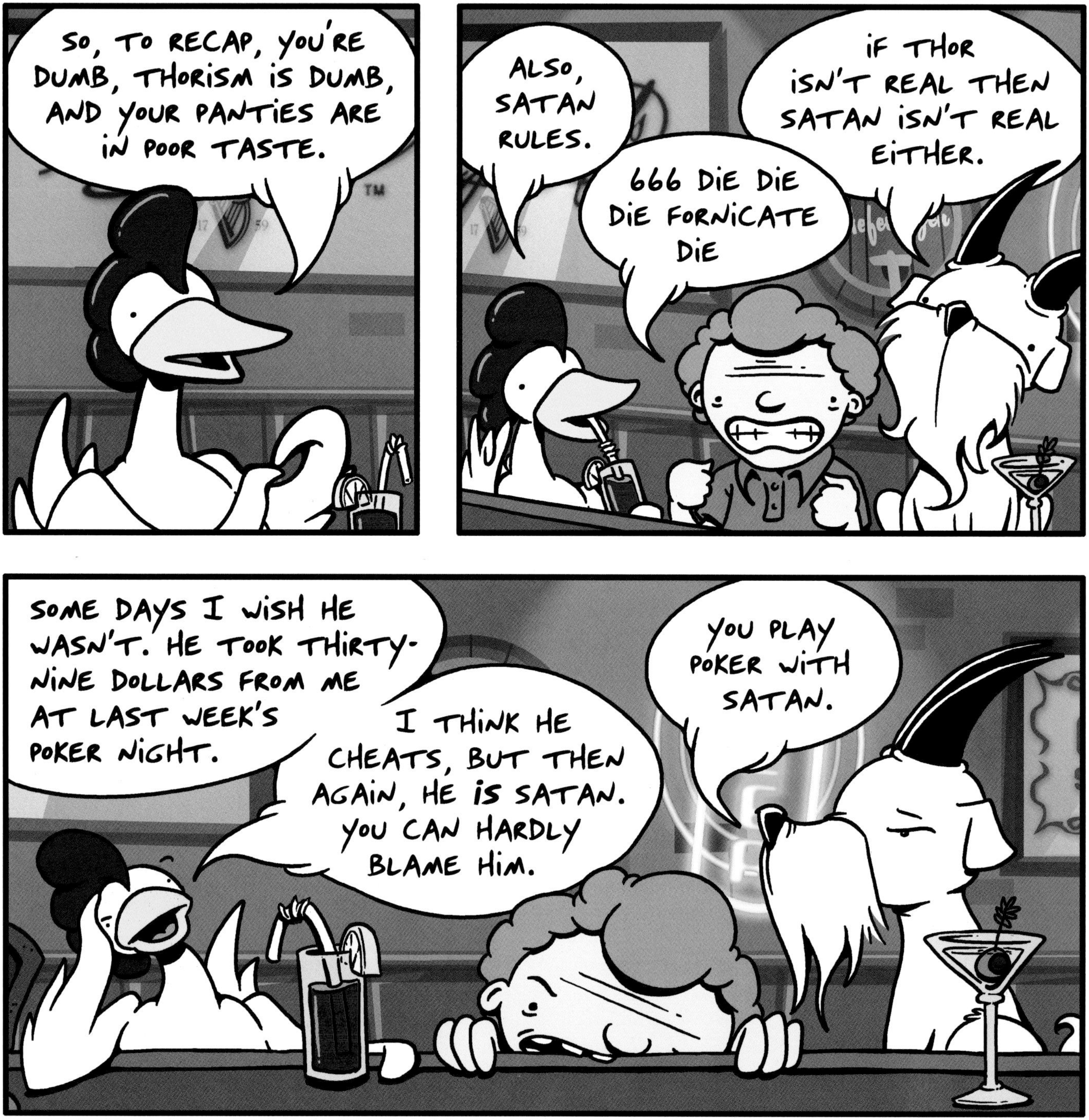
SO, TO RECAP, YOU'RE DUMB, THORISM IS DUMB, AND YOUR PANTIES ARE IN POOR TASTE.
ALSO, SATAN RULES.
666 DIE DIE DIE FORNICATE DIE
IF THOR ISN'T REAL THEN SATAN ISN'T REAL EITHER.
SOME DAYS I WISH HE WASN'T. HE TOOK THIRTY-NINE DOLLARS FROM ME AT LAST WEEK'S POKER NIGHT.
I THINK HE CHEATS, BUT THEN AGAIN, HE IS SATAN. YOU CAN HARDLY BLAME HIM.
YOU PLAY POKER WITH SATAN.

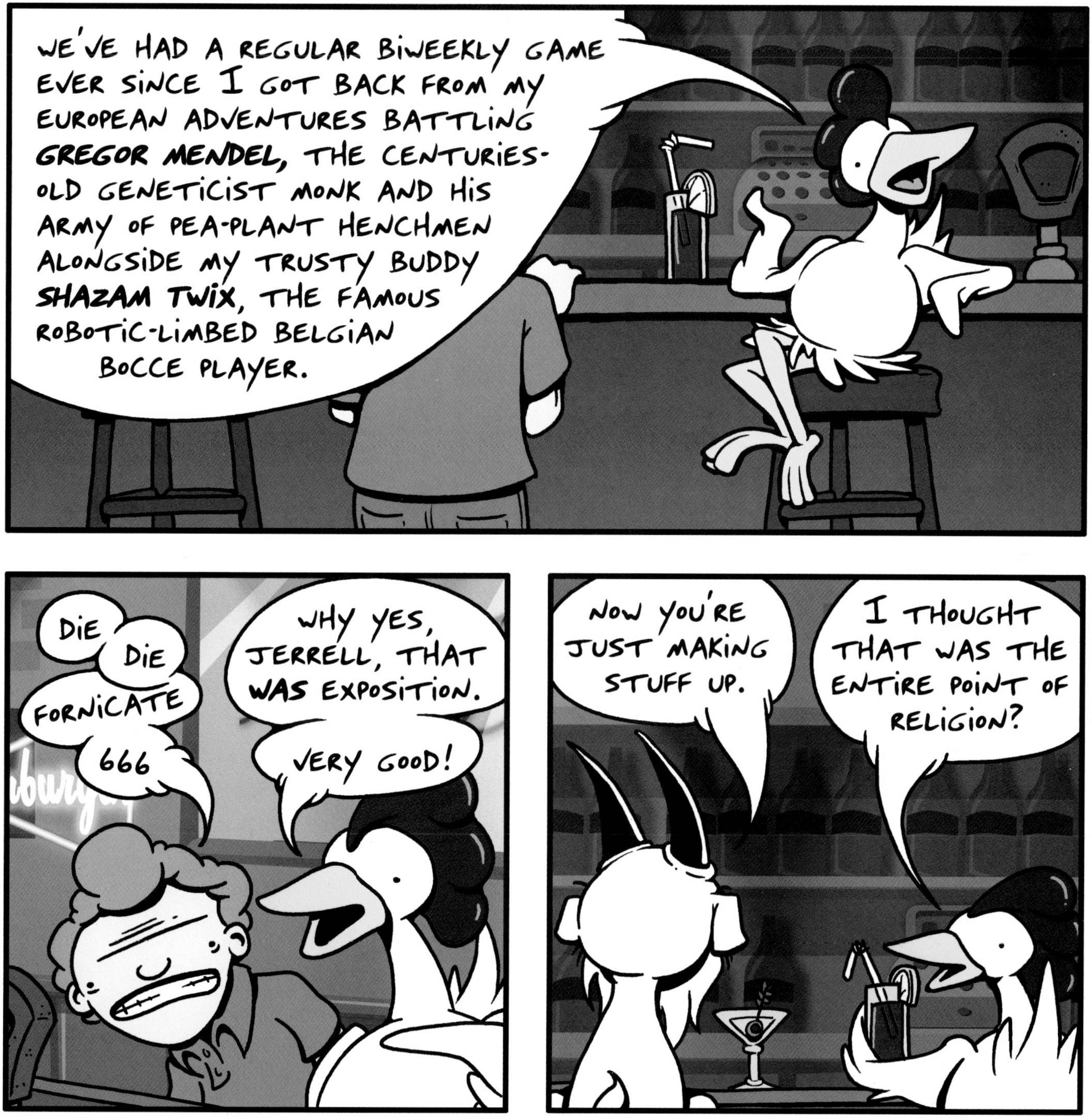
WE'VE HAD A REGULAR BIWEEKLY GAME EVER SINCE I GOT BACK FROM MY EUROPEAN ADVENTURES BATTLING **GREGOR MENDEL**, THE CENTURIES-OLD GENETICIST MONK AND HIS ARMY OF PEA-PLANT HENCHMEN ALONGSIDE MY TRUSTY BUDDY **SHAZAM TWIX**, THE FAMOUS ROBOTIC-LIMBED BELGIAN BOCCE PLAYER.
DIE
DIE
FORNICATE
666
WHY YES, JERRELL, THAT **WAS** EXPOSITION.
VERY GOOD!
NOW YOU'RE JUST MAKING STUFF UP.
I THOUGHT THAT WAS THE ENTIRE POINT OF RELIGION?

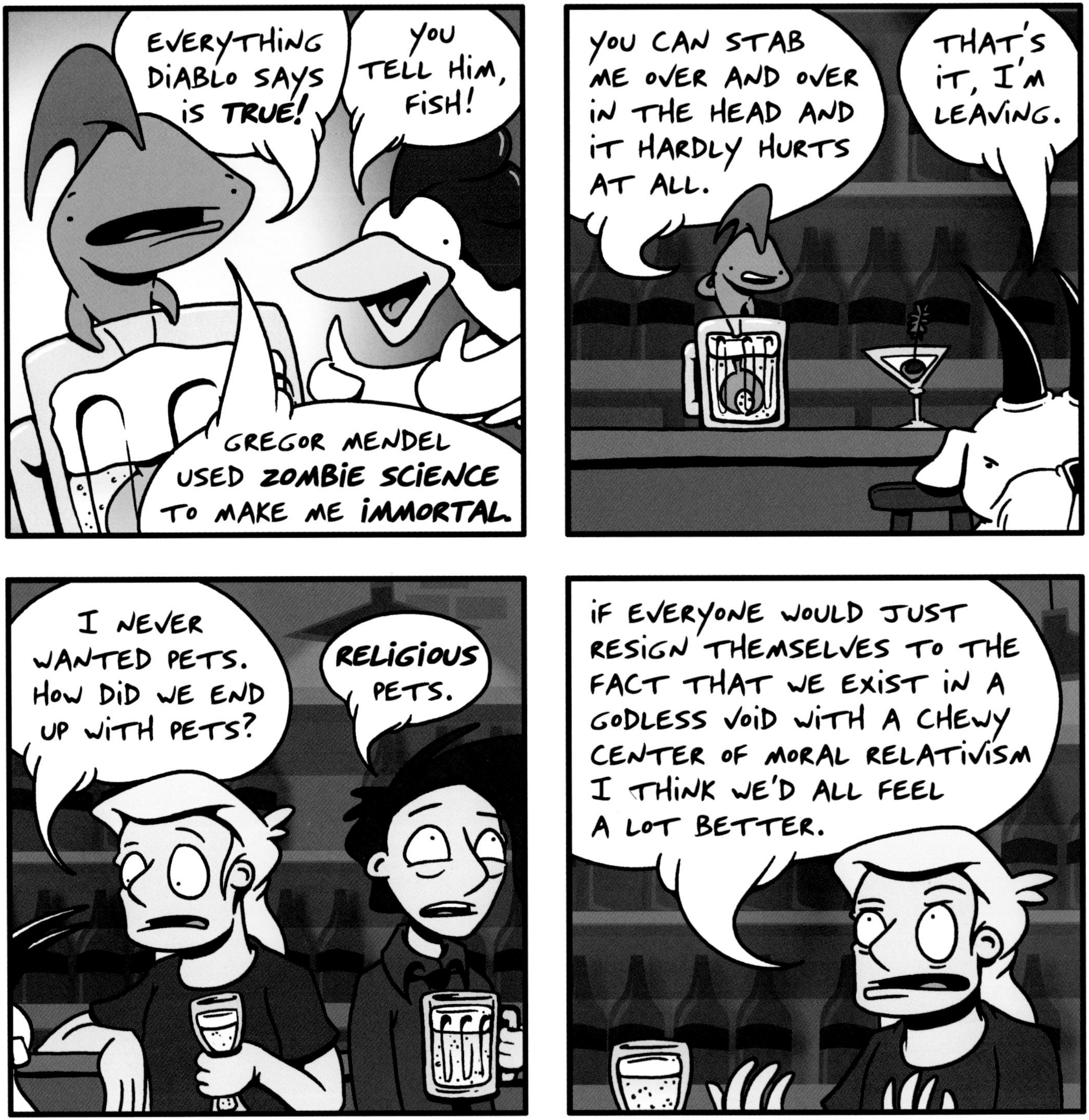
EVERYTHING DIABLO SAYS IS TRUE!
YOU TELL HIM, FISH!
GREGOR MENDEL USED ZOMBIE SCIENCE TO MAKE ME IMMORTAL.
YOU CAN STAB ME OVER AND OVER IN THE HEAD AND IT HARDLY HURTS AT ALL.
THAT'S IT, I'M LEAVING.
I NEVER WANTED PETS. HOW DID WE END UP WITH PETS?
RELIGIOUS PETS.
IF EVERYONE WOULD JUST RESIGN THEMSELVES TO THE FACT THAT WE EXIST IN A GODLESS VOID WITH A CHEWY CENTER OF MORAL RELATIVISM I THINK WE'D ALL FEEL A LOT BETTER.

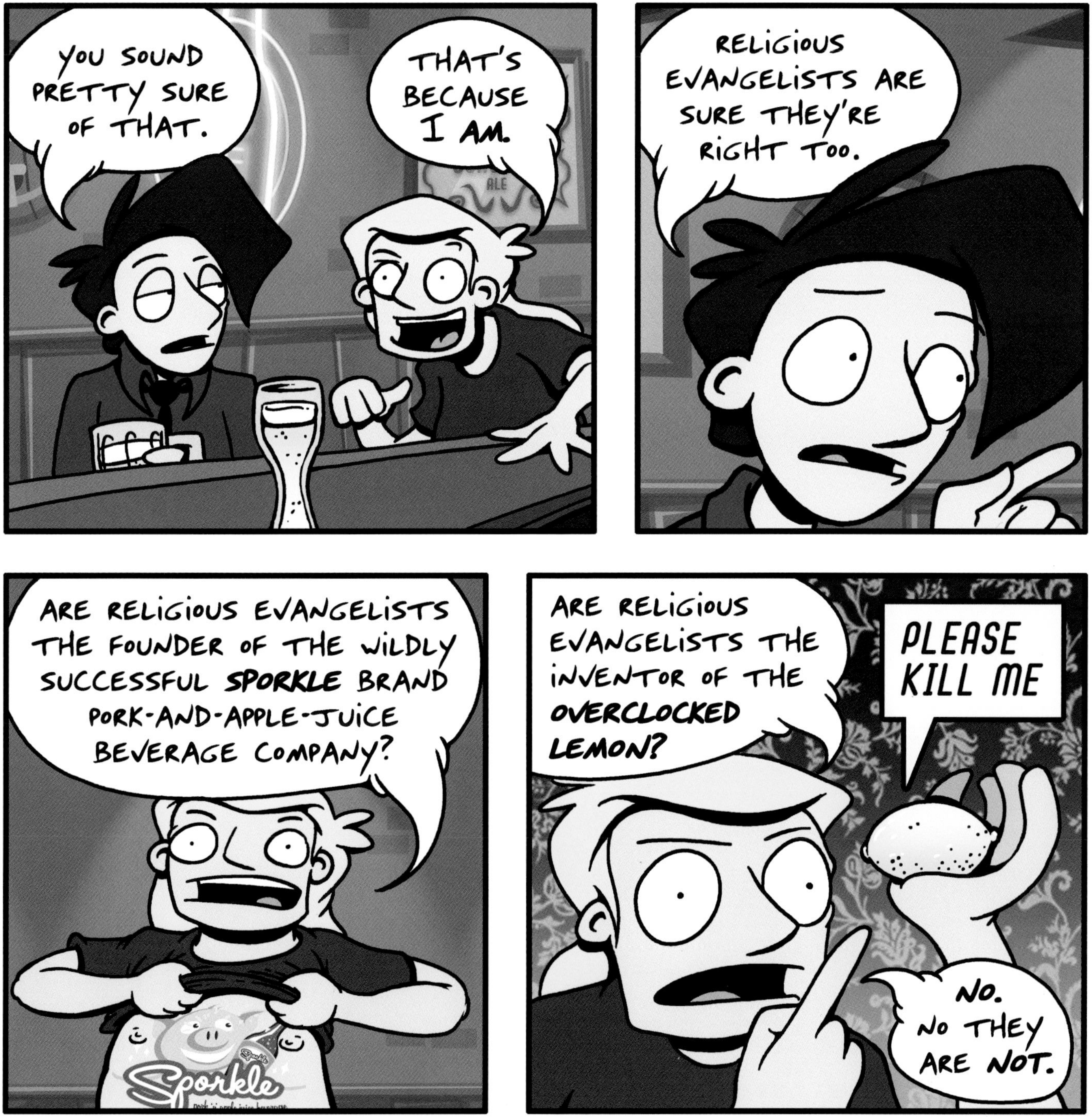
YOU SOUND PRETTY SURE OF THAT.
THAT'S BECAUSE I AM.
RELIGIOUS EVANGELISTS ARE SURE THEY'RE RIGHT TOO.
ARE RELIGIOUS EVANGELISTS THE FOUNDER OF THE WILDLY SUCCESSFUL SPORKLE BRAND PORK-AND-APPLE-JUICE BEVERAGE COMPANY?
Sporkle
ARE RELIGIOUS EVANGELISTS THE INVENTOR OF THE OVERCLOCKED LEMON?
PLEASE KILL ME
NO. NO THEY ARE NOT.

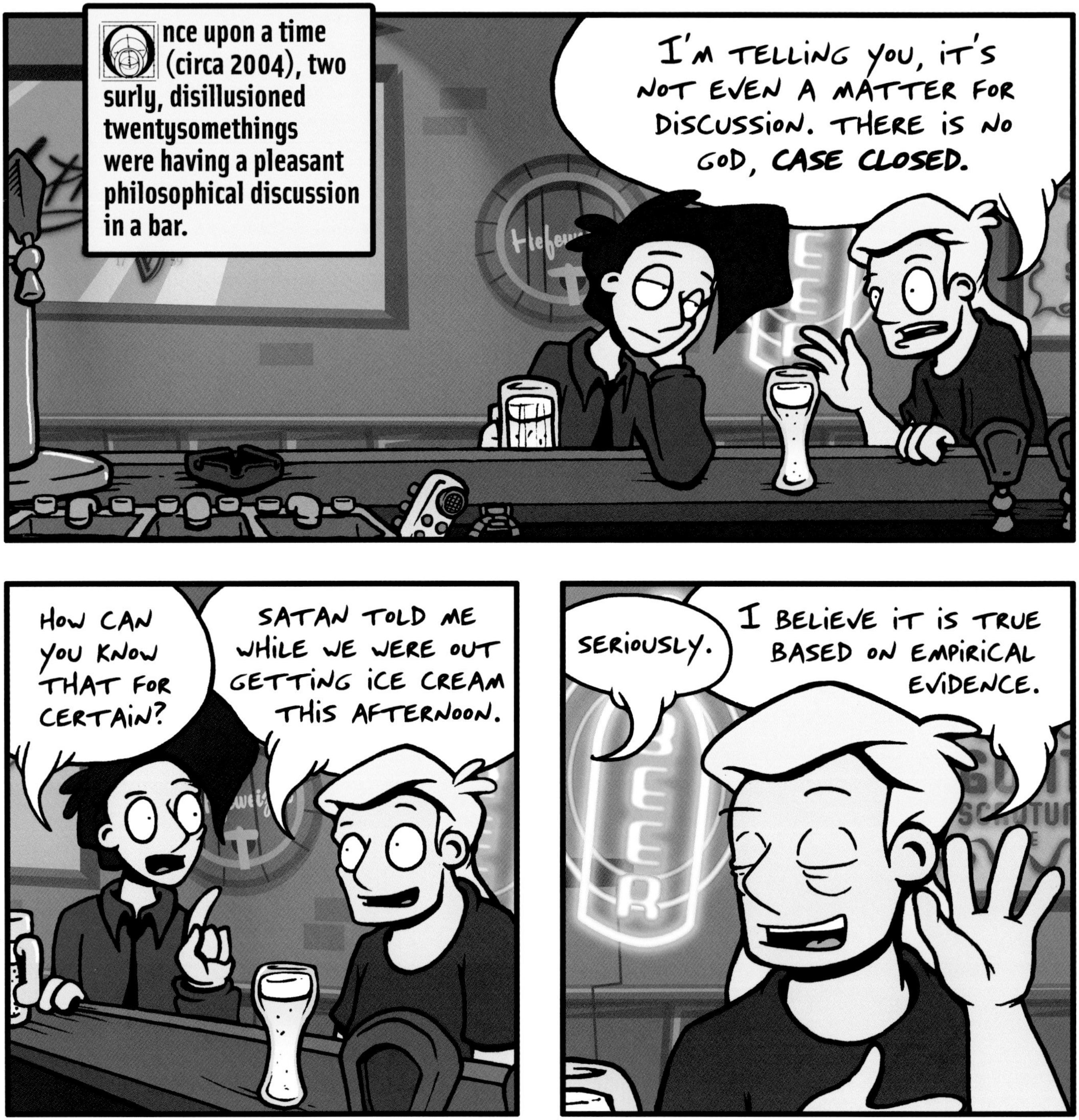
Once upon a time (circa 2004), two surly, disillusioned twentysomethings were having a pleasant philosophical discussion in a bar.
I'M TELLING YOU, IT'S NOT EVEN A MATTER FOR DISCUSSION. THERE IS NO GOD, CASE CLOSED.
HOW CAN YOU KNOW THAT FOR CERTAIN?
SATAN TOLD ME WHILE WE WERE OUT GETTING ICE CREAM THIS AFTERNOON.
SERIOUSLY.
I BELIEVE IT IS TRUE BASED ON EMPIRICAL EVIDENCE.

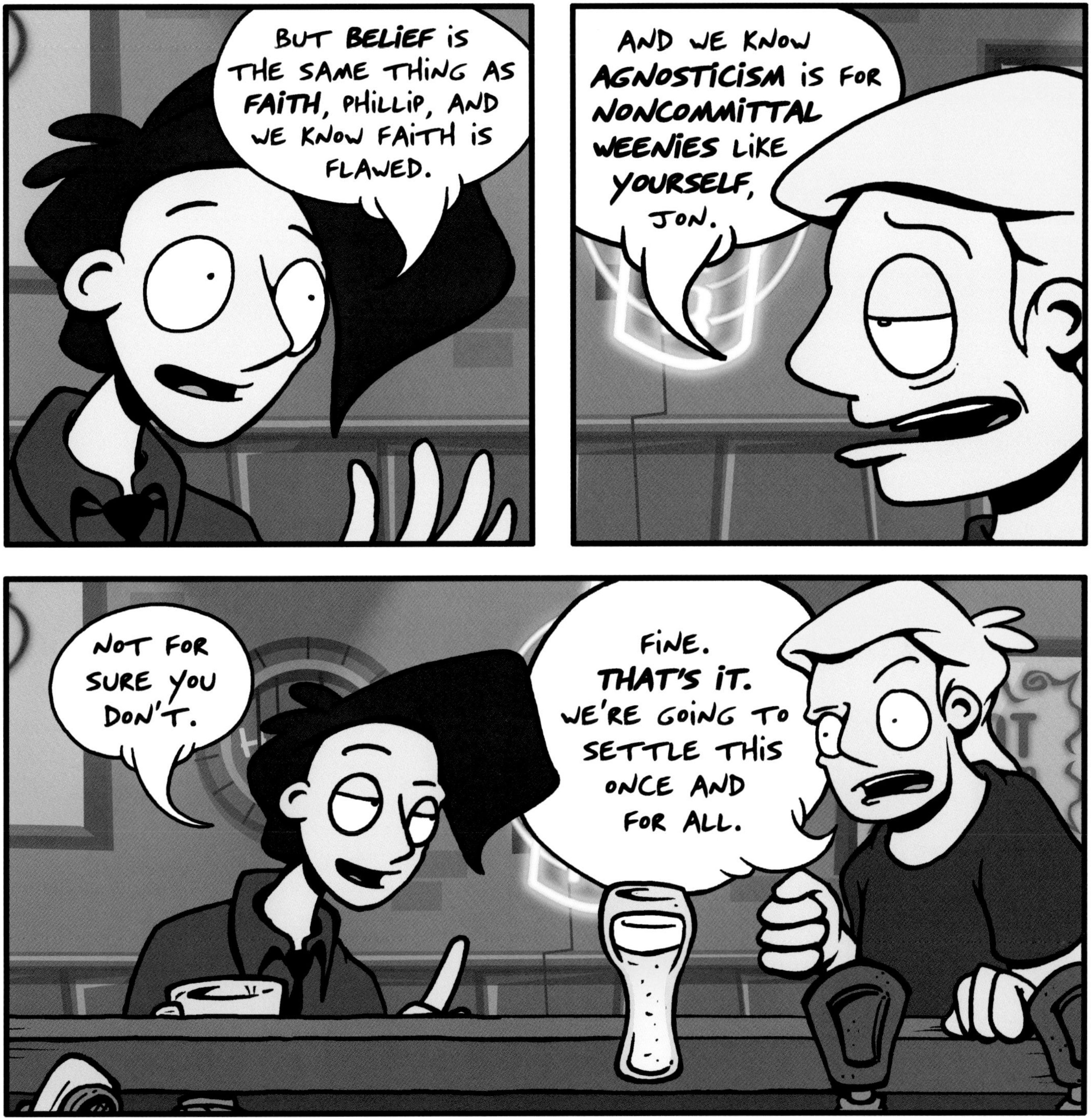
BUT BELIEF IS THE SAME THING AS FAITH, PHILLIP, AND WE KNOW FAITH IS FLAWED.
AND WE KNOW AGNOSTICISM IS FOR NONCOMMITTAL WEENIES LIKE YOURSELF, JON.
NOT FOR SURE YOU DON'T.
FINE. THAT'S IT. WE'RE GOING TO SETTLE THIS ONCE AND FOR ALL.

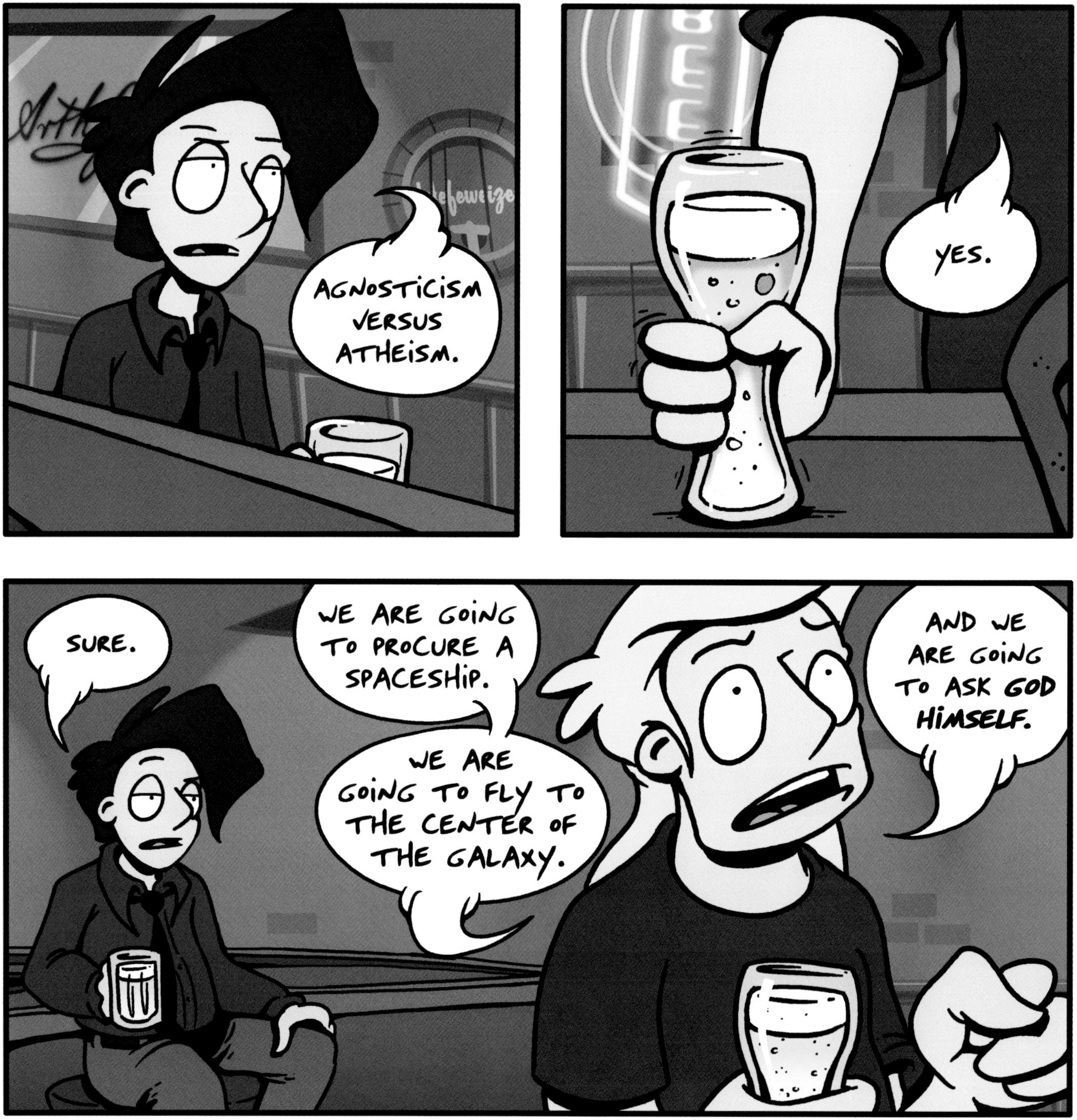
AGNOSTICISM VERSUS ATHEISM.
YES.
SURE.
WE ARE GOING TO PROCURE A SPACESHIP.
WE ARE GOING TO FLY TO THE CENTER OF THE GALAXY.
AND WE ARE GOING TO ASK GOD HIMSELF.

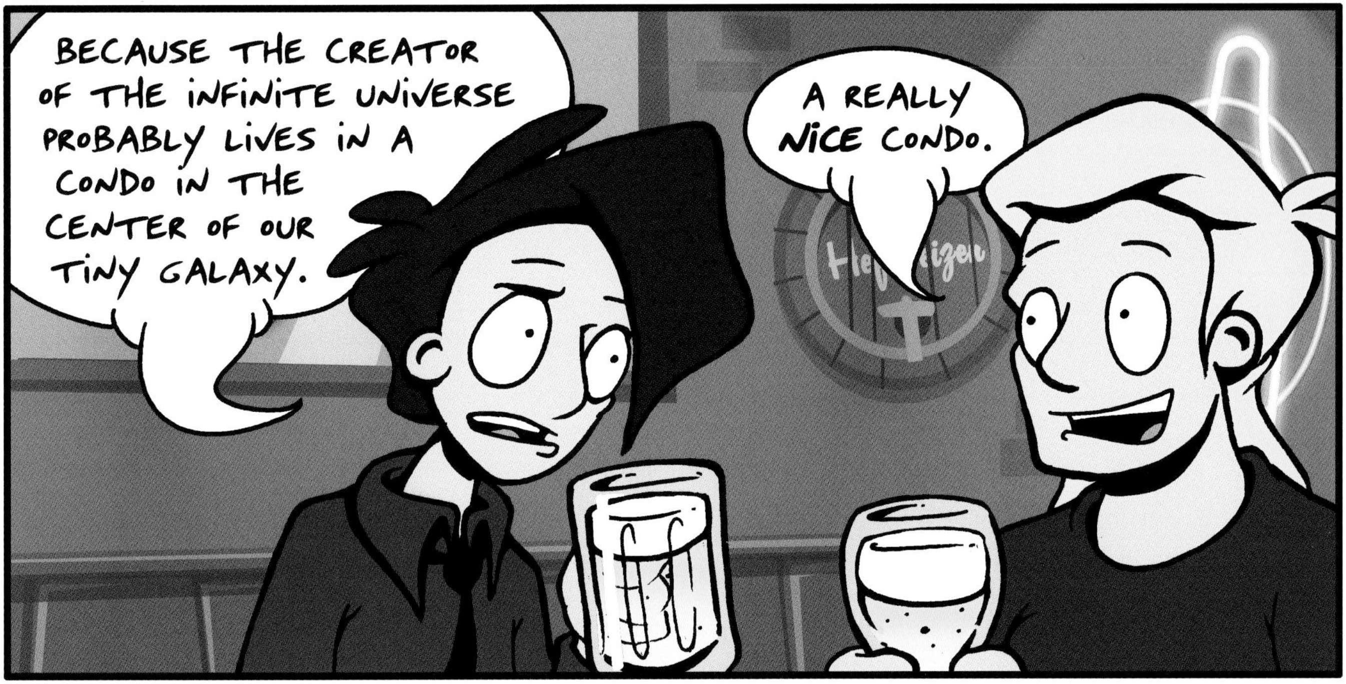
BECAUSE THE CREATOR OF THE INFINITE UNIVERSE PROBABLY LIVES IN A CONDO IN THE CENTER OF OUR TINY GALAXY.
A REALLY NICE CONDO.
Hefeweizen

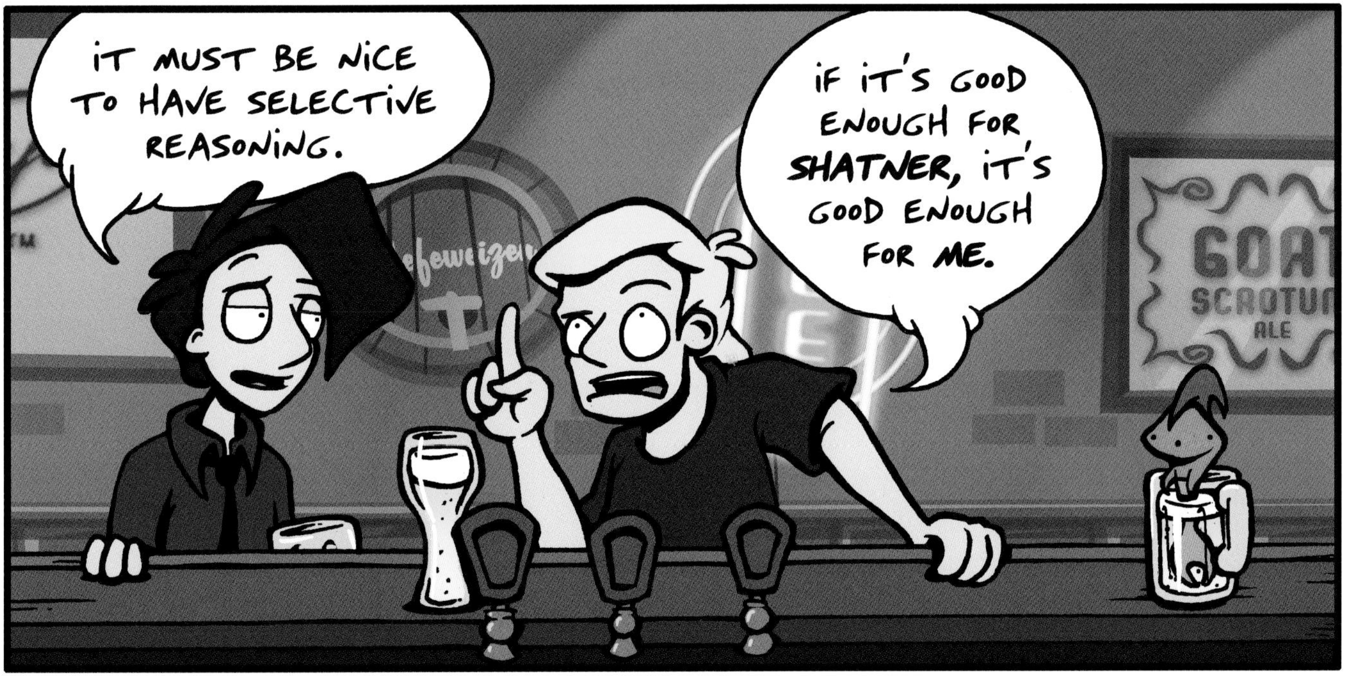
IT MUST BE NICE TO HAVE SELECTIVE REASONING.
IF IT'S GOOD ENOUGH FOR SHATNER, IT'S GOOD ENOUGH FOR ME.
Hefeweizen
GOAT SCROTUM ALE

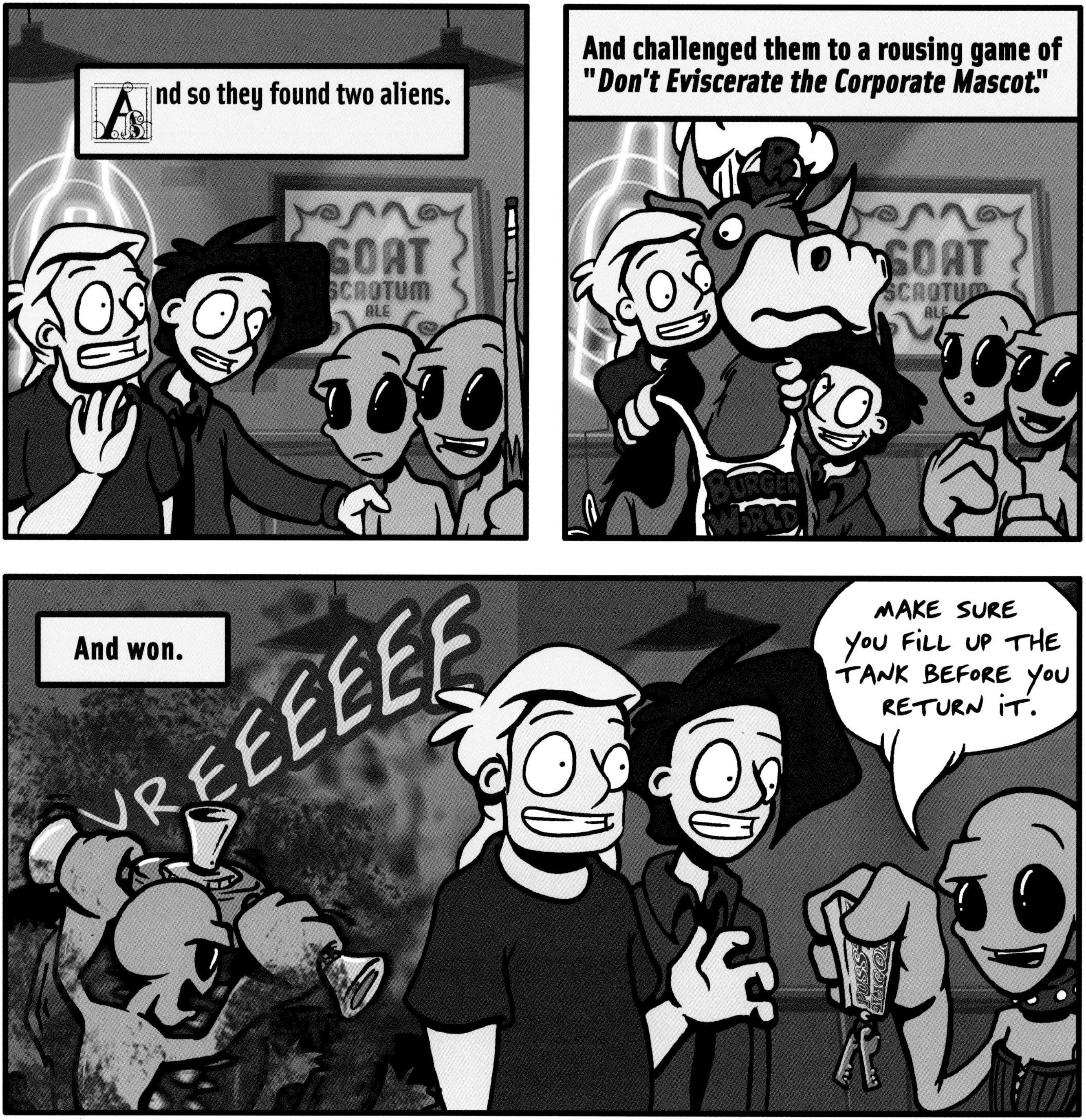
And so they found two aliens.
GOAT SCROTUM ALE
And challenged them to a rousing game of "*Don't Eviscerate the Corporate Mascot.*"
GOAT SCROTUM ALE
BURGER WORLD
And won.
VREEEEEEEE
MAKE SURE YOU FILL UP THE TANK BEFORE YOU RETURN IT.

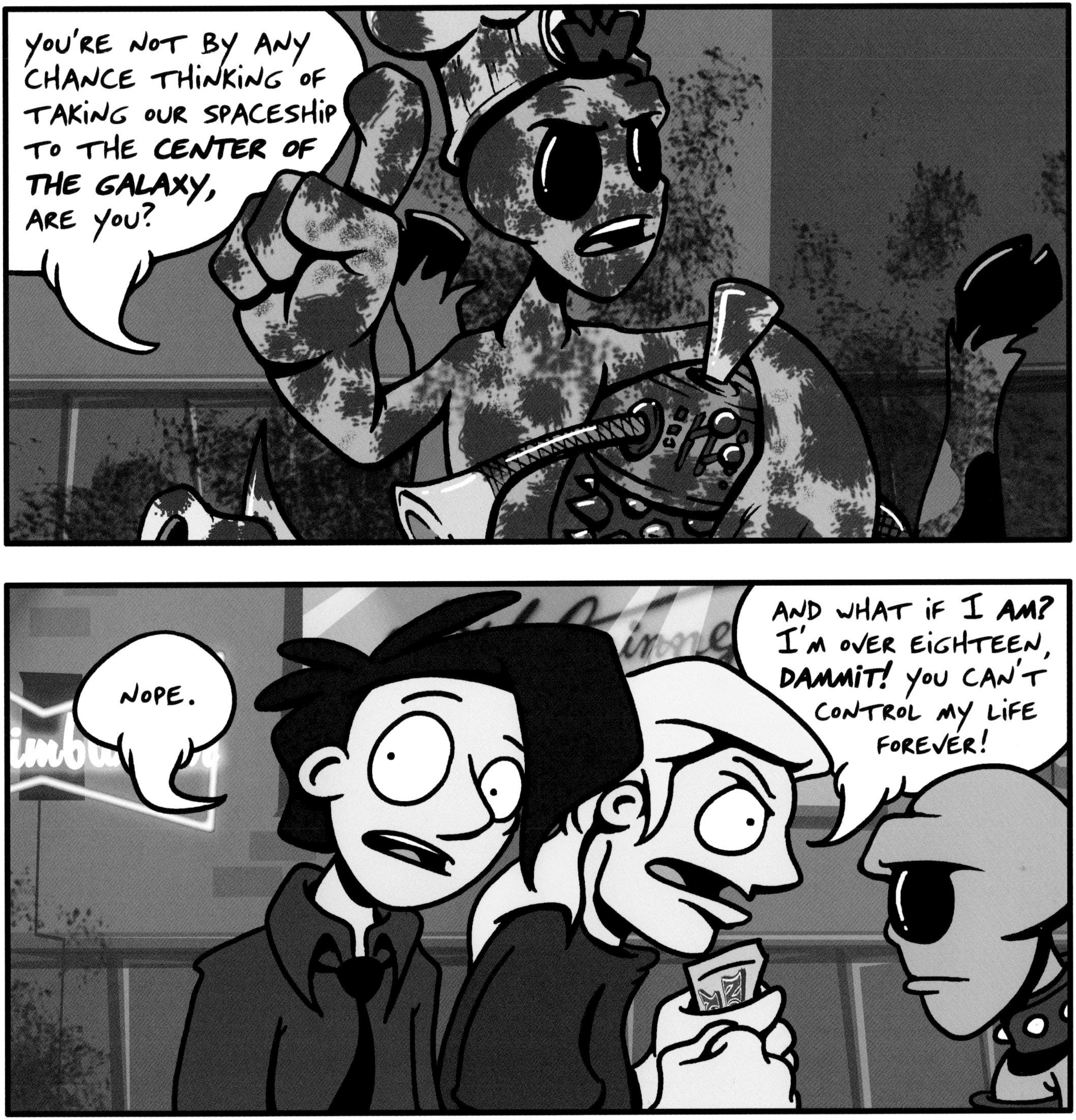
YOU'RE NOT BY ANY CHANCE THINKING OF TAKING OUR SPACESHIP TO THE **CENTER OF THE GALAXY**, ARE YOU?
NOPE.
AND WHAT IF I **AM?** I'M OVER EIGHTEEN, **DAMMIT!** YOU CAN'T CONTROL MY LIFE FOREVER!

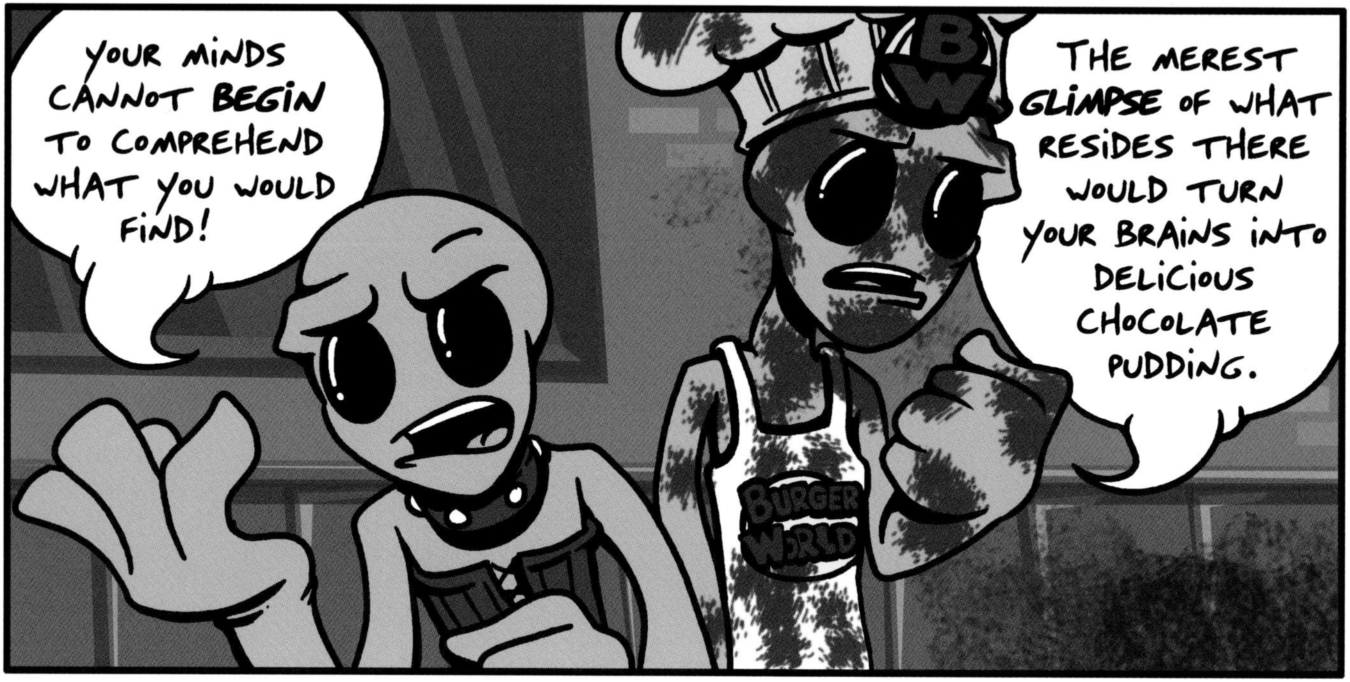
YOUR MINDS CANNOT BEGIN TO COMPREHEND WHAT YOU WOULD FIND!
THE MEREST GLIMPSE OF WHAT RESIDES THERE WOULD TURN YOUR BRAINS INTO DELICIOUS CHOCOLATE PUDDING.
BW
BURGER WORLD
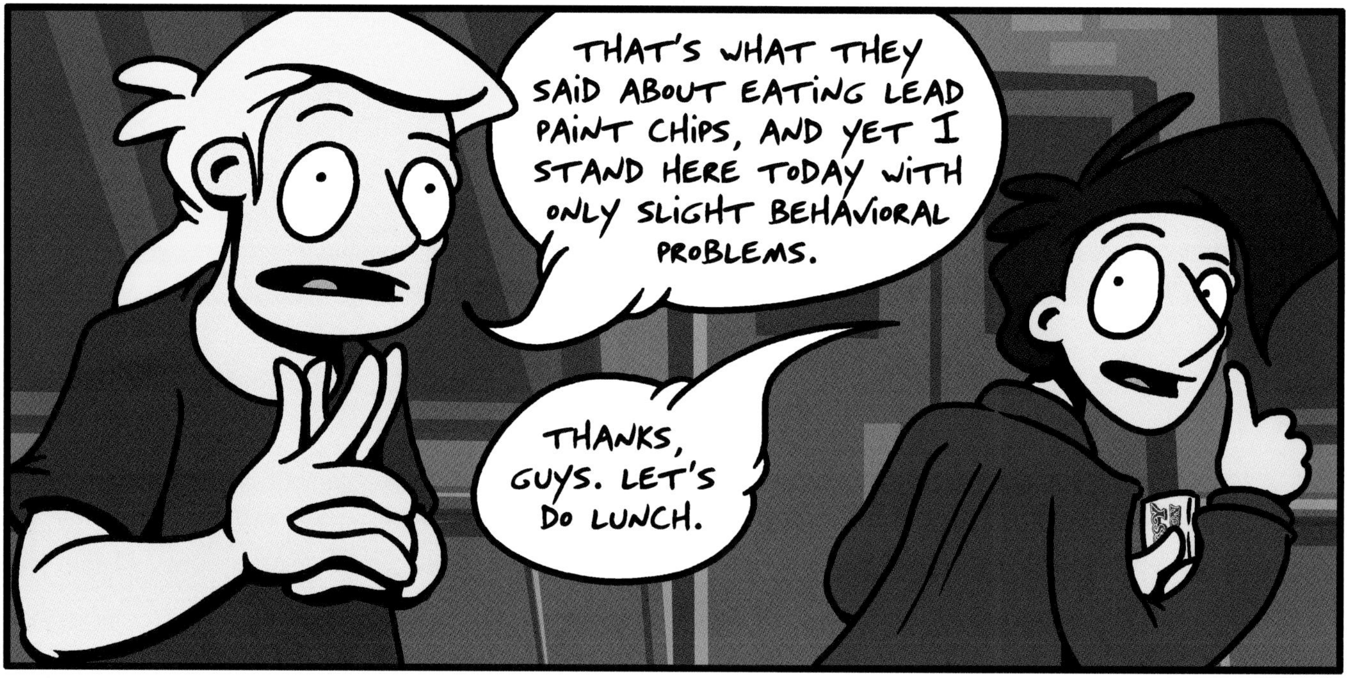
THAT'S WHAT THEY SAID ABOUT EATING LEAD PAINT CHIPS, AND YET I STAND HERE TODAY WITH ONLY SLIGHT BEHAVIORAL PROBLEMS.
THANKS, GUYS. LET'S DO LUNCH.

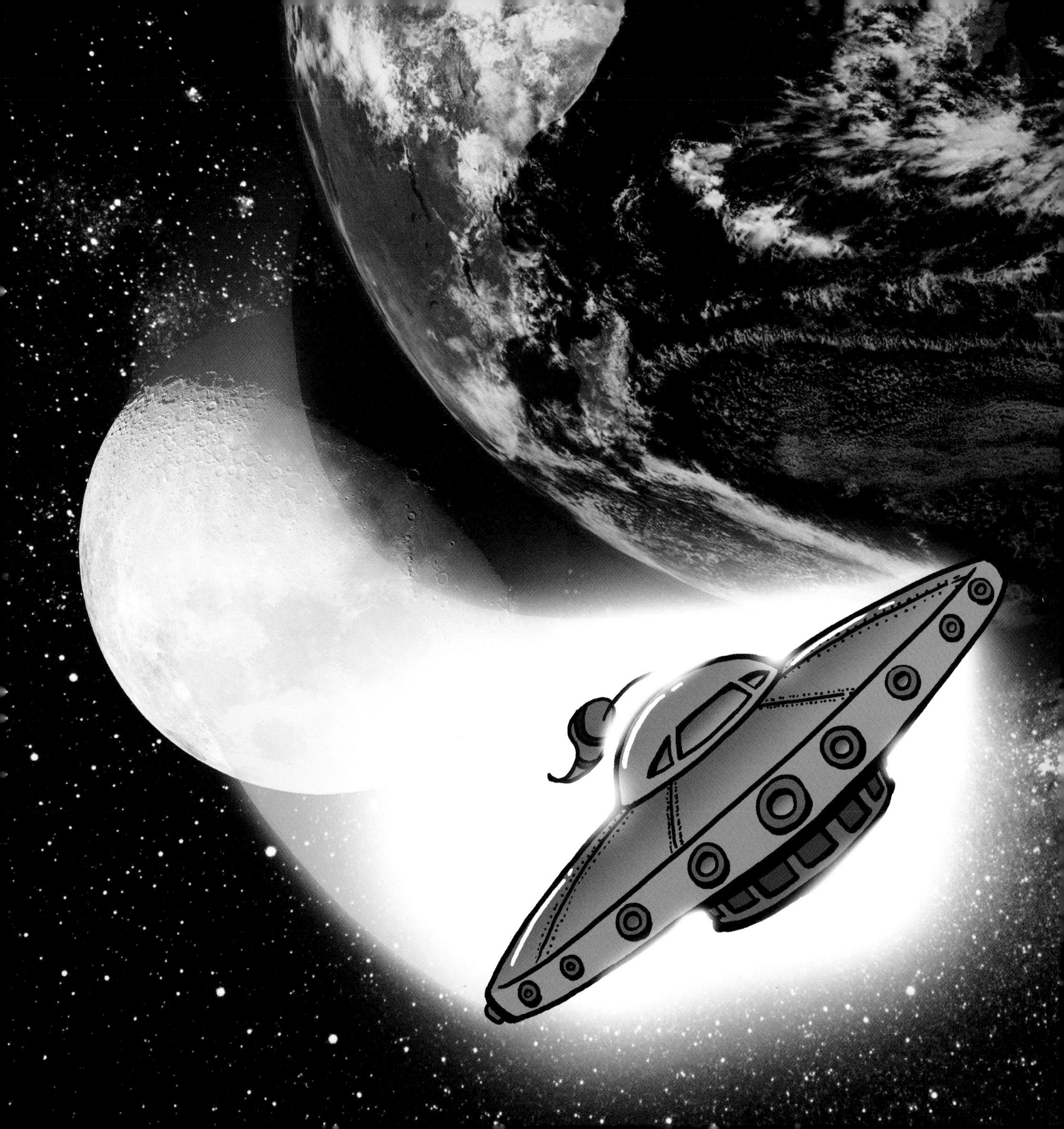

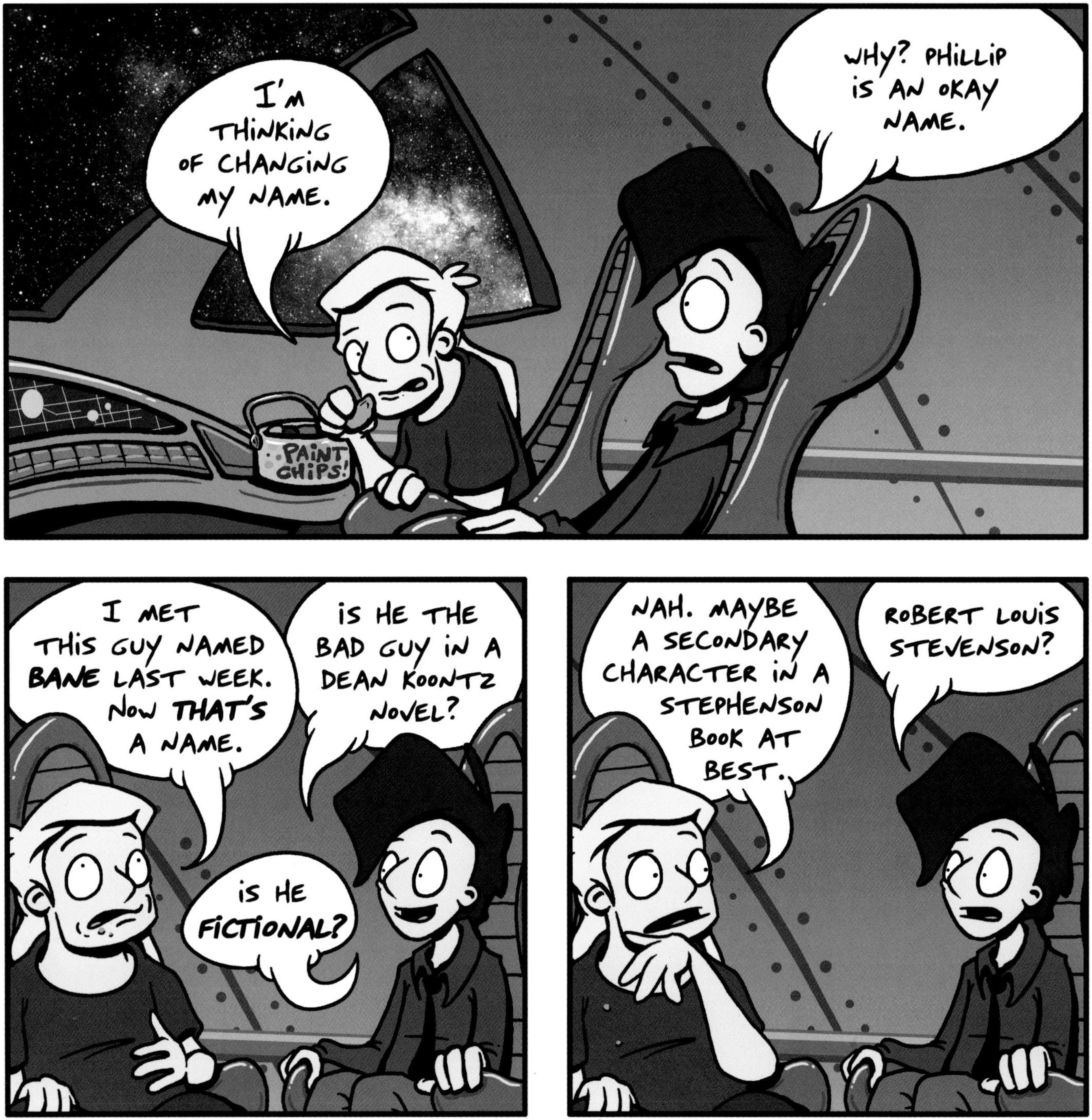
I'M THINKING OF CHANGING MY NAME.
WHY? PHILLIP IS AN OKAY NAME.
PAINT CHIPS!
I MET THIS GUY NAMED BANE LAST WEEK. NOW THAT'S A NAME.
IS HE THE BAD GUY IN A DEAN KOONTZ NOVEL?
IS HE FICTIONAL?
NAH. MAYBE A SECONDARY CHARACTER IN A STEPHENSON BOOK AT BEST.
ROBERT LOUIS STEVENSON?

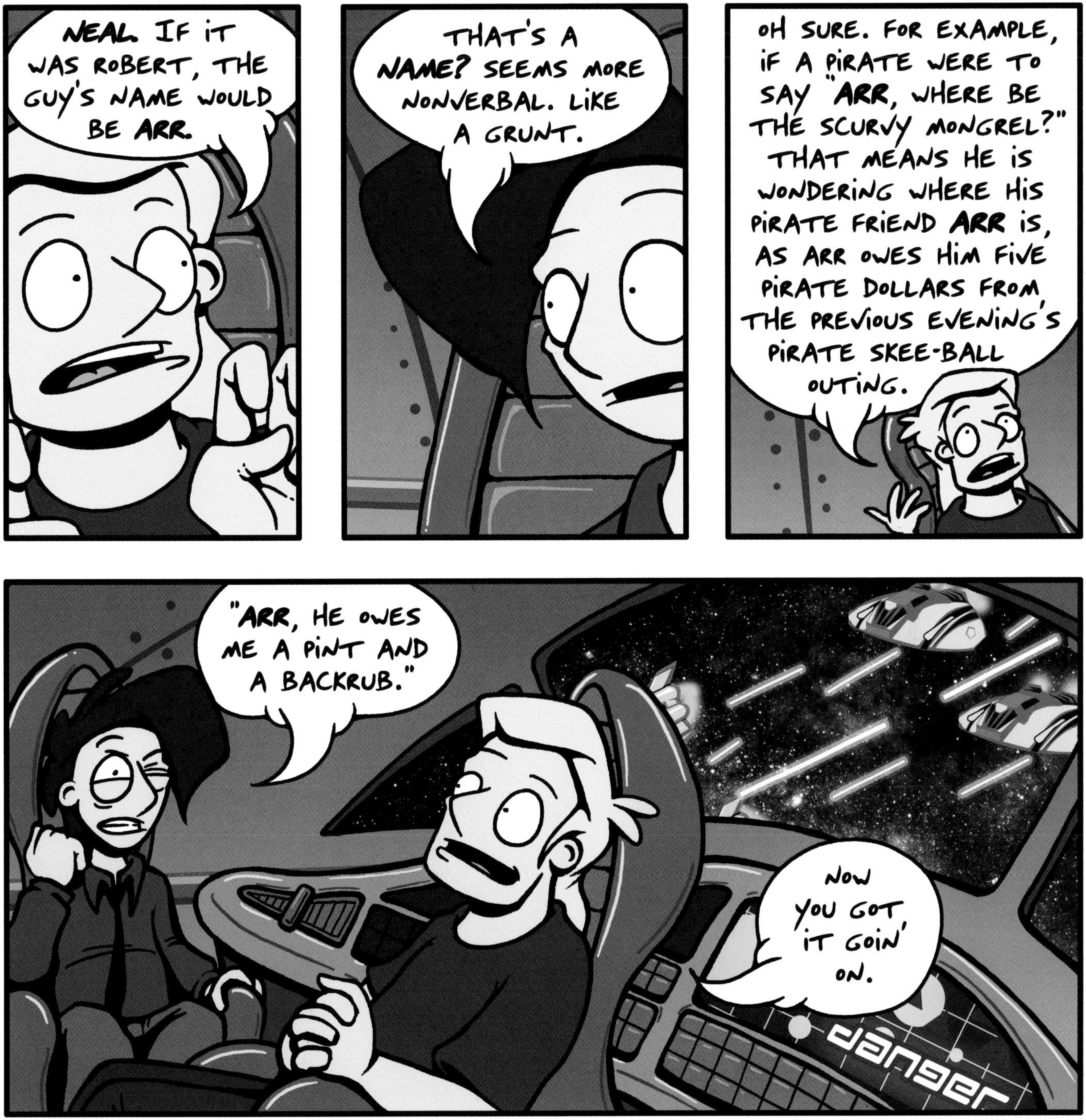
NEAL. IF IT WAS ROBERT, THE GUY'S NAME WOULD BE ARR.
THAT'S A NAME? SEEMS MORE NONVERBAL. LIKE A GRUNT.
OH SURE. FOR EXAMPLE, IF A PIRATE WERE TO SAY "ARR, WHERE BE THE SCURVY MONGREL?" THAT MEANS HE IS WONDERING WHERE HIS PIRATE FRIEND ARR IS, AS ARR OWES HIM FIVE PIRATE DOLLARS FROM THE PREVIOUS EVENING'S PIRATE SKEE-BALL OUTING.
"ARR, HE OWES ME A PINT AND A BACKRUB."
NOW YOU GOT IT GOIN' ON.
danger

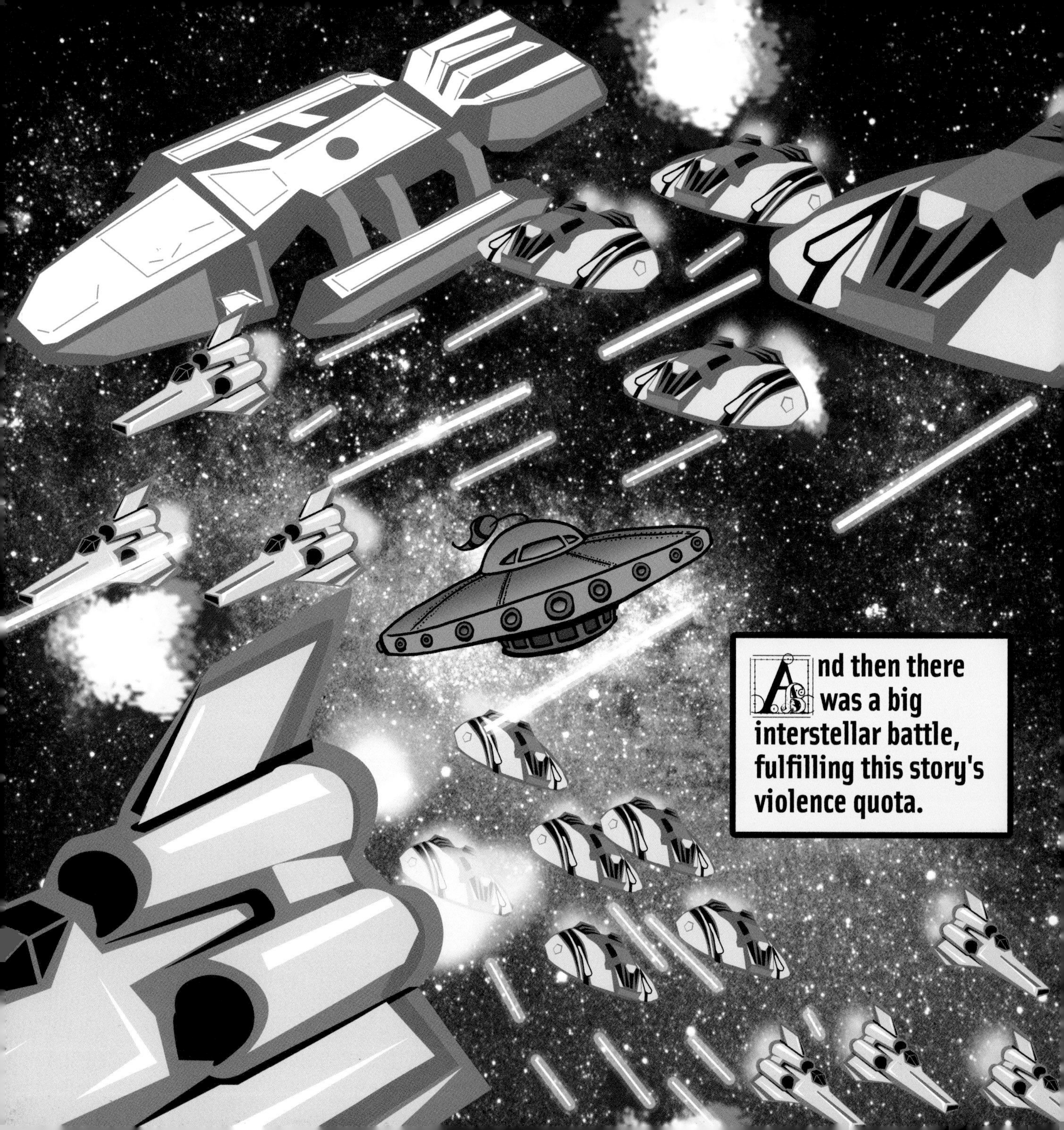
And then there was a big interstellar battle, fulfilling this story's violence quota.

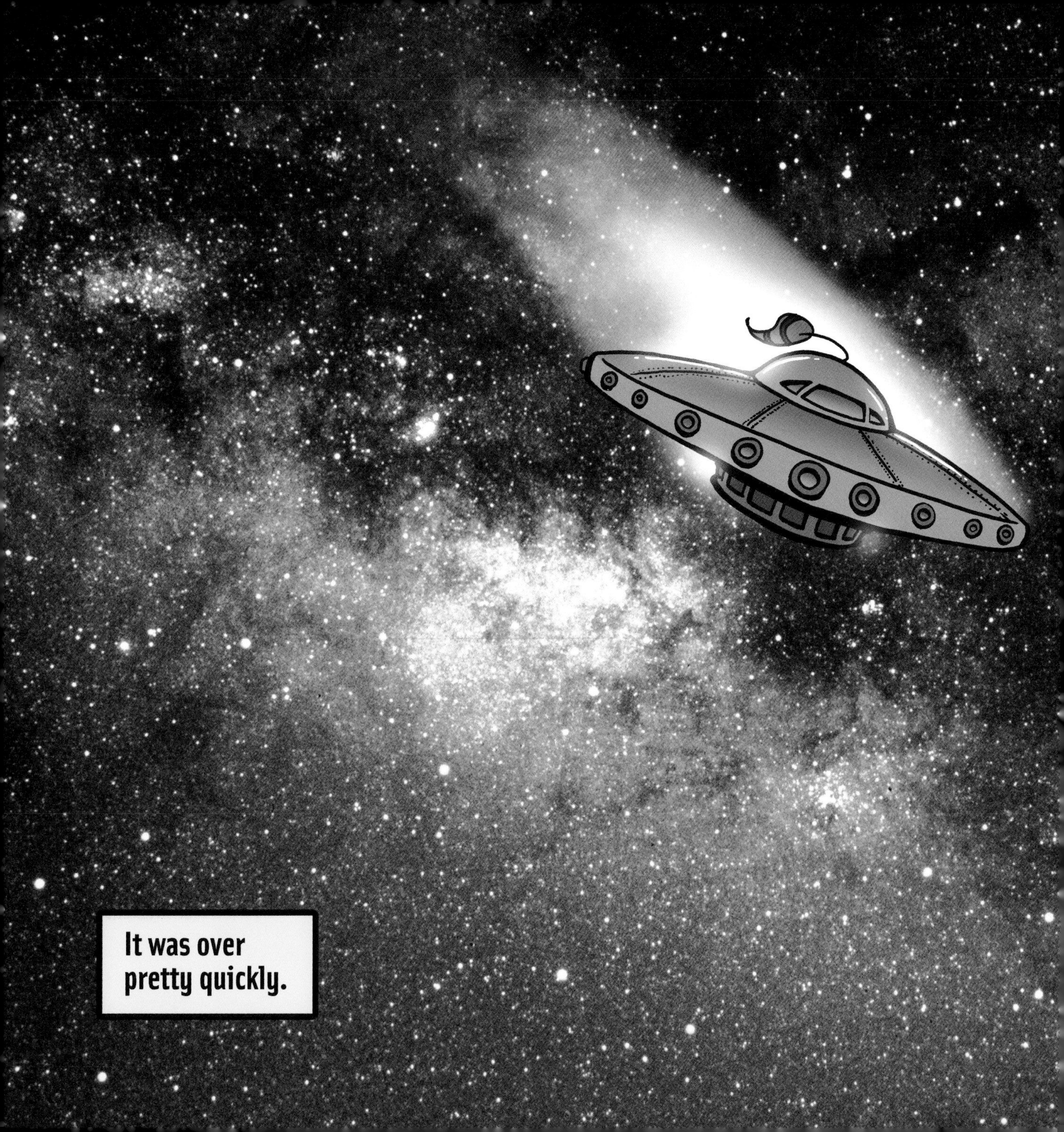
It was over pretty quickly.

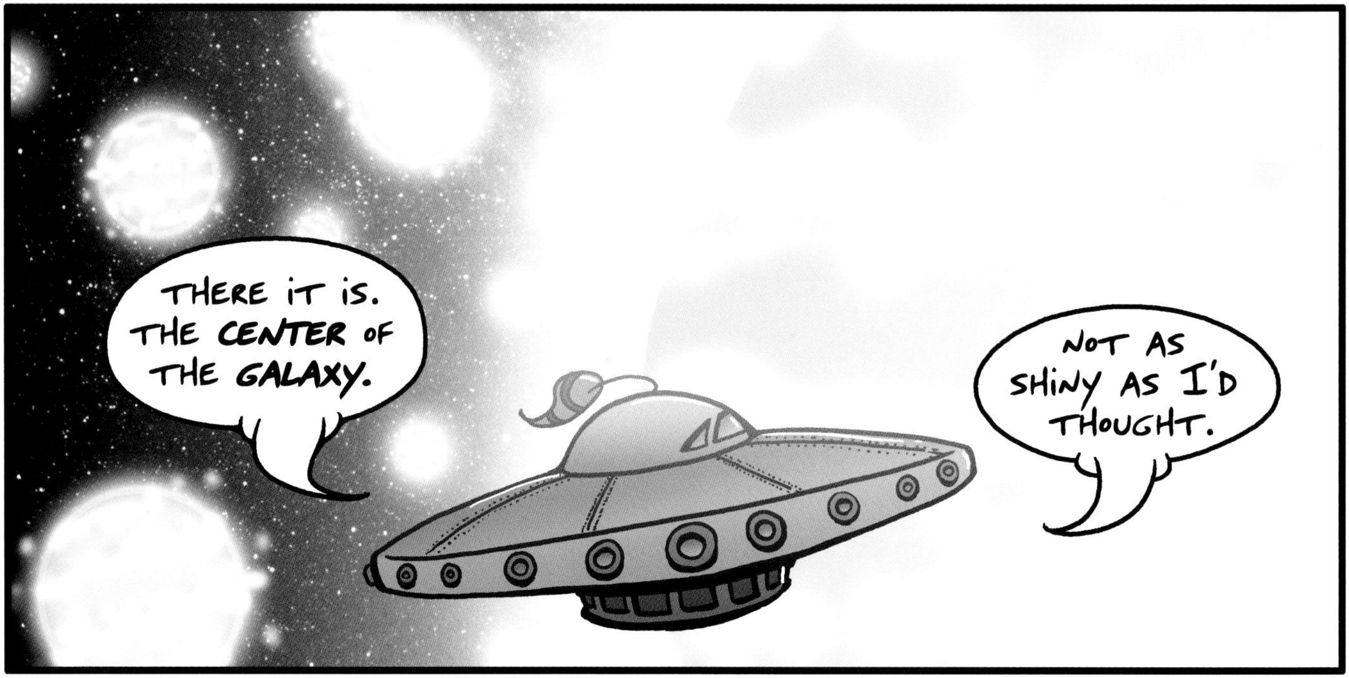
THERE IT IS. THE CENTER OF THE GALAXY.
NOT AS SHINY AS I'D THOUGHT.
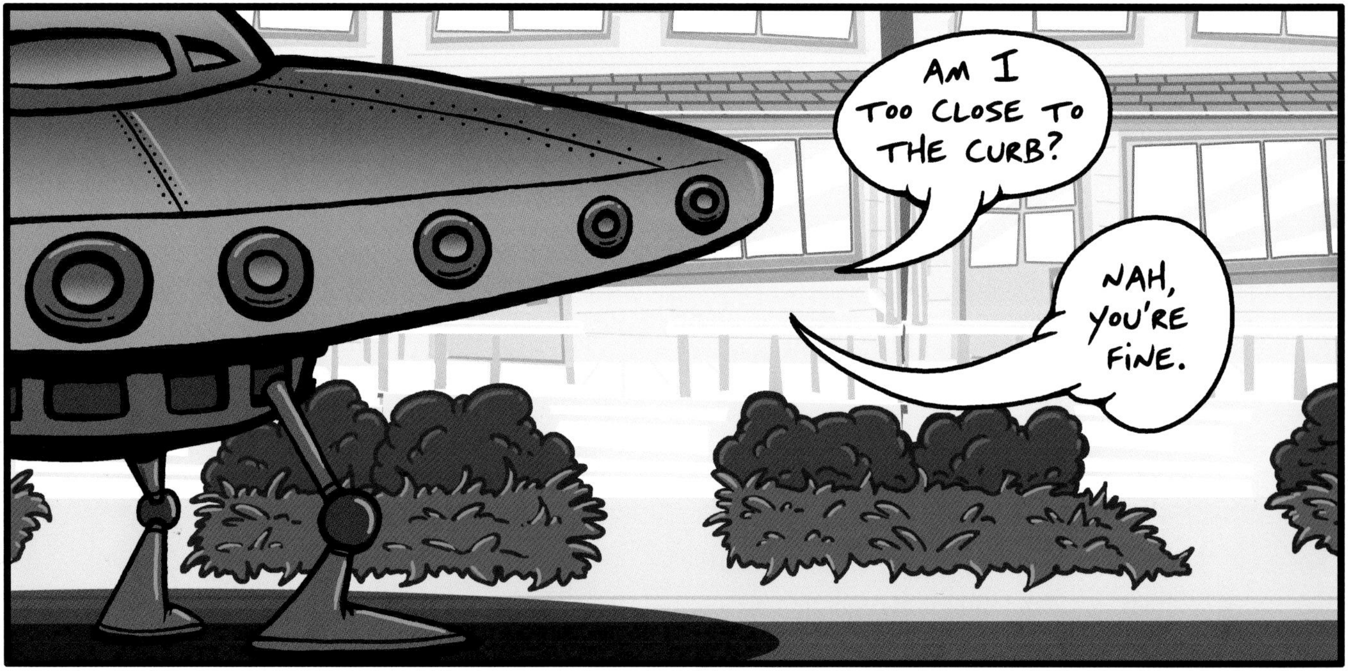
AM I TOO CLOSE TO THE CURB?
NAH, YOU'RE FINE.

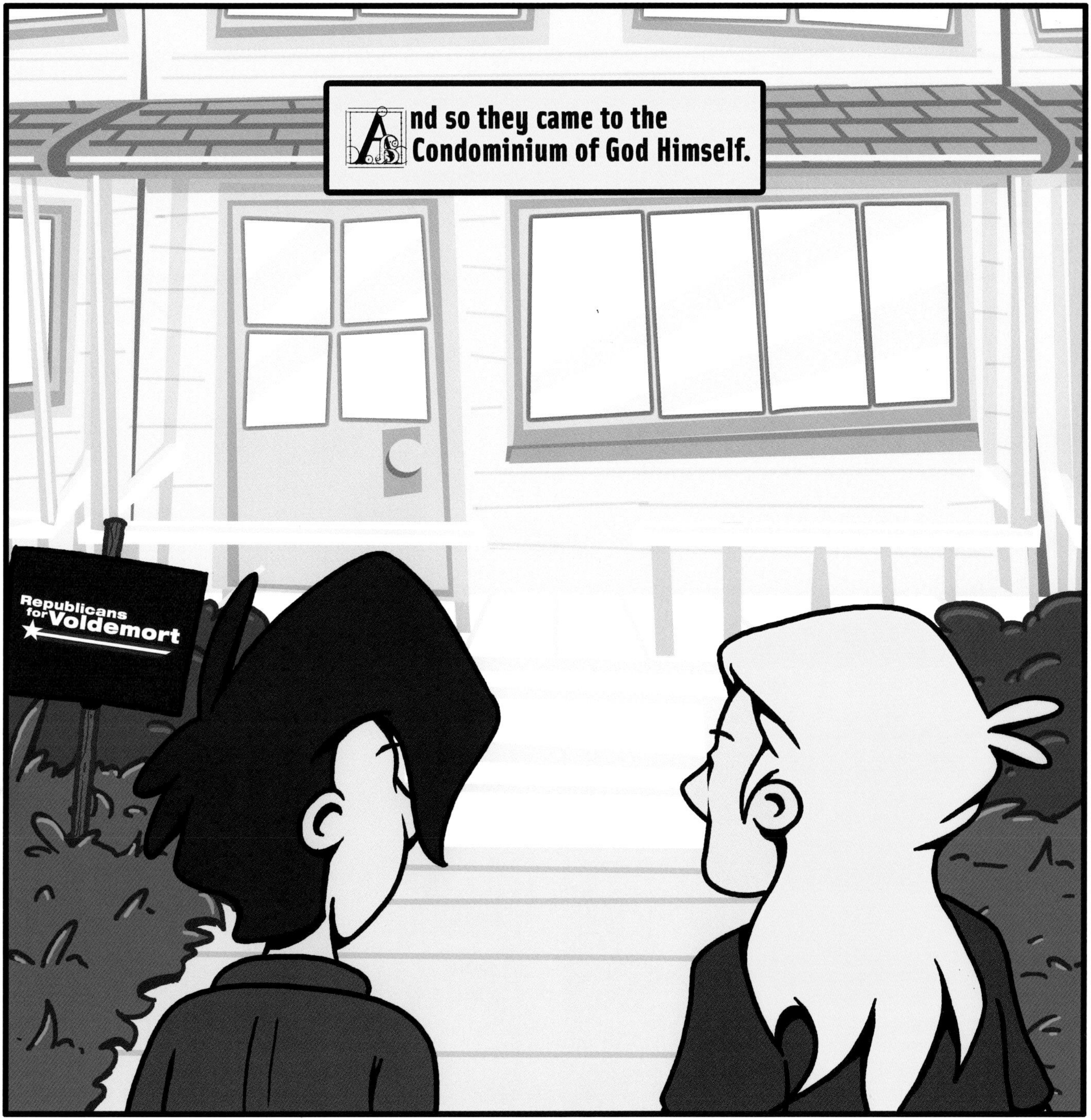
And so they came to the Condominium of God Himself.
Republicans for Voldemort

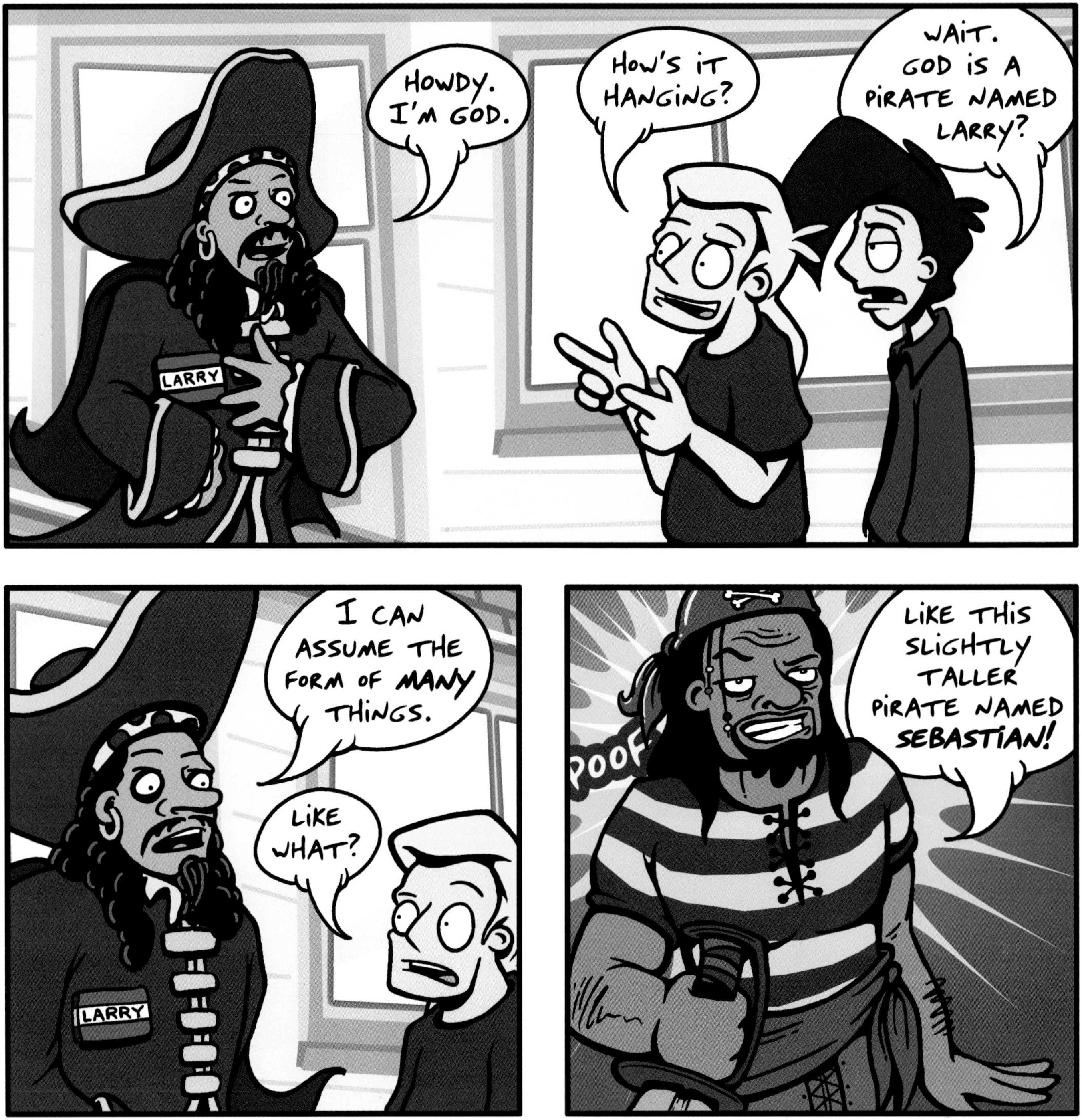
HOWDY. I'M GOD.
HOW'S IT HANGING?
WAIT. GOD IS A PIRATE NAMED LARRY?
LARRY
I CAN ASSUME THE FORM OF MANY THINGS.
LIKE WHAT?
LARRY
POOF
LIKE THIS SLIGHTLY TALLER PIRATE NAMED SEBASTIAN!

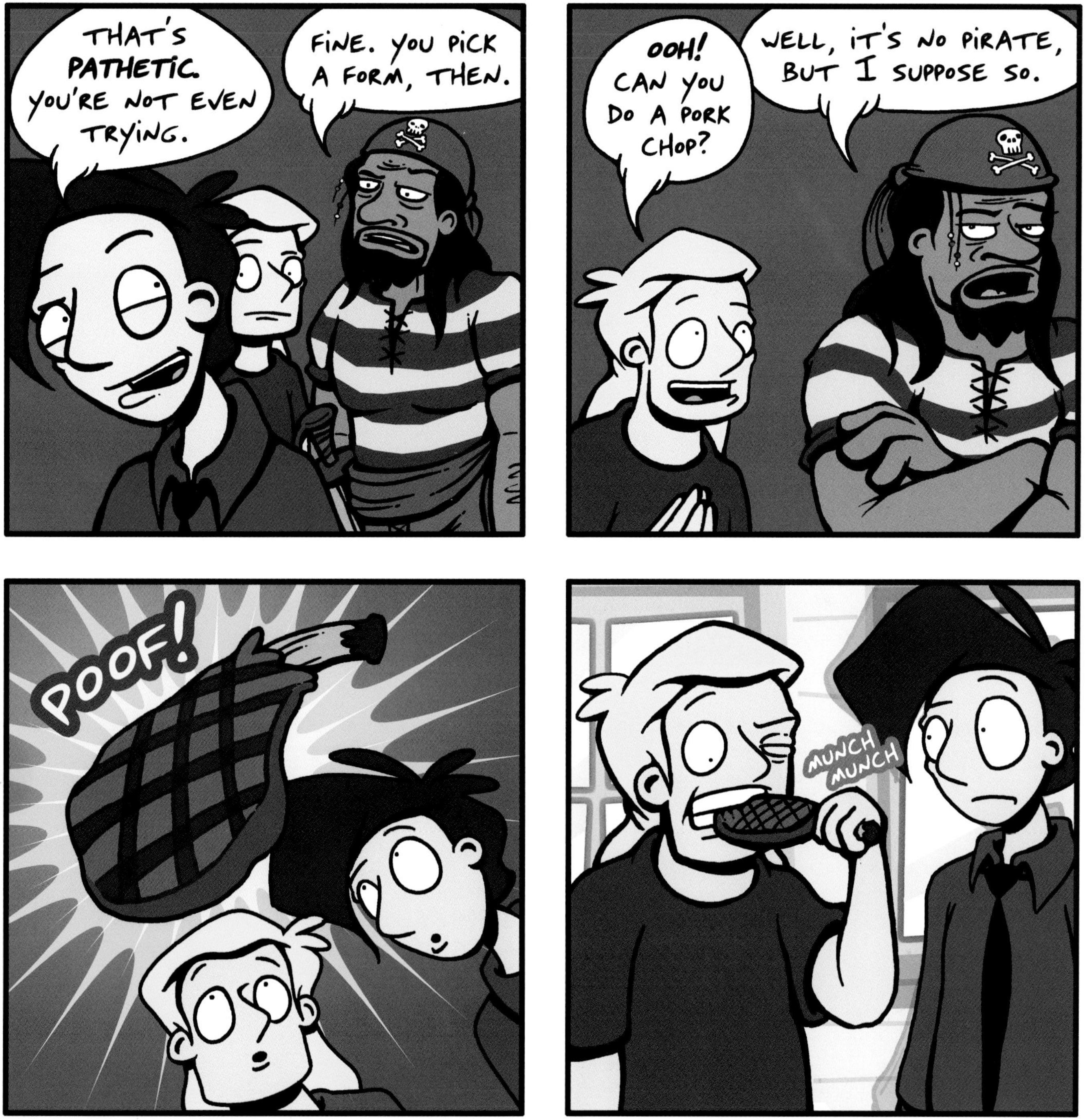
THAT'S **PATHETIC.** YOU'RE NOT EVEN TRYING.
FINE. YOU PICK A FORM, THEN.
OOH! CAN YOU DO A PORK CHOP?
WELL, IT'S NO PIRATE, BUT I SUPPOSE SO.
POOF!
MUNCH MUNCH

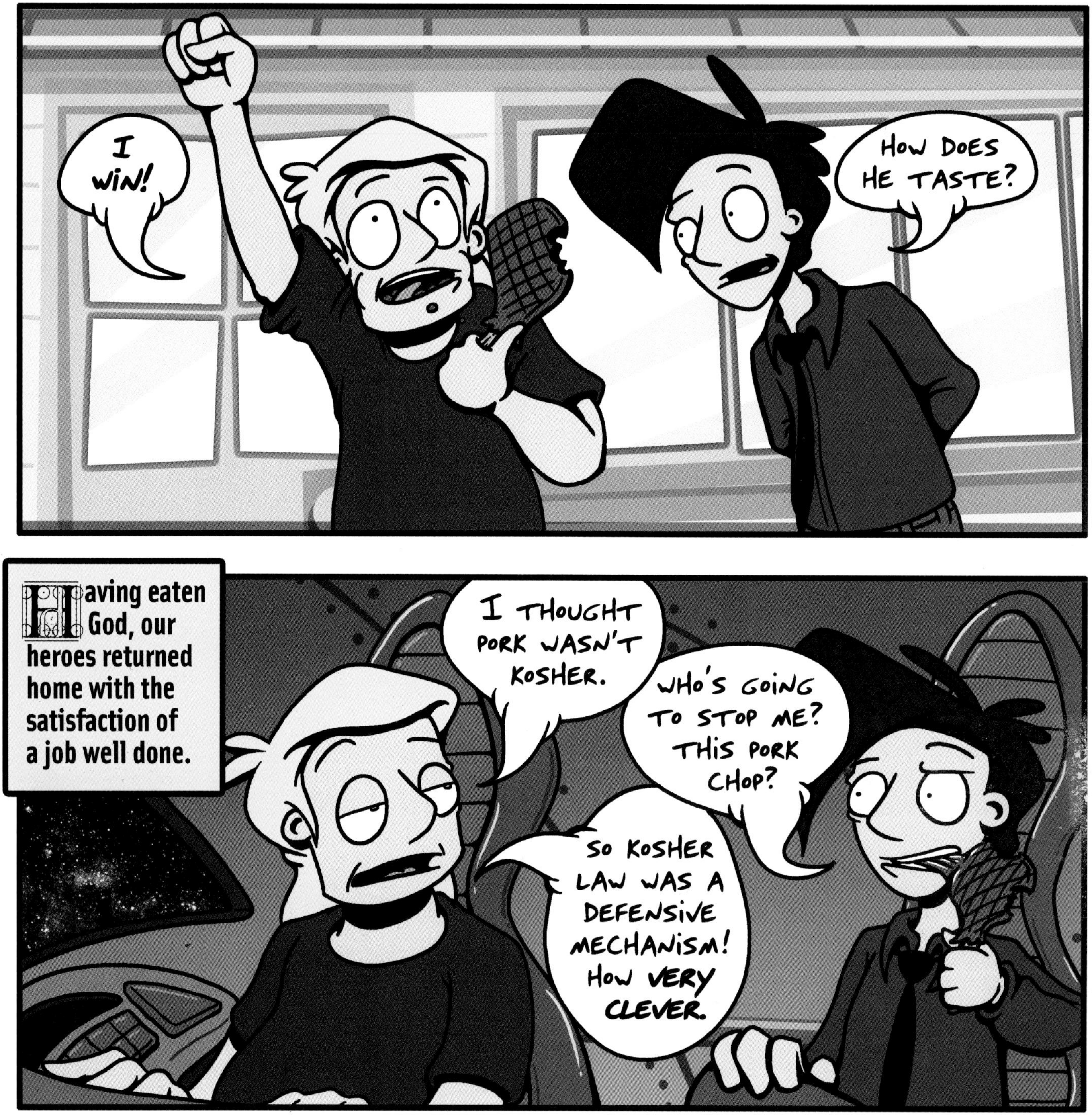
I WIN!
HOW DOES HE TASTE?
Having eaten God, our heroes returned home with the satisfaction of a job well done.
I THOUGHT PORK WASN'T KOSHER.
WHO'S GOING TO STOP ME? THIS PORK CHOP?
SO KOSHER LAW WAS A DEFENSIVE MECHANISM! HOW VERY CLEVER.

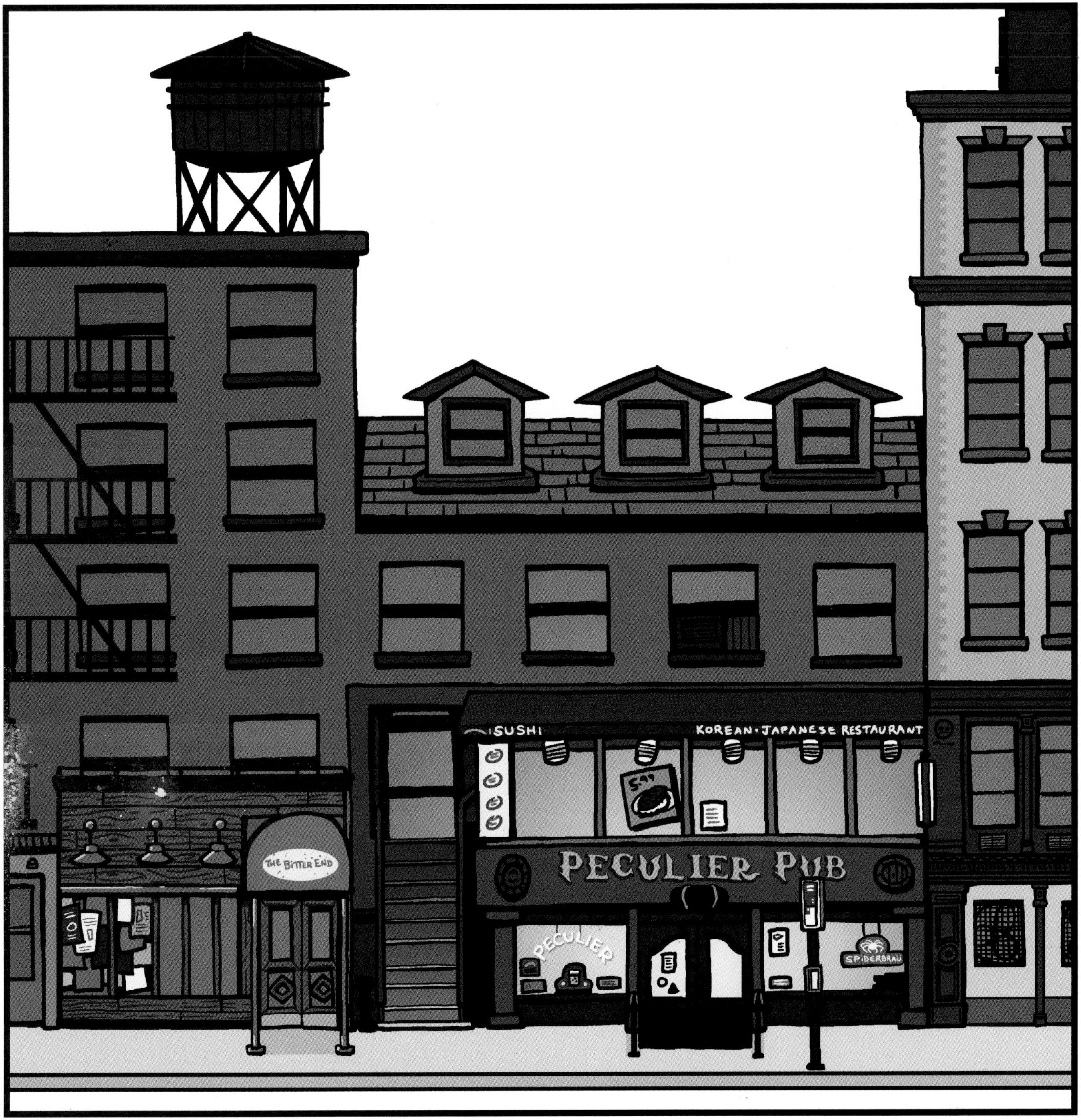
SUSHI
KOREAN · JAPANESE RESTAURANT
5.99
THE BITTER END
PECULIER PUB
PECULIER
SPIDERBRAU

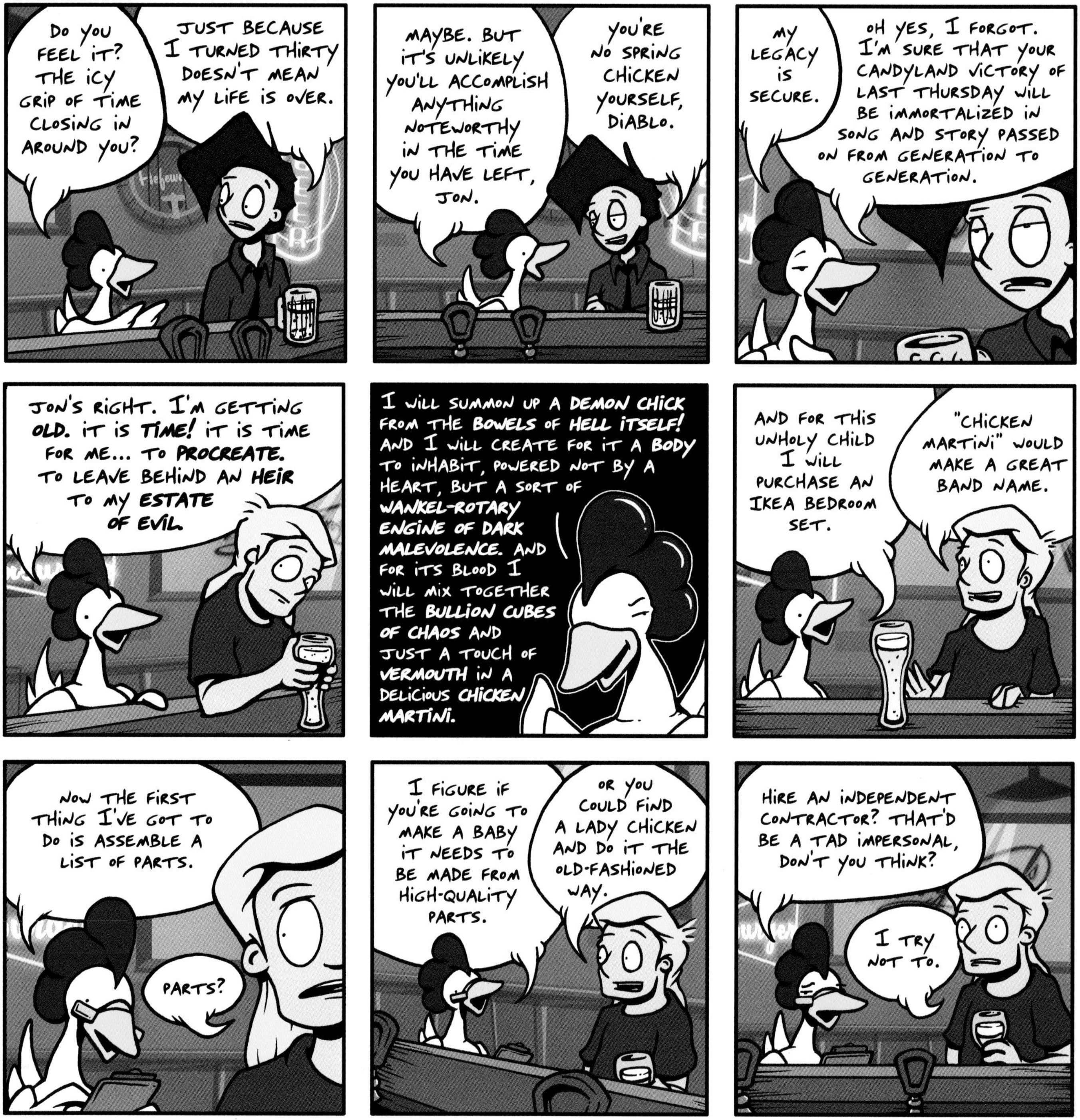
Do you feel it? The icy grip of time closing in around you?
Just because I turned thirty doesn't mean my life is over.
Maybe. But it's unlikely you'll accomplish anything noteworthy in the time you have left, Jon.
You're no spring chicken yourself, Diablo.
My legacy is secure.
Oh yes, I forgot. I'm sure that your Candyland victory of last Thursday will be immortalized in song and story passed on from generation to generation.
Jon's right. I'm getting old. It is time! It is time for me... to procreate. To leave behind an heir to my estate of evil.
I will summon up a demon chick from the bowels of hell itself! And I will create for it a body to inhabit, powered not by a heart, but a sort of Wankel-rotary engine of dark malevolence. And for its blood I will mix together the bullion cubes of chaos and just a touch of vermouth in a delicious chicken martini.
And for this unholy child I will purchase an IKEA bedroom set.
"Chicken martini" would make a great band name.
Now the first thing I've got to do is assemble a list of parts.
Parts?
I figure if you're going to make a baby it needs to be made from high-quality parts.
Or you could find a lady chicken and do it the old-fashioned way.
Hire an independent contractor? That'd be a tad impersonal, don't you think?
I try not to.

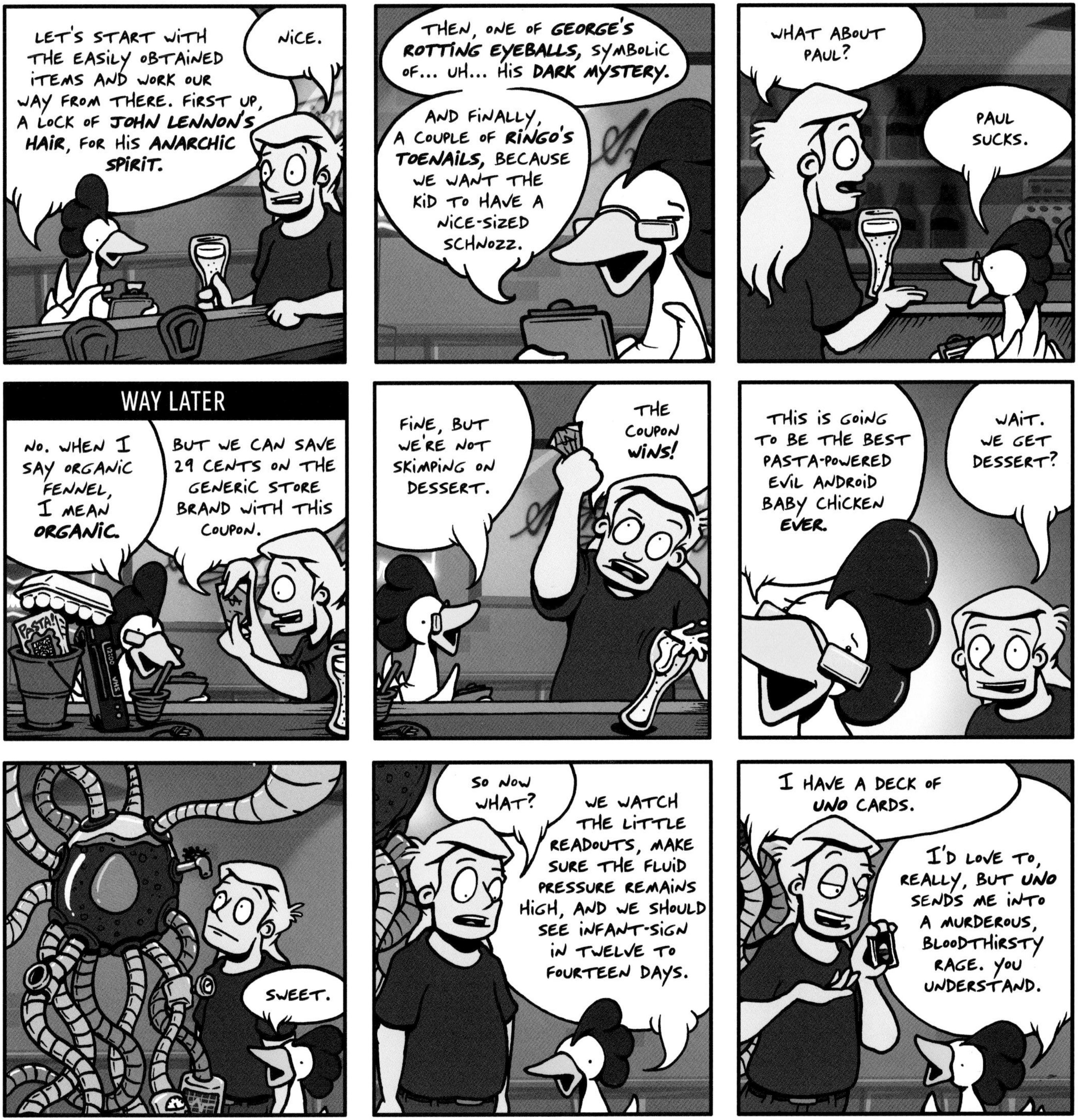
LET'S START WITH THE EASILY OBTAINED ITEMS AND WORK OUR WAY FROM THERE. FIRST UP, A LOCK OF JOHN LENNON'S HAIR, FOR HIS ANARCHIC SPIRIT.
NICE.
THEN, ONE OF GEORGE'S ROTTING EYEBALLS, SYMBOLIC OF... UH... HIS DARK MYSTERY.
AND FINALLY, A COUPLE OF RINGO'S TOENAILS, BECAUSE WE WANT THE KID TO HAVE A NICE-SIZED SCHNOZZ.
WHAT ABOUT PAUL?
PAUL SUCKS.
WAY LATER
NO. WHEN I SAY ORGANIC FENNEL, I MEAN ORGANIC.
BUT WE CAN SAVE 29 CENTS ON THE GENERIC STORE BRAND WITH THIS COUPON.
PASTA!
FINE, BUT WE'RE NOT SKIMPING ON DESSERT.
THE COUPON WINS!
THIS IS GOING TO BE THE BEST PASTA-POWERED EVIL ANDROID BABY CHICKEN EVER.
WAIT. WE GET DESSERT?
SWEET.
SO NOW WHAT?
WE WATCH THE LITTLE READOUTS, MAKE SURE THE FLUID PRESSURE REMAINS HIGH, AND WE SHOULD SEE INFANT-SIGN IN TWELVE TO FOURTEEN DAYS.
I HAVE A DECK OF UNO CARDS.
I'D LOVE TO, REALLY, BUT UNO SENDS ME INTO A MURDEROUS, BLOODTHIRSTY RAGE. YOU UNDERSTAND.

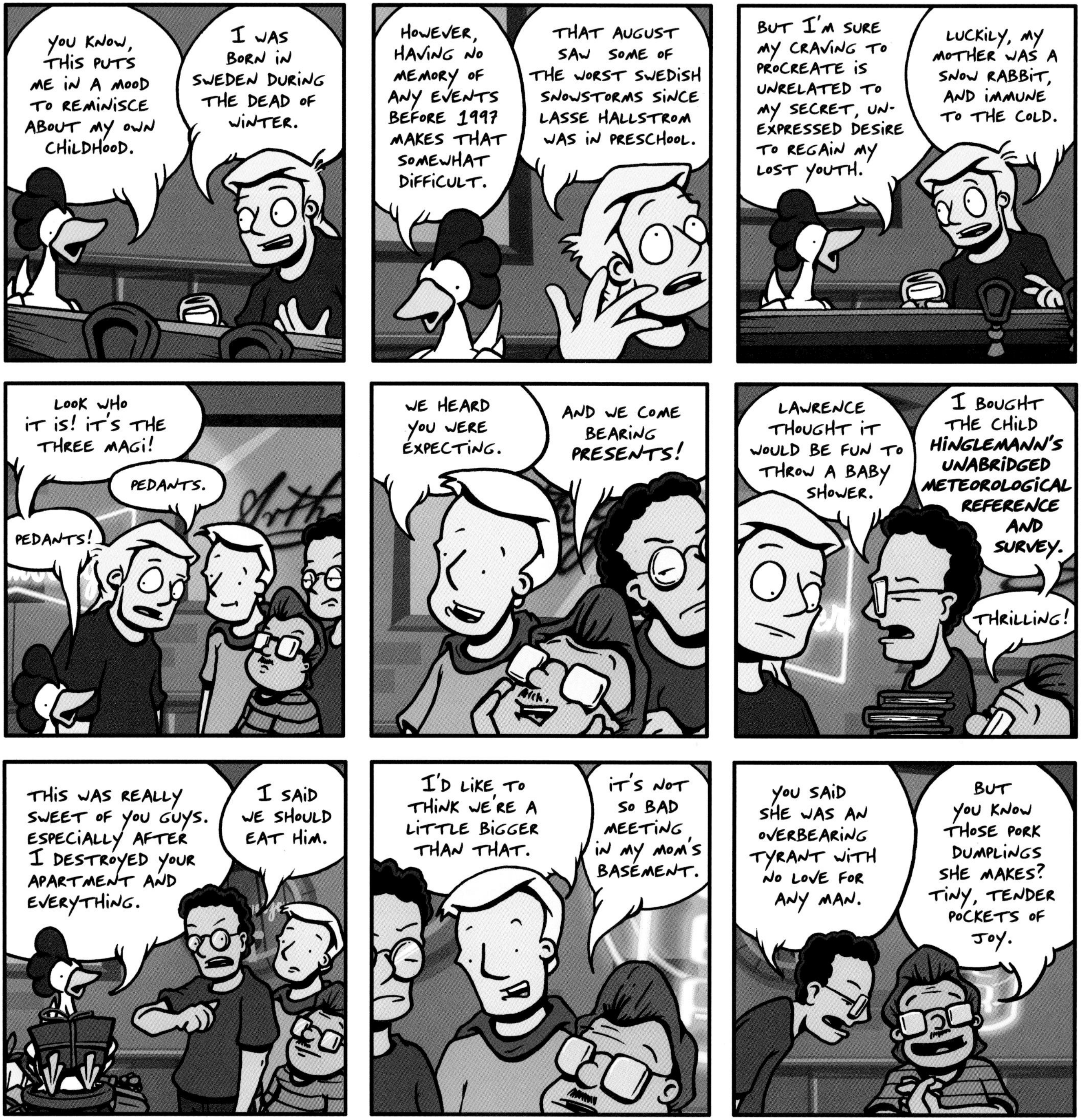
YOU KNOW, THIS PUTS ME IN A MOOD TO REMINISCE ABOUT MY OWN CHILDHOOD.
I WAS BORN IN SWEDEN DURING THE DEAD OF WINTER.
HOWEVER, HAVING NO MEMORY OF ANY EVENTS BEFORE 1997 MAKES THAT SOMEWHAT DIFFICULT.
THAT AUGUST SAW SOME OF THE WORST SWEDISH SNOWSTORMS SINCE LASSE HALLSTROM WAS IN PRESCHOOL.
BUT I'M SURE MY CRAVING TO PROCREATE IS UNRELATED TO MY SECRET, UN-EXPRESSED DESIRE TO REGAIN MY LOST YOUTH.
LUCKILY, MY MOTHER WAS A SNOW RABBIT, AND IMMUNE TO THE COLD.
LOOK WHO IT IS! IT'S THE THREE MAGI!
PEDANTS.
PEDANTS!
WE HEARD YOU WERE EXPECTING.
AND WE COME BEARING **PRESENTS**!
LAWRENCE THOUGHT IT WOULD BE FUN TO THROW A BABY SHOWER.
I BOUGHT THE CHILD **HINGLEMANN'S UNABRIDGED METEOROLOGICAL REFERENCE AND SURVEY.**
THRILLING!
THIS WAS REALLY SWEET OF YOU GUYS. ESPECIALLY AFTER I DESTROYED YOUR APARTMENT AND EVERYTHING.
I SAID WE SHOULD EAT HIM.
I'D LIKE TO THINK WE'RE A LITTLE BIGGER THAN THAT.
IT'S NOT SO BAD MEETING IN MY MOM'S BASEMENT.
YOU SAID SHE WAS AN OVERBEARING TYRANT WITH NO LOVE FOR ANY MAN.
BUT YOU KNOW THOSE PORK DUMPLINGS SHE MAKES? TINY, TENDER POCKETS OF JOY.

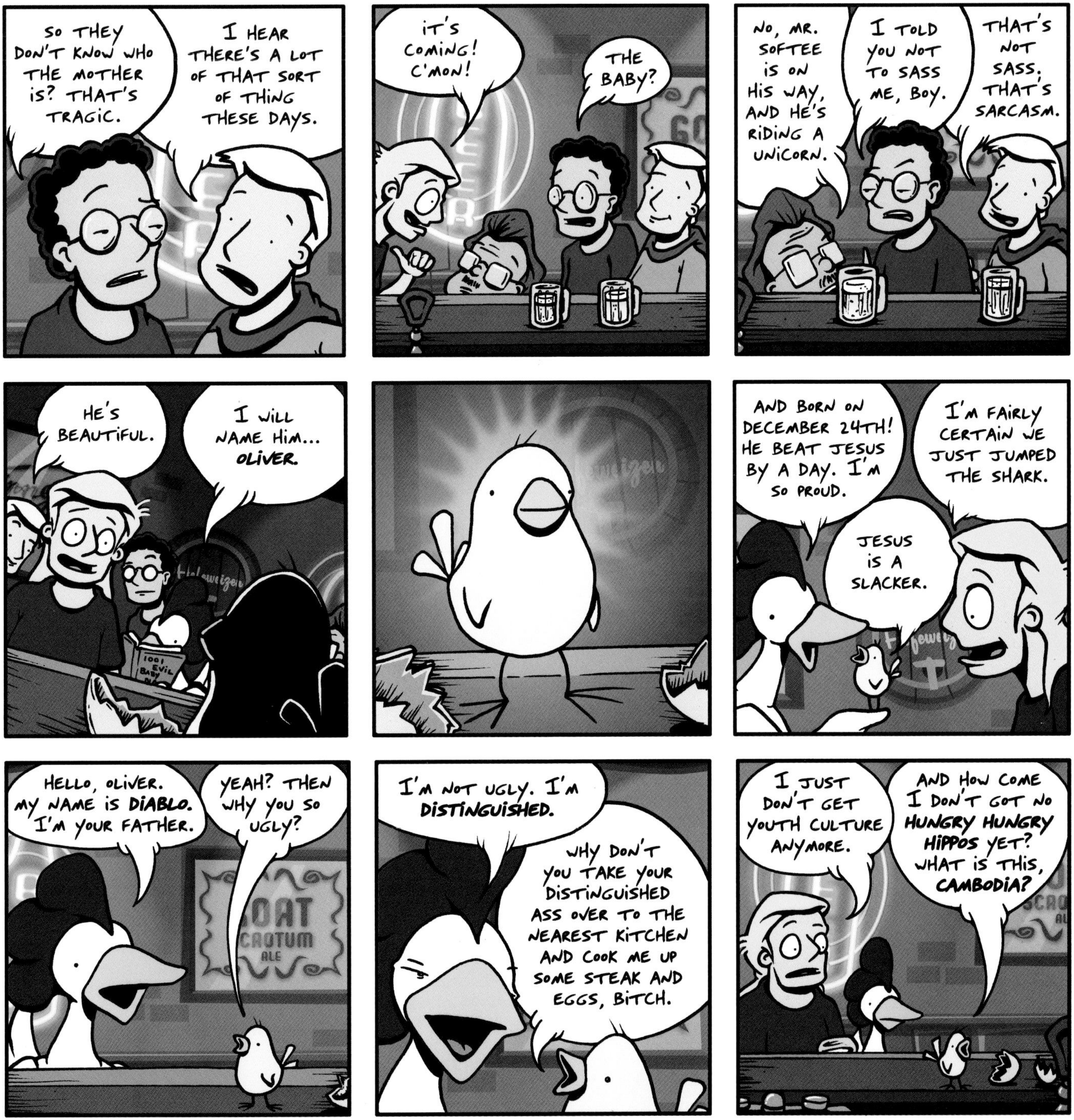
SO THEY DON'T KNOW WHO THE MOTHER IS? THAT'S TRAGIC.
I HEAR THERE'S A LOT OF THAT SORT OF THING THESE DAYS.
IT'S COMING! C'MON!
THE BABY?
NO, MR. SOFTEE IS ON HIS WAY, AND HE'S RIDING A UNICORN.
I TOLD YOU NOT TO SASS ME, BOY.
THAT'S NOT SASS, THAT'S SARCASM.
HE'S BEAUTIFUL.
I WILL NAME HIM... **OLIVER.**
AND BORN ON DECEMBER 24TH! HE BEAT JESUS BY A DAY. I'M SO PROUD.
I'M FAIRLY CERTAIN WE JUST JUMPED THE SHARK.
JESUS IS A SLACKER.
HELLO, OLIVER. MY NAME IS **DIABLO.** I'M YOUR FATHER.
YEAH? THEN WHY YOU SO UGLY?
I'M NOT UGLY. I'M **DISTINGUISHED.**
WHY DON'T YOU TAKE YOUR DISTINGUISHED ASS OVER TO THE NEAREST KITCHEN AND COOK ME UP SOME STEAK AND EGGS, BITCH.
I JUST DON'T GET YOUTH CULTURE ANYMORE.
AND HOW COME I DON'T GOT NO **HUNGRY HUNGRY HIPPOS** YET? WHAT IS THIS, **CAMBODIA?**

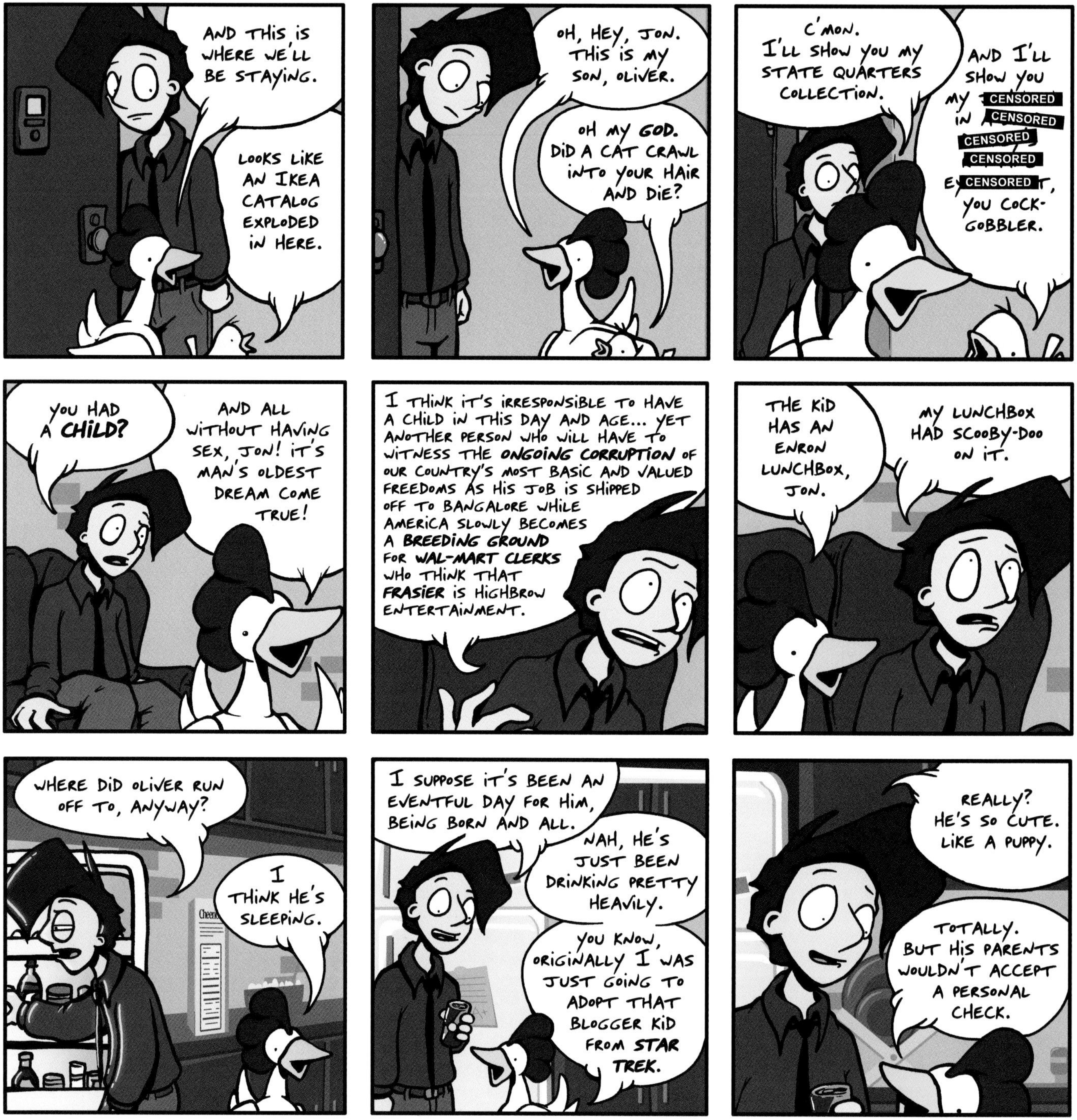
AND THIS IS WHERE WE'LL BE STAYING.
LOOKS LIKE AN IKEA CATALOG EXPLODED IN HERE.
OH, HEY, JON. THIS IS MY SON, OLIVER.
OH MY **GOD.** DID A CAT CRAWL INTO YOUR HAIR AND DIE?
C'MON. I'LL SHOW YOU MY STATE QUARTERS COLLECTION.
AND I'LL SHOW YOU MY CENSORED IN CENSORED CENSORED CENSORED CENSORED, YOU COCK-GOBBLER.
YOU HAD A **CHILD?**
AND ALL WITHOUT HAVING SEX, JON! IT'S MAN'S OLDEST DREAM COME TRUE!
I THINK IT'S IRRESPONSIBLE TO HAVE A CHILD IN THIS DAY AND AGE... YET ANOTHER PERSON WHO WILL HAVE TO WITNESS THE **ONGOING CORRUPTION** OF OUR COUNTRY'S MOST BASIC AND VALUED FREEDOMS AS HIS JOB IS SHIPPED OFF TO BANGALORE WHILE AMERICA SLOWLY BECOMES A **BREEDING GROUND** FOR **WAL-MART CLERKS** WHO THINK THAT **FRASIER** IS HIGHBROW ENTERTAINMENT.
THE KID HAS AN ENRON LUNCHBOX, JON.
MY LUNCHBOX HAD SCOOBY-DOO ON IT.
WHERE DID OLIVER RUN OFF TO, ANYWAY?
I THINK HE'S SLEEPING.
I SUPPOSE IT'S BEEN AN EVENTFUL DAY FOR HIM, BEING BORN AND ALL.
NAH, HE'S JUST BEEN DRINKING PRETTY HEAVILY.
YOU KNOW, ORIGINALLY I WAS JUST GOING TO ADOPT THAT BLOGGER KID FROM **STAR TREK.**
REALLY? HE'S SO CUTE. LIKE A PUPPY.
TOTALLY. BUT HIS PARENTS WOULDN'T ACCEPT A PERSONAL CHECK.

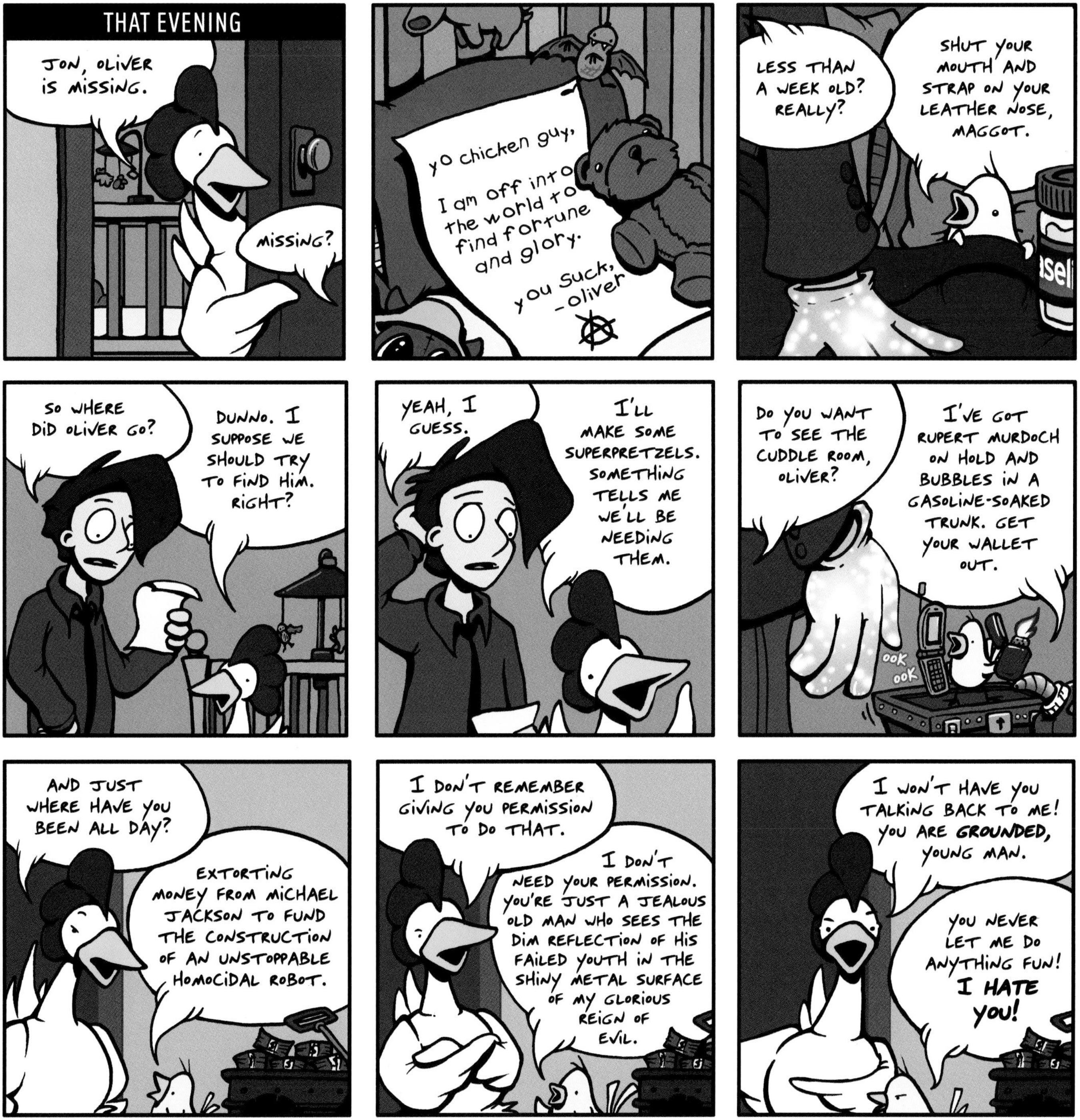
THAT EVENING
JON, OLIVER IS MISSING.
MISSING?
yo chicken guy, I am off into the world to find fortune and glory. you suck, -oliver
LESS THAN A WEEK OLD? REALLY?
SHUT YOUR MOUTH AND STRAP ON YOUR LEATHER NOSE, MAGGOT.
SO WHERE DID OLIVER GO?
DUNNO. I SUPPOSE WE SHOULD TRY TO FIND HIM. RIGHT?
YEAH, I GUESS.
I'LL MAKE SOME SUPERPRETZELS. SOMETHING TELLS ME WE'LL BE NEEDING THEM.
DO YOU WANT TO SEE THE CUDDLE ROOM, OLIVER?
I'VE GOT RUPERT MURDOCH ON HOLD AND BUBBLES IN A GASOLINE-SOAKED TRUNK. GET YOUR WALLET OUT.
OOK OOK
AND JUST WHERE HAVE YOU BEEN ALL DAY?
EXTORTING MONEY FROM MICHAEL JACKSON TO FUND THE CONSTRUCTION OF AN UNSTOPPABLE HOMOCIDAL ROBOT.
I DON'T REMEMBER GIVING YOU PERMISSION TO DO THAT.
I DON'T NEED YOUR PERMISSION. YOU'RE JUST A JEALOUS OLD MAN WHO SEES THE DIM REFLECTION OF HIS FAILED YOUTH IN THE SHINY METAL SURFACE OF MY GLORIOUS REIGN OF EVIL.
I WON'T HAVE YOU TALKING BACK TO ME! YOU ARE **GROUNDED**, YOUNG MAN.
YOU NEVER LET ME DO ANYTHING FUN! **I HATE YOU!**

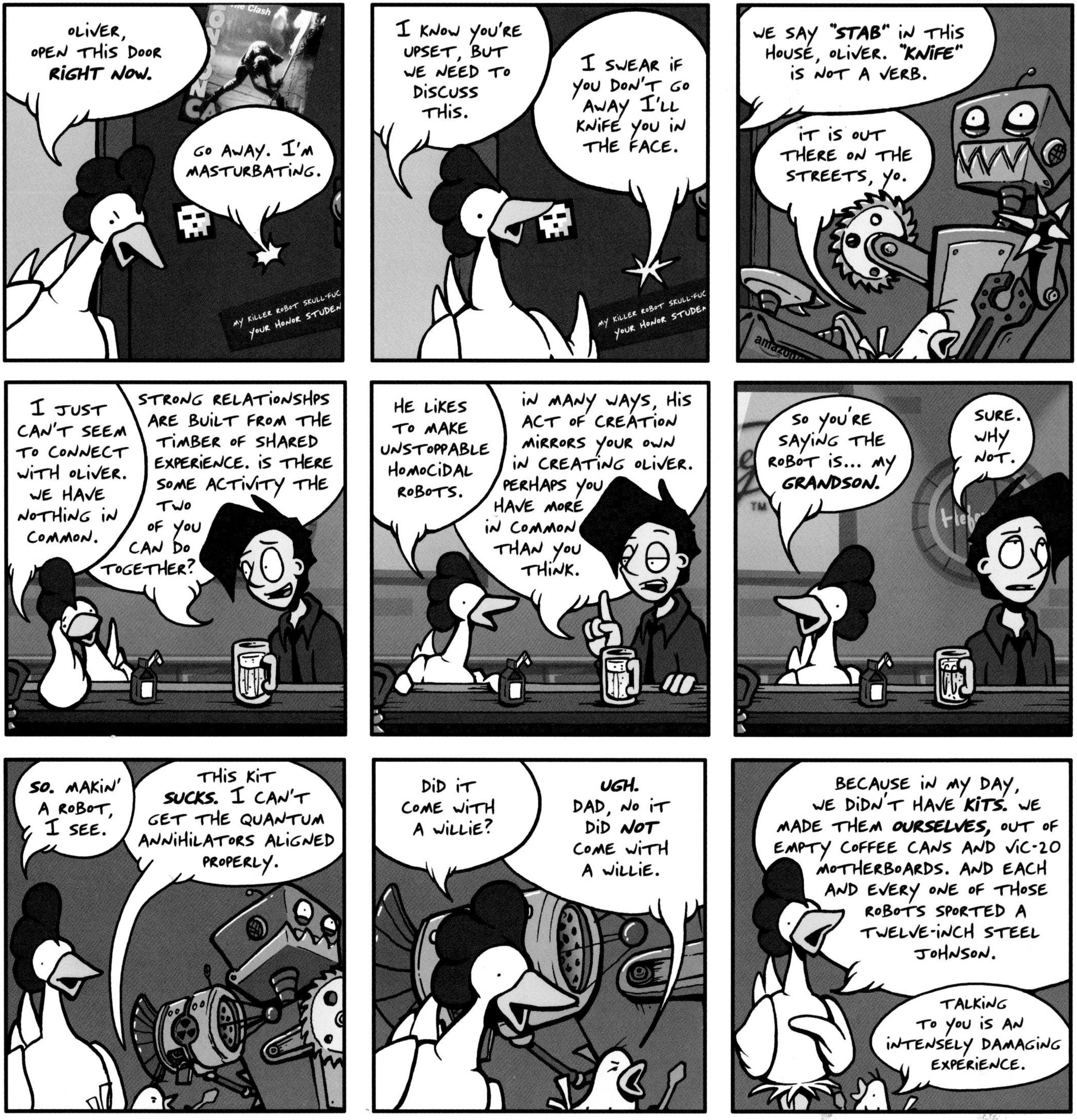
The Clash
OLIVER, OPEN THIS DOOR **RIGHT NOW.**
GO AWAY. I'M MASTURBATING.
MY KILLER ROBOT SKULL-FUC
YOUR HONOR STUDEN
I KNOW YOU'RE UPSET, BUT WE NEED TO DISCUSS THIS.
I SWEAR IF YOU DON'T GO AWAY I'LL KNIFE YOU IN THE FACE.
MY KILLER ROBOT SKULL-FUC
YOUR HONOR STUDEN
WE SAY **"STAB"** IN THIS HOUSE, OLIVER. **"KNIFE"** IS NOT A VERB.
IT IS OUT THERE ON THE STREETS, YO.
I JUST CAN'T SEEM TO CONNECT WITH OLIVER. WE HAVE NOTHING IN COMMON.
STRONG RELATIONSHPS ARE BUILT FROM THE TIMBER OF SHARED EXPERIENCE. IS THERE SOME ACTIVITY THE TWO OF YOU CAN DO TOGETHER?
HE LIKES TO MAKE UNSTOPPABLE HOMOCIDAL ROBOTS.
IN MANY WAYS, HIS ACT OF CREATION MIRRORS YOUR OWN IN CREATING OLIVER. PERHAPS YOU HAVE MORE IN COMMON THAN YOU THINK.
SO YOU'RE SAYING THE ROBOT IS... MY **GRANDSON.**
SURE. WHY NOT.
SO. MAKIN' A ROBOT, I SEE.
THIS KIT **SUCKS.** I CAN'T GET THE QUANTUM ANNIHILATORS ALIGNED PROPERLY.
DID IT COME WITH A WILLIE?
UGH. DAD, NO IT DID **NOT** COME WITH A WILLIE.
BECAUSE IN MY DAY, WE DIDN'T HAVE **KITS.** WE MADE THEM **OURSELVES,** OUT OF EMPTY COFFEE CANS AND VIC-20 MOTHERBOARDS. AND EACH AND EVERY ONE OF THOSE ROBOTS SPORTED A TWELVE-INCH STEEL JOHNSON.
TALKING TO YOU IS AN INTENSELY DAMAGING EXPERIENCE.

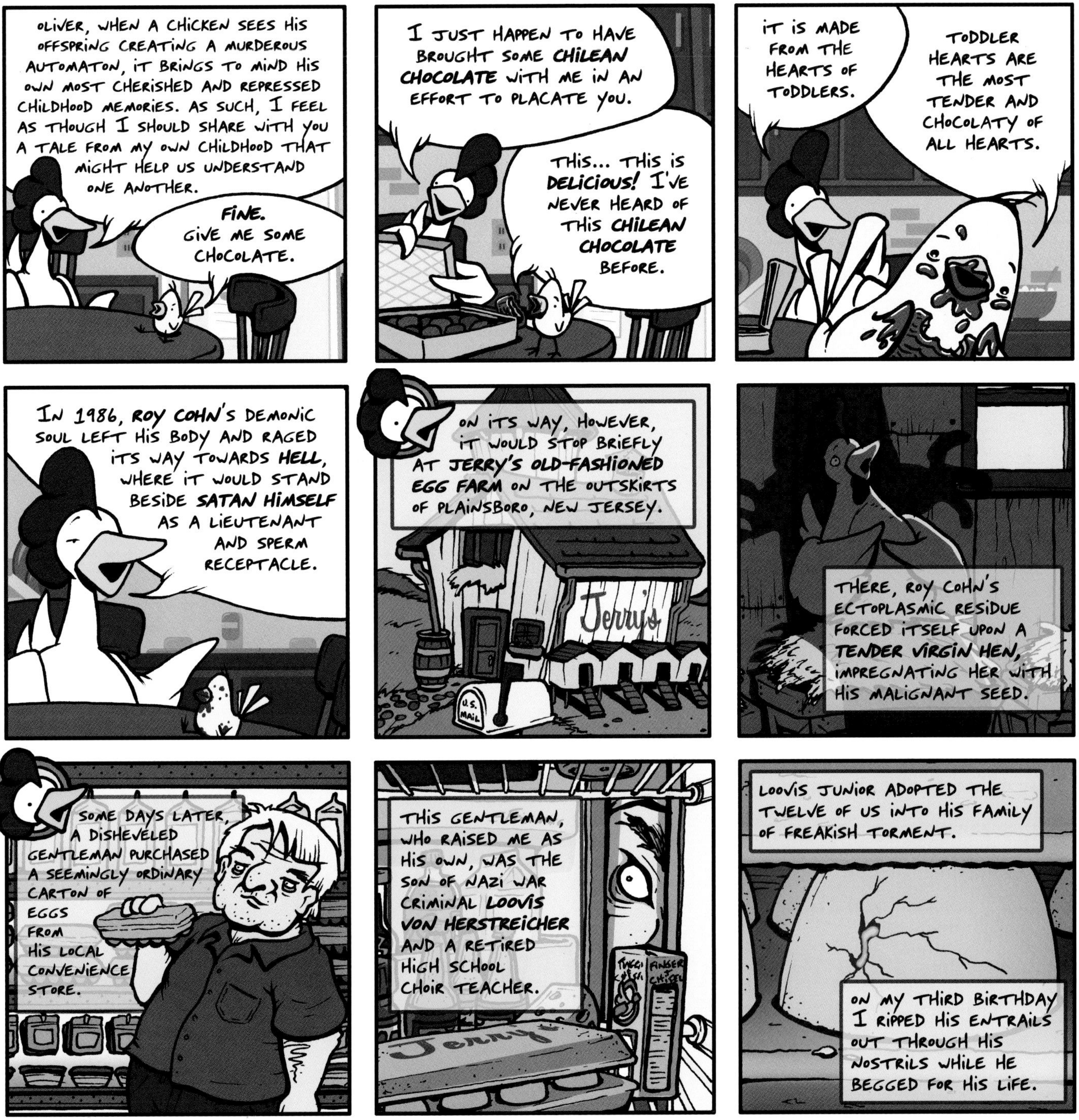
OLIVER, WHEN A CHICKEN SEES HIS OFFSPRING CREATING A MURDEROUS AUTOMATON, IT BRINGS TO MIND HIS OWN MOST CHERISHED AND REPRESSED CHILDHOOD MEMORIES. AS SUCH, I FEEL AS THOUGH I SHOULD SHARE WITH YOU A TALE FROM MY OWN CHILDHOOD THAT MIGHT HELP US UNDERSTAND ONE ANOTHER.
FINE. GIVE ME SOME CHOCOLATE.
I JUST HAPPEN TO HAVE BROUGHT SOME **CHILEAN CHOCOLATE** WITH ME IN AN EFFORT TO PLACATE YOU.
THIS... THIS IS **DELICIOUS!** I'VE NEVER HEARD OF THIS **CHILEAN CHOCOLATE** BEFORE.
IT IS MADE FROM THE HEARTS OF TODDLERS.
TODDLER HEARTS ARE THE MOST TENDER AND CHOCOLATY OF ALL HEARTS.
IN 1986, **ROY COHN**'S DEMONIC SOUL LEFT HIS BODY AND RAGED ITS WAY TOWARDS **HELL**, WHERE IT WOULD STAND BESIDE **SATAN HIMSELF** AS A LIEUTENANT AND SPERM RECEPTACLE.
ON ITS WAY, HOWEVER, IT WOULD STOP BRIEFLY AT **JERRY'S OLD-FASHIONED EGG FARM** ON THE OUTSKIRTS OF PLAINSBORO, NEW JERSEY.
Jerry's
U.S. MAIL
THERE, ROY COHN'S ECTOPLASMIC RESIDUE FORCED ITSELF UPON A **TENDER VIRGIN HEN**, IMPREGNATING HER WITH HIS MALIGNANT SEED.
SOME DAYS LATER, A DISHEVELED GENTLEMAN PURCHASED A SEEMINGLY ORDINARY CARTON OF EGGS FROM HIS LOCAL CONVENIENCE STORE.
THIS GENTLEMAN, WHO RAISED ME AS HIS OWN, WAS THE SON OF NAZI WAR CRIMINAL **LOOVIS VON HERSTREICHER** AND A RETIRED HIGH SCHOOL CHOIR TEACHER.
Jerry's
LOOVIS JUNIOR ADOPTED THE TWELVE OF US INTO HIS FAMILY OF FREAKISH TORMENT.
ON MY THIRD BIRTHDAY I RIPPED HIS ENTRAILS OUT THROUGH HIS NOSTRILS WHILE HE BEGGED FOR HIS LIFE.

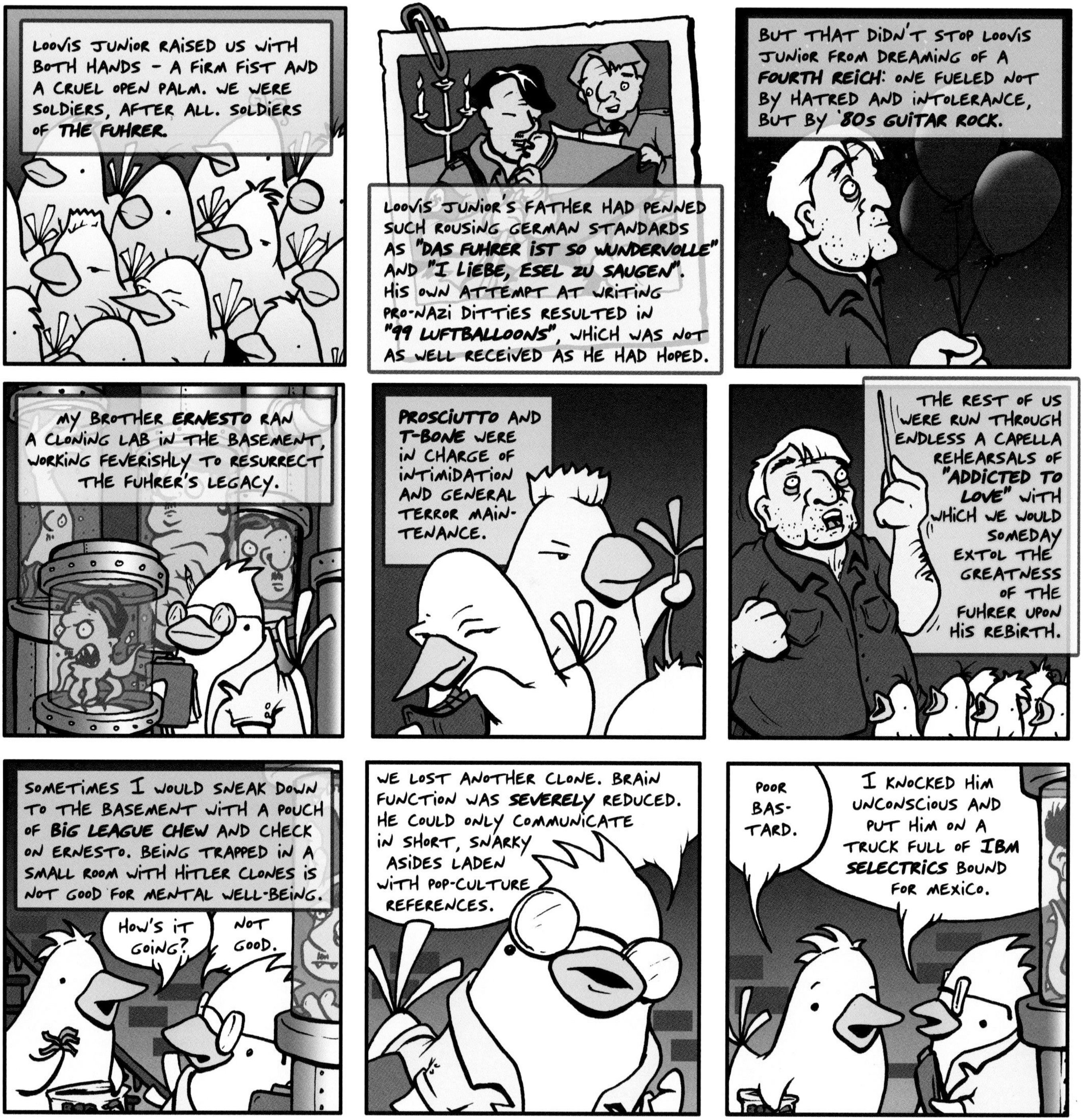
LOOVIS JUNIOR RAISED US WITH BOTH HANDS – A FIRM FIST AND A CRUEL OPEN PALM. WE WERE SOLDIERS, AFTER ALL. SOLDIERS OF THE FUHRER.
LOOVIS JUNIOR'S FATHER HAD PENNED SUCH ROUSING GERMAN STANDARDS AS "DAS FUHRER IST SO WUNDERVOLLE" AND "I LIEBE, ESEL ZU SAUGEN". HIS OWN ATTEMPT AT WRITING PRO-NAZI DITTIES RESULTED IN "99 LUFTBALLOONS", WHICH WAS NOT AS WELL RECEIVED AS HE HAD HOPED.
BUT THAT DIDN'T STOP LOOVIS JUNIOR FROM DREAMING OF A FOURTH REICH: ONE FUELED NOT BY HATRED AND INTOLERANCE, BUT BY '80S GUITAR ROCK.
MY BROTHER ERNESTO RAN A CLONING LAB IN THE BASEMENT, WORKING FEVERISHLY TO RESURRECT THE FUHRER'S LEGACY.
PROSCIUTTO AND T-BONE WERE IN CHARGE OF INTIMIDATION AND GENERAL TERROR MAIN-TENANCE.
THE REST OF US WERE RUN THROUGH ENDLESS A CAPELLA REHEARSALS OF "ADDICTED TO LOVE" WITH WHICH WE WOULD SOMEDAY EXTOL THE GREATNESS OF THE FUHRER UPON HIS REBIRTH.
SOMETIMES I WOULD SNEAK DOWN TO THE BASEMENT WITH A POUCH OF BIG LEAGUE CHEW AND CHECK ON ERNESTO. BEING TRAPPED IN A SMALL ROOM WITH HITLER CLONES IS NOT GOOD FOR MENTAL WELL-BEING.
HOW'S IT GOING?
NOT GOOD.
WE LOST ANOTHER CLONE. BRAIN FUNCTION WAS SEVERELY REDUCED. HE COULD ONLY COMMUNICATE IN SHORT, SNARKY ASIDES LADEN WITH POP-CULTURE REFERENCES.
POOR BAS-TARD.
I KNOCKED HIM UNCONSCIOUS AND PUT HIM ON A TRUCK FULL OF IBM SELECTRICS BOUND FOR MEXICO.

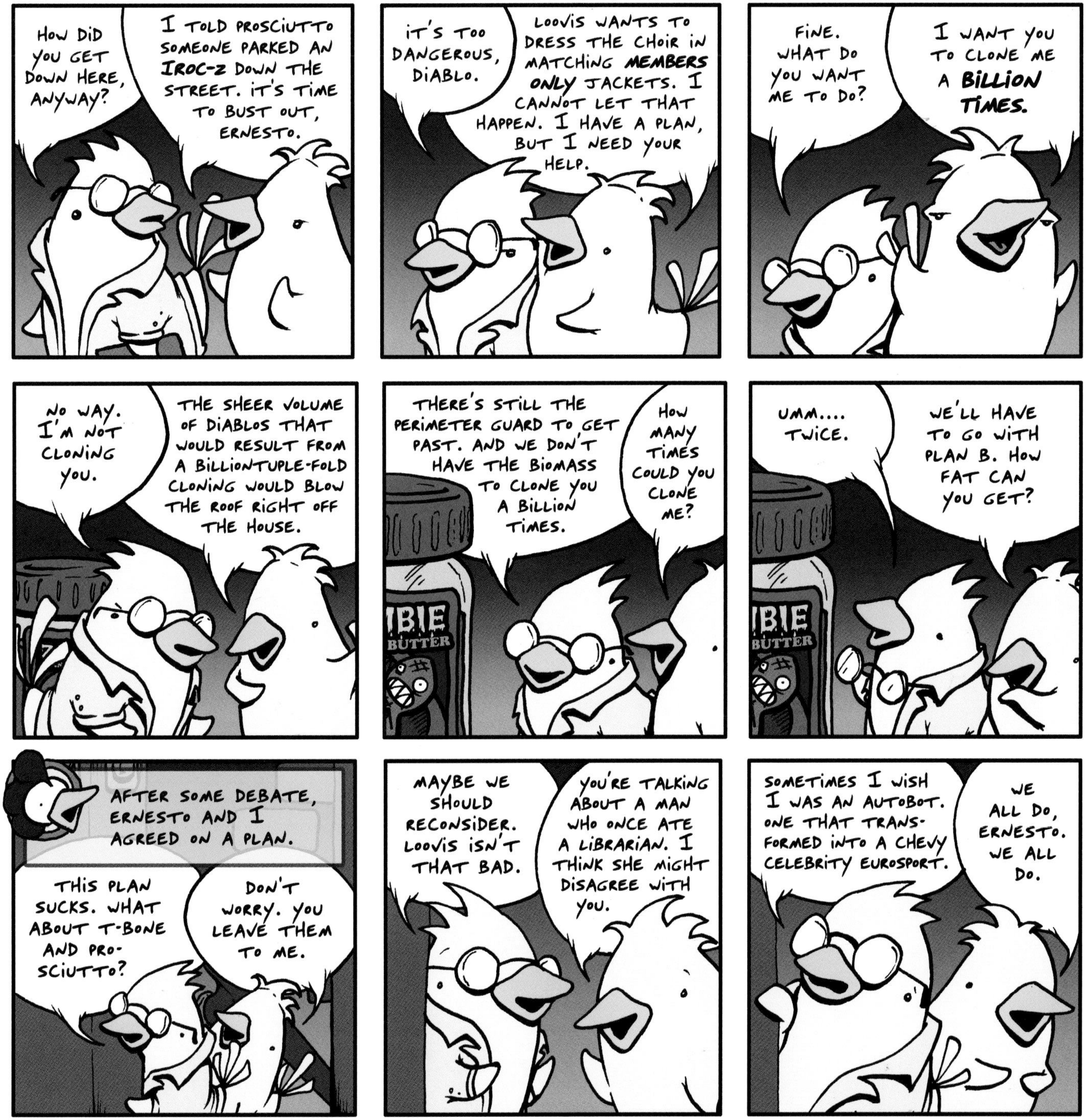

HOW DID YOU GET DOWN HERE, ANYWAY?
I TOLD PROSCIUTTO SOMEONE PARKED AN **IROC-Z** DOWN THE STREET. IT'S TIME TO BUST OUT, ERNESTO.
IT'S TOO DANGEROUS, DIABLO.
LOOVIS WANTS TO DRESS THE CHOIR IN MATCHING ***MEMBERS ONLY*** JACKETS. I CANNOT LET THAT HAPPEN. I HAVE A PLAN, BUT I NEED YOUR HELP.
FINE. WHAT DO YOU WANT ME TO DO?
I WANT YOU TO CLONE ME A **BILLION TIMES.**
NO WAY. I'M NOT CLONING YOU.
THE SHEER VOLUME OF DIABLOS THAT WOULD RESULT FROM A BILLIONTUPLE-FOLD CLONING WOULD BLOW THE ROOF RIGHT OFF THE HOUSE.
THERE'S STILL THE PERIMETER GUARD TO GET PAST. AND WE DON'T HAVE THE BIOMASS TO CLONE YOU A BILLION TIMES.
HOW MANY TIMES COULD YOU CLONE ME?
UMM.... TWICE.
WE'LL HAVE TO GO WITH PLAN B. HOW FAT CAN YOU GET?
AFTER SOME DEBATE, ERNESTO AND I AGREED ON A PLAN.
THIS PLAN SUCKS. WHAT ABOUT T-BONE AND PRO-SCIUTTO?
DON'T WORRY. YOU LEAVE THEM TO ME.
MAYBE WE SHOULD RECONSIDER. LOOVIS ISN'T THAT BAD.
YOU'RE TALKING ABOUT A MAN WHO ONCE ATE A LIBRARIAN. I THINK SHE MIGHT DISAGREE WITH YOU.
SOMETIMES I WISH I WAS AN AUTOBOT. ONE THAT TRANS-FORMED INTO A CHEVY CELEBRITY EUROSPORT.
WE ALL DO, ERNESTO. WE ALL DO.

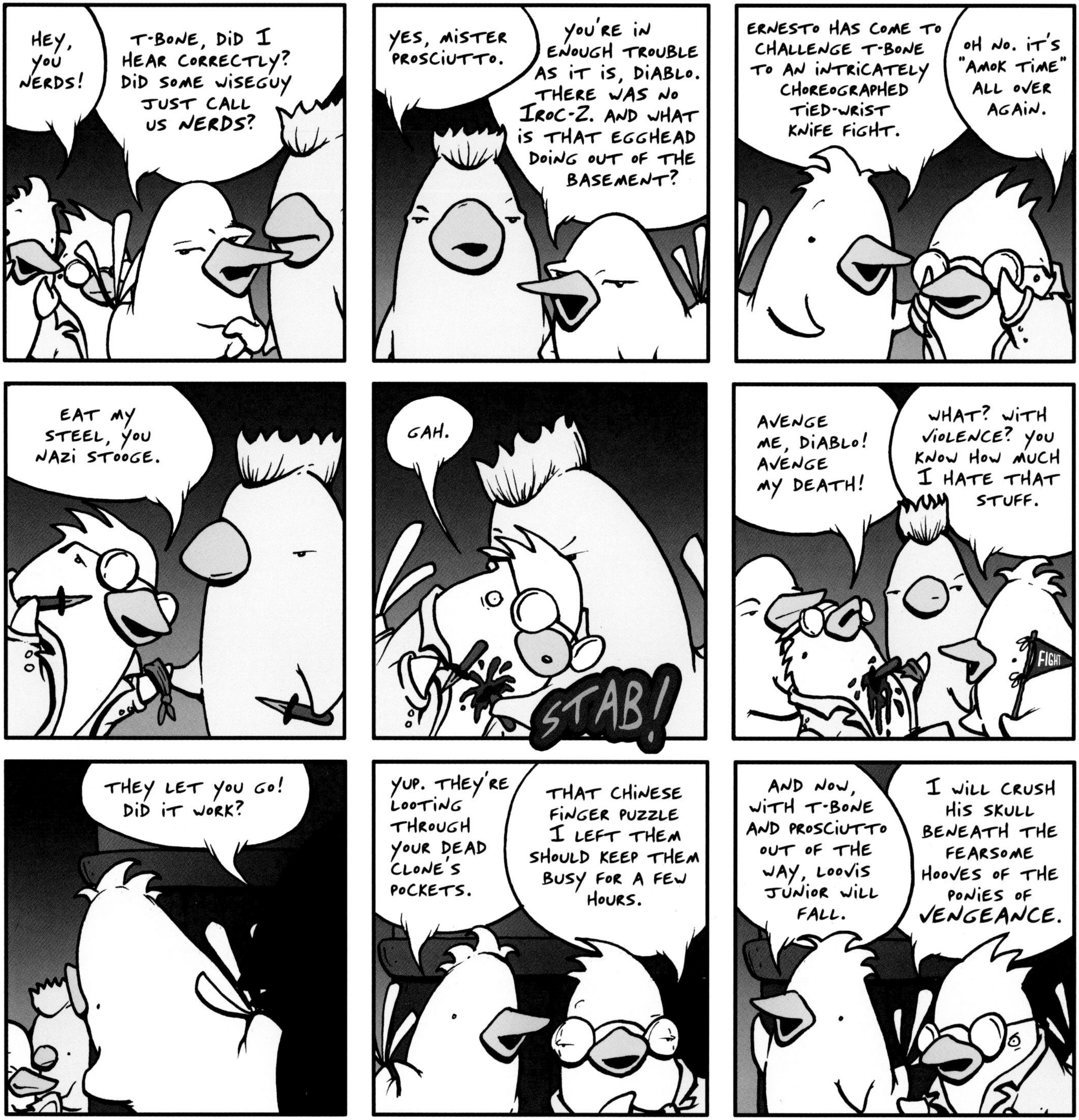
HEY, YOU NERDS!
T-BONE, DID I HEAR CORRECTLY? DID SOME WISEGUY JUST CALL US NERDS?
YES, MISTER PROSCIUTTO.
YOU'RE IN ENOUGH TROUBLE AS IT IS, DIABLO. THERE WAS NO IROC-Z. AND WHAT IS THAT EGGHEAD DOING OUT OF THE BASEMENT?
ERNESTO HAS COME TO CHALLENGE T-BONE TO AN INTRICATELY CHOREOGRAPHED TIED-WRIST KNIFE FIGHT.
OH NO. IT'S "AMOK TIME" ALL OVER AGAIN.
EAT MY STEEL, YOU NAZI STOOGE.
GAH.
STAB!
AVENGE ME, DIABLO! AVENGE MY DEATH!
WHAT? WITH VIOLENCE? YOU KNOW HOW MUCH I HATE THAT STUFF.
FIGHT
THEY LET YOU GO! DID IT WORK?
YUP. THEY'RE LOOTING THROUGH YOUR DEAD CLONE'S POCKETS.
THAT CHINESE FINGER PUZZLE I LEFT THEM SHOULD KEEP THEM BUSY FOR A FEW HOURS.
AND NOW, WITH T-BONE AND PROSCIUTTO OUT OF THE WAY, LOOVIS JUNIOR WILL FALL.
I WILL CRUSH HIS SKULL BENEATH THE FEARSOME HOOVES OF THE PONIES OF VENGEANCE.

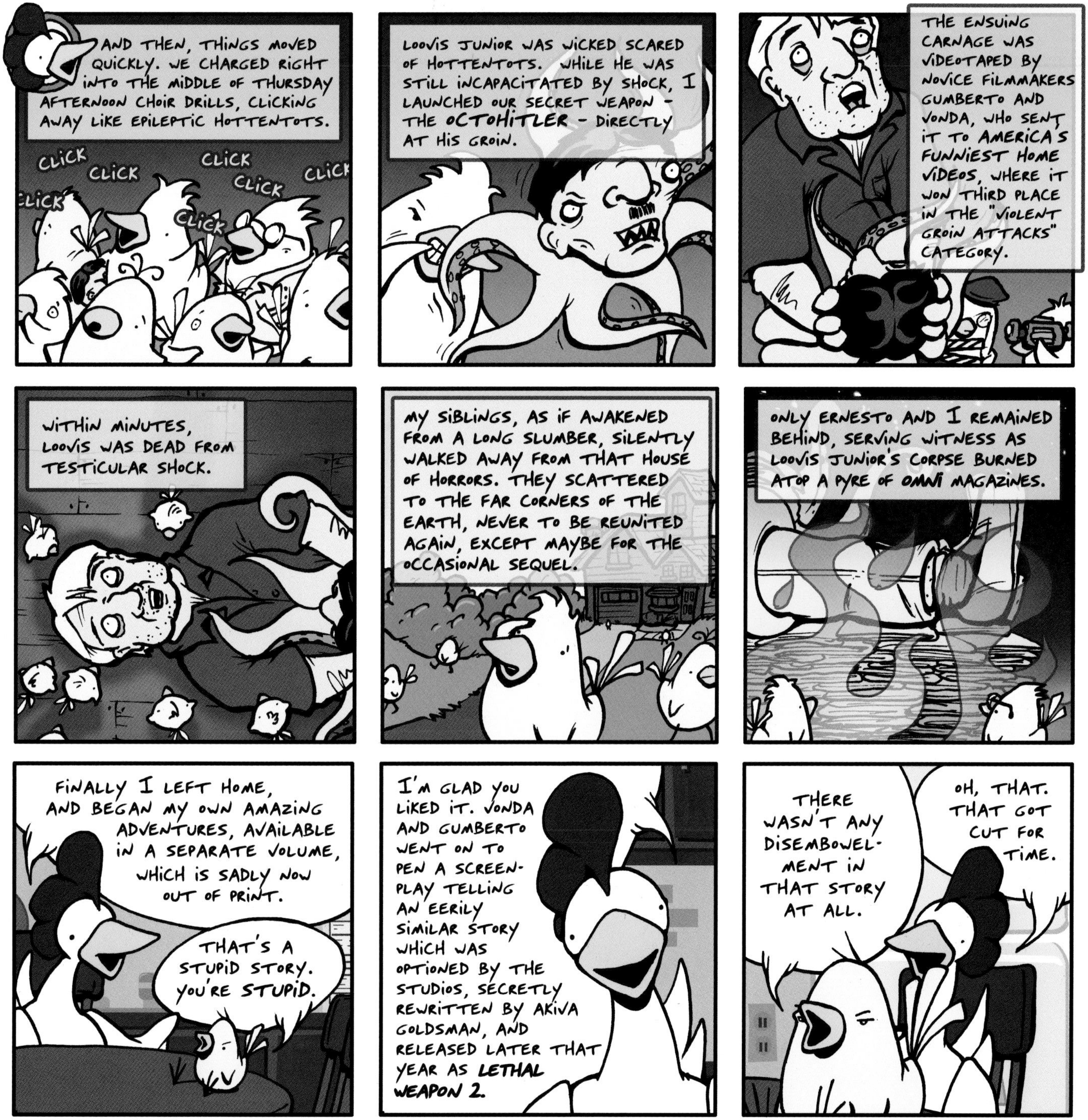
AND THEN, THINGS MOVED QUICKLY. WE CHARGED RIGHT INTO THE MIDDLE OF THURSDAY AFTERNOON CHOIR DRILLS, CLICKING AWAY LIKE EPILEPTIC HOTTENTOTS.
CLICK CLICK CLICK CLICK CLICK CLICK CLICK
LOOVIS JUNIOR WAS WICKED SCARED OF HOTTENTOTS. WHILE HE WAS STILL INCAPACITATED BY SHOCK, I LAUNCHED OUR SECRET WEAPON – THE OCTOHITLER – DIRECTLY AT HIS GROIN.
THE ENSUING CARNAGE WAS VIDEOTAPED BY NOVICE FILMMAKERS GUMBERTO AND VONDA, WHO SENT IT TO AMERICA'S FUNNIEST HOME VIDEOS, WHERE IT WON THIRD PLACE IN THE "VIOLENT GROIN ATTACKS" CATEGORY.
WITHIN MINUTES, LOOVIS WAS DEAD FROM TESTICULAR SHOCK.
MY SIBLINGS, AS IF AWAKENED FROM A LONG SLUMBER, SILENTLY WALKED AWAY FROM THAT HOUSE OF HORRORS. THEY SCATTERED TO THE FAR CORNERS OF THE EARTH, NEVER TO BE REUNITED AGAIN, EXCEPT MAYBE FOR THE OCCASIONAL SEQUEL.
ONLY ERNESTO AND I REMAINED BEHIND, SERVING WITNESS AS LOOVIS JUNIOR'S CORPSE BURNED ATOP A PYRE OF OMNI MAGAZINES.
FINALLY I LEFT HOME, AND BEGAN MY OWN AMAZING ADVENTURES, AVAILABLE IN A SEPARATE VOLUME, WHICH IS SADLY NOW OUT OF PRINT.
THAT'S A STUPID STORY. YOU'RE STUPID.
I'M GLAD YOU LIKED IT. VONDA AND GUMBERTO WENT ON TO PEN A SCREENPLAY TELLING AN EERILY SIMILAR STORY WHICH WAS OPTIONED BY THE STUDIOS, SECRETLY REWRITTEN BY AKIVA GOLDSMAN, AND RELEASED LATER THAT YEAR AS LETHAL WEAPON 2.
THERE WASN'T ANY DISEMBOWELMENT IN THAT STORY AT ALL.
OH, THAT. THAT GOT CUT FOR TIME.

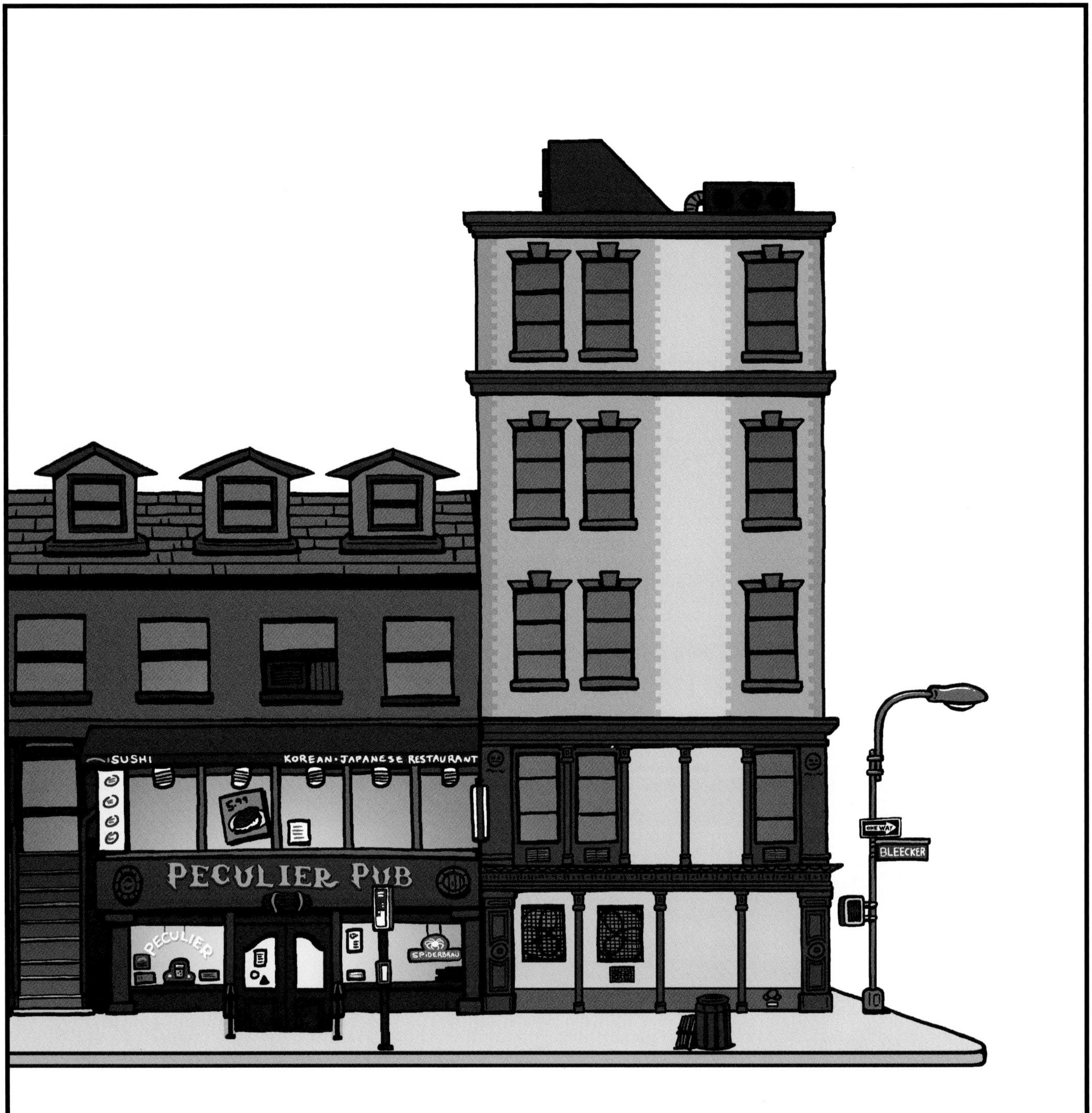
SUSHI
KOREAN·JAPANESE RESTAURANT
PECULIER PUB
PECULIER
SPIDERBRAU
ONE WAY
BLEECKER

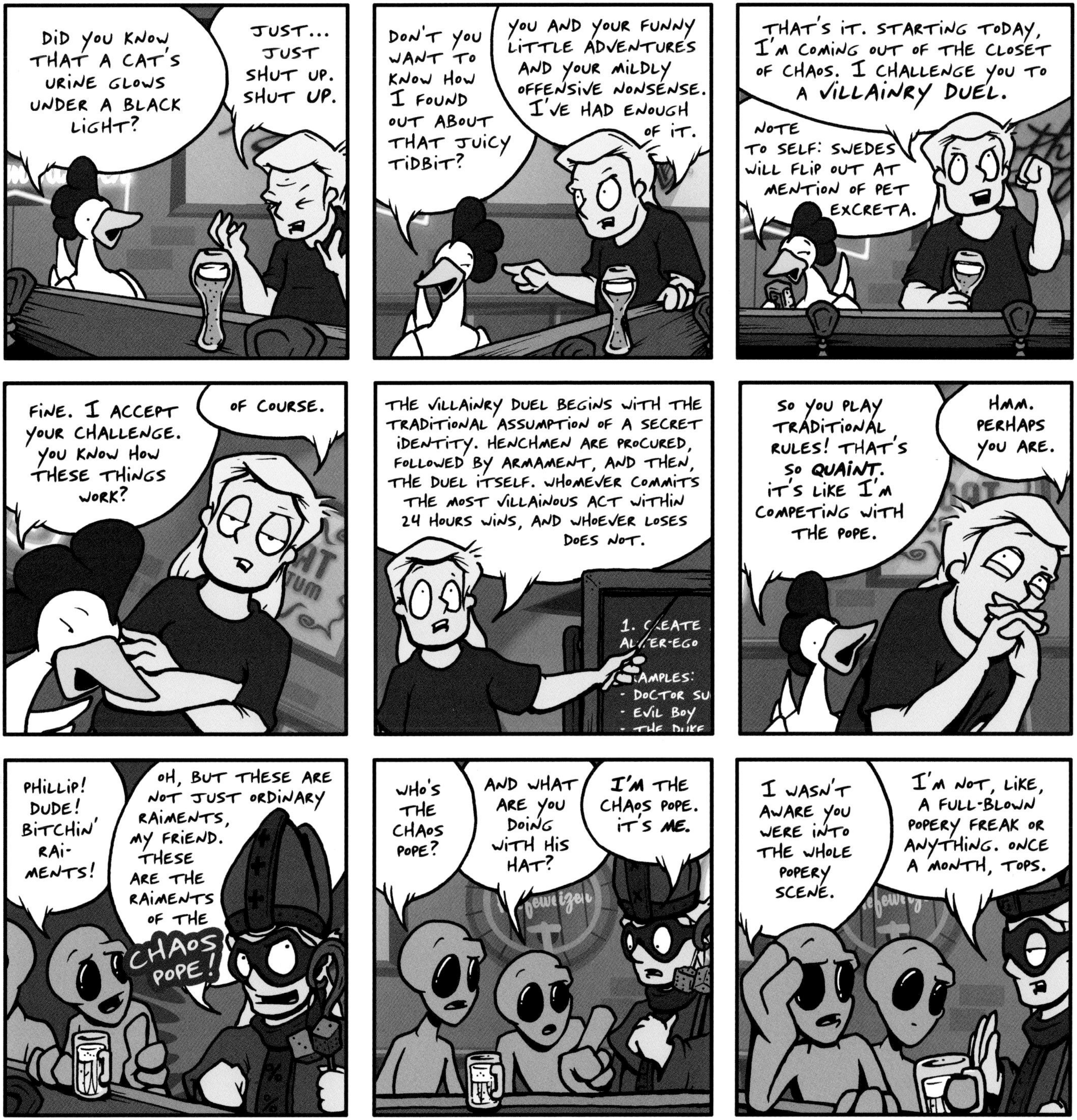
DID YOU KNOW THAT A CAT'S URINE GLOWS UNDER A BLACK LIGHT?
JUST... JUST SHUT UP. SHUT UP.
DON'T YOU WANT TO KNOW HOW I FOUND OUT ABOUT THAT JUICY TIDBIT?
YOU AND YOUR FUNNY LITTLE ADVENTURES AND YOUR MILDLY OFFENSIVE NONSENSE. I'VE HAD ENOUGH OF IT.
THAT'S IT. STARTING TODAY, I'M COMING OUT OF THE CLOSET OF CHAOS. I CHALLENGE YOU TO A VILLAINRY DUEL.
NOTE TO SELF: SWEDES WILL FLIP OUT AT MENTION OF PET EXCRETA.
FINE. I ACCEPT YOUR CHALLENGE. YOU KNOW HOW THESE THINGS WORK?
OF COURSE.
THE VILLAINRY DUEL BEGINS WITH THE TRADITIONAL ASSUMPTION OF A SECRET IDENTITY. HENCHMEN ARE PROCURED, FOLLOWED BY ARMAMENT, AND THEN, THE DUEL ITSELF. WHOMEVER COMMITS THE MOST VILLAINOUS ACT WITHIN 24 HOURS WINS, AND WHOEVER LOSES DOES NOT.
SO YOU PLAY TRADITIONAL RULES! THAT'S SO QUAINT. IT'S LIKE I'M COMPETING WITH THE POPE.
HMM. PERHAPS YOU ARE.
PHILLIP! DUDE! BITCHIN' RAI-MENTS!
OH, BUT THESE ARE NOT JUST ORDINARY RAIMENTS, MY FRIEND. THESE ARE THE RAIMENTS OF THE CHAOS POPE!
WHO'S THE CHAOS POPE?
AND WHAT ARE YOU DOING WITH HIS HAT?
I'M THE CHAOS POPE. IT'S ME.
I WASN'T AWARE YOU WERE INTO THE WHOLE POPERY SCENE.
I'M NOT, LIKE, A FULL-BLOWN POPERY FREAK OR ANYTHING. ONCE A MONTH, TOPS.

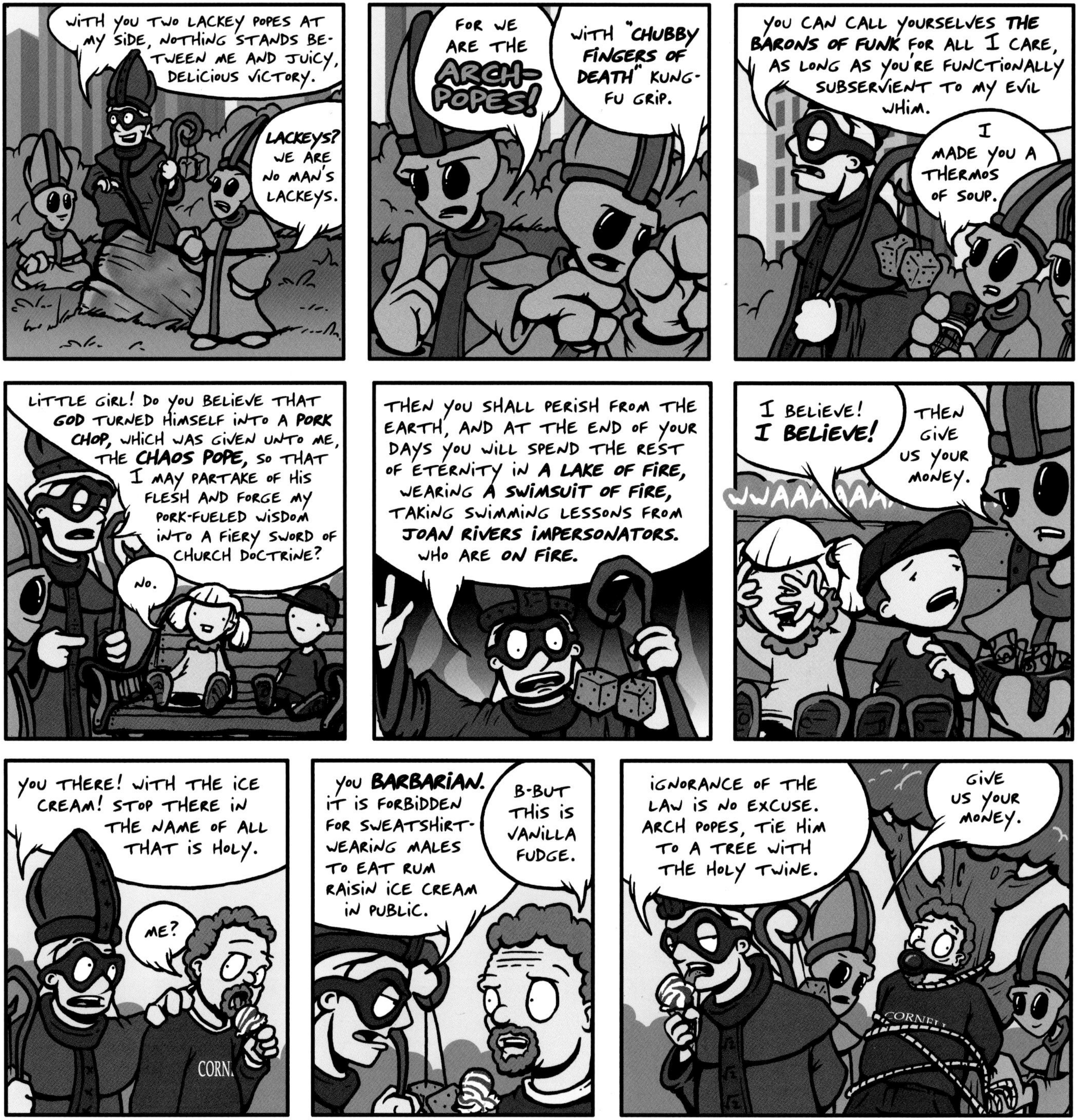
WITH YOU TWO LACKEY POPES AT MY SIDE, NOTHING STANDS BETWEEN ME AND JUICY, DELICIOUS VICTORY.
LACKEYS? WE ARE NO MAN'S LACKEYS.
FOR WE ARE THE ARCH-POPES!
WITH "CHUBBY FINGERS OF DEATH" KUNG-FU GRIP.
YOU CAN CALL YOURSELVES THE BARONS OF FUNK FOR ALL I CARE, AS LONG AS YOU'RE FUNCTIONALLY SUBSERVIENT TO MY EVIL WHIM.
I MADE YOU A THERMOS OF SOUP.
LITTLE GIRL! DO YOU BELIEVE THAT GOD TURNED HIMSELF INTO A PORK CHOP, WHICH WAS GIVEN UNTO ME, THE CHAOS POPE, SO THAT I MAY PARTAKE OF HIS FLESH AND FORGE MY PORK-FUELED WISDOM INTO A FIERY SWORD OF CHURCH DOCTRINE?
NO.
THEN YOU SHALL PERISH FROM THE EARTH, AND AT THE END OF YOUR DAYS YOU WILL SPEND THE REST OF ETERNITY IN A LAKE OF FIRE, WEARING A SWIMSUIT OF FIRE, TAKING SWIMMING LESSONS FROM JOAN RIVERS IMPERSONATORS. WHO ARE ON FIRE.
WWAAAAAAAA
I BELIEVE! I BELIEVE!
THEN GIVE US YOUR MONEY.
YOU THERE! WITH THE ICE CREAM! STOP THERE IN THE NAME OF ALL THAT IS HOLY.
ME?
CORN
YOU BARBARIAN. IT IS FORBIDDEN FOR SWEATSHIRT-WEARING MALES TO EAT RUM RAISIN ICE CREAM IN PUBLIC.
B-BUT THIS IS VANILLA FUDGE.
IGNORANCE OF THE LAW IS NO EXCUSE. ARCH POPES, TIE HIM TO A TREE WITH THE HOLY TWINE.
GIVE US YOUR MONEY.
CORNELL

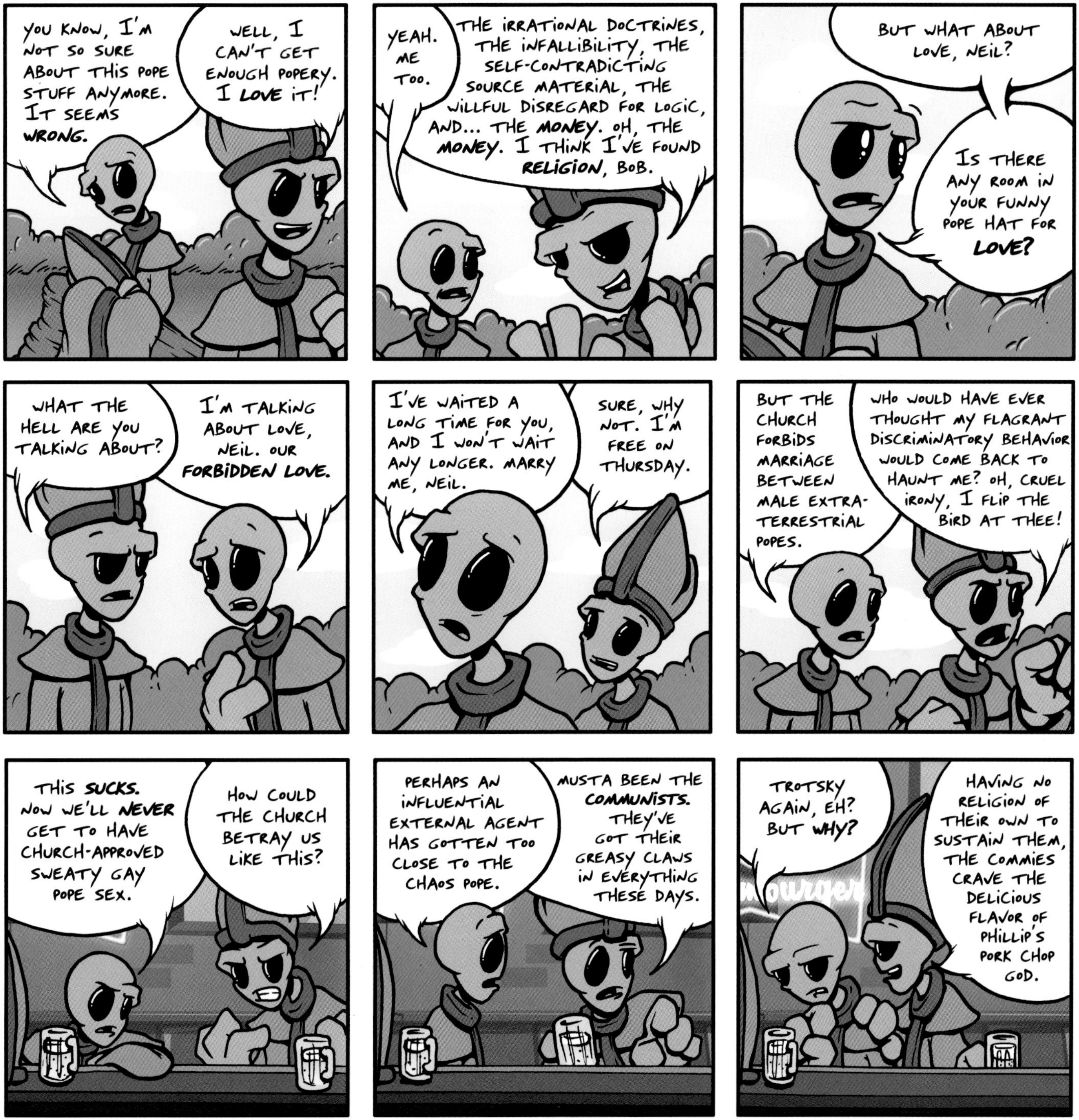
YOU KNOW, I'M NOT SO SURE ABOUT THIS POPE STUFF ANYMORE. IT SEEMS WRONG.
WELL, I CAN'T GET ENOUGH POPERY. I LOVE IT!
YEAH. ME TOO.
THE IRRATIONAL DOCTRINES, THE INFALLIBILITY, THE SELF-CONTRADICTING SOURCE MATERIAL, THE WILLFUL DISREGARD FOR LOGIC, AND... THE MONEY. OH, THE MONEY. I THINK I'VE FOUND RELIGION, BOB.
BUT WHAT ABOUT LOVE, NEIL?
IS THERE ANY ROOM IN YOUR FUNNY POPE HAT FOR LOVE?
WHAT THE HELL ARE YOU TALKING ABOUT?
I'M TALKING ABOUT LOVE, NEIL. OUR FORBIDDEN LOVE.
I'VE WAITED A LONG TIME FOR YOU, AND I WON'T WAIT ANY LONGER. MARRY ME, NEIL.
SURE, WHY NOT. I'M FREE ON THURSDAY.
BUT THE CHURCH FORBIDS MARRIAGE BETWEEN MALE EXTRA-TERRESTRIAL POPES.
WHO WOULD HAVE EVER THOUGHT MY FLAGRANT DISCRIMINATORY BEHAVIOR WOULD COME BACK TO HAUNT ME? OH, CRUEL IRONY, I FLIP THE BIRD AT THEE!
THIS SUCKS. NOW WE'LL NEVER GET TO HAVE CHURCH-APPROVED SWEATY GAY POPE SEX.
HOW COULD THE CHURCH BETRAY US LIKE THIS?
PERHAPS AN INFLUENTIAL EXTERNAL AGENT HAS GOTTEN TOO CLOSE TO THE CHAOS POPE.
MUSTA BEEN THE COMMUNISTS. THEY'VE GOT THEIR GREASY CLAWS IN EVERYTHING THESE DAYS.
TROTSKY AGAIN, EH? BUT WHY?
HAVING NO RELIGION OF THEIR OWN TO SUSTAIN THEM, THE COMMIES CRAVE THE DELICIOUS FLAVOR OF PHILLIP'S PORK CHOP GOD.

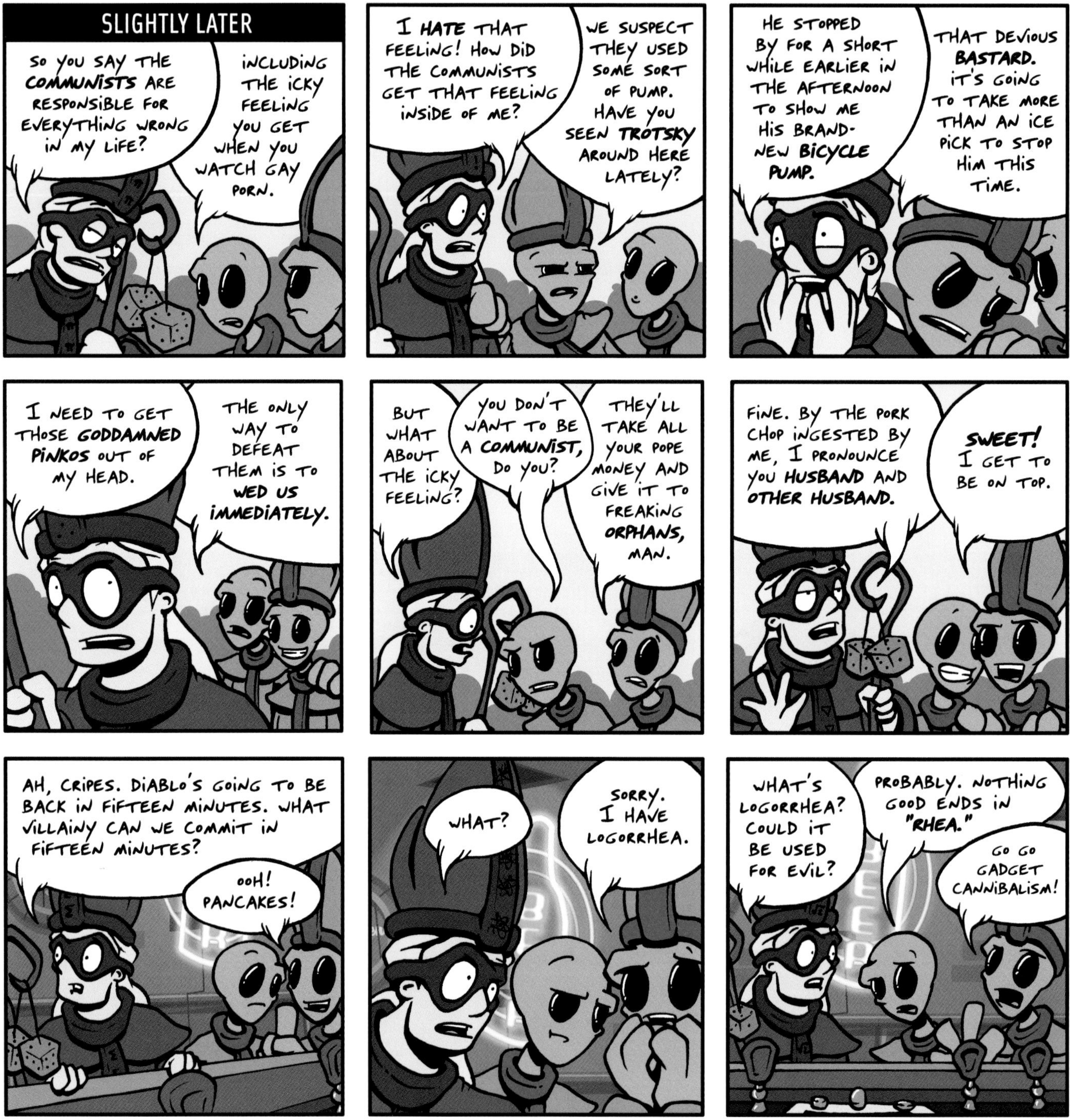
SLIGHTLY LATER
SO YOU SAY THE COMMUNISTS ARE RESPONSIBLE FOR EVERYTHING WRONG IN MY LIFE?
INCLUDING THE ICKY FEELING YOU GET WHEN YOU WATCH GAY PORN.
I HATE THAT FEELING! HOW DID THE COMMUNISTS GET THAT FEELING INSIDE OF ME?
WE SUSPECT THEY USED SOME SORT OF PUMP. HAVE YOU SEEN TROTSKY AROUND HERE LATELY?
HE STOPPED BY FOR A SHORT WHILE EARLIER IN THE AFTERNOON TO SHOW ME HIS BRAND-NEW BICYCLE PUMP.
THAT DEVIOUS BASTARD. IT'S GOING TO TAKE MORE THAN AN ICE PICK TO STOP HIM THIS TIME.
I NEED TO GET THOSE GODDAMNED PINKOS OUT OF MY HEAD.
THE ONLY WAY TO DEFEAT THEM IS TO WED US IMMEDIATELY.
BUT WHAT ABOUT THE ICKY FEELING?
YOU DON'T WANT TO BE A COMMUNIST, DO YOU?
THEY'LL TAKE ALL YOUR POPE MONEY AND GIVE IT TO FREAKING ORPHANS, MAN.
FINE. BY THE PORK CHOP INGESTED BY ME, I PRONOUNCE YOU HUSBAND AND OTHER HUSBAND.
SWEET! I GET TO BE ON TOP.
AH, CRIPES. DIABLO'S GOING TO BE BACK IN FIFTEEN MINUTES. WHAT VILLAINY CAN WE COMMIT IN FIFTEEN MINUTES?
OOH! PANCAKES!
WHAT?
SORRY. I HAVE LOGORRHEA.
WHAT'S LOGORRHEA? COULD IT BE USED FOR EVIL?
PROBABLY. NOTHING GOOD ENDS IN "RHEA."
GO GO GADGET CANNIBALISM!

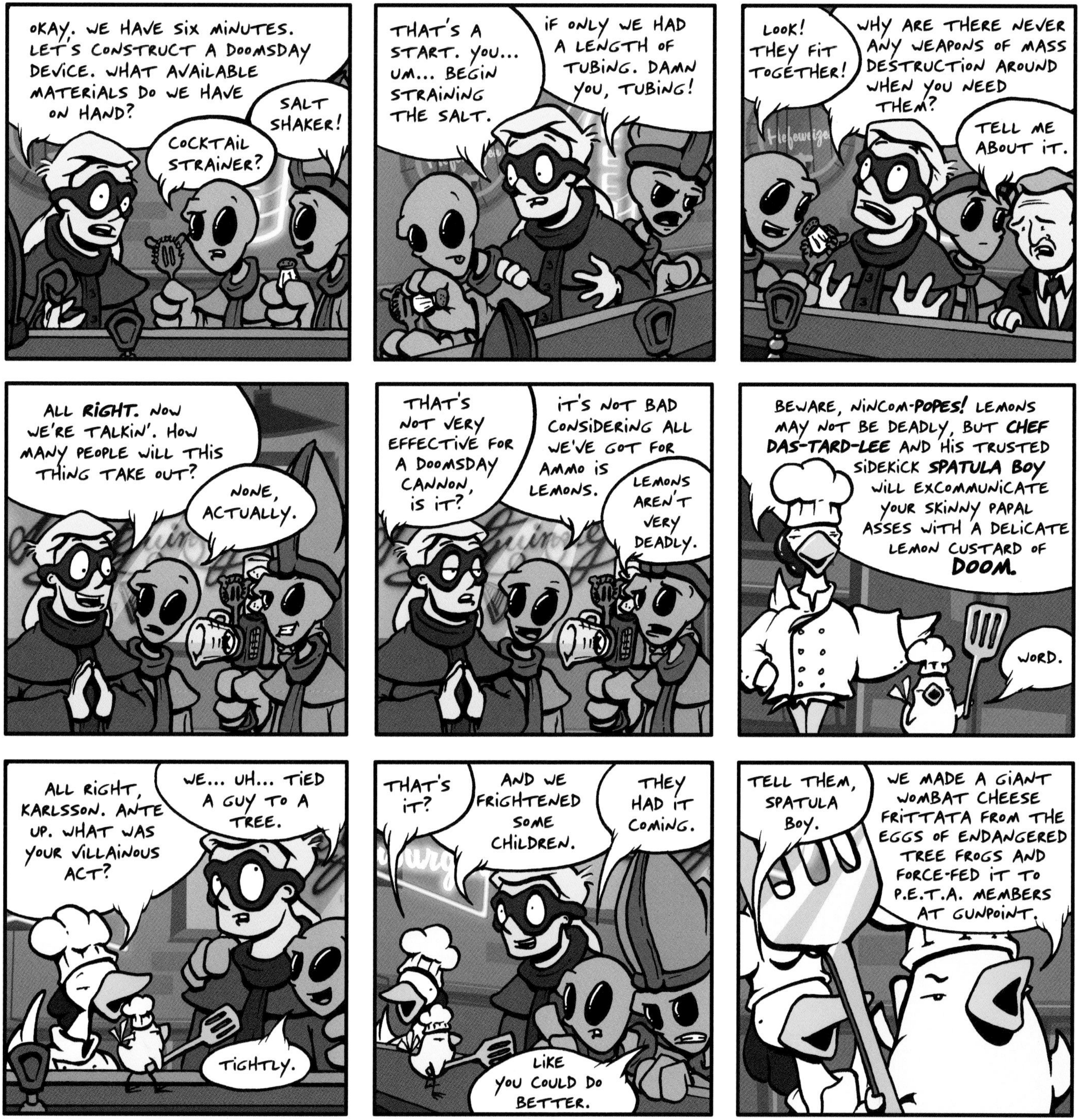
OKAY. WE HAVE SIX MINUTES. LET'S CONSTRUCT A DOOMSDAY DEVICE. WHAT AVAILABLE MATERIALS DO WE HAVE ON HAND?
COCKTAIL STRAINER?
SALT SHAKER!
THAT'S A START. YOU... UM... BEGIN STRAINING THE SALT.
IF ONLY WE HAD A LENGTH OF TUBING. DAMN YOU, TUBING!
LOOK! THEY FIT TOGETHER!
WHY ARE THERE NEVER ANY WEAPONS OF MASS DESTRUCTION AROUND WHEN YOU NEED THEM?
TELL ME ABOUT IT.
ALL **RIGHT**. NOW WE'RE TALKIN'. HOW MANY PEOPLE WILL THIS THING TAKE OUT?
NONE, ACTUALLY.
THAT'S NOT VERY EFFECTIVE FOR A DOOMSDAY CANNON, IS IT?
IT'S NOT BAD CONSIDERING ALL WE'VE GOT FOR AMMO IS LEMONS.
LEMONS AREN'T VERY DEADLY.
BEWARE, NINCOM-**POPES!** LEMONS MAY NOT BE DEADLY, BUT **CHEF DAS-TARD-LEE** AND HIS TRUSTED SIDEKICK **SPATULA BOY** WILL EXCOMMUNICATE YOUR SKINNY PAPAL ASSES WITH A DELICATE LEMON CUSTARD OF **DOOM.**
WORD.
ALL RIGHT, KARLSSON. ANTE UP. WHAT WAS YOUR VILLAINOUS ACT?
WE... UH... TIED A GUY TO A TREE.
TIGHTLY.
THAT'S IT?
AND WE FRIGHTENED SOME CHILDREN.
THEY HAD IT COMING.
LIKE YOU COULD DO BETTER.
TELL THEM, SPATULA BOY.
WE MADE A GIANT WOMBAT CHEESE FRITTATA FROM THE EGGS OF ENDANGERED TREE FROGS AND FORCE-FED IT TO P.E.T.A. MEMBERS AT GUNPOINT.

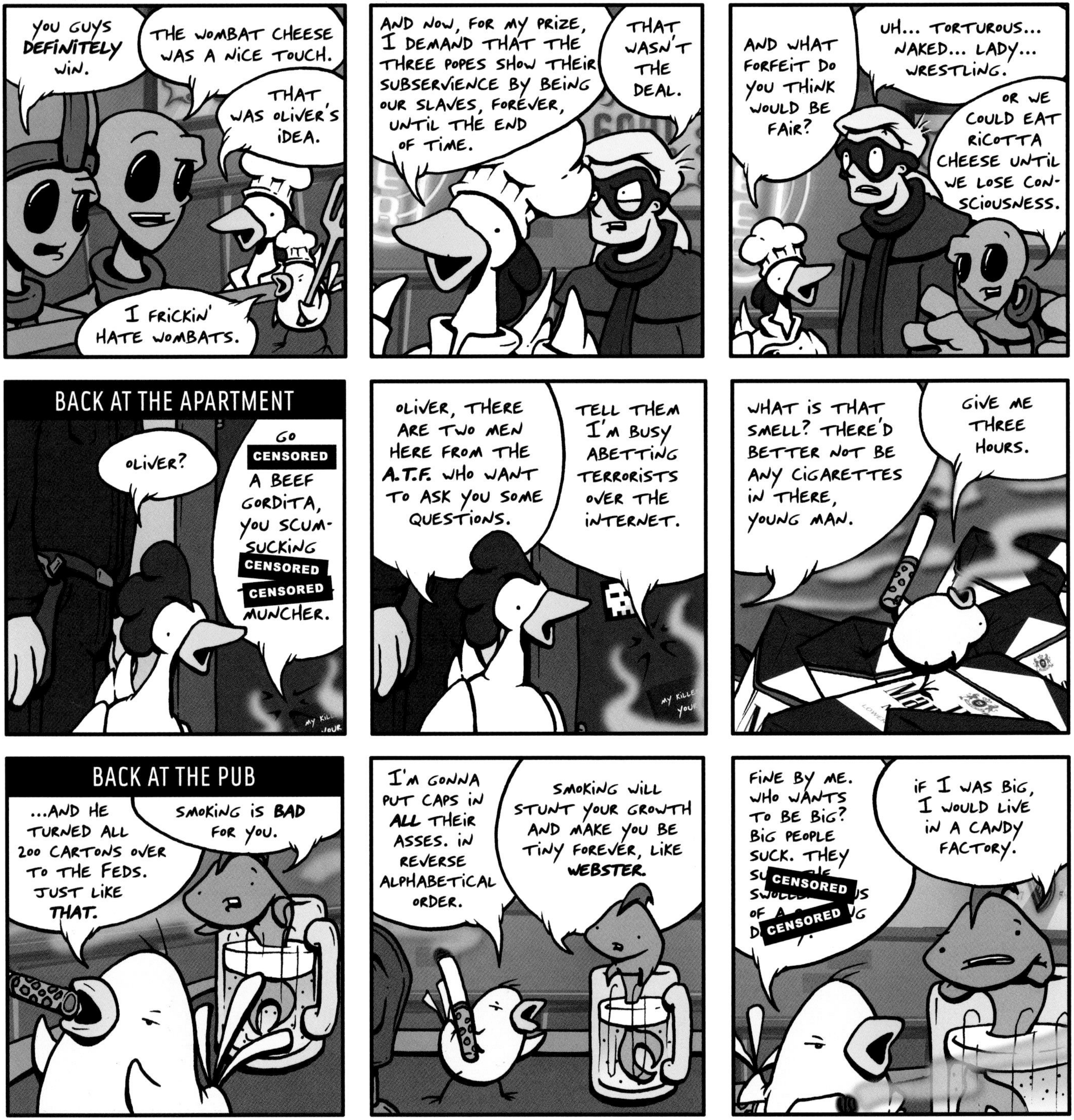
YOU GUYS **DEFINITELY** WIN.
THE WOMBAT CHEESE WAS A NICE TOUCH.
THAT WAS OLIVER'S IDEA.
I FRICKIN' HATE WOMBATS.
AND NOW, FOR MY PRIZE, I DEMAND THAT THE THREE POPES SHOW THEIR SUBSERVIENCE BY BEING OUR SLAVES, FOREVER, UNTIL THE END OF TIME.
THAT WASN'T THE DEAL.
AND WHAT FORFEIT DO YOU THINK WOULD BE FAIR?
UH... TORTUROUS... NAKED... LADY... WRESTLING.
OR WE COULD EAT RICOTTA CHEESE UNTIL WE LOSE CONSCIOUSNESS.
BACK AT THE APARTMENT
OLIVER?
GO CENSORED A BEEF GORDITA, YOU SCUM-SUCKING CENSORED CENSORED MUNCHER.
OLIVER, THERE ARE TWO MEN HERE FROM THE **A.T.F.** WHO WANT TO ASK YOU SOME QUESTIONS.
TELL THEM I'M BUSY ABETTING TERRORISTS OVER THE INTERNET.
WHAT IS THAT SMELL? THERE'D BETTER NOT BE ANY CIGARETTES IN THERE, YOUNG MAN.
GIVE ME THREE HOURS.
BACK AT THE PUB
...AND HE TURNED ALL 200 CARTONS OVER TO THE FEDS. JUST LIKE **THAT.**
SMOKING IS **BAD** FOR YOU.
I'M GONNA PUT CAPS IN **ALL** THEIR ASSES. IN REVERSE ALPHABETICAL ORDER.
SMOKING WILL STUNT YOUR GROWTH AND MAKE YOU BE TINY FOREVER, LIKE **WEBSTER.**
FINE BY ME. WHO WANTS TO BE BIG? BIG PEOPLE SUCK. THEY CENSORED CENSORED
IF I WAS BIG, I WOULD LIVE IN A CANDY FACTORY.

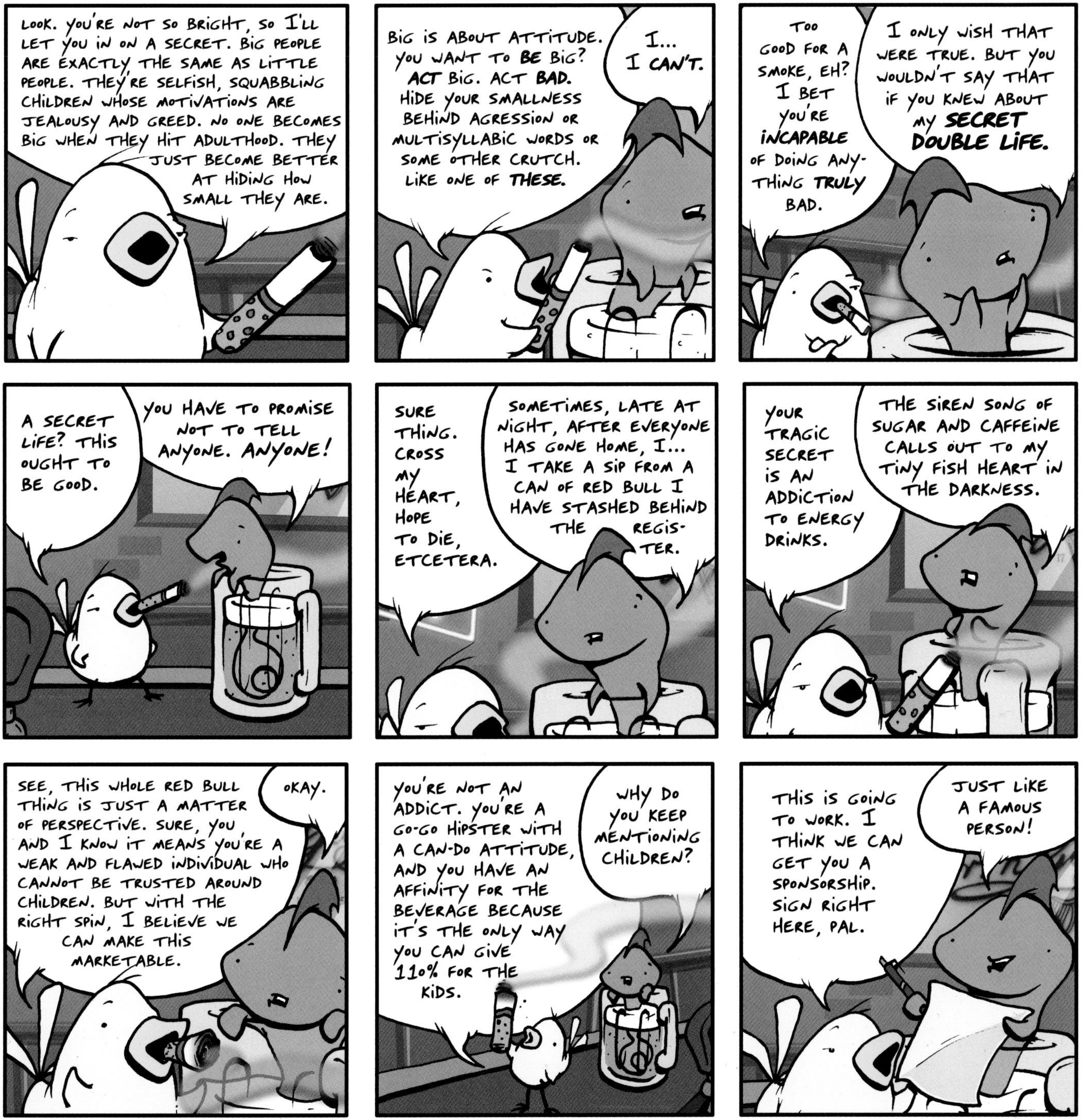
LOOK. YOU'RE NOT SO BRIGHT, SO I'LL LET YOU IN ON A SECRET. BIG PEOPLE ARE EXACTLY THE SAME AS LITTLE PEOPLE. THEY'RE SELFISH, SQUABBLING CHILDREN WHOSE MOTIVATIONS ARE JEALOUSY AND GREED. NO ONE BECOMES BIG WHEN THEY HIT ADULTHOOD. THEY JUST BECOME BETTER AT HIDING HOW SMALL THEY ARE.
BIG IS ABOUT ATTITUDE. YOU WANT TO **BE** BIG? **ACT** BIG. ACT **BAD.** HIDE YOUR SMALLNESS BEHIND AGRESSION OR MULTISYLLABIC WORDS OR SOME OTHER CRUTCH. LIKE ONE OF **THESE.**
I... I **CAN'T.**
TOO GOOD FOR A SMOKE, EH? I BET YOU'RE **INCAPABLE** OF DOING ANYTHING **TRULY** BAD.
I ONLY WISH THAT WERE TRUE. BUT YOU WOULDN'T SAY THAT IF YOU KNEW ABOUT MY **SECRET DOUBLE LIFE.**
A SECRET LIFE? THIS OUGHT TO BE GOOD.
YOU HAVE TO PROMISE NOT TO TELL ANYONE. *ANYONE!*
SURE THING. CROSS MY HEART, HOPE TO DIE, ETCETERA.
SOMETIMES, LATE AT NIGHT, AFTER EVERYONE HAS GONE HOME, I... I TAKE A SIP FROM A CAN OF RED BULL I HAVE STASHED BEHIND THE REGISTER.
YOUR TRAGIC SECRET IS AN ADDICTION TO ENERGY DRINKS.
THE SIREN SONG OF SUGAR AND CAFFEINE CALLS OUT TO MY TINY FISH HEART IN THE DARKNESS.
SEE, THIS WHOLE RED BULL THING IS JUST A MATTER OF PERSPECTIVE. SURE, YOU AND I KNOW IT MEANS YOU'RE A WEAK AND FLAWED INDIVIDUAL WHO CANNOT BE TRUSTED AROUND CHILDREN. BUT WITH THE RIGHT SPIN, I BELIEVE WE CAN MAKE THIS MARKETABLE.
OKAY.
YOU'RE NOT AN ADDICT. YOU'RE A GO-GO HIPSTER WITH A CAN-DO ATTITUDE, AND YOU HAVE AN AFFINITY FOR THE BEVERAGE BECAUSE IT'S THE ONLY WAY YOU CAN GIVE 110% FOR THE KIDS.
WHY DO YOU KEEP MENTIONING CHILDREN?
THIS IS GOING TO WORK. I THINK WE CAN GET YOU A SPONSORSHIP. SIGN RIGHT HERE, PAL.
JUST LIKE A FAMOUS PERSON!

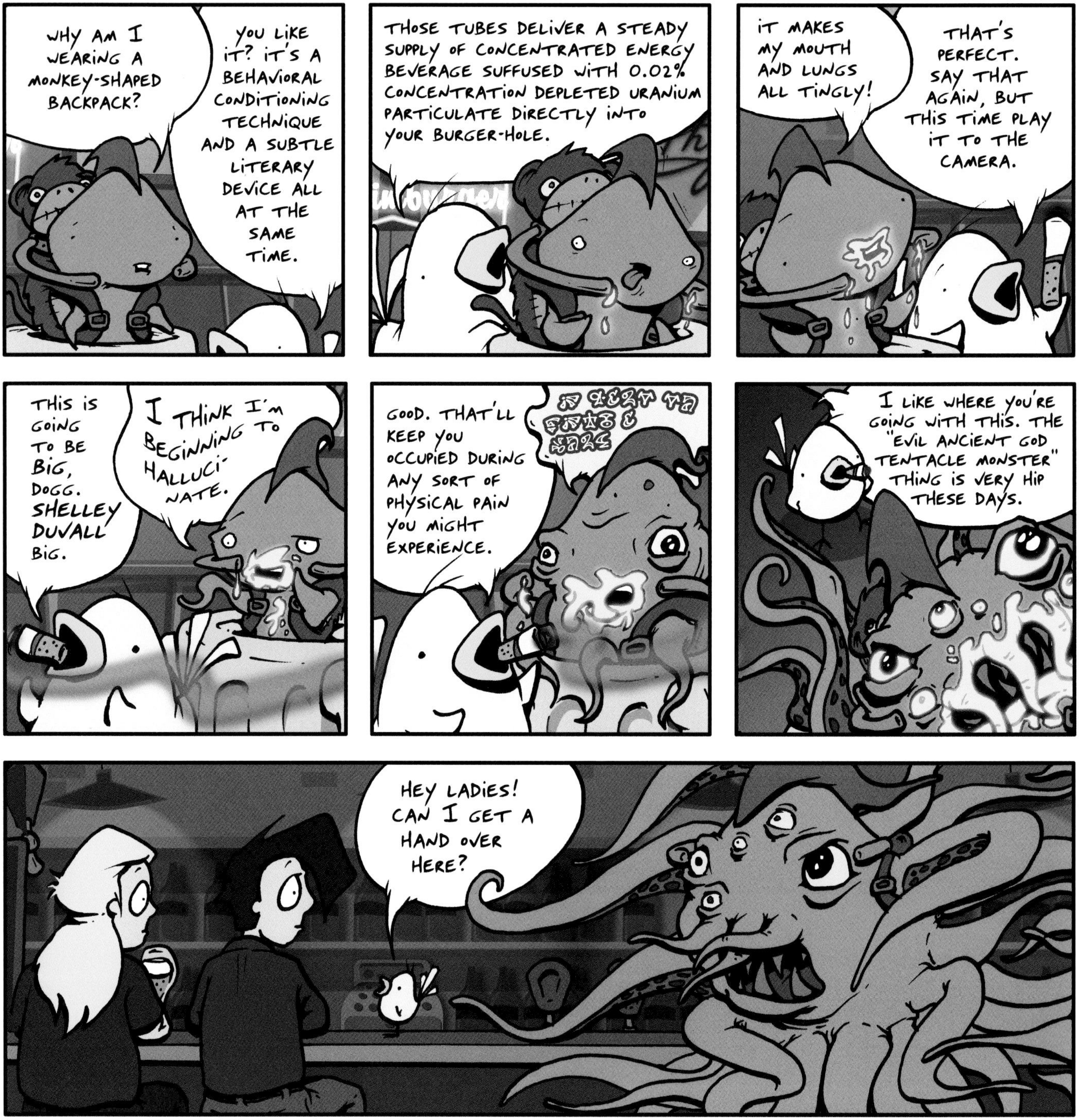
WHY AM I WEARING A MONKEY-SHAPED BACKPACK?
YOU LIKE IT? IT'S A BEHAVIORAL CONDITIONING TECHNIQUE AND A SUBTLE LITERARY DEVICE ALL AT THE SAME TIME.
THOSE TUBES DELIVER A STEADY SUPPLY OF CONCENTRATED ENERGY BEVERAGE SUFFUSED WITH 0.02% CONCENTRATION DEPLETED URANIUM PARTICULATE DIRECTLY INTO YOUR BURGER-HOLE.
IT MAKES MY MOUTH AND LUNGS ALL TINGLY!
THAT'S PERFECT. SAY THAT AGAIN, BUT THIS TIME PLAY IT TO THE CAMERA.
THIS IS GOING TO BE BIG, DOGG. SHELLEY DUVALL BIG.
I THINK I'M BEGINNING TO HALLUCI-NATE.
GOOD. THAT'LL KEEP YOU OCCUPIED DURING ANY SORT OF PHYSICAL PAIN YOU MIGHT EXPERIENCE.
I LIKE WHERE YOU'RE GOING WITH THIS. THE "EVIL ANCIENT GOD TENTACLE MONSTER" THING IS VERY HIP THESE DAYS.
HEY LADIES! CAN I GET A HAND OVER HERE?

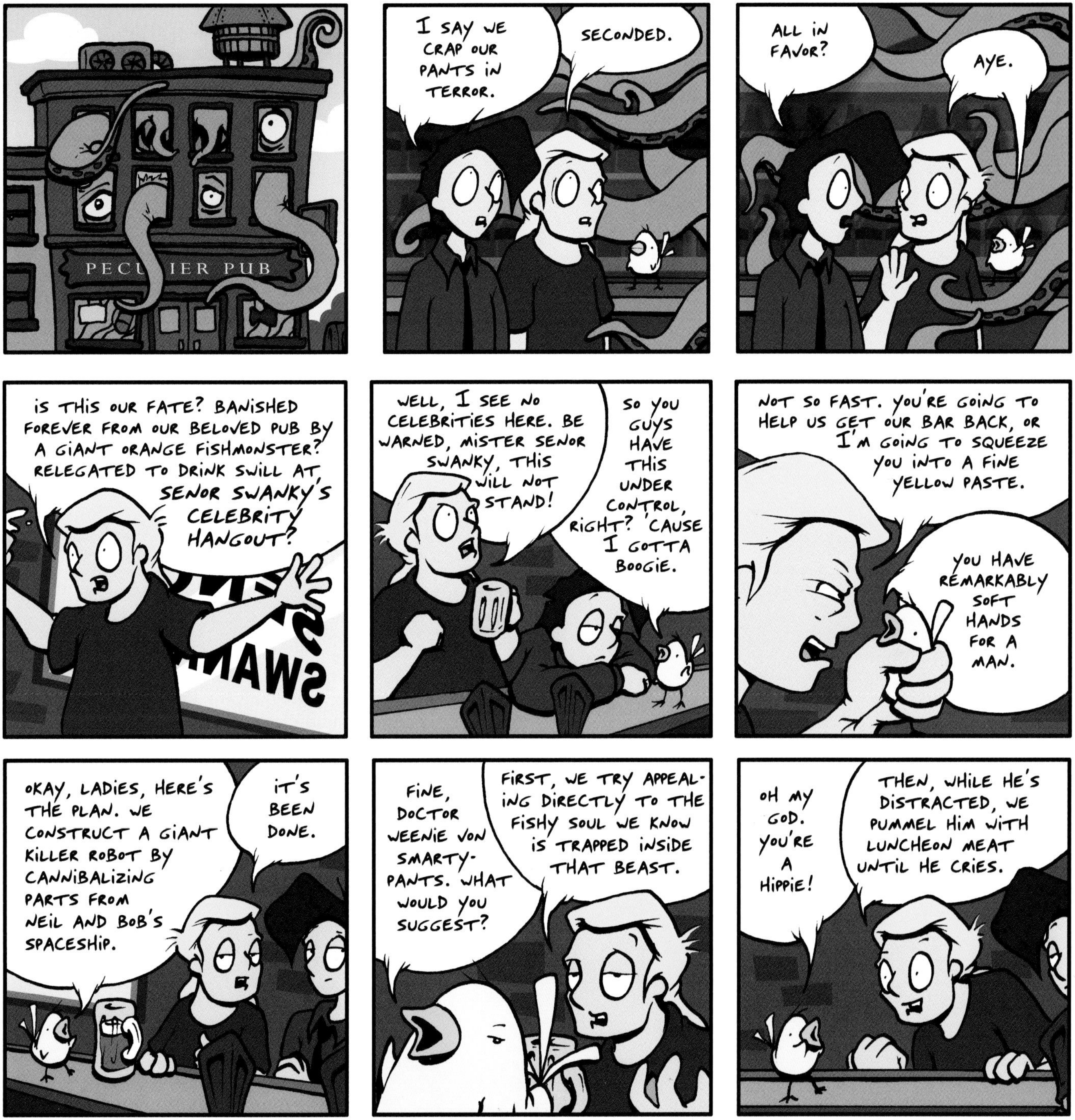
PECULIER PUB
I SAY WE CRAP OUR PANTS IN TERROR.
SECONDED.
ALL IN FAVOR?
AYE.
IS THIS OUR FATE? BANISHED FOREVER FROM OUR BELOVED PUB BY A GIANT ORANGE FISHMONSTER? RELEGATED TO DRINK SWILL AT SENOR SWANKY'S CELEBRITY HANGOUT?
WELL, I SEE NO CELEBRITIES HERE. BE WARNED, MISTER SENOR SWANKY, THIS WILL NOT STAND!
SO YOU GUYS HAVE THIS UNDER CONTROL, RIGHT? 'CAUSE I GOTTA BOOGIE.
NOT SO FAST. YOU'RE GOING TO HELP US GET OUR BAR BACK, OR I'M GOING TO SQUEEZE YOU INTO A FINE YELLOW PASTE.
YOU HAVE REMARKABLY SOFT HANDS FOR A MAN.
OKAY, LADIES, HERE'S THE PLAN. WE CONSTRUCT A GIANT KILLER ROBOT BY CANNIBALIZING PARTS FROM NEIL AND BOB'S SPACESHIP.
IT'S BEEN DONE.
FINE, DOCTOR WEENIE VON SMARTY-PANTS. WHAT WOULD YOU SUGGEST?
FIRST, WE TRY APPEALING DIRECTLY TO THE FISHY SOUL WE KNOW IS TRAPPED INSIDE THAT BEAST.
OH MY GOD. YOU'RE A HIPPIE!
THEN, WHILE HE'S DISTRACTED, WE PUMMEL HIM WITH LUNCHEON MEAT UNTIL HE CRIES.

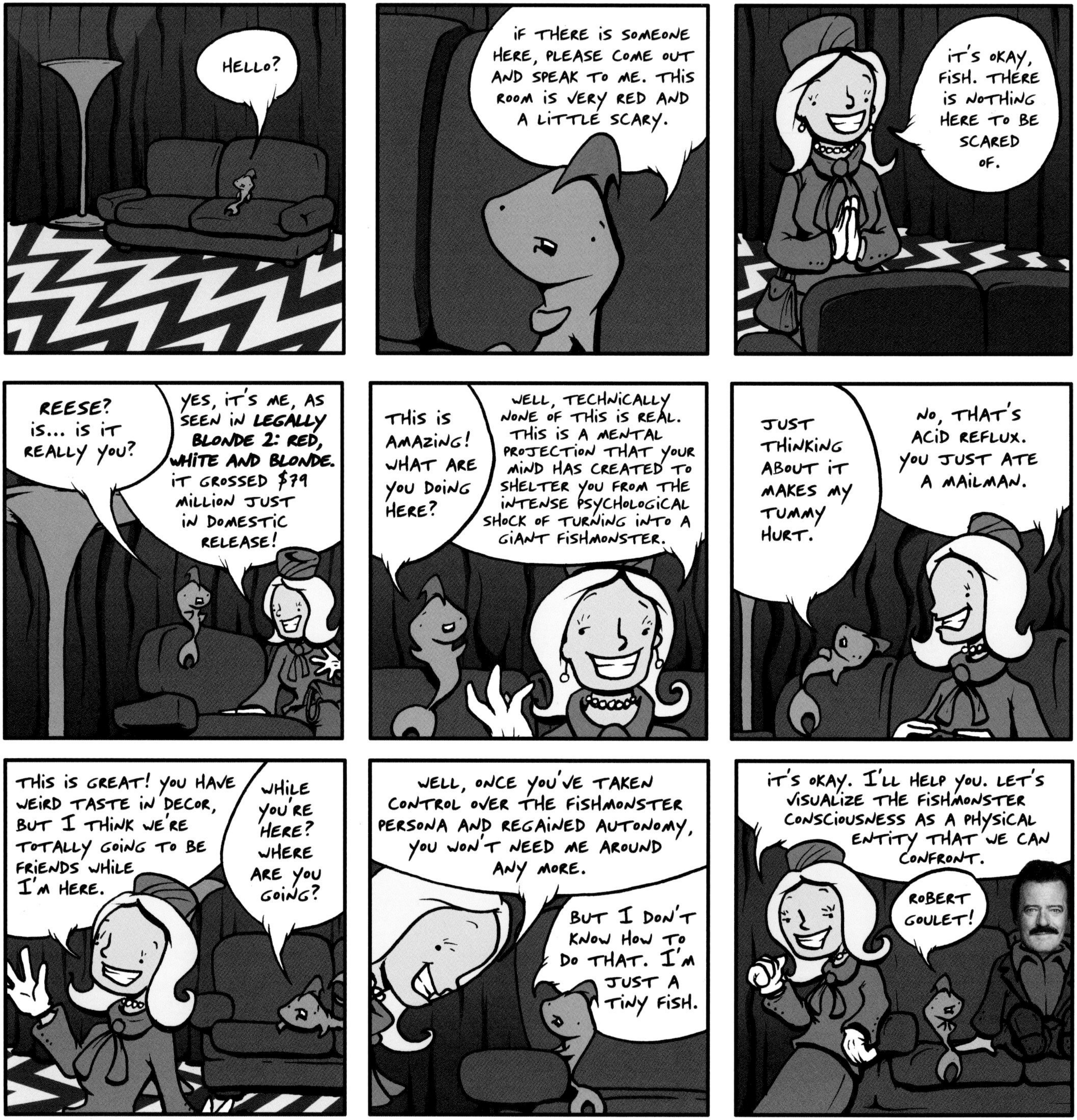
HELLO?
IF THERE IS SOMEONE HERE, PLEASE COME OUT AND SPEAK TO ME. THIS ROOM IS VERY RED AND A LITTLE SCARY.
IT'S OKAY, FISH. THERE IS NOTHING HERE TO BE SCARED OF.
REESE? IS... IS IT REALLY YOU?
YES, IT'S ME, AS SEEN IN **LEGALLY BLONDE 2: RED, WHITE AND BLONDE.** IT GROSSED $79 MILLION JUST IN DOMESTIC RELEASE!
THIS IS AMAZING! WHAT ARE YOU DOING HERE?
WELL, TECHNICALLY NONE OF THIS IS REAL. THIS IS A MENTAL PROJECTION THAT YOUR MIND HAS CREATED TO SHELTER YOU FROM THE INTENSE PSYCHOLOGICAL SHOCK OF TURNING INTO A GIANT FISHMONSTER.
JUST THINKING ABOUT IT MAKES MY TUMMY HURT.
NO, THAT'S ACID REFLUX. YOU JUST ATE A MAILMAN.
THIS IS GREAT! YOU HAVE WEIRD TASTE IN DECOR, BUT I THINK WE'RE TOTALLY GOING TO BE FRIENDS WHILE I'M HERE.
WHILE YOU'RE HERE? WHERE ARE YOU GOING?
WELL, ONCE YOU'VE TAKEN CONTROL OVER THE FISHMONSTER PERSONA AND REGAINED AUTONOMY, YOU WON'T NEED ME AROUND ANY MORE.
BUT I DON'T KNOW HOW TO DO THAT. I'M JUST A TINY FISH.
IT'S OKAY. I'LL HELP YOU. LET'S VISUALIZE THE FISHMONSTER CONSCIOUSNESS AS A PHYSICAL ENTITY THAT WE CAN CONFRONT.
ROBERT GOULET!

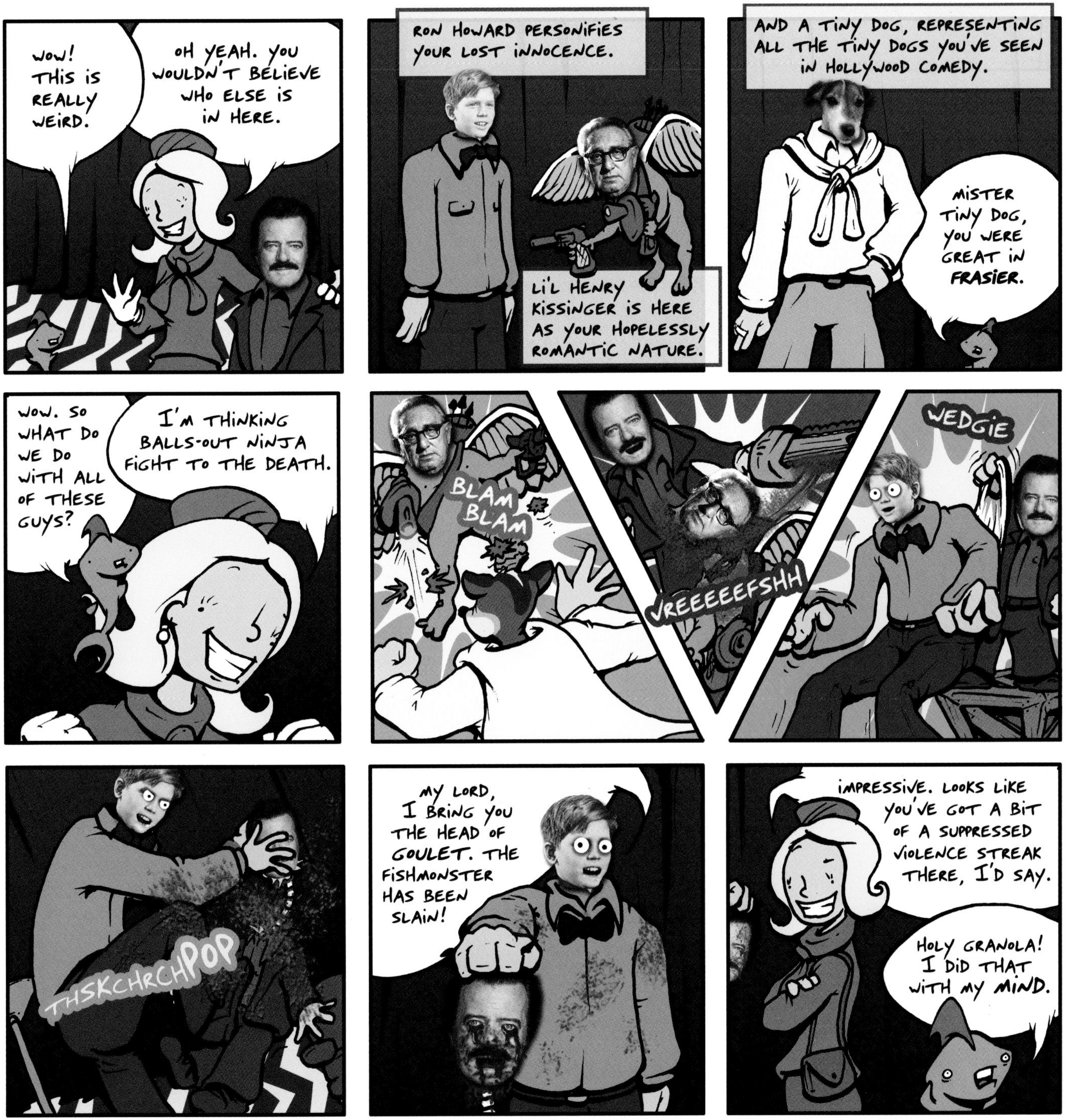
WOW! THIS IS REALLY WEIRD.
OH YEAH. YOU WOULDN'T BELIEVE WHO ELSE IS IN HERE.
RON HOWARD PERSONIFIES YOUR LOST INNOCENCE.
LI'L HENRY KISSINGER IS HERE AS YOUR HOPELESSLY ROMANTIC NATURE.
AND A TINY DOG, REPRESENTING ALL THE TINY DOGS YOU'VE SEEN IN HOLLYWOOD COMEDY.
MISTER TINY DOG, YOU WERE GREAT IN FRASIER.
WOW. SO WHAT DO WE DO WITH ALL OF THESE GUYS?
I'M THINKING BALLS-OUT NINJA FIGHT TO THE DEATH.
BLAM BLAM
VREEEEEEFSHH
WEDGIE
THSKCHRCHPOP
MY LORD, I BRING YOU THE HEAD OF GOULET. THE FISHMONSTER HAS BEEN SLAIN!
IMPRESSIVE. LOOKS LIKE YOU'VE GOT A BIT OF A SUPPRESSED VIOLENCE STREAK THERE, I'D SAY.
HOLY GRANOLA! I DID THAT WITH MY MIND.

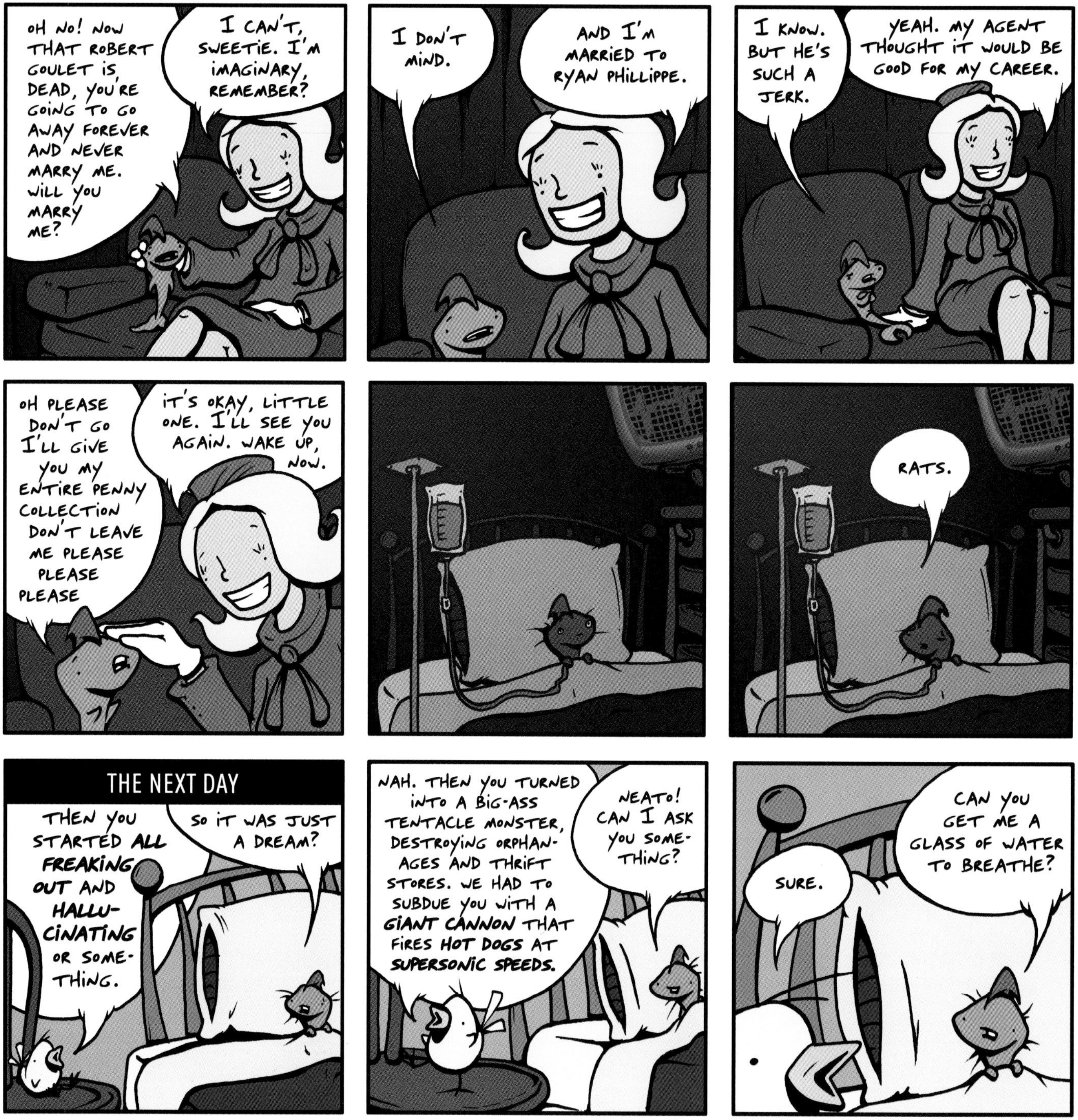
OH NO! NOW THAT ROBERT GOULET IS, DEAD, YOU'RE GOING TO GO AWAY FOREVER AND NEVER MARRY ME. WILL YOU MARRY ME?
I CAN'T, SWEETIE. I'M IMAGINARY, REMEMBER?
I DON'T MIND.
AND I'M MARRIED TO RYAN PHILLIPPE.
I KNOW. BUT HE'S SUCH A JERK.
YEAH. MY AGENT THOUGHT IT WOULD BE GOOD FOR MY CAREER.
OH PLEASE DON'T GO I'LL GIVE YOU MY ENTIRE PENNY COLLECTION DON'T LEAVE ME PLEASE PLEASE PLEASE
IT'S OKAY, LITTLE ONE. I'LL SEE YOU AGAIN. WAKE UP, NOW.
RATS.
THE NEXT DAY
THEN YOU STARTED **ALL FREAKING OUT** AND **HALLUCINATING** OR SOMETHING.
SO IT WAS JUST A DREAM?
NAH. THEN YOU TURNED INTO A BIG-ASS TENTACLE MONSTER, DESTROYING ORPHANAGES AND THRIFT STORES. WE HAD TO SUBDUE YOU WITH A **GIANT CANNON** THAT FIRES **HOT DOGS** AT **SUPERSONIC SPEEDS.**
NEATO! CAN I ASK YOU SOMETHING?
CAN YOU GET ME A GLASS OF WATER TO BREATHE?
SURE.

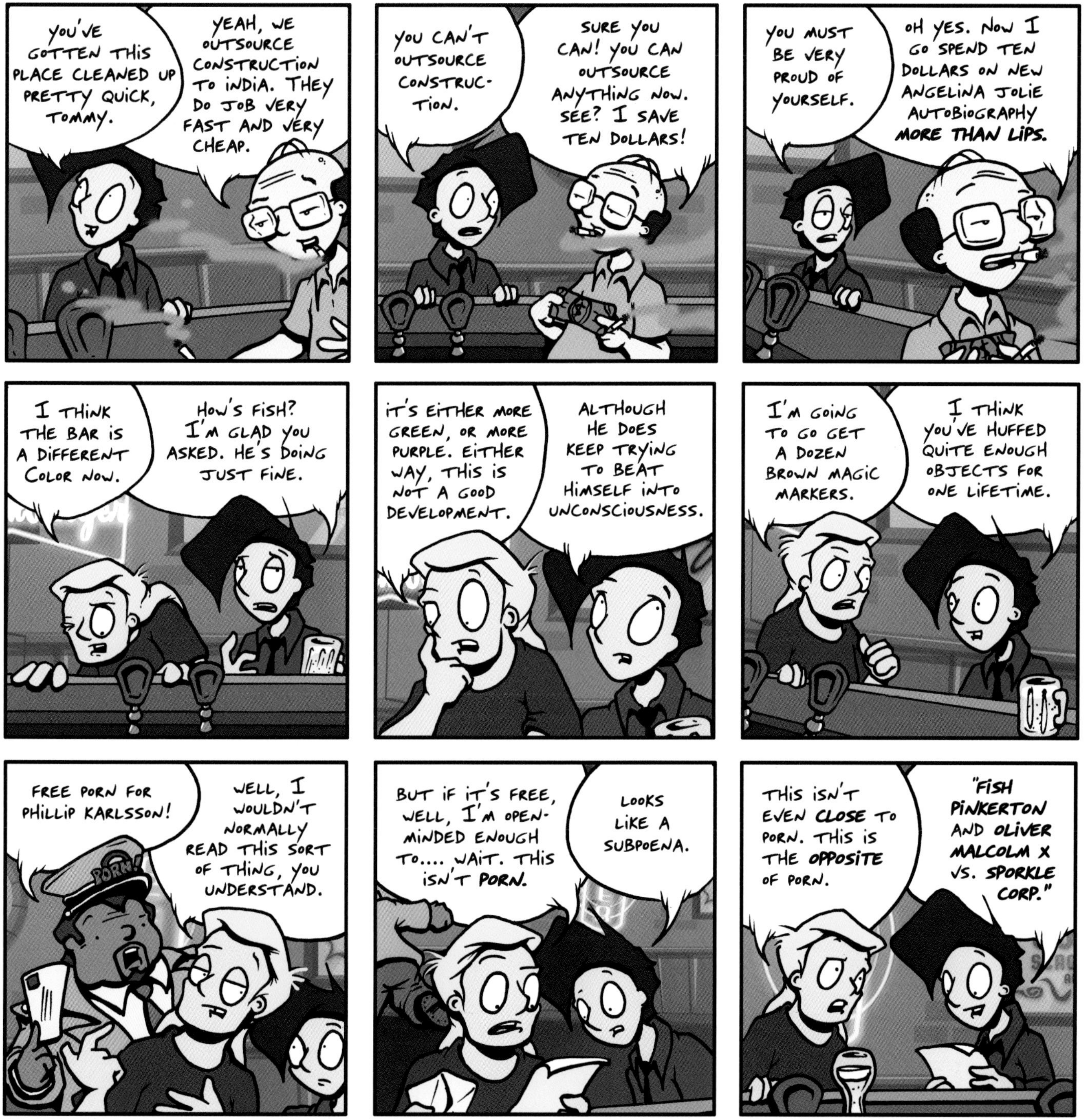
YOU'VE GOTTEN THIS PLACE CLEANED UP PRETTY QUICK, TOMMY.
YEAH, WE OUTSOURCE CONSTRUCTION TO INDIA. THEY DO JOB VERY FAST AND VERY CHEAP.
YOU CAN'T OUTSOURCE CONSTRUC-TION.
SURE YOU CAN! YOU CAN OUTSOURCE ANYTHING NOW. SEE? I SAVE TEN DOLLARS!
YOU MUST BE VERY PROUD OF YOURSELF.
OH YES. NOW I GO SPEND TEN DOLLARS ON NEW ANGELINA JOLIE AUTOBIOGRAPHY MORE THAN LIPS.
I THINK THE BAR IS A DIFFERENT COLOR NOW.
HOW'S FISH? I'M GLAD YOU ASKED. HE'S DOING JUST FINE.
IT'S EITHER MORE GREEN, OR MORE PURPLE. EITHER WAY, THIS IS NOT A GOOD DEVELOPMENT.
ALTHOUGH HE DOES KEEP TRYING TO BEAT HIMSELF INTO UNCONSCIOUSNESS.
I'M GOING TO GO GET A DOZEN BROWN MAGIC MARKERS.
I THINK YOU'VE HUFFED QUITE ENOUGH OBJECTS FOR ONE LIFETIME.
FREE PORN FOR PHILLIP KARLSSON!
PORN!
WELL, I WOULDN'T NORMALLY READ THIS SORT OF THING, YOU UNDERSTAND.
BUT IF IT'S FREE, WELL, I'M OPEN-MINDED ENOUGH TO.... WAIT. THIS ISN'T PORN.
LOOKS LIKE A SUBPOENA.
THIS ISN'T EVEN CLOSE TO PORN. THIS IS THE OPPOSITE OF PORN.
"FISH PINKERTON AND OLIVER MALCOLM X VS. SPORKLE CORP."

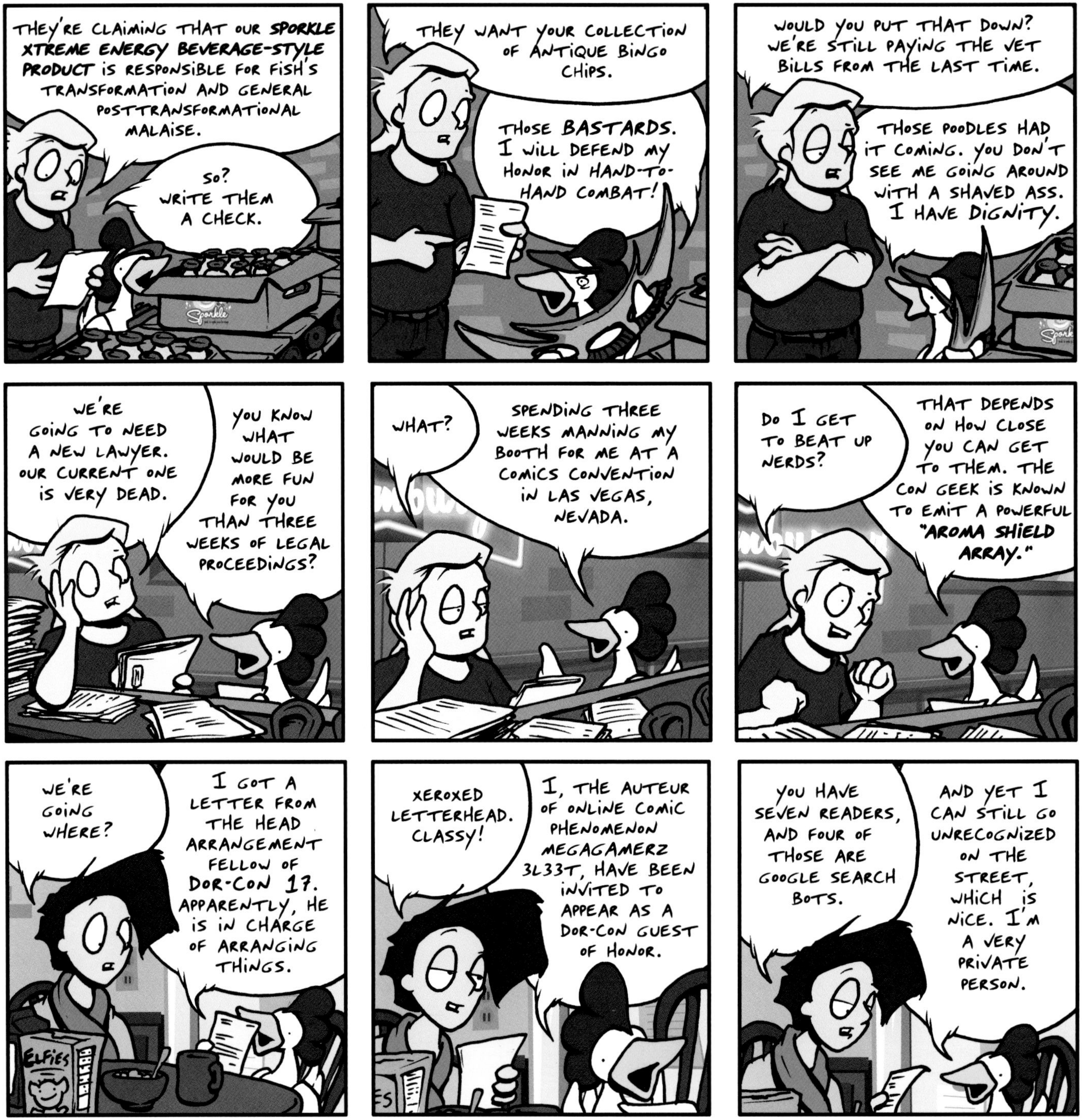
THEY'RE CLAIMING THAT OUR SPORKLE XTREME ENERGY BEVERAGE-STYLE PRODUCT IS RESPONSIBLE FOR FISH'S TRANSFORMATION AND GENERAL POSTTRANSFORMATIONAL MALAISE.
SO? WRITE THEM A CHECK.
Sporkle
THEY WANT YOUR COLLECTION OF ANTIQUE BINGO CHIPS.
THOSE BASTARDS. I WILL DEFEND MY HONOR IN HAND-TO-HAND COMBAT!
WOULD YOU PUT THAT DOWN? WE'RE STILL PAYING THE VET BILLS FROM THE LAST TIME.
THOSE POODLES HAD IT COMING. YOU DON'T SEE ME GOING AROUND WITH A SHAVED ASS. I HAVE DIGNITY.
WE'RE GOING TO NEED A NEW LAWYER. OUR CURRENT ONE IS VERY DEAD.
YOU KNOW WHAT WOULD BE MORE FUN FOR YOU THAN THREE WEEKS OF LEGAL PROCEEDINGS?
WHAT?
SPENDING THREE WEEKS MANNING MY BOOTH FOR ME AT A COMICS CONVENTION IN LAS VEGAS, NEVADA.
DO I GET TO BEAT UP NERDS?
THAT DEPENDS ON HOW CLOSE YOU CAN GET TO THEM. THE CON GEEK IS KNOWN TO EMIT A POWERFUL "AROMA SHIELD ARRAY."
WE'RE GOING WHERE?
I GOT A LETTER FROM THE HEAD ARRANGEMENT FELLOW OF DOR-CON 17. APPARENTLY, HE IS IN CHARGE OF ARRANGING THINGS.
ELFIES
XEROXED LETTERHEAD. CLASSY!
I, THE AUTEUR OF ONLINE COMIC PHENOMENON MEGAGAMERZ 3L33T, HAVE BEEN INVITED TO APPEAR AS A DOR-CON GUEST OF HONOR.
YOU HAVE SEVEN READERS, AND FOUR OF THOSE ARE GOOGLE SEARCH BOTS.
AND YET I CAN STILL GO UNRECOGNIZED ON THE STREET, WHICH IS NICE. I'M A VERY PRIVATE PERSON.

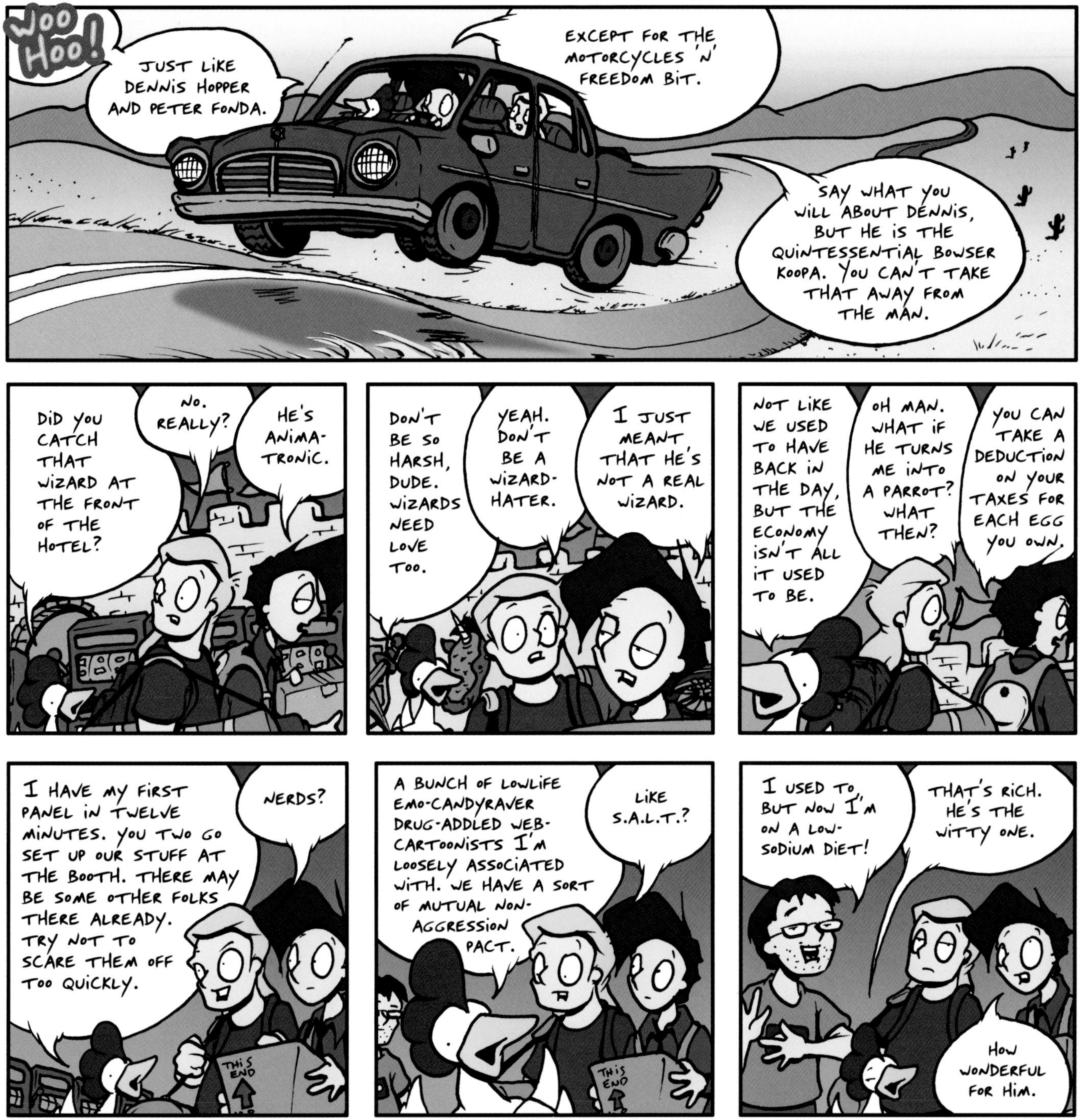
WOO HOO!
JUST LIKE DENNIS HOPPER AND PETER FONDA.
EXCEPT FOR THE MOTORCYCLES 'N' FREEDOM BIT.
SAY WHAT YOU WILL ABOUT DENNIS, BUT HE IS THE QUINTESSENTIAL BOWSER KOOPA. YOU CAN'T TAKE THAT AWAY FROM THE MAN.
DID YOU CATCH THAT WIZARD AT THE FRONT OF THE HOTEL?
NO. REALLY?
HE'S ANIMA-TRONIC.
DON'T BE SO HARSH, DUDE. WIZARDS NEED LOVE TOO.
YEAH. DON'T BE A WIZARD-HATER.
I JUST MEANT THAT HE'S NOT A REAL WIZARD.
NOT LIKE WE USED TO HAVE BACK IN THE DAY, BUT THE ECONOMY ISN'T ALL IT USED TO BE.
OH MAN. WHAT IF HE TURNS ME INTO A PARROT? WHAT THEN?
YOU CAN TAKE A DEDUCTION ON YOUR TAXES FOR EACH EGG YOU OWN.
I HAVE MY FIRST PANEL IN TWELVE MINUTES. YOU TWO GO SET UP OUR STUFF AT THE BOOTH. THERE MAY BE SOME OTHER FOLKS THERE ALREADY. TRY NOT TO SCARE THEM OFF TOO QUICKLY.
NERDS?
THIS END
A BUNCH OF LOWLIFE EMO-CANDYRAVER DRUG-ADDLED WEB-CARTOONISTS I'M LOOSELY ASSOCIATED WITH. WE HAVE A SORT OF MUTUAL NON-AGGRESSION PACT.
LIKE S.A.L.T.?
THIS END
I USED TO, BUT NOW I'M ON A LOW-SODIUM DIET!
THAT'S RICH. HE'S THE WITTY ONE.
HOW WONDERFUL FOR HIM.

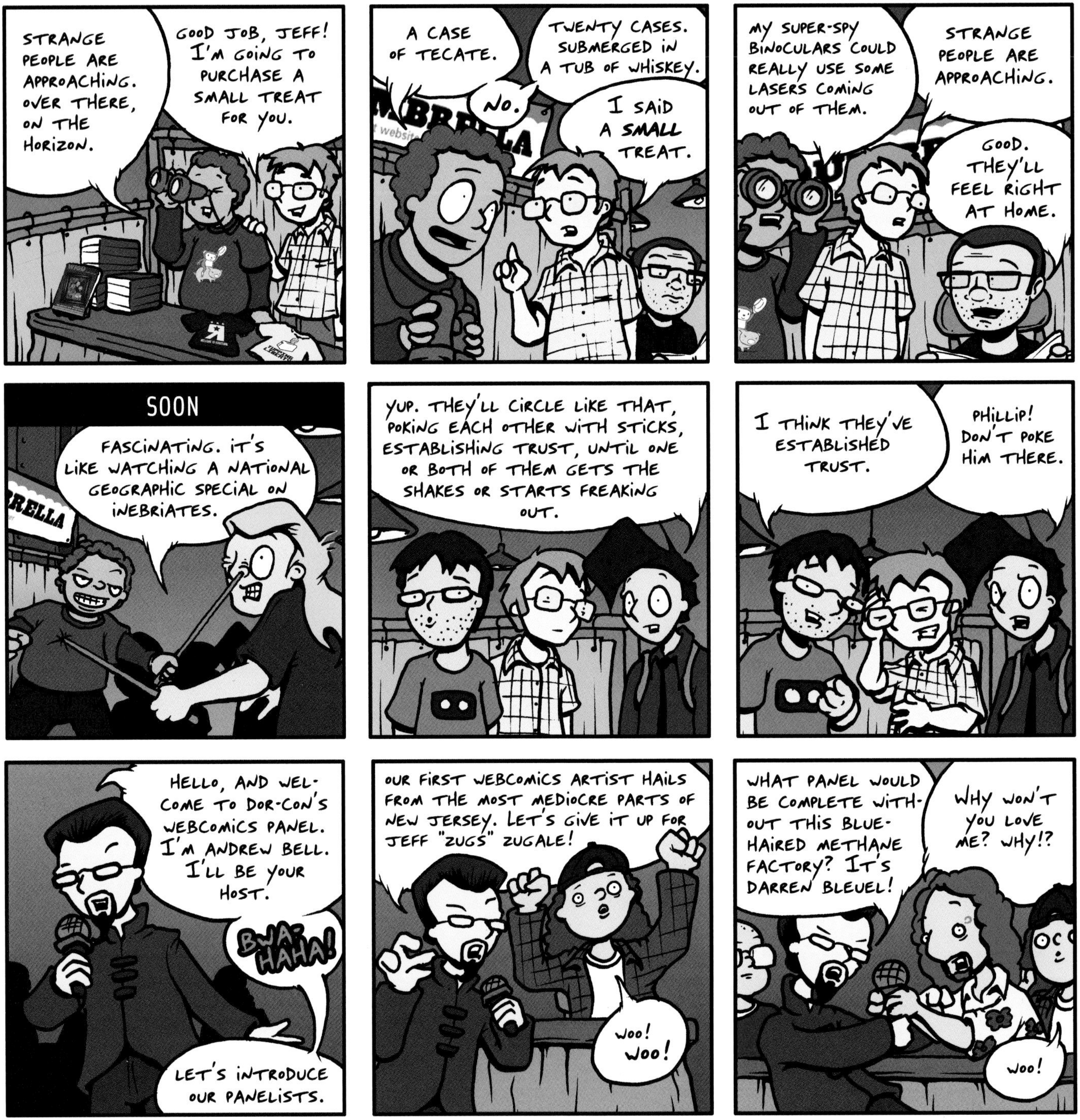
STRANGE PEOPLE ARE APPROACHING. OVER THERE, ON THE HORIZON.
GOOD JOB, JEFF! I'M GOING TO PURCHASE A SMALL TREAT FOR YOU.
A CASE OF TECATE.
TWENTY CASES. SUBMERGED IN A TUB OF WHISKEY.
NO.
I SAID A SMALL TREAT.
MY SUPER-SPY BINOCULARS COULD REALLY USE SOME LASERS COMING OUT OF THEM.
STRANGE PEOPLE ARE APPROACHING.
GOOD. THEY'LL FEEL RIGHT AT HOME.
SOON
FASCINATING. IT'S LIKE WATCHING A NATIONAL GEOGRAPHIC SPECIAL ON INEBRIATES.
YUP. THEY'LL CIRCLE LIKE THAT, POKING EACH OTHER WITH STICKS, ESTABLISHING TRUST, UNTIL ONE OR BOTH OF THEM GETS THE SHAKES OR STARTS FREAKING OUT.
I THINK THEY'VE ESTABLISHED TRUST.
PHILLIP! DON'T POKE HIM THERE.
HELLO, AND WELCOME TO DOR-CON'S WEBCOMICS PANEL. I'M ANDREW BELL. I'LL BE YOUR HOST.
BWAHAHA!
LET'S INTRODUCE OUR PANELISTS.
OUR FIRST WEBCOMICS ARTIST HAILS FROM THE MOST MEDIOCRE PARTS OF NEW JERSEY. LET'S GIVE IT UP FOR JEFF "ZUGS" ZUGALE!
WOO! WOO!
WHAT PANEL WOULD BE COMPLETE WITHOUT THIS BLUE-HAIRED METHANE FACTORY? IT'S DARREN BLEUEL!
WHY WON'T YOU LOVE ME? WHY!?
WOO!

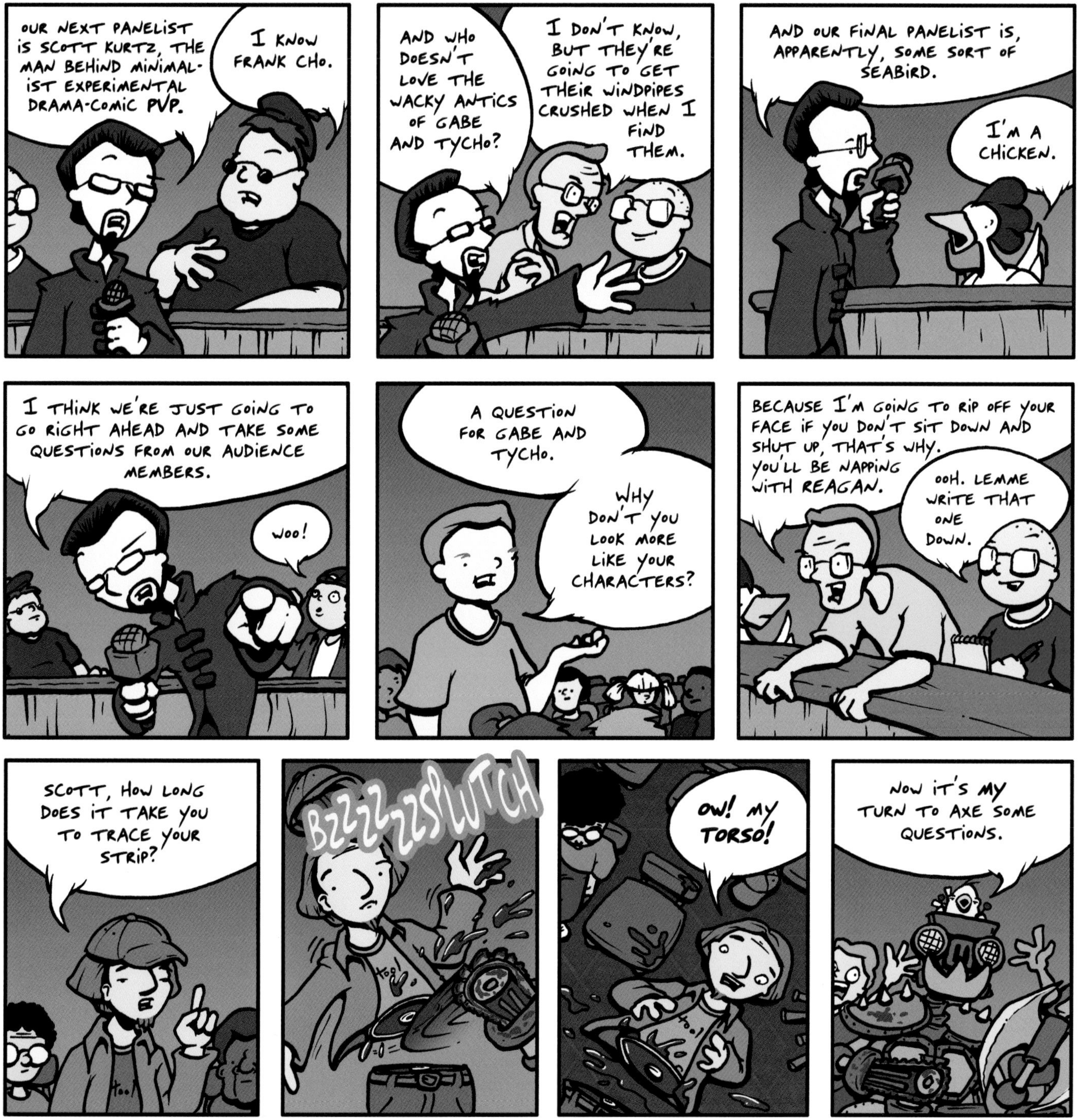

OUR NEXT PANELIST IS SCOTT KURTZ, THE MAN BEHIND MINIMAL-IST EXPERIMENTAL DRAMA-COMIC PVP.
I KNOW FRANK CHO.
AND WHO DOESN'T LOVE THE WACKY ANTICS OF GABE AND TYCHO?
I DON'T KNOW, BUT THEY'RE GOING TO GET THEIR WINDPIPES CRUSHED WHEN I FIND THEM.
AND OUR FINAL PANELIST IS, APPARENTLY, SOME SORT OF SEABIRD.
I'M A CHICKEN.
I THINK WE'RE JUST GOING TO GO RIGHT AHEAD AND TAKE SOME QUESTIONS FROM OUR AUDIENCE MEMBERS.
WOO!
A QUESTION FOR GABE AND TYCHO.
WHY DON'T YOU LOOK MORE LIKE YOUR CHARACTERS?
BECAUSE I'M GOING TO RIP OFF YOUR FACE IF YOU DON'T SIT DOWN AND SHUT UP, THAT'S WHY. YOU'LL BE NAPPING WITH REAGAN.
OOH. LEMME WRITE THAT ONE DOWN.
SCOTT, HOW LONG DOES IT TAKE YOU TO TRACE YOUR STRIP?
BZZZZZZSPLUTCH
OW! MY TORSO!
NOW IT'S MY TURN TO AXE SOME QUESTIONS.

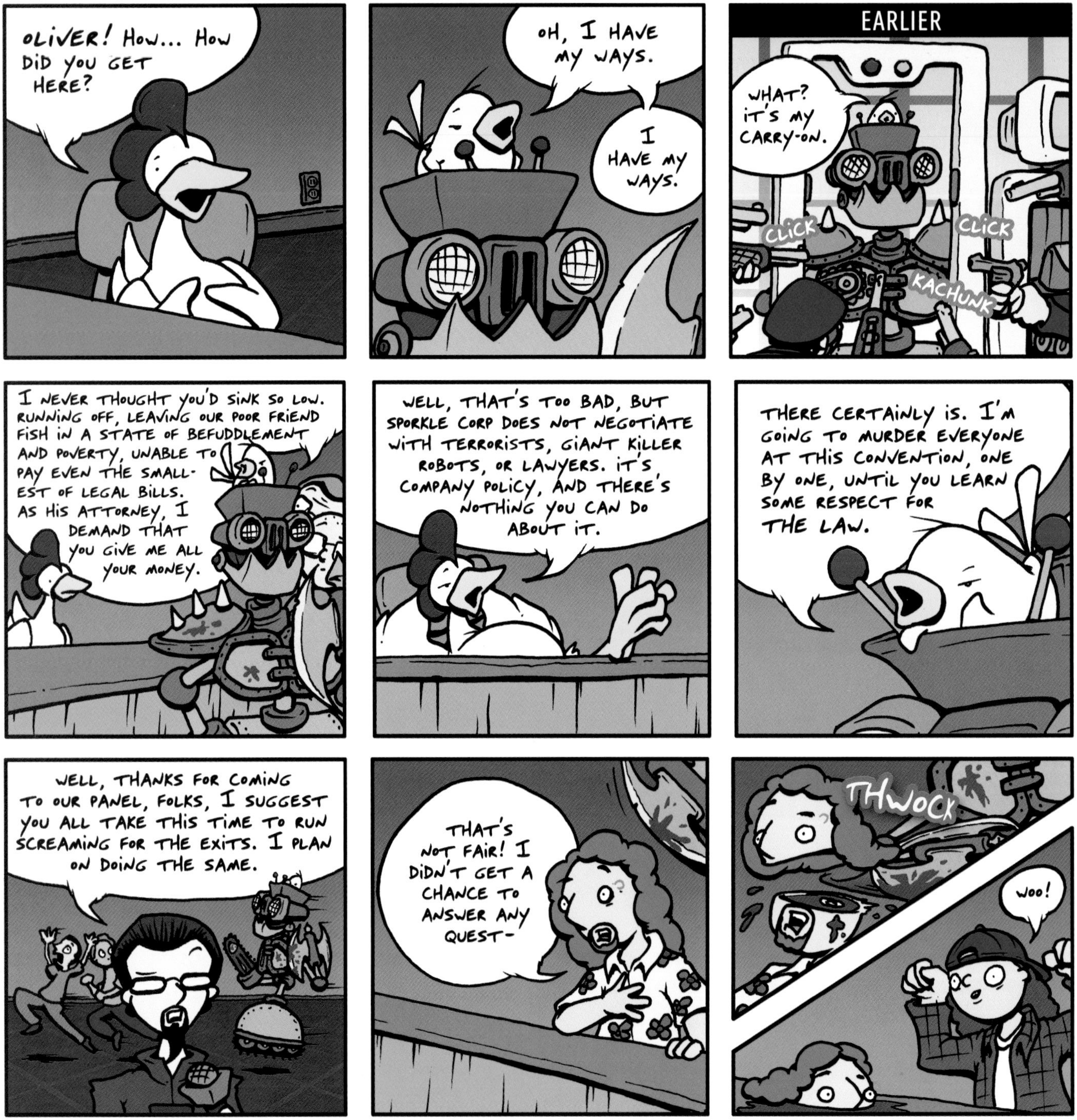
OLIVER! HOW... HOW DID YOU GET HERE?
OH, I HAVE MY WAYS.
I HAVE MY WAYS.
EARLIER
WHAT? IT'S MY CARRY-ON.
CLICK
CLICK
KACHUNK
I NEVER THOUGHT YOU'D SINK SO LOW. RUNNING OFF, LEAVING OUR POOR FRIEND FISH IN A STATE OF BEFUDDLEMENT AND POVERTY, UNABLE TO PAY EVEN THE SMALLEST OF LEGAL BILLS. AS HIS ATTORNEY, I DEMAND THAT YOU GIVE ME ALL YOUR MONEY.
WELL, THAT'S TOO BAD, BUT SPORKLE CORP DOES NOT NEGOTIATE WITH TERRORISTS, GIANT KILLER ROBOTS, OR LAWYERS. IT'S COMPANY POLICY, AND THERE'S NOTHING YOU CAN DO ABOUT IT.
THERE CERTAINLY IS. I'M GOING TO MURDER EVERYONE AT THIS CONVENTION, ONE BY ONE, UNTIL YOU LEARN SOME RESPECT FOR THE LAW.
WELL, THANKS FOR COMING TO OUR PANEL, FOLKS, I SUGGEST YOU ALL TAKE THIS TIME TO RUN SCREAMING FOR THE EXITS. I PLAN ON DOING THE SAME.
THAT'S NOT FAIR! I DIDN'T GET A CHANCE TO ANSWER ANY QUEST-
THWOCK
WOO!

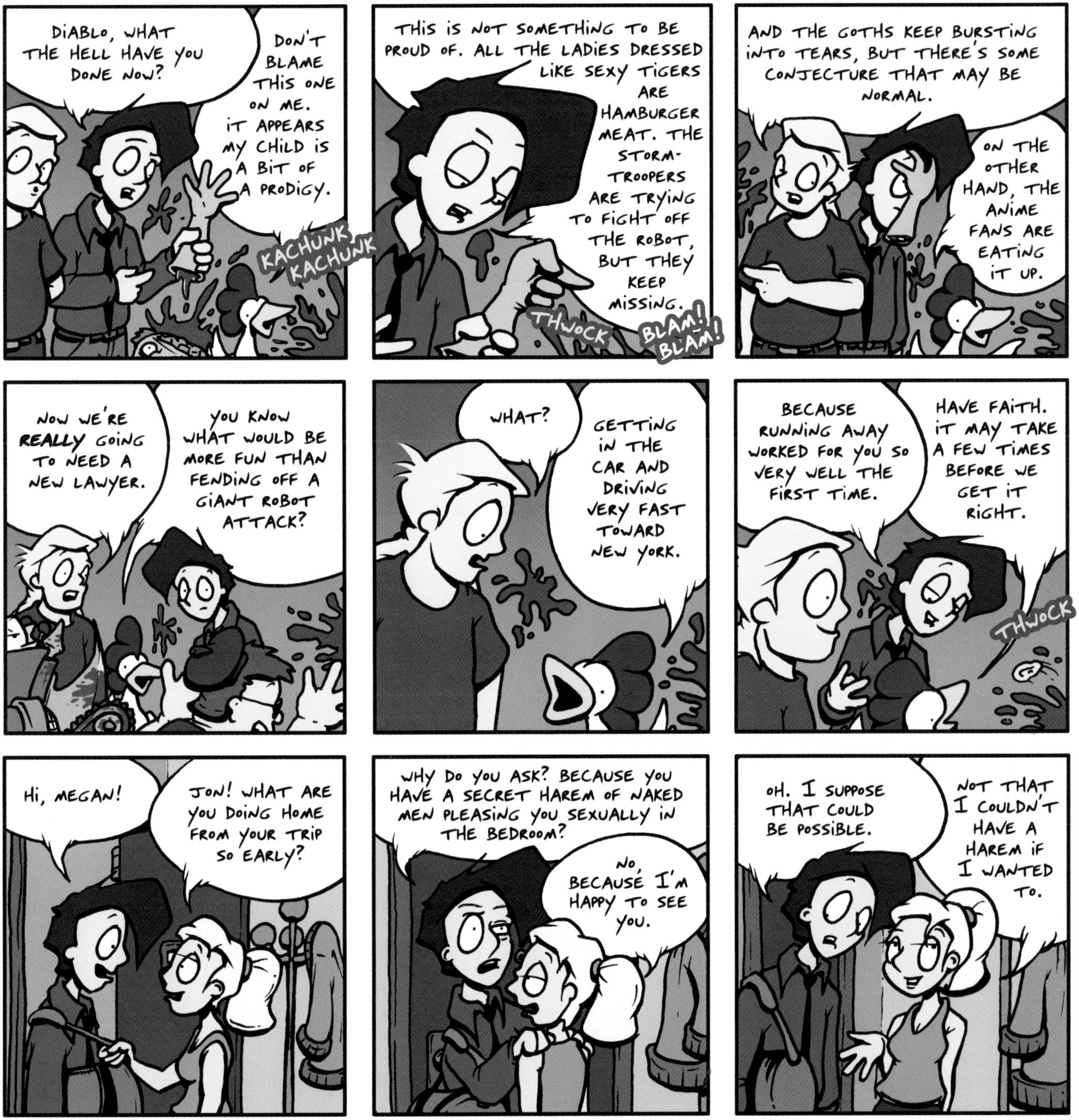
DIABLO, WHAT THE HELL HAVE YOU DONE NOW?
DON'T BLAME THIS ONE ON ME. IT APPEARS MY CHILD IS A BIT OF A PRODIGY.
KACHUNK KACHUNK
THIS IS NOT SOMETHING TO BE PROUD OF. ALL THE LADIES DRESSED LIKE SEXY TIGERS ARE HAMBURGER MEAT. THE STORM-TROOPERS ARE TRYING TO FIGHT OFF THE ROBOT, BUT THEY KEEP MISSING.
THWOCK
BLAM! BLAM!
AND THE GOTHS KEEP BURSTING INTO TEARS, BUT THERE'S SOME CONJECTURE THAT MAY BE NORMAL.
ON THE OTHER HAND, THE ANIME FANS ARE EATING IT UP.
NOW WE'RE **REALLY** GOING TO NEED A NEW LAWYER.
YOU KNOW WHAT WOULD BE MORE FUN THAN FENDING OFF A GIANT ROBOT ATTACK?
WHAT?
GETTING IN THE CAR AND DRIVING VERY FAST TOWARD NEW YORK.
BECAUSE RUNNING AWAY WORKED FOR YOU SO VERY WELL THE FIRST TIME.
HAVE FAITH. IT MAY TAKE A FEW TIMES BEFORE WE GET IT RIGHT.
THWOCK
HI, MEGAN!
JON! WHAT ARE YOU DOING HOME FROM YOUR TRIP SO EARLY?
WHY DO YOU ASK? BECAUSE YOU HAVE A SECRET HAREM OF NAKED MEN PLEASING YOU SEXUALLY IN THE BEDROOM?
NO, BECAUSE I'M HAPPY TO SEE YOU.
OH. I SUPPOSE THAT COULD BE POSSIBLE.
NOT THAT I COULDN'T HAVE A HAREM IF I WANTED TO.

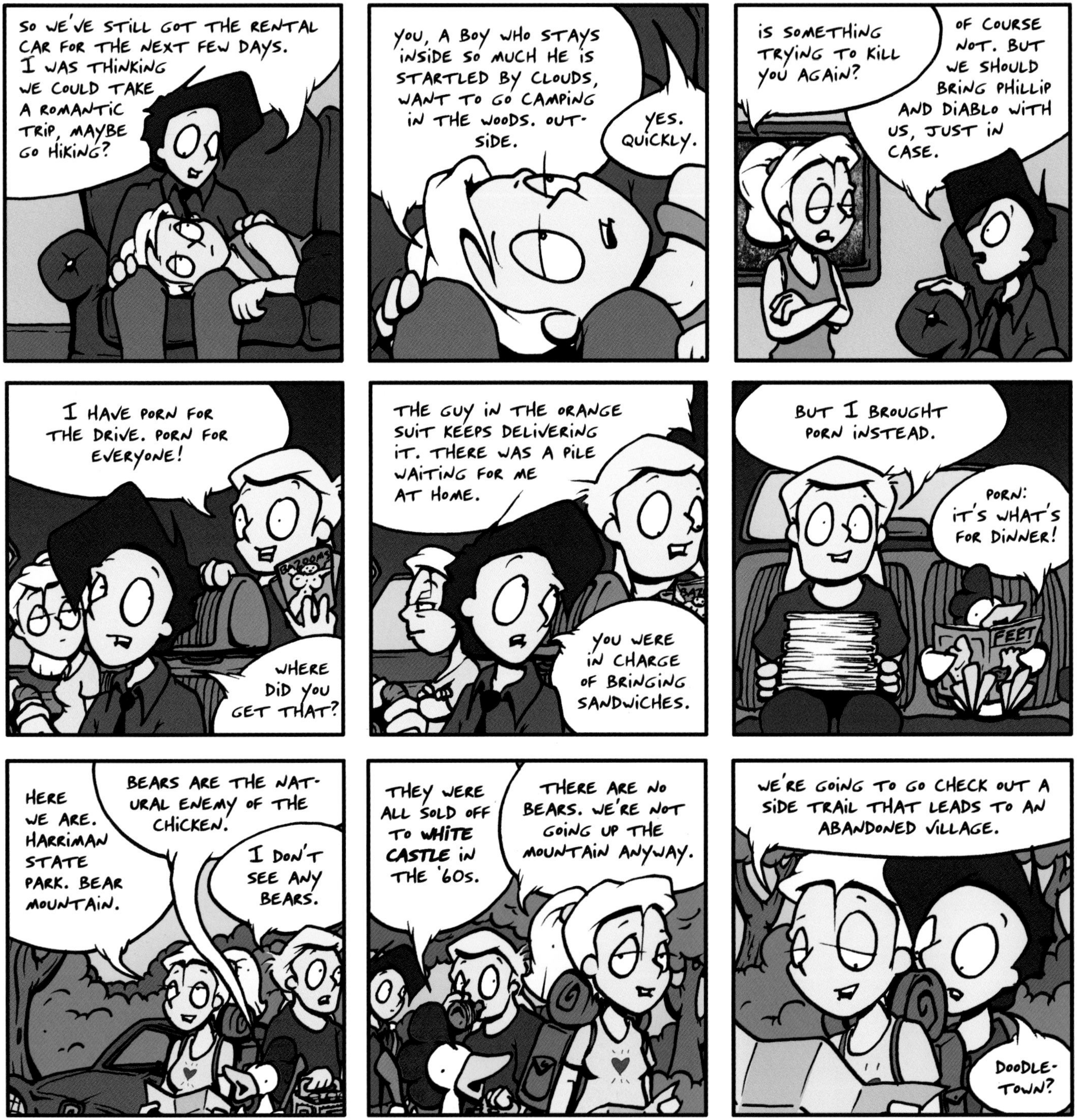
SO WE'VE STILL GOT THE RENTAL CAR FOR THE NEXT FEW DAYS. I WAS THINKING WE COULD TAKE A ROMANTIC TRIP, MAYBE GO HIKING?
YOU, A BOY WHO STAYS INSIDE SO MUCH HE IS STARTLED BY CLOUDS, WANT TO GO CAMPING IN THE WOODS. OUTSIDE.
YES. QUICKLY.
IS SOMETHING TRYING TO KILL YOU AGAIN?
OF COURSE NOT. BUT WE SHOULD BRING PHILLIP AND DIABLO WITH US, JUST IN CASE.
I HAVE PORN FOR THE DRIVE. PORN FOR EVERYONE!
BAZOOMS
WHERE DID YOU GET THAT?
THE GUY IN THE ORANGE SUIT KEEPS DELIVERING IT. THERE WAS A PILE WAITING FOR ME AT HOME.
YOU WERE IN CHARGE OF BRINGING SANDWICHES.
BUT I BROUGHT PORN INSTEAD.
PORN: IT'S WHAT'S FOR DINNER!
FEET
HERE WE ARE. HARRIMAN STATE PARK. BEAR MOUNTAIN.
BEARS ARE THE NATURAL ENEMY OF THE CHICKEN.
I DON'T SEE ANY BEARS.
THEY WERE ALL SOLD OFF TO WHITE CASTLE IN THE '60S.
THERE ARE NO BEARS. WE'RE NOT GOING UP THE MOUNTAIN ANYWAY.
WE'RE GOING TO GO CHECK OUT A SIDE TRAIL THAT LEADS TO AN ABANDONED VILLAGE.
DOODLETOWN?

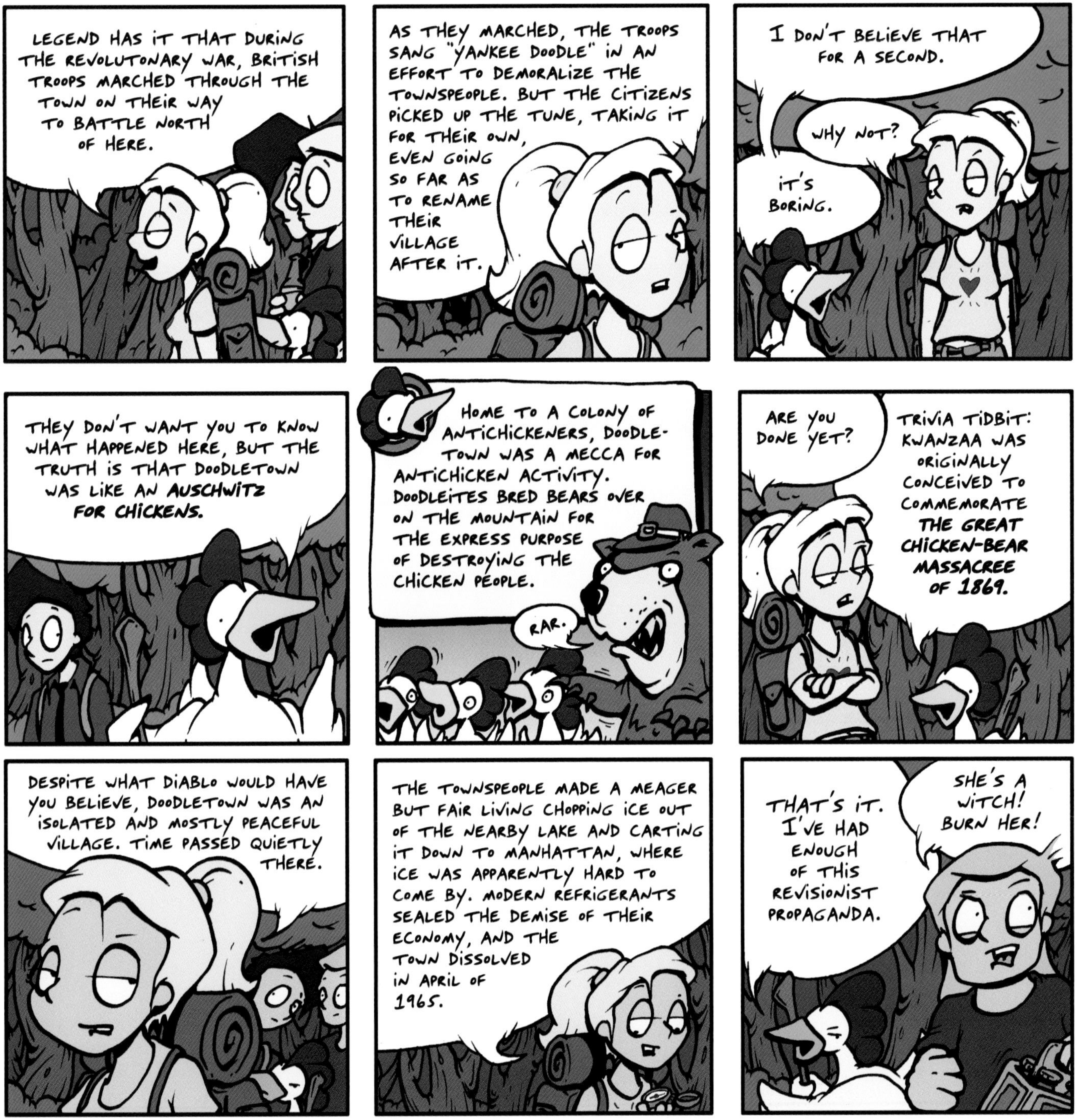
LEGEND HAS IT THAT DURING THE REVOLUTONARY WAR, BRITISH TROOPS MARCHED THROUGH THE TOWN ON THEIR WAY TO BATTLE NORTH OF HERE.
AS THEY MARCHED, THE TROOPS SANG "YANKEE DOODLE" IN AN EFFORT TO DEMORALIZE THE TOWNSPEOPLE. BUT THE CITIZENS PICKED UP THE TUNE, TAKING IT FOR THEIR OWN, EVEN GOING SO FAR AS TO RENAME THEIR VILLAGE AFTER IT.
I DON'T BELIEVE THAT FOR A SECOND.
WHY NOT?
IT'S BORING.
THEY DON'T WANT YOU TO KNOW WHAT HAPPENED HERE, BUT THE TRUTH IS THAT DOODLETOWN WAS LIKE AN AUSCHWITZ FOR CHICKENS.
HOME TO A COLONY OF ANTICHICKENERS, DOODLETOWN WAS A MECCA FOR ANTICHICKEN ACTIVITY. DOODLEITES BRED BEARS OVER ON THE MOUNTAIN FOR THE EXPRESS PURPOSE OF DESTROYING THE CHICKEN PEOPLE.
RAR.
ARE YOU DONE YET?
TRIVIA TIDBIT: KWANZAA WAS ORIGINALLY CONCEIVED TO COMMEMORATE THE GREAT CHICKEN-BEAR MASSACREE OF 1869.
DESPITE WHAT DIABLO WOULD HAVE YOU BELIEVE, DOODLETOWN WAS AN ISOLATED AND MOSTLY PEACEFUL VILLAGE. TIME PASSED QUIETLY THERE.
THE TOWNSPEOPLE MADE A MEAGER BUT FAIR LIVING CHOPPING ICE OUT OF THE NEARBY LAKE AND CARTING IT DOWN TO MANHATTAN, WHERE ICE WAS APPARENTLY HARD TO COME BY. MODERN REFRIGERANTS SEALED THE DEMISE OF THEIR ECONOMY, AND THE TOWN DISSOLVED IN APRIL OF 1965.
THAT'S IT. I'VE HAD ENOUGH OF THIS REVISIONIST PROPAGANDA.
SHE'S A WITCH! BURN HER!

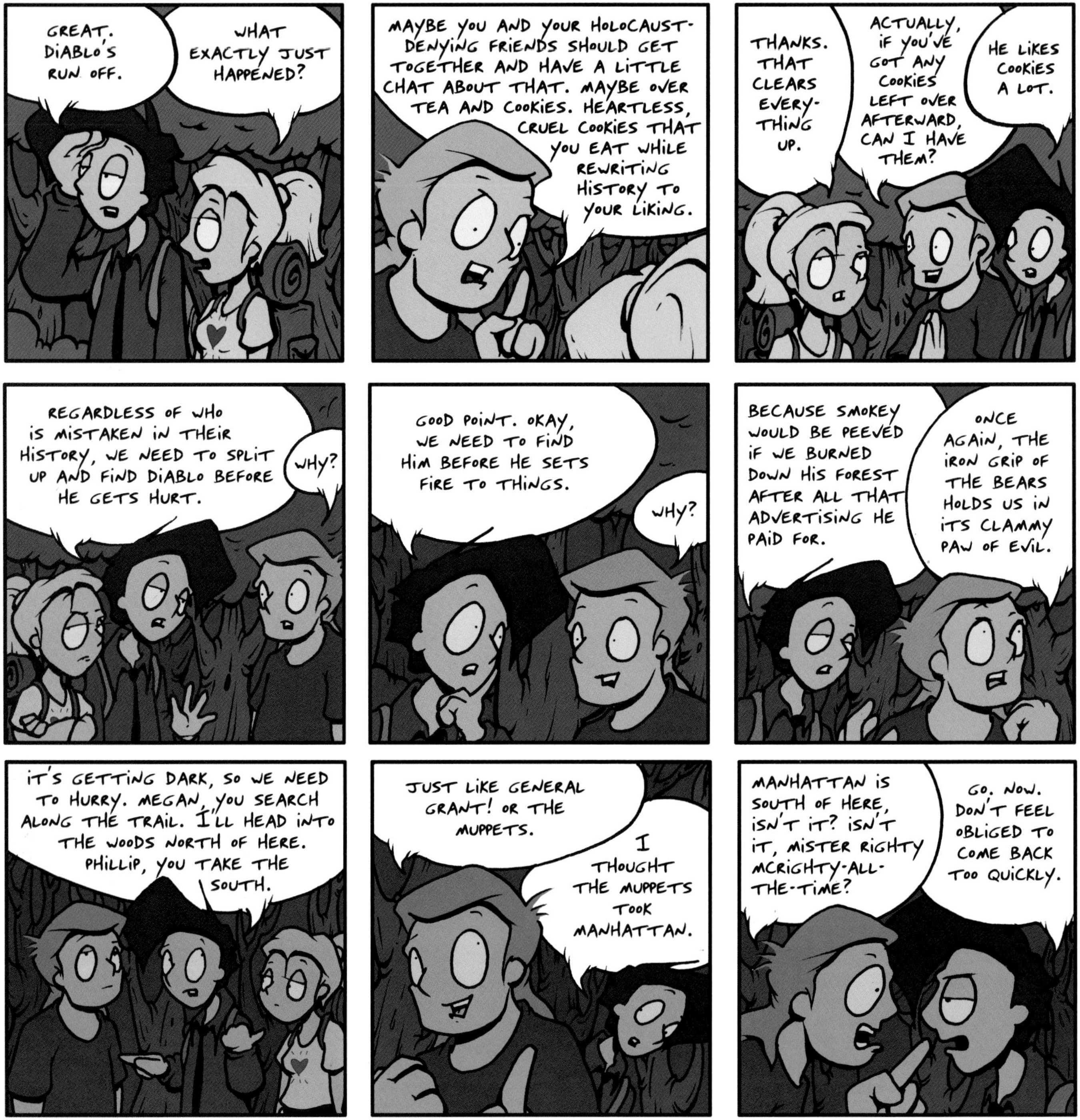
GREAT. DIABLO'S RUN OFF.
WHAT EXACTLY JUST HAPPENED?
MAYBE YOU AND YOUR HOLOCAUST-DENYING FRIENDS SHOULD GET TOGETHER AND HAVE A LITTLE CHAT ABOUT THAT. MAYBE OVER TEA AND COOKIES. HEARTLESS, CRUEL COOKIES THAT YOU EAT WHILE REWRITING HISTORY TO YOUR LIKING.
THANKS. THAT CLEARS EVERY-THING UP.
ACTUALLY, IF YOU'VE GOT ANY COOKIES LEFT OVER AFTERWARD, CAN I HAVE THEM?
HE LIKES COOKIES A LOT.
REGARDLESS OF WHO IS MISTAKEN IN THEIR HISTORY, WE NEED TO SPLIT UP AND FIND DIABLO BEFORE HE GETS HURT.
WHY?
GOOD POINT. OKAY, WE NEED TO FIND HIM BEFORE HE SETS FIRE TO THINGS.
WHY?
BECAUSE SMOKEY WOULD BE PEEVED IF WE BURNED DOWN HIS FOREST AFTER ALL THAT ADVERTISING HE PAID FOR.
ONCE AGAIN, THE IRON GRIP OF THE BEARS HOLDS US IN ITS CLAMMY PAW OF EVIL.
IT'S GETTING DARK, SO WE NEED TO HURRY. MEGAN, YOU SEARCH ALONG THE TRAIL. I'LL HEAD INTO THE WOODS NORTH OF HERE. PHILLIP, YOU TAKE THE SOUTH.
JUST LIKE GENERAL GRANT! OR THE MUPPETS.
I THOUGHT THE MUPPETS TOOK MANHATTAN.
MANHATTAN IS SOUTH OF HERE, ISN'T IT? ISN'T IT, MISTER RIGHTY MCRIGHTY-ALL-THE-TIME?
GO. NOW. DON'T FEEL OBLIGED TO COME BACK TOO QUICKLY.

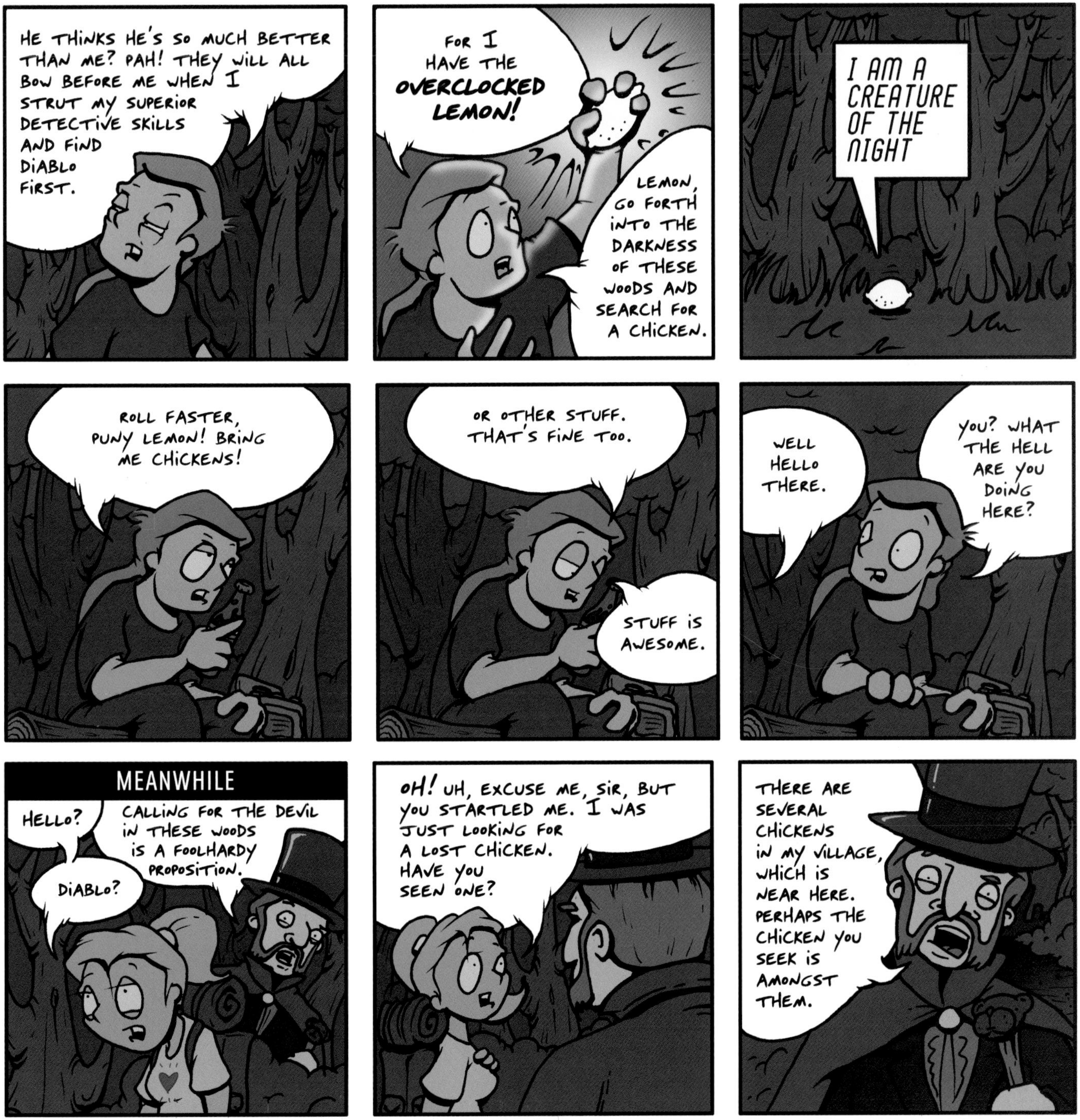
HE THINKS HE'S SO MUCH BETTER THAN ME? PAH! THEY WILL ALL BOW BEFORE ME WHEN I STRUT MY SUPERIOR DETECTIVE SKILLS AND FIND DIABLO FIRST.
FOR I HAVE THE OVERCLOCKED LEMON!
LEMON, GO FORTH INTO THE DARKNESS OF THESE WOODS AND SEARCH FOR A CHICKEN.
I AM A CREATURE OF THE NIGHT
ROLL FASTER, PUNY LEMON! BRING ME CHICKENS!
OR OTHER STUFF. THAT'S FINE TOO.
STUFF IS AWESOME.
WELL HELLO THERE.
YOU? WHAT THE HELL ARE YOU DOING HERE?
MEANWHILE
HELLO?
DIABLO?
CALLING FOR THE DEVIL IN THESE WOODS IS A FOOLHARDY PROPOSITION.
OH! UH, EXCUSE ME, SIR, BUT YOU STARTLED ME. I WAS JUST LOOKING FOR A LOST CHICKEN. HAVE YOU SEEN ONE?
THERE ARE SEVERAL CHICKENS IN MY VILLAGE, WHICH IS NEAR HERE. PERHAPS THE CHICKEN YOU SEEK IS AMONGST THEM.

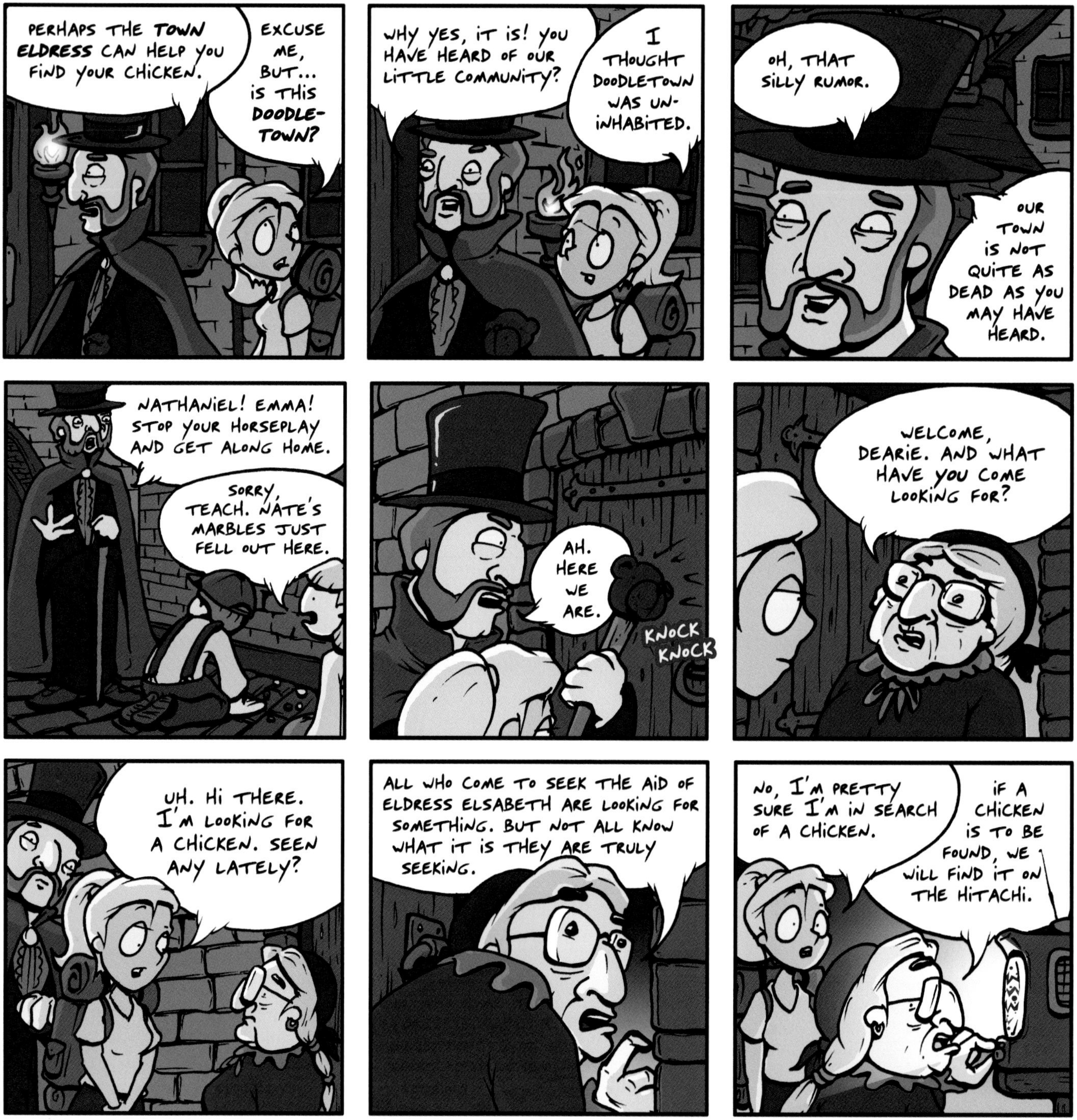
PERHAPS THE TOWN ELDRESS CAN HELP YOU FIND YOUR CHICKEN.
EXCUSE ME, BUT... IS THIS DOODLE-TOWN?
WHY YES, IT IS! YOU HAVE HEARD OF OUR LITTLE COMMUNITY?
I THOUGHT DOODLETOWN WAS UN-INHABITED.
OH, THAT SILLY RUMOR.
OUR TOWN IS NOT QUITE AS DEAD AS YOU MAY HAVE HEARD.
NATHANIEL! EMMA! STOP YOUR HORSEPLAY AND GET ALONG HOME.
SORRY, TEACH. NATE'S MARBLES JUST FELL OUT HERE.
AH. HERE WE ARE.
KNOCK KNOCK
WELCOME, DEARIE. AND WHAT HAVE YOU COME LOOKING FOR?
UH. HI THERE. I'M LOOKING FOR A CHICKEN. SEEN ANY LATELY?
ALL WHO COME TO SEEK THE AID OF ELDRESS ELSABETH ARE LOOKING FOR SOMETHING. BUT NOT ALL KNOW WHAT IT IS THEY ARE TRULY SEEKING.
NO, I'M PRETTY SURE I'M IN SEARCH OF A CHICKEN.
IF A CHICKEN IS TO BE FOUND, WE WILL FIND IT ON THE HITACHI.

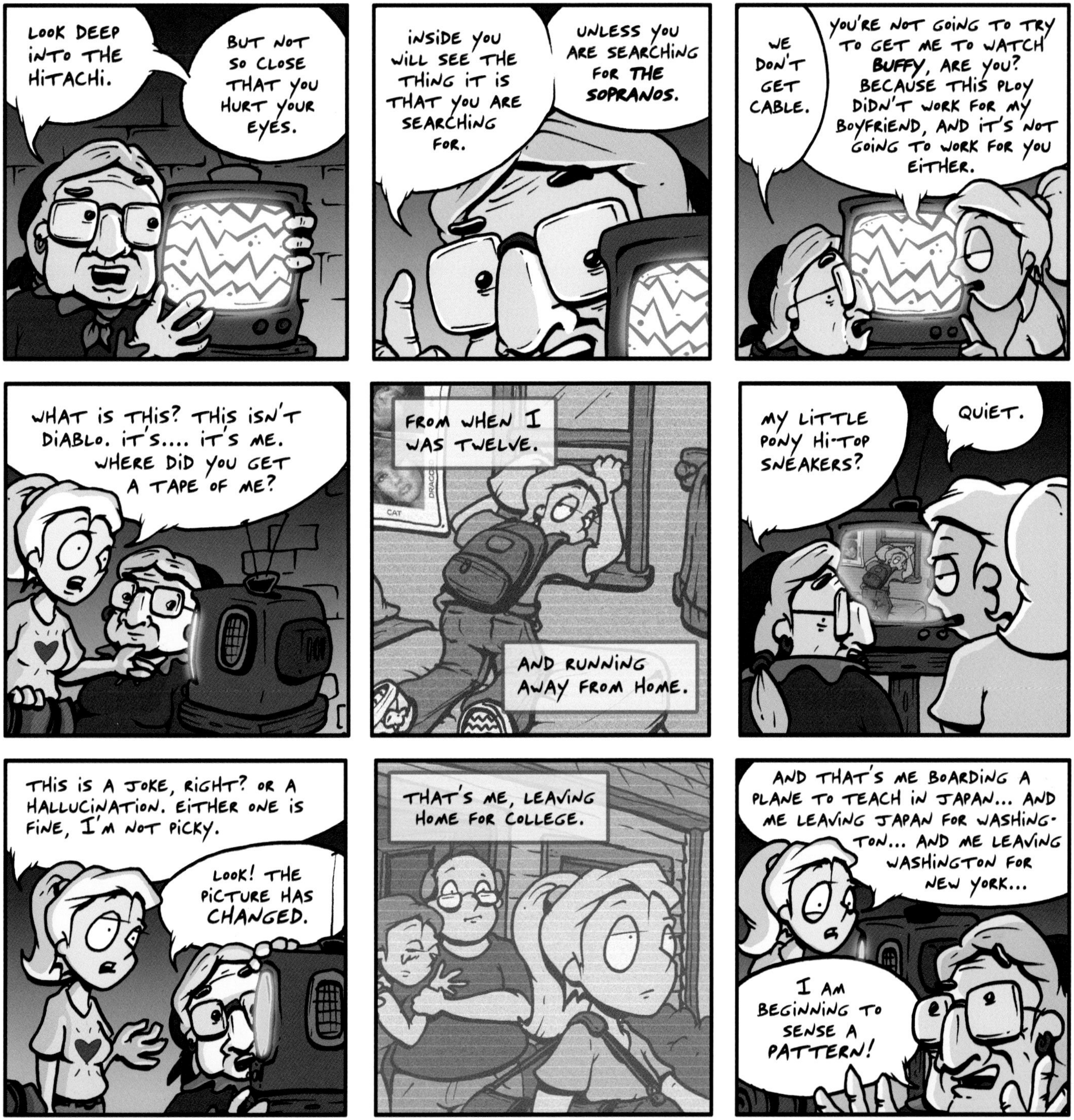
LOOK DEEP INTO THE HITACHI.
BUT NOT SO CLOSE THAT YOU HURT YOUR EYES.
INSIDE YOU WILL SEE THE THING IT IS THAT YOU ARE SEARCHING FOR.
UNLESS YOU ARE SEARCHING FOR **THE SOPRANOS**.
WE DON'T GET CABLE.
YOU'RE NOT GOING TO TRY TO GET ME TO WATCH **BUFFY**, ARE YOU? BECAUSE THIS PLOY DIDN'T WORK FOR MY BOYFRIEND, AND IT'S NOT GOING TO WORK FOR YOU EITHER.
WHAT IS THIS? THIS ISN'T DIABLO. IT'S.... IT'S ME. WHERE DID YOU GET A TAPE OF ME?
FROM WHEN I WAS TWELVE.
AND RUNNING AWAY FROM HOME.
MY LITTLE PONY HI-TOP SNEAKERS?
QUIET.
THIS IS A JOKE, RIGHT? OR A HALLUCINATION. EITHER ONE IS FINE, I'M NOT PICKY.
LOOK! THE PICTURE HAS CHANGED.
THAT'S ME, LEAVING HOME FOR COLLEGE.
AND THAT'S ME BOARDING A PLANE TO TEACH IN JAPAN... AND ME LEAVING JAPAN FOR WASHINGTON... AND ME LEAVING WASHINGTON FOR NEW YORK...
I AM BEGINNING TO SENSE A PATTERN!

YOU SENSE A PATTERN.

THE HITACHI SHOWS YOU SEARCHING ENDLESSLY FOR SOMETHING YOU HAVE NOT YET FOUND.

IT IS NOT DESPITE YOUR TRAVELS THAT YOU HAVE NOT FOUND THE OBJECT OF YOUR QUEST, BUT **BECAUSE** OF THEM.

THIS IS THE PART WHERE YOU TELL ME TO GO FIGHT DARTH VADER IN THE TREE CAVE, RIGHT?

IT IS STABILITY THAT YOU SEEK. IT IS A PLACE TO CALL HOME.

LOOK, THIS HAS BEEN FUN, BUT... WELL, NO. IT HASN'T BEEN FUN. IT'S BEEN CREEPY AND I REALLY SHOULD BE GOING.

SEE? YOU ARE ALWAYS LEAVING.

THERE IS NO NEED TO LEAVE, THOUGH. NOT THIS TIME. YOU CAN MAKE YOUR HOME HERE WITH US, IN DOODLETOWN. STAY HERE AND I PROMISE YOU WILL NOT GO WANDERING AGAIN.

YES. YOU... YOU'RE RIGHT. I'LL STAY.

I'LL STAY FOREVER.

DIABLO! C'MON! I DON'T HAVE TIME FOR THIS.

WHAT DO YOU WANT? A BRIBE?

WHAT IS IT YOU WANT THIS TIME? MONEY? POWER?

BECAUSE YOU'RE NOT GETTING ME TO SING STEPHEN SONDHEIM TUNES AGAIN. EVER.

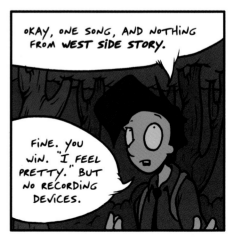

OKAY, ONE SONG, AND NOTHING FROM **WEST SIDE STORY**.

FINE. YOU WIN. "I FEEL PRETTY." BUT NO RECORDING DEVICES.

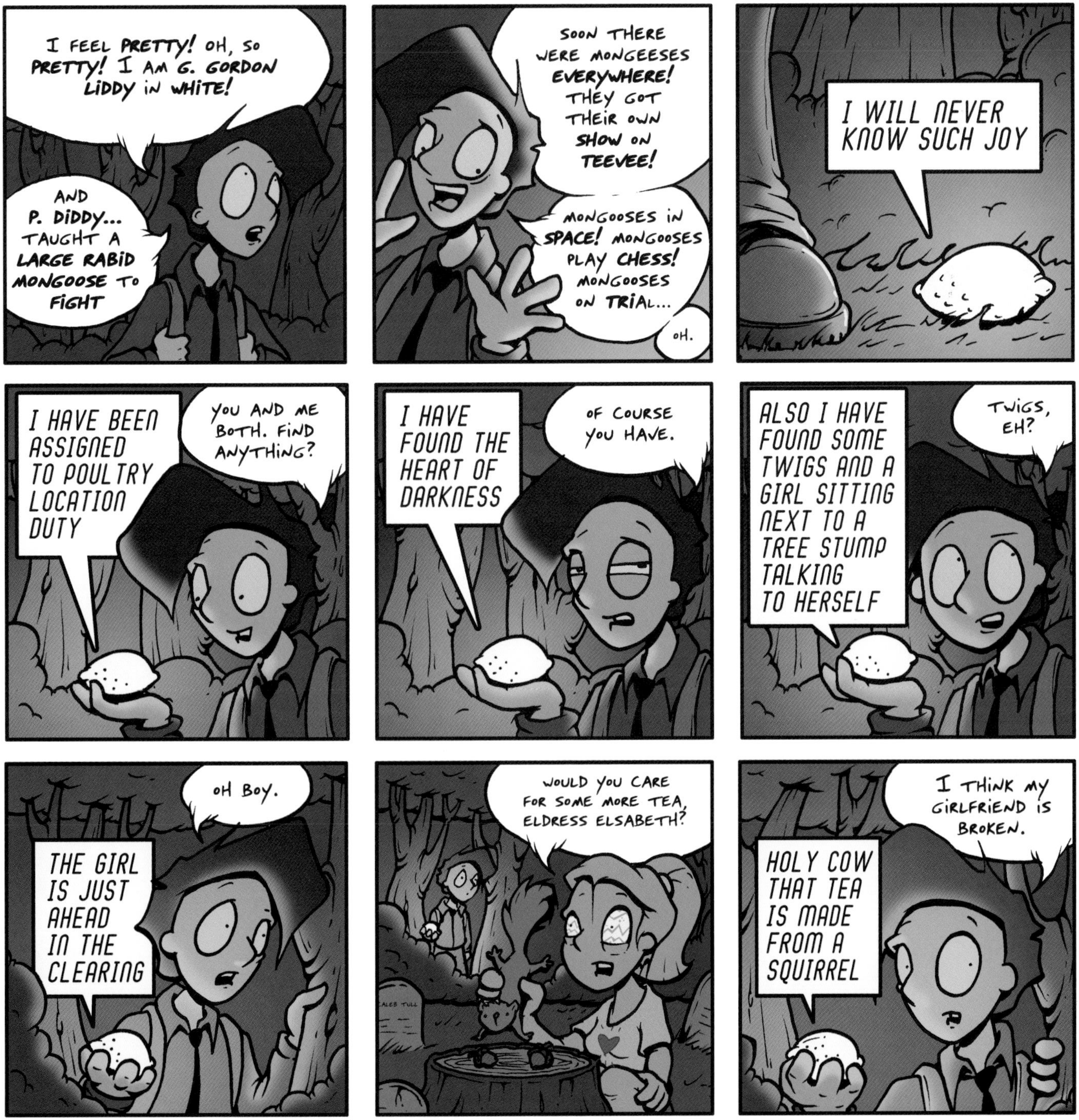
I FEEL PRETTY! OH, SO PRETTY! I AM G. GORDON LIDDY IN WHITE!
AND P. DIDDY... TAUGHT A LARGE RABID MONGOOSE TO FIGHT
SOON THERE WERE MONGEESES EVERYWHERE! THEY GOT THEIR OWN SHOW ON TEEVEE!
MONGOOSES IN SPACE! MONGOOSES PLAY CHESS! MONGOOSES ON TRIAL...
OH.
I WILL NEVER KNOW SUCH JOY
I HAVE BEEN ASSIGNED TO POULTRY LOCATION DUTY
YOU AND ME BOTH. FIND ANYTHING?
I HAVE FOUND THE HEART OF DARKNESS
OF COURSE YOU HAVE.
ALSO I HAVE FOUND SOME TWIGS AND A GIRL SITTING NEXT TO A TREE STUMP TALKING TO HERSELF
TWIGS, EH?
OH BOY.
THE GIRL IS JUST AHEAD IN THE CLEARING
WOULD YOU CARE FOR SOME MORE TEA, ELDRESS ELSABETH?
CALEB TULL
HOLY COW THAT TEA IS MADE FROM A SQUIRREL
I THINK MY GIRLFRIEND IS BROKEN.

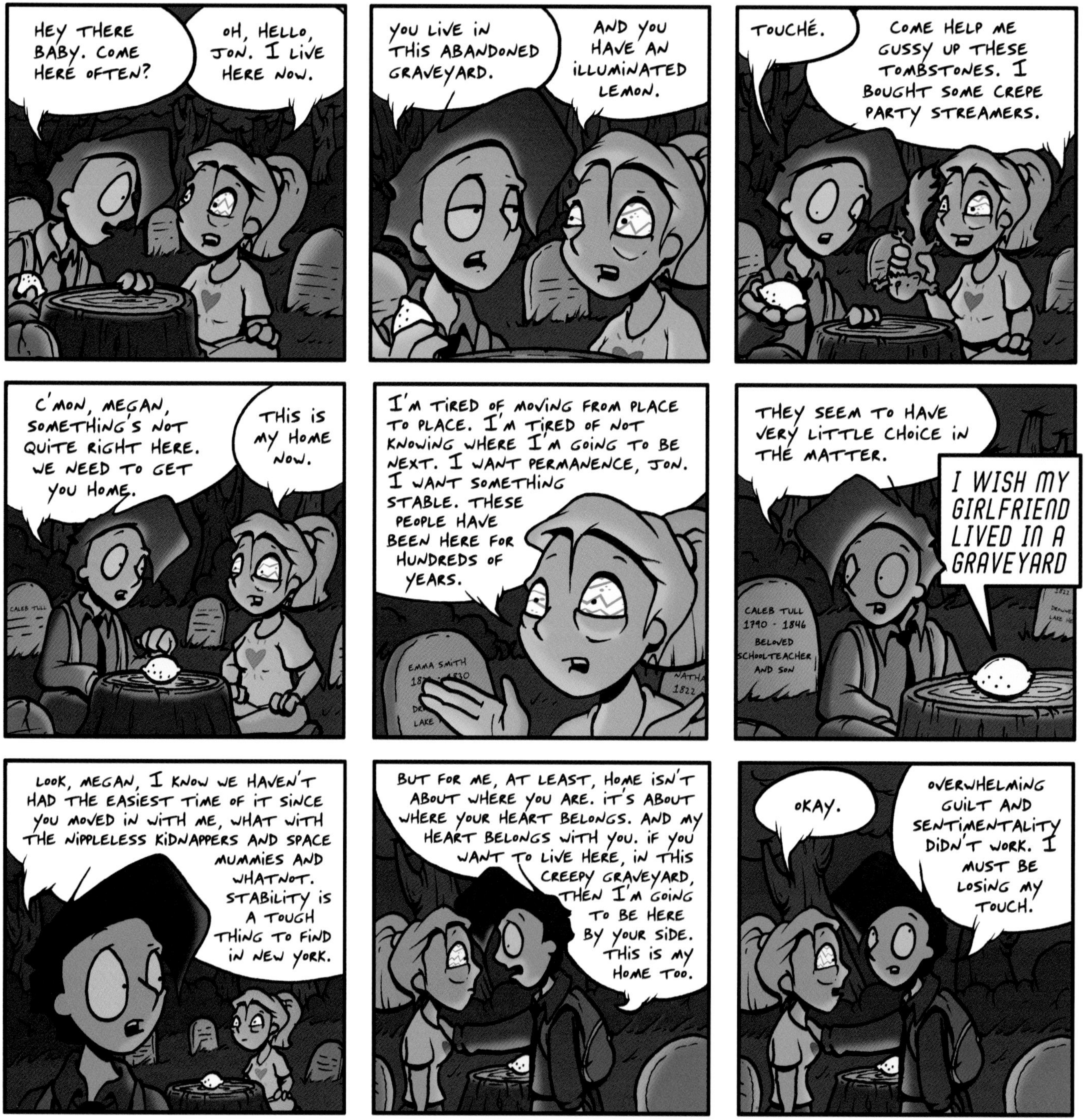
HEY THERE BABY. COME HERE OFTEN?
OH, HELLO, JON. I LIVE HERE NOW.
YOU LIVE IN THIS ABANDONED GRAVEYARD.
AND YOU HAVE AN ILLUMINATED LEMON.
TOUCHÉ.
COME HELP ME GUSSY UP THESE TOMBSTONES. I BOUGHT SOME CREPE PARTY STREAMERS.
C'MON, MEGAN, SOMETHING'S NOT QUITE RIGHT HERE. WE NEED TO GET YOU HOME.
THIS IS MY HOME NOW.
I'M TIRED OF MOVING FROM PLACE TO PLACE. I'M TIRED OF NOT KNOWING WHERE I'M GOING TO BE NEXT. I WANT PERMANENCE, JON. I WANT SOMETHING STABLE. THESE PEOPLE HAVE BEEN HERE FOR HUNDREDS OF YEARS.
EMMA SMITH
THEY SEEM TO HAVE VERY LITTLE CHOICE IN THE MATTER.
CALEB TULL
1790 - 1846
BELOVED SCHOOLTEACHER AND SON
I WISH MY GIRLFRIEND LIVED IN A GRAVEYARD
LOOK, MEGAN, I KNOW WE HAVEN'T HAD THE EASIEST TIME OF IT SINCE YOU MOVED IN WITH ME, WHAT WITH THE NIPPLELESS KIDNAPPERS AND SPACE MUMMIES AND WHATNOT. STABILITY IS A TOUGH THING TO FIND IN NEW YORK.
BUT FOR ME, AT LEAST, HOME ISN'T ABOUT WHERE YOU ARE. IT'S ABOUT WHERE YOUR HEART BELONGS. AND MY HEART BELONGS WITH YOU. IF YOU WANT TO LIVE HERE, IN THIS CREEPY GRAVEYARD, THEN I'M GOING TO BE HERE BY YOUR SIDE. THIS IS MY HOME TOO.
OKAY.
OVERWHELMING GUILT AND SENTIMENTALITY DIDN'T WORK. I MUST BE LOSING MY TOUCH.

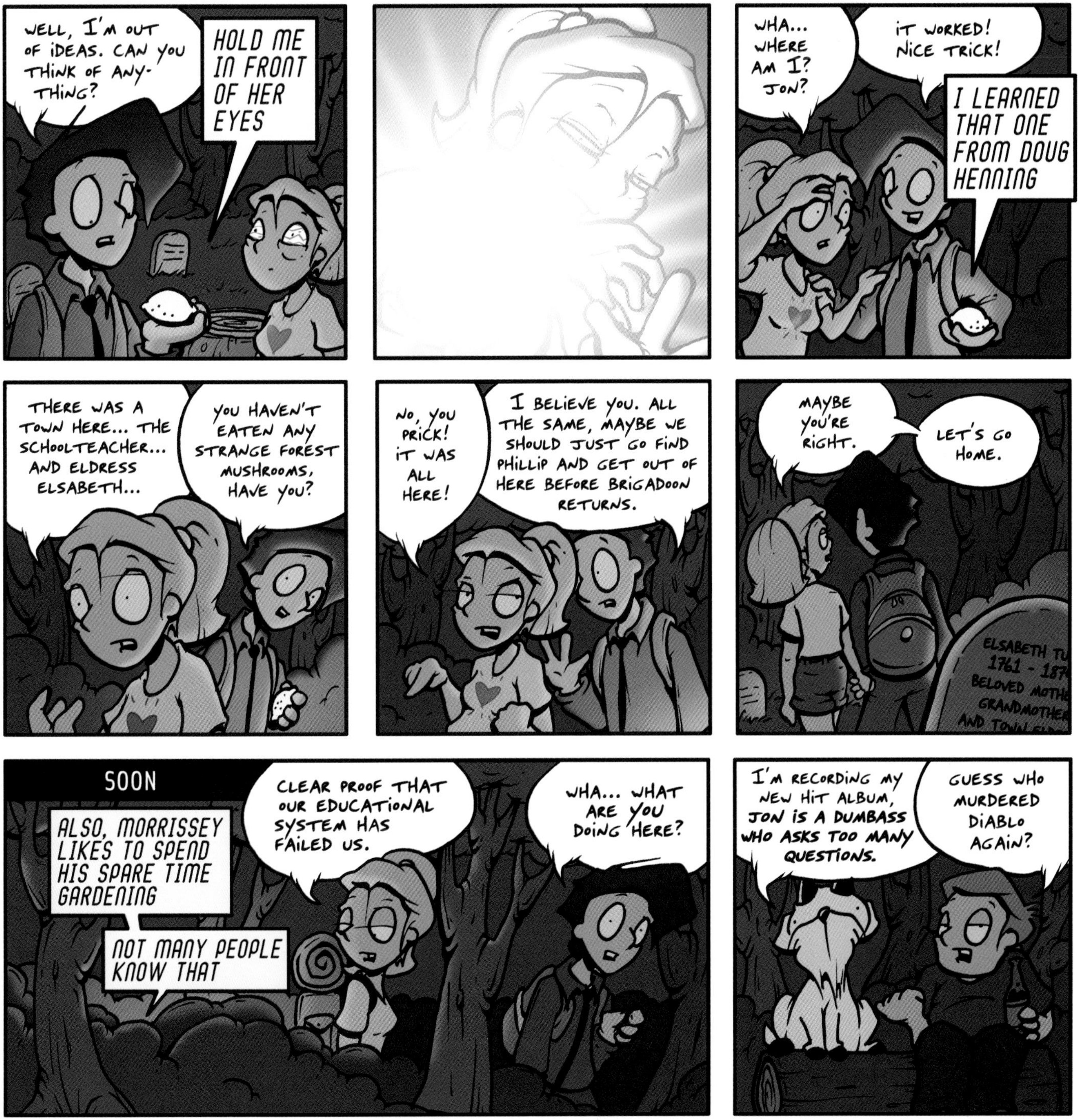
WELL, I'M OUT OF iDEAS. CAN YOU THINK OF ANY-THING?
HOLD ME IN FRONT OF HER EYES
WHA... WHERE AM I? JON?
iT WORKED! NiCE TRiCK!
I LEARNED THAT ONE FROM DOUG HENNING
THERE WAS A TOWN HERE... THE SCHOOLTEACHER... AND ELDRESS ELSABETH...
YOU HAVEN'T EATEN ANY STRANGE FOREST MUSHROOMS, HAVE YOU?
NO, YOU PRiCK! iT WAS ALL HERE!
I BELiEVE YOU. ALL THE SAME, MAYBE WE SHOULD JUST GO FiND PHiLLiP AND GET OUT OF HERE BEFORE BRiGADOON RETURNS.
MAYBE YOU'RE RiGHT.
LET'S GO HOME.
ELSABETH TU
1761 - 187
BELOVED MOTHE
GRANDMOTHER
SOON
ALSO, MORRISSEY LIKES TO SPEND HIS SPARE TIME GARDENING
NOT MANY PEOPLE KNOW THAT
CLEAR PROOF THAT OUR EDUCATiONAL SYSTEM HAS FAiLED US.
WHA... WHAT ARE YOU DOiNG HERE?
I'M RECORDiNG MY NEW HiT ALBUM, JON IS A DUMBASS WHO ASKS TOO MANY QUESTiONS.
GUESS WHO MURDERED DiABLO AGAiN?

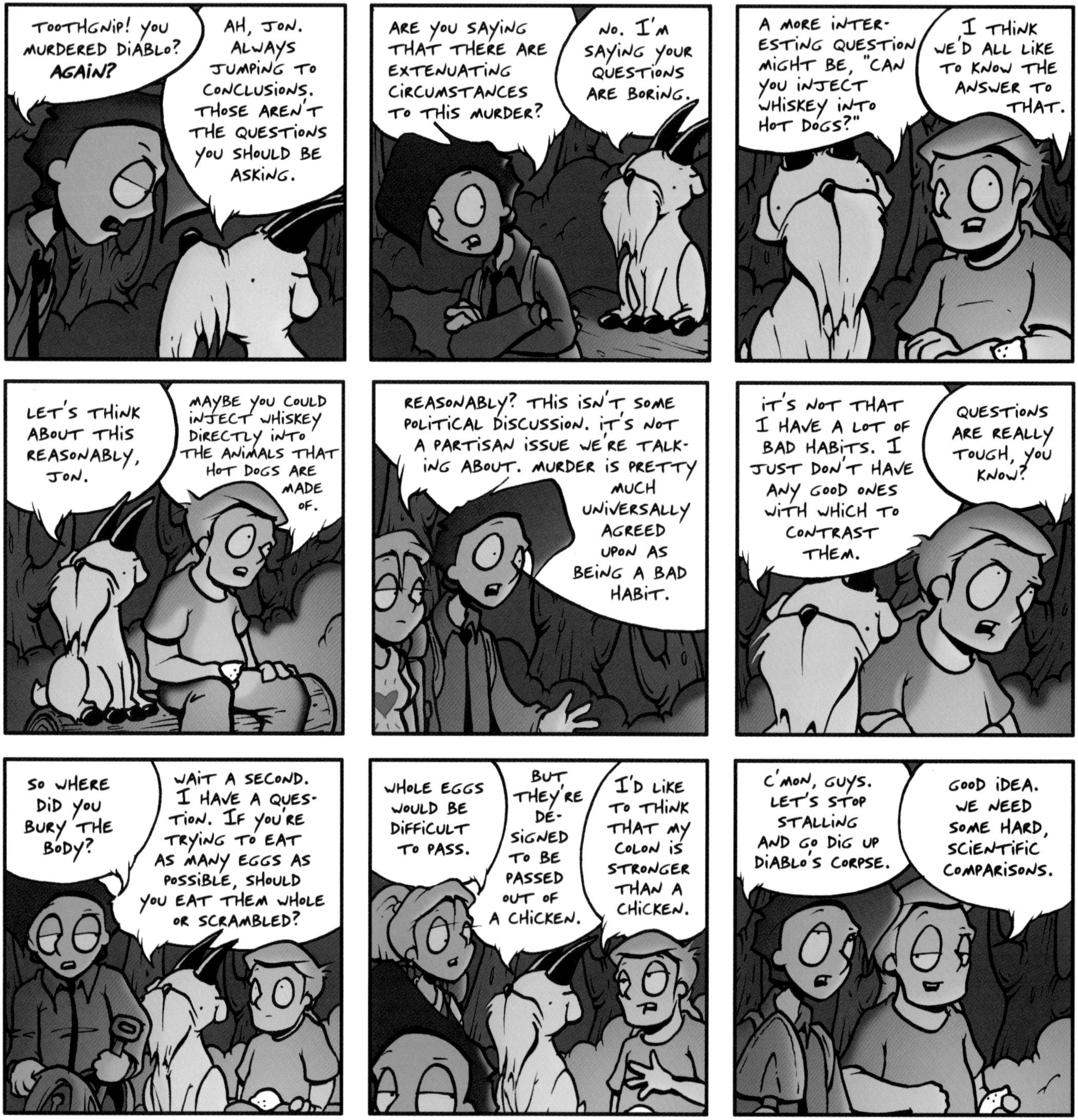
TOOTHGNIP! YOU MURDERED DIABLO? AGAIN?
AH, JON. ALWAYS JUMPING TO CONCLUSIONS. THOSE AREN'T THE QUESTIONS YOU SHOULD BE ASKING.
ARE YOU SAYING THAT THERE ARE EXTENUATING CIRCUMSTANCES TO THIS MURDER?
NO. I'M SAYING YOUR QUESTIONS ARE BORING.
A MORE INTERESTING QUESTION MIGHT BE, "CAN YOU INJECT WHISKEY INTO HOT DOGS?"
I THINK WE'D ALL LIKE TO KNOW THE ANSWER TO THAT.
LET'S THINK ABOUT THIS REASONABLY, JON.
MAYBE YOU COULD INJECT WHISKEY DIRECTLY INTO THE ANIMALS THAT HOT DOGS ARE MADE OF.
REASONABLY? THIS ISN'T SOME POLITICAL DISCUSSION. IT'S NOT A PARTISAN ISSUE WE'RE TALKING ABOUT. MURDER IS PRETTY MUCH UNIVERSALLY AGREED UPON AS BEING A BAD HABIT.
IT'S NOT THAT I HAVE A LOT OF BAD HABITS. I JUST DON'T HAVE ANY GOOD ONES WITH WHICH TO CONTRAST THEM.
QUESTIONS ARE REALLY TOUGH, YOU KNOW?
SO WHERE DID YOU BURY THE BODY?
WAIT A SECOND. I HAVE A QUESTION. IF YOU'RE TRYING TO EAT AS MANY EGGS AS POSSIBLE, SHOULD YOU EAT THEM WHOLE OR SCRAMBLED?
WHOLE EGGS WOULD BE DIFFICULT TO PASS.
BUT THEY'RE DESIGNED TO BE PASSED OUT OF A CHICKEN.
I'D LIKE TO THINK THAT MY COLON IS STRONGER THAN A CHICKEN.
C'MON, GUYS. LET'S STOP STALLING AND GO DIG UP DIABLO'S CORPSE.
GOOD IDEA. WE NEED SOME HARD, SCIENTIFIC COMPARISONS.

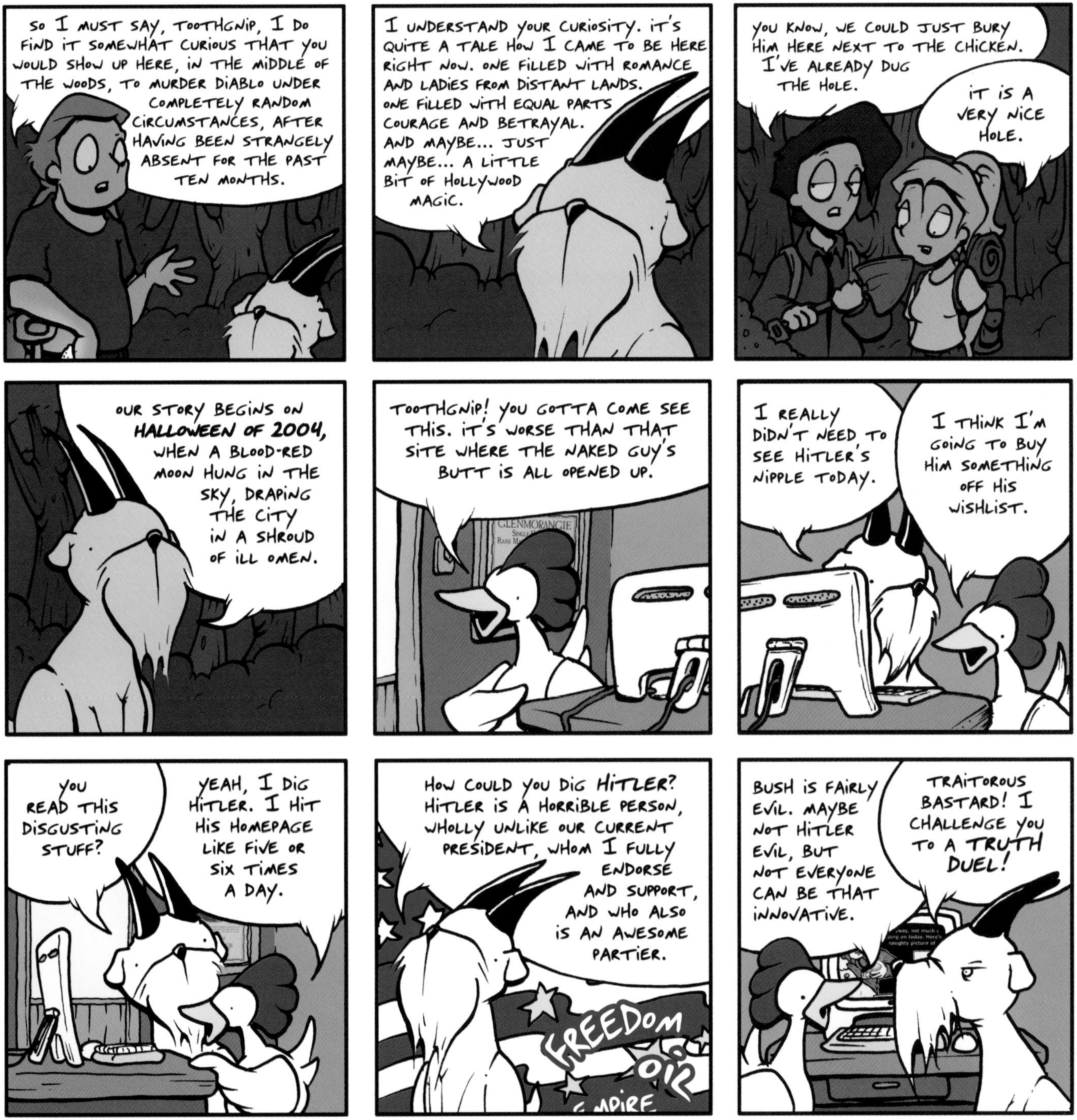
SO I MUST SAY, TOOTHGNIP, I DO FIND IT SOMEWHAT CURIOUS THAT YOU WOULD SHOW UP HERE, IN THE MIDDLE OF THE WOODS, TO MURDER DIABLO UNDER COMPLETELY RANDOM CIRCUMSTANCES, AFTER HAVING BEEN STRANGELY ABSENT FOR THE PAST TEN MONTHS.
I UNDERSTAND YOUR CURIOSITY. IT'S QUITE A TALE HOW I CAME TO BE HERE RIGHT NOW. ONE FILLED WITH ROMANCE AND LADIES FROM DISTANT LANDS. ONE FILLED WITH EQUAL PARTS COURAGE AND BETRAYAL. AND MAYBE... JUST MAYBE... A LITTLE BIT OF HOLLYWOOD MAGIC.
YOU KNOW, WE COULD JUST BURY HIM HERE NEXT TO THE CHICKEN. I'VE ALREADY DUG THE HOLE.
IT IS A VERY NICE HOLE.
OUR STORY BEGINS ON **HALLOWEEN OF 2004,** WHEN A BLOOD-RED MOON HUNG IN THE SKY, DRAPING THE CITY IN A SHROUD OF ILL OMEN.
TOOTHGNIP! YOU GOTTA COME SEE THIS. IT'S WORSE THAN THAT SITE WHERE THE NAKED GUY'S BUTT IS ALL OPENED UP.
GLENMORANGIE
I REALLY DIDN'T NEED TO SEE HITLER'S NIPPLE TODAY.
I THINK I'M GOING TO BUY HIM SOMETHING OFF HIS WISHLIST.
YOU READ THIS DISGUSTING STUFF?
YEAH, I DIG HITLER. I HIT HIS HOMEPAGE LIKE FIVE OR SIX TIMES A DAY.
HOW COULD YOU DIG **HITLER**? HITLER IS A HORRIBLE PERSON, WHOLLY UNLIKE OUR CURRENT PRESIDENT, WHOM I FULLY ENDORSE AND SUPPORT, AND WHO ALSO IS AN AWESOME PARTIER.
FREEDOM
OIL
BUSH IS FAIRLY EVIL. MAYBE NOT HITLER EVIL, BUT NOT EVERYONE CAN BE THAT INNOVATIVE.
TRAITOROUS BASTARD! I CHALLENGE YOU TO A **TRUTH DUEL!**

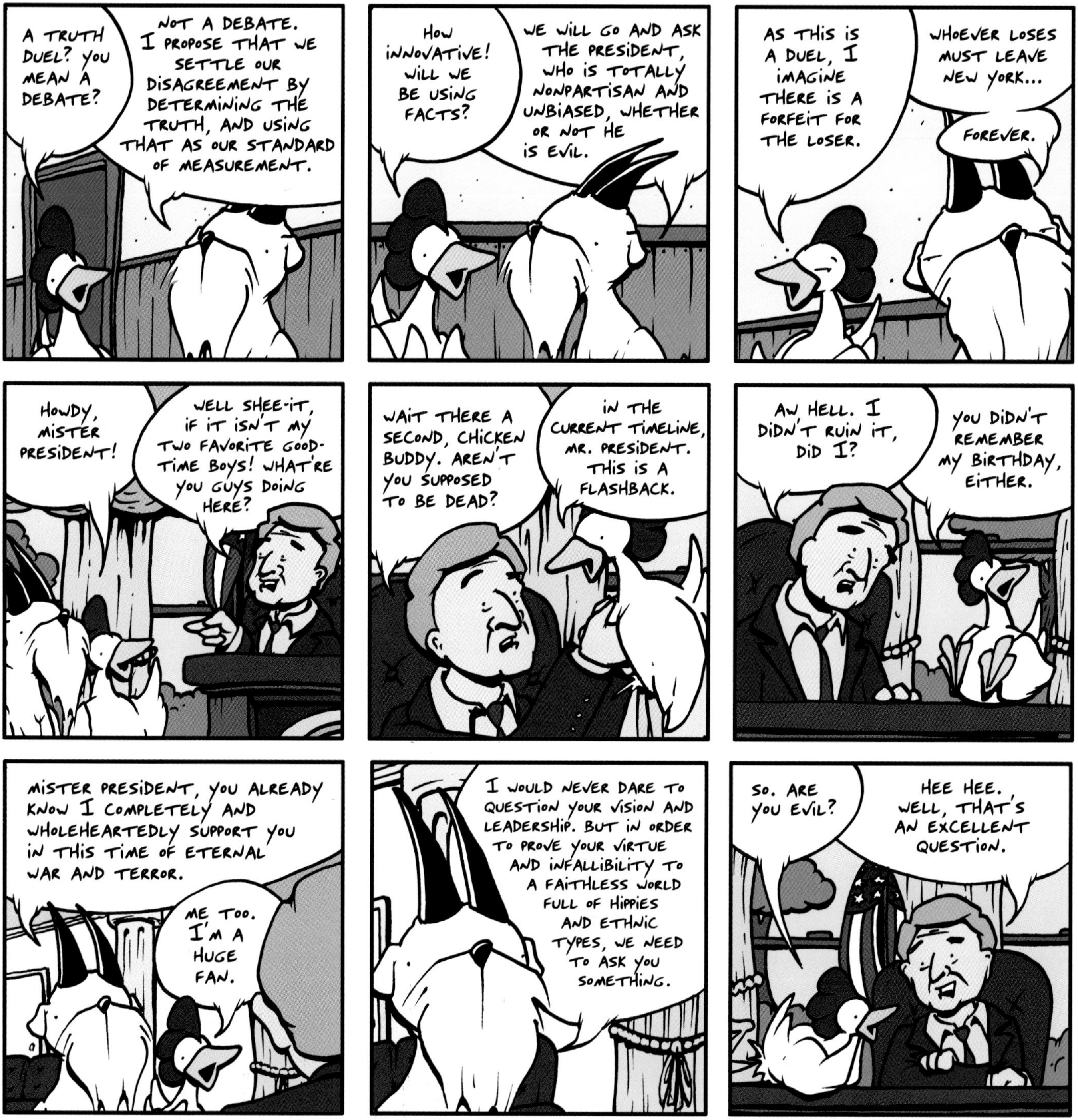
A TRUTH DUEL? YOU MEAN A DEBATE?
NOT A DEBATE. I PROPOSE THAT WE SETTLE OUR DISAGREEMENT BY DETERMINING THE TRUTH, AND USING THAT AS OUR STANDARD OF MEASUREMENT.
HOW INNOVATIVE! WILL WE BE USING FACTS?
WE WILL GO AND ASK THE PRESIDENT, WHO IS TOTALLY NONPARTISAN AND UNBIASED, WHETHER OR NOT HE IS EVIL.
AS THIS IS A DUEL, I IMAGINE THERE IS A FORFEIT FOR THE LOSER.
WHOEVER LOSES MUST LEAVE NEW YORK...
FOREVER.
HOWDY, MISTER PRESIDENT!
WELL SHEE-IT, IF IT ISN'T MY TWO FAVORITE GOOD-TIME BOYS! WHAT'RE YOU GUYS DOING HERE?
WAIT THERE A SECOND, CHICKEN BUDDY. AREN'T YOU SUPPOSED TO BE DEAD?
IN THE CURRENT TIMELINE, MR. PRESIDENT. THIS IS A FLASHBACK.
AW, HELL. I DIDN'T RUIN IT, DID I?
YOU DIDN'T REMEMBER MY BIRTHDAY, EITHER.
MISTER PRESIDENT, YOU ALREADY KNOW I COMPLETELY AND WHOLEHEARTEDLY SUPPORT YOU IN THIS TIME OF ETERNAL WAR AND TERROR.
ME TOO. I'M A HUGE FAN.
I WOULD NEVER DARE TO QUESTION YOUR VISION AND LEADERSHIP. BUT IN ORDER TO PROVE YOUR VIRTUE AND INFALLIBILITY TO A FAITHLESS WORLD FULL OF HIPPIES AND ETHNIC TYPES, WE NEED TO ASK YOU SOMETHING.
SO. ARE YOU EVIL?
HEE HEE. WELL, THAT'S AN EXCELLENT QUESTION.

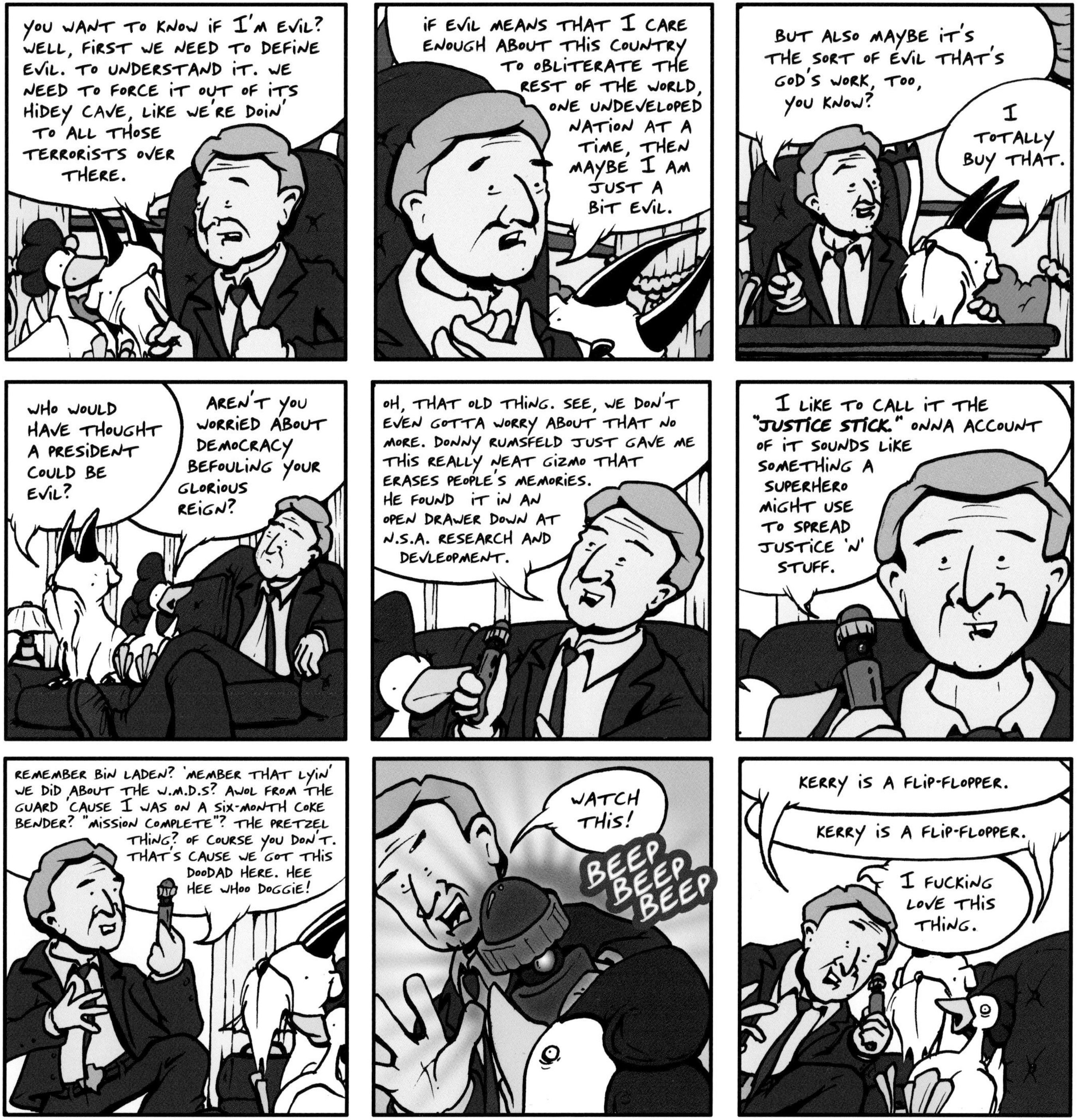
YOU WANT TO KNOW IF I'M EVIL? WELL, FIRST WE NEED TO DEFINE EVIL. TO UNDERSTAND IT. WE NEED TO FORCE IT OUT OF ITS HIDEY CAVE, LIKE WE'RE DOIN' TO ALL THOSE TERRORISTS OVER THERE.
IF EVIL MEANS THAT I CARE ENOUGH ABOUT THIS COUNTRY TO OBLITERATE THE REST OF THE WORLD, ONE UNDEVELOPED NATION AT A TIME, THEN MAYBE I AM JUST A BIT EVIL.
BUT ALSO MAYBE IT'S THE SORT OF EVIL THAT'S GOD'S WORK, TOO, YOU KNOW?
I TOTALLY BUY THAT.
WHO WOULD HAVE THOUGHT A PRESIDENT COULD BE EVIL?
AREN'T YOU WORRIED ABOUT DEMOCRACY BEFOULING YOUR GLORIOUS REIGN?
OH, THAT OLD THING. SEE, WE DON'T EVEN GOTTA WORRY ABOUT THAT NO MORE. DONNY RUMSFELD JUST GAVE ME THIS REALLY NEAT GIZMO THAT ERASES PEOPLE'S MEMORIES. HE FOUND IT IN AN OPEN DRAWER DOWN AT N.S.A. RESEARCH AND DEVLEOPMENT.
I LIKE TO CALL IT THE "JUSTICE STICK." ONNA ACCOUNT OF IT SOUNDS LIKE SOMETHING A SUPERHERO MIGHT USE TO SPREAD JUSTICE 'N' STUFF.
REMEMBER BIN LADEN? 'MEMBER THAT LYIN' WE DID ABOUT THE W.M.D.S? AWOL FROM THE GUARD 'CAUSE I WAS ON A SIX-MONTH COKE BENDER? "MISSION COMPLETE"? THE PRETZEL THING? OF COURSE YOU DON'T. THAT'S CAUSE WE GOT THIS DOODAD HERE. HEE HEE WHOO DOGGIE!
WATCH THIS!
BEEP BEEP BEEP
KERRY IS A FLIP-FLOPPER.
KERRY IS A FLIP-FLOPPER.
I FUCKING LOVE THIS THING.

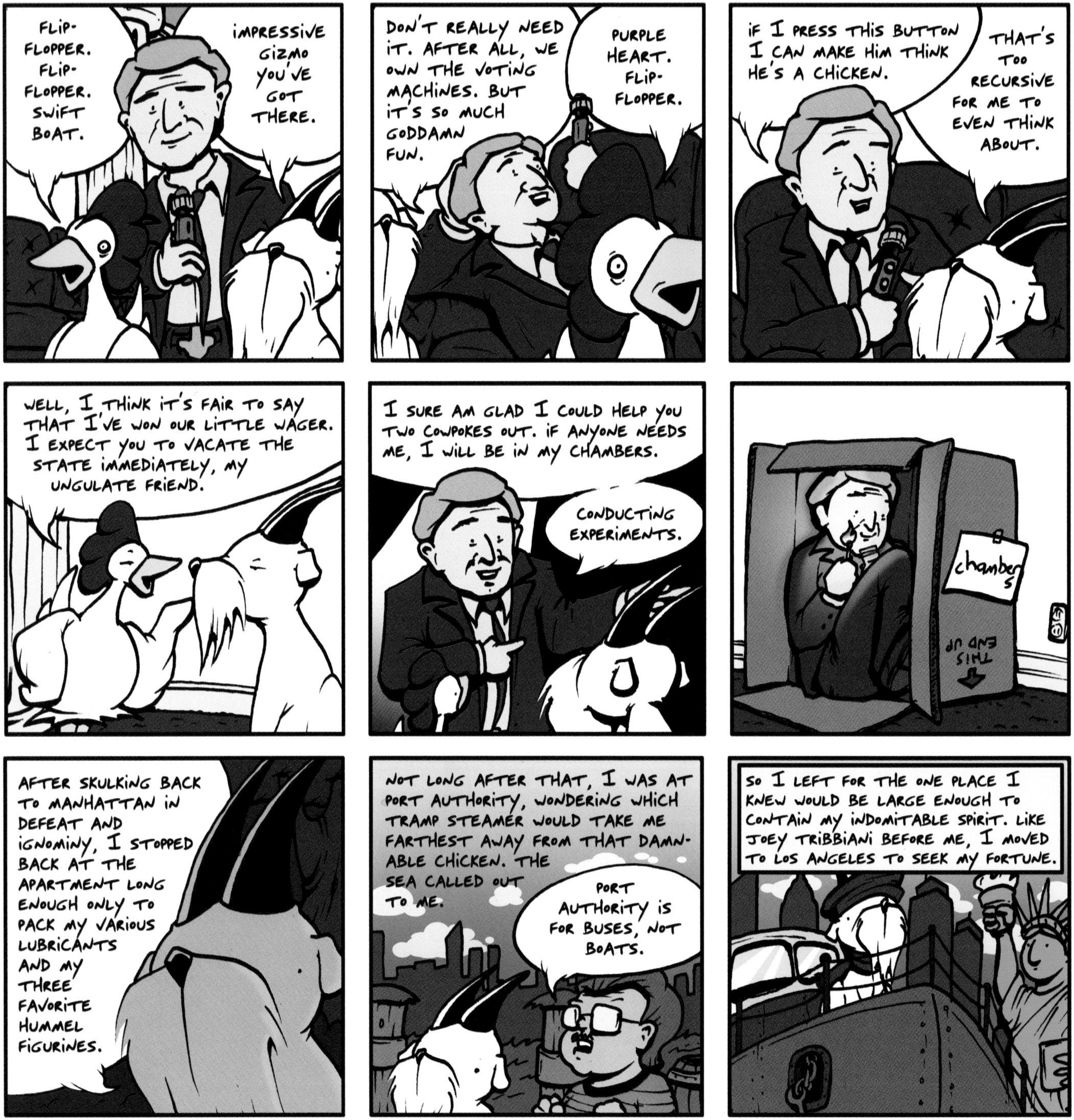

FLIP-FLOPPER. FLIP-FLOPPER. SWIFT BOAT.
IMPRESSIVE GIZMO YOU'VE GOT THERE.
DON'T REALLY NEED IT. AFTER ALL, WE OWN THE VOTING MACHINES. BUT IT'S SO MUCH GODDAMN FUN.
PURPLE HEART. FLIP-FLOPPER.
IF I PRESS THIS BUTTON I CAN MAKE HIM THINK HE'S A CHICKEN.
THAT'S TOO RECURSIVE FOR ME TO EVEN THINK ABOUT.
WELL, I THINK IT'S FAIR TO SAY THAT I'VE WON OUR LITTLE WAGER. I EXPECT YOU TO VACATE THE STATE IMMEDIATELY, MY UNGULATE FRIEND.
I SURE AM GLAD I COULD HELP YOU TWO COWPOKES OUT. IF ANYONE NEEDS ME, I WILL BE IN MY CHAMBERS.
CONDUCTING EXPERIMENTS.
chambers
THIS END UP
AFTER SKULKING BACK TO MANHATTAN IN DEFEAT AND IGNOMINY, I STOPPED BACK AT THE APARTMENT LONG ENOUGH ONLY TO PACK MY VARIOUS LUBRICANTS AND MY THREE FAVORITE HUMMEL FIGURINES.
NOT LONG AFTER THAT, I WAS AT PORT AUTHORITY, WONDERING WHICH TRAMP STEAMER WOULD TAKE ME FARTHEST AWAY FROM THAT DAMNABLE CHICKEN. THE SEA CALLED OUT TO ME.
PORT AUTHORITY IS FOR BUSES, NOT BOATS.
SO I LEFT FOR THE ONE PLACE I KNEW WOULD BE LARGE ENOUGH TO CONTAIN MY INDOMITABLE SPIRIT. LIKE JOEY TRIBBIANI BEFORE ME, I MOVED TO LOS ANGELES TO SEEK MY FORTUNE.

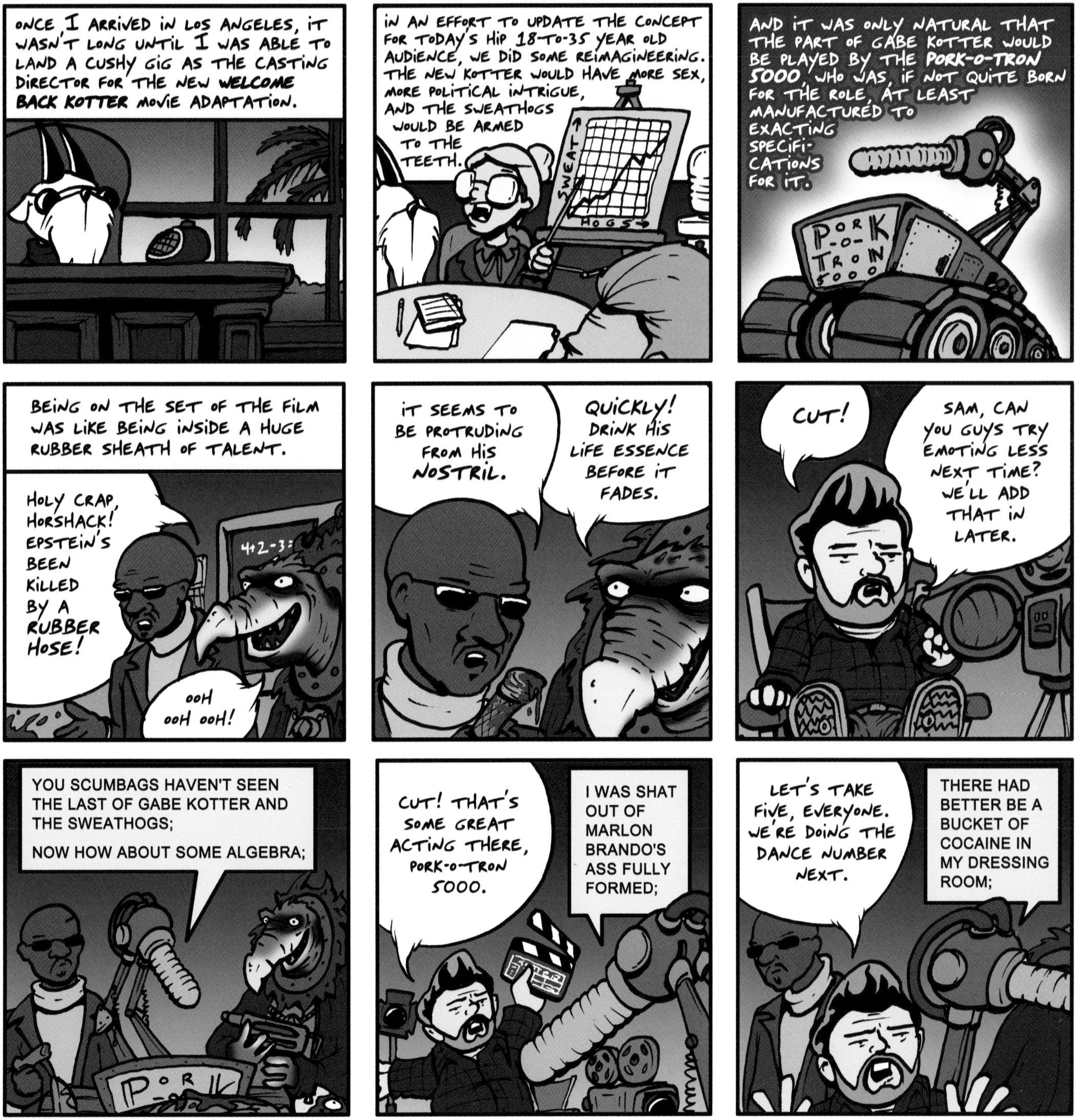
ONCE I ARRIVED IN LOS ANGELES, IT WASN'T LONG UNTIL I WAS ABLE TO LAND A CUSHY GIG AS THE CASTING DIRECTOR FOR THE NEW WELCOME BACK KOTTER MOVIE ADAPTATION.
IN AN EFFORT TO UPDATE THE CONCEPT FOR TODAY'S HIP 18-TO-35 YEAR OLD AUDIENCE, WE DID SOME REIMAGINEERING. THE NEW KOTTER WOULD HAVE MORE SEX, MORE POLITICAL INTRIGUE, AND THE SWEATHOGS WOULD BE ARMED TO THE TEETH.
SWEAT
HOGS
AND IT WAS ONLY NATURAL THAT THE PART OF GABE KOTTER WOULD BE PLAYED BY THE PORK-O-TRON 5000, WHO WAS, IF NOT QUITE BORN FOR THE ROLE, AT LEAST MANUFACTURED TO EXACTING SPECIFICATIONS FOR IT.
PORK-O-TRON 5000
BEING ON THE SET OF THE FILM WAS LIKE BEING INSIDE A HUGE RUBBER SHEATH OF TALENT.
HOLY CRAP, HORSHACK! EPSTEIN'S BEEN KILLED BY A RUBBER HOSE!
4+2-3=
OOH OOH OOH!
IT SEEMS TO BE PROTRUDING FROM HIS NOSTRIL.
QUICKLY! DRINK HIS LIFE ESSENCE BEFORE IT FADES.
CUT!
SAM, CAN YOU GUYS TRY EMOTING LESS NEXT TIME? WE'LL ADD THAT IN LATER.
YOU SCUMBAGS HAVEN'T SEEN THE LAST OF GABE KOTTER AND THE SWEATHOGS;
NOW HOW ABOUT SOME ALGEBRA;
CUT! THAT'S SOME GREAT ACTING THERE, PORK-O-TRON 5000.
I WAS SHAT OUT OF MARLON BRANDO'S ASS FULLY FORMED;
LET'S TAKE FIVE, EVERYONE. WE'RE DOING THE DANCE NUMBER NEXT.
THERE HAD BETTER BE A BUCKET OF COCAINE IN MY DRESSING ROOM;

DID THE PORK-O-TRON HAVE A LASER?

NO HE DID NOT HAVE A LASER.

WELL WHY THE HELL NOT?

YOU CAN'T USE A LASER FOR PORKING. NOW SHUT UP.

I GREATLY ADMIRED PORK-O-TRON 5000 FOR BOTH HIS PORKING AND ACTING ABILITIES. WHICH MADE IT SUPER-PAINFUL AND SLIGHTLY IRONIC WHEN I LATER CAUSED HIS DEATH.

WE WERE OUT IN WIL WHEATON'S VOLKSWAGEN BUS ONE NIGHT AFTER THE SHOOT RAN LATE. ONE OF HIS HEROIN MULES HAD JUST TAKEN A FIVE-THOUSAND-DOLLAR DUMP AND WE WERE IN RARE FORM.

NOW REMEMBER, WHEATON'S A METHOD ACTOR. I HAD CAST HIM AS GUMMY, THE DISAFFECTED SKATE-BOARDER WHO HAS TO DECIDE BETWEEN HIS HEART AND HIS HOMELAND WHEN HE FALLS IN LOVE WITH A FEMALE TERRORIST.

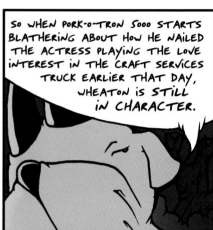

SO WHEN PORK-O-TRON 5000 STARTS BLATHERING ABOUT HOW HE NAILED THE ACTRESS PLAYING THE LOVE INTEREST IN THE CRAFT SERVICES TRUCK EARLIER THAT DAY, WHEATON IS STILL IN CHARACTER.

THEN I SWITCHED TO ACCESSORY TWELVE;

ONLY A PROFESSIONAL ACTRESS CAN ACCOMMODATE THAT ACCESSORY LOL;

SHUT UP, MAN. THAT'S ENOUGH.

IT SOUNDS LIKE THERE WAS A GREAT CONJUNCTION, YES.

TO THIS DAY I STILL DON'T KNOW WHERE THAT GUN CAME FROM.

MAYBE SEARS.

THAT'S IT. NO ONE IS LEAVING THIS MICROBUS ALIVE.

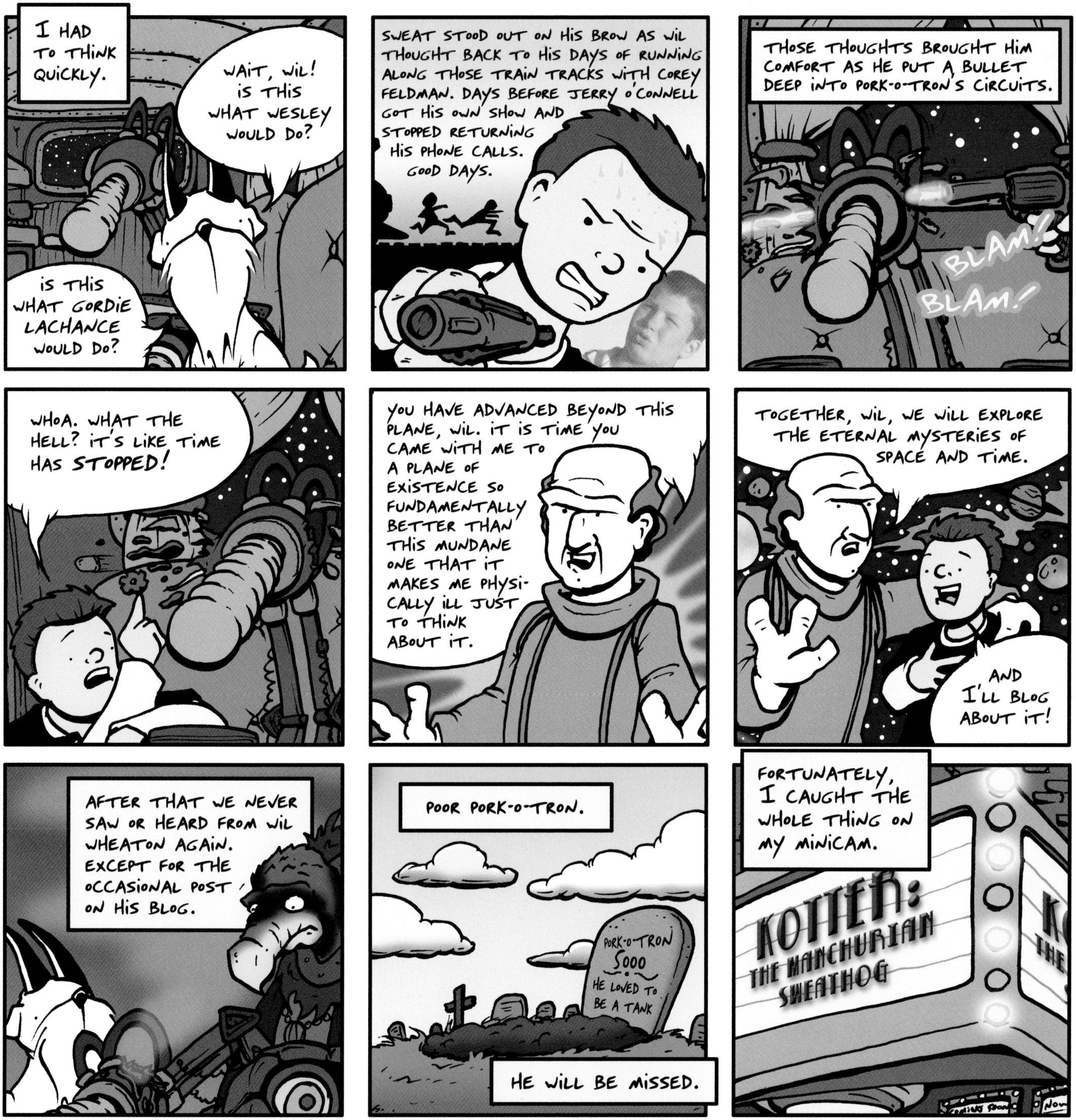

I HAD TO THINK QUICKLY.
WAIT, WIL! IS THIS WHAT WESLEY WOULD DO?
IS THIS WHAT GORDIE LACHANCE WOULD DO?
SWEAT STOOD OUT ON HIS BROW AS WIL THOUGHT BACK TO HIS DAYS OF RUNNING ALONG THOSE TRAIN TRACKS WITH COREY FELDMAN. DAYS BEFORE JERRY O'CONNELL GOT HIS OWN SHOW AND STOPPED RETURNING HIS PHONE CALLS. GOOD DAYS.
THOSE THOUGHTS BROUGHT HIM COMFORT AS HE PUT A BULLET DEEP INTO PORK-O-TRON'S CIRCUITS.
BLAM!
BLAM!
WHOA. WHAT THE HELL? IT'S LIKE TIME HAS STOPPED!
YOU HAVE ADVANCED BEYOND THIS PLANE, WIL. IT IS TIME YOU CAME WITH ME TO A PLANE OF EXISTENCE SO FUNDAMENTALLY BETTER THAN THIS MUNDANE ONE THAT IT MAKES ME PHYSICALLY ILL JUST TO THINK ABOUT IT.
TOGETHER, WIL, WE WILL EXPLORE THE ETERNAL MYSTERIES OF SPACE AND TIME.
AND I'LL BLOG ABOUT IT!
AFTER THAT WE NEVER SAW OR HEARD FROM WIL WHEATON AGAIN. EXCEPT FOR THE OCCASIONAL POST ON HIS BLOG.
POOR PORK-O-TRON.
PORK-O-TRON 5000
HE LOVED TO BE A TANK
HE WILL BE MISSED.
FORTUNATELY, I CAUGHT THE WHOLE THING ON MY MINICAM.
KOTTER: THE MANCHURIAN SWEATHOG

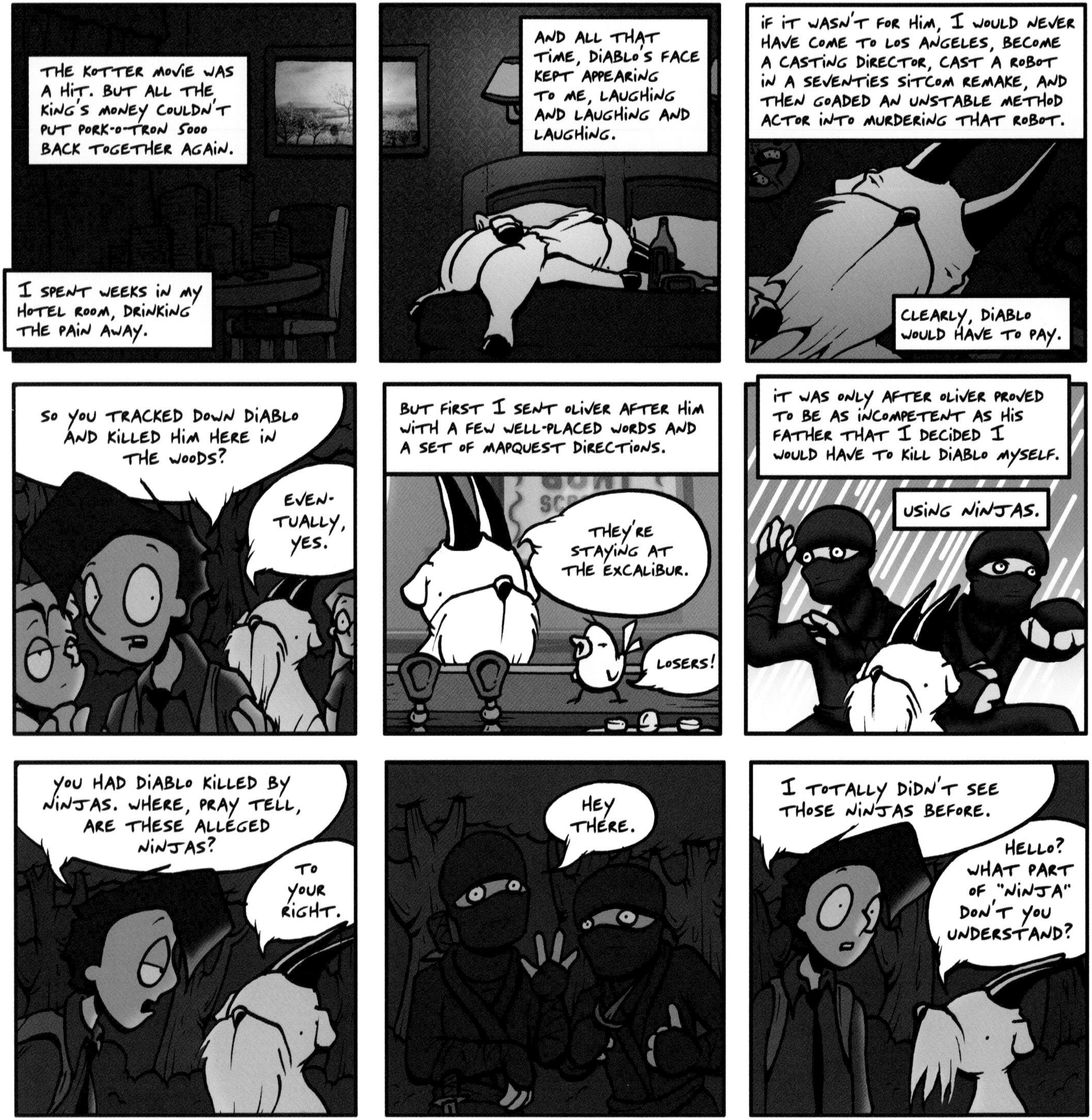
THE KOTTER MOVIE WAS A HIT. BUT ALL THE KING'S MONEY COULDN'T PUT PORK-O-TRON 5000 BACK TOGETHER AGAIN.
I SPENT WEEKS IN MY HOTEL ROOM, DRINKING THE PAIN AWAY.
AND ALL THAT TIME, DIABLO'S FACE KEPT APPEARING TO ME, LAUGHING AND LAUGHING AND LAUGHING.
IF IT WASN'T FOR HIM, I WOULD NEVER HAVE COME TO LOS ANGELES, BECOME A CASTING DIRECTOR, CAST A ROBOT IN A SEVENTIES SITCOM REMAKE, AND THEN GOADED AN UNSTABLE METHOD ACTOR INTO MURDERING THAT ROBOT.
CLEARLY, DIABLO WOULD HAVE TO PAY.
SO YOU TRACKED DOWN DIABLO AND KILLED HIM HERE IN THE WOODS?
EVEN-TUALLY, YES.
BUT FIRST I SENT OLIVER AFTER HIM WITH A FEW WELL-PLACED WORDS AND A SET OF MAPQUEST DIRECTIONS.
THEY'RE STAYING AT THE EXCALIBUR.
LOSERS!
IT WAS ONLY AFTER OLIVER PROVED TO BE AS INCOMPETENT AS HIS FATHER THAT I DECIDED I WOULD HAVE TO KILL DIABLO MYSELF.
USING NINJAS.
YOU HAD DIABLO KILLED BY NINJAS. WHERE, PRAY TELL, ARE THESE ALLEGED NINJAS?
TO YOUR RIGHT.
HEY THERE.
I TOTALLY DIDN'T SEE THOSE NINJAS BEFORE.
HELLO? WHAT PART OF "NINJA" DON'T YOU UNDERSTAND?

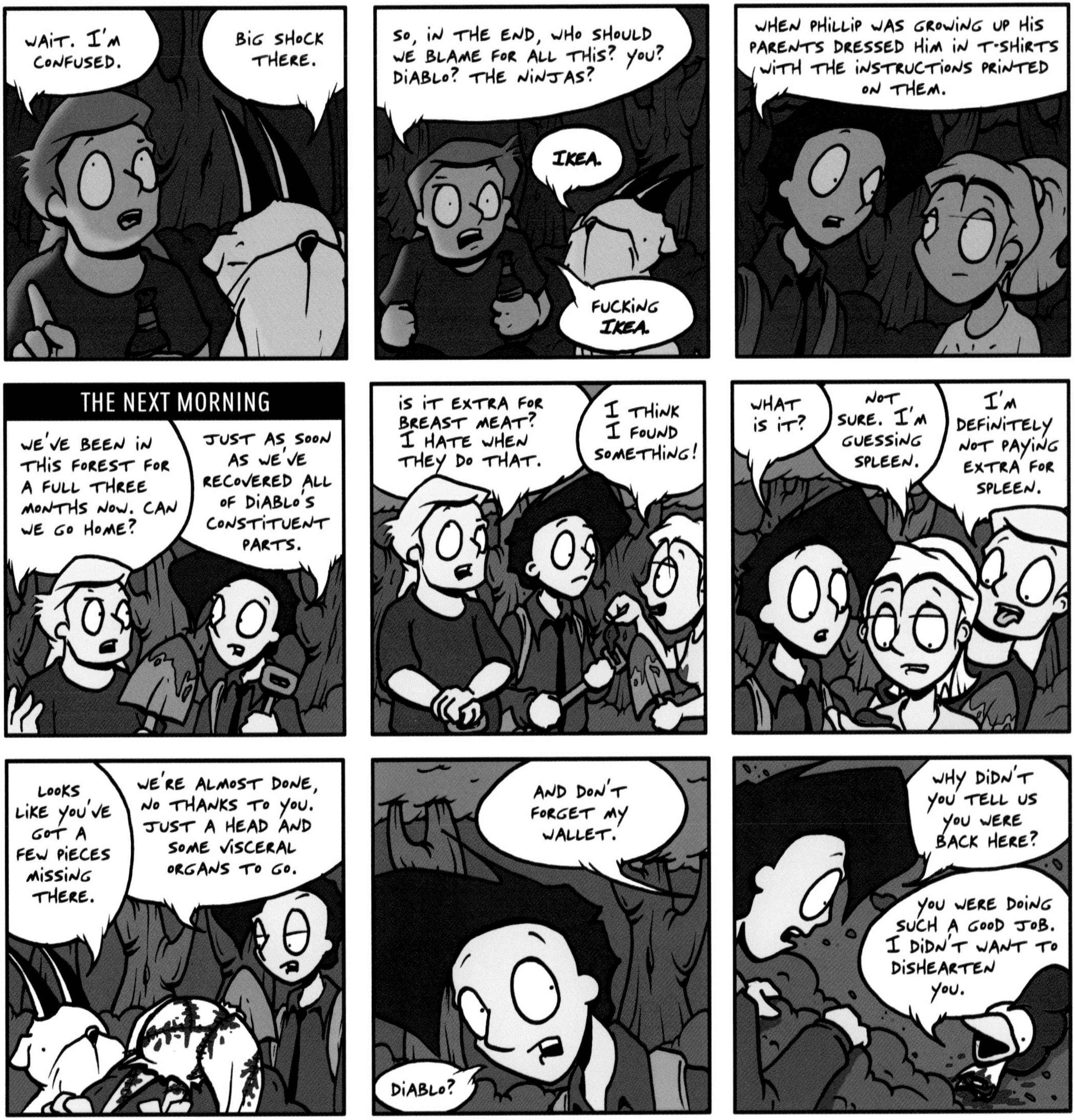
WAIT. I'M CONFUSED.
BIG SHOCK THERE.
SO, IN THE END, WHO SHOULD WE BLAME FOR ALL THIS? YOU? DIABLO? THE NINJAS?
IKEA.
FUCKING IKEA.
WHEN PHILLIP WAS GROWING UP HIS PARENTS DRESSED HIM IN T-SHIRTS WITH THE INSTRUCTIONS PRINTED ON THEM.
THE NEXT MORNING
WE'VE BEEN IN THIS FOREST FOR A FULL THREE MONTHS NOW. CAN WE GO HOME?
JUST AS SOON AS WE'VE RECOVERED ALL OF DIABLO'S CONSTITUENT PARTS.
IS IT EXTRA FOR BREAST MEAT? I HATE WHEN THEY DO THAT.
I THINK I FOUND SOMETHING!
WHAT IS IT?
NOT SURE. I'M GUESSING SPLEEN.
I'M DEFINITELY NOT PAYING EXTRA FOR SPLEEN.
LOOKS LIKE YOU'VE GOT A FEW PIECES MISSING THERE.
WE'RE ALMOST DONE, NO THANKS TO YOU. JUST A HEAD AND SOME VISCERAL ORGANS TO GO.
AND DON'T FORGET MY WALLET.
DIABLO?
WHY DIDN'T YOU TELL US YOU WERE BACK HERE?
YOU WERE DOING SUCH A GOOD JOB. I DIDN'T WANT TO DISHEARTEN YOU.

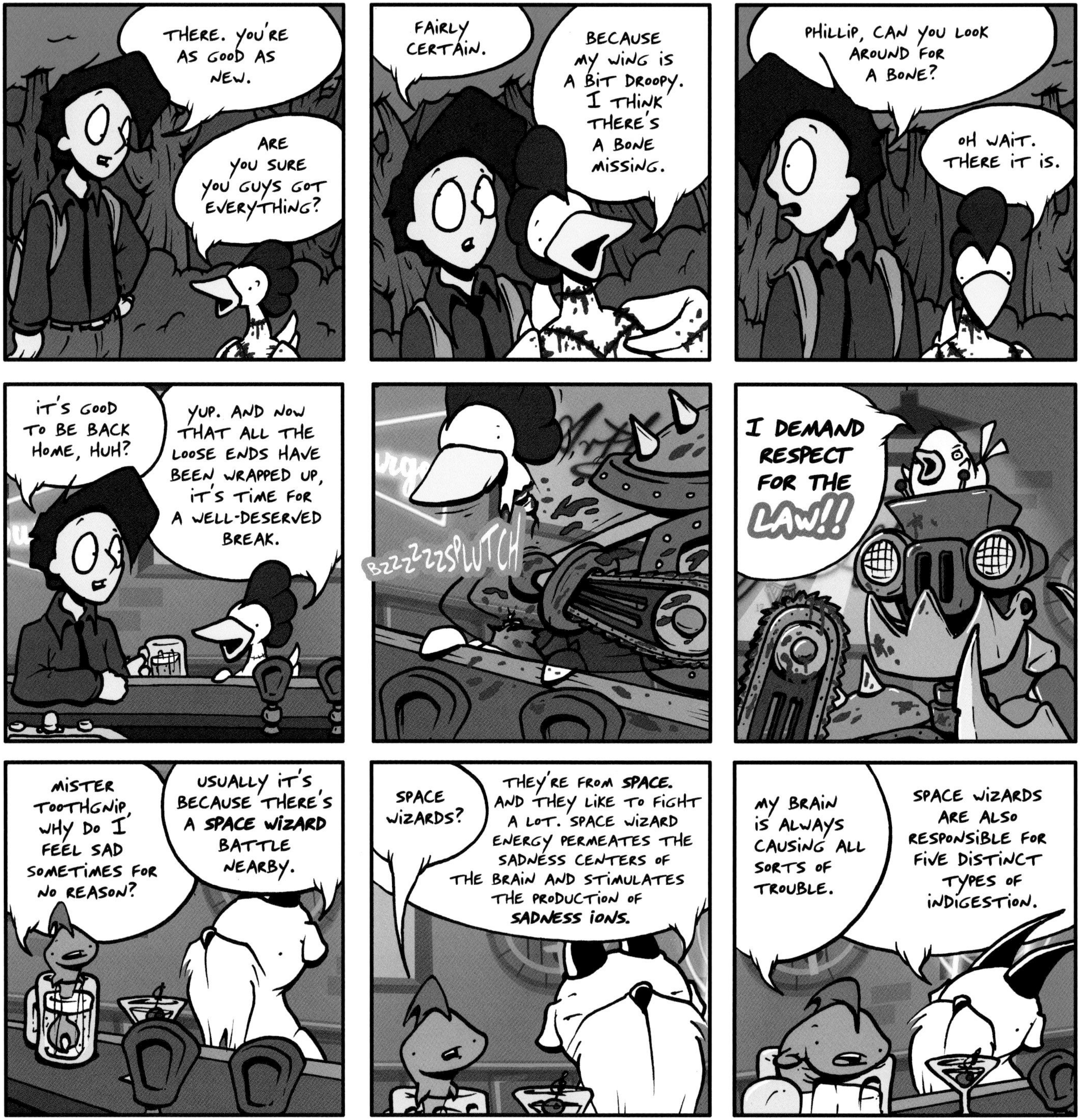
THERE. YOU'RE AS GOOD AS NEW.
ARE YOU SURE YOU GUYS GOT EVERYTHING?
FAIRLY CERTAIN.
BECAUSE MY WING IS A BIT DROOPY. I THINK THERE'S A BONE MISSING.
PHILLIP, CAN YOU LOOK AROUND FOR A BONE?
OH WAIT. THERE IT IS.
IT'S GOOD TO BE BACK HOME, HUH?
YUP. AND NOW THAT ALL THE LOOSE ENDS HAVE BEEN WRAPPED UP, IT'S TIME FOR A WELL-DESERVED BREAK.
BZZZZZZSPLUTCH
I DEMAND RESPECT FOR THE LAW!!
MISTER TOOTHGNIP, WHY DO I FEEL SAD SOMETIMES FOR NO REASON?
USUALLY IT'S BECAUSE THERE'S A SPACE WIZARD BATTLE NEARBY.
SPACE WIZARDS?
THEY'RE FROM SPACE. AND THEY LIKE TO FIGHT A LOT. SPACE WIZARD ENERGY PERMEATES THE SADNESS CENTERS OF THE BRAIN AND STIMULATES THE PRODUCTION OF SADNESS IONS.
MY BRAIN IS ALWAYS CAUSING ALL SORTS OF TROUBLE.
SPACE WIZARDS ARE ALSO RESPONSIBLE FOR FIVE DISTINCT TYPES OF INDIGESTION.

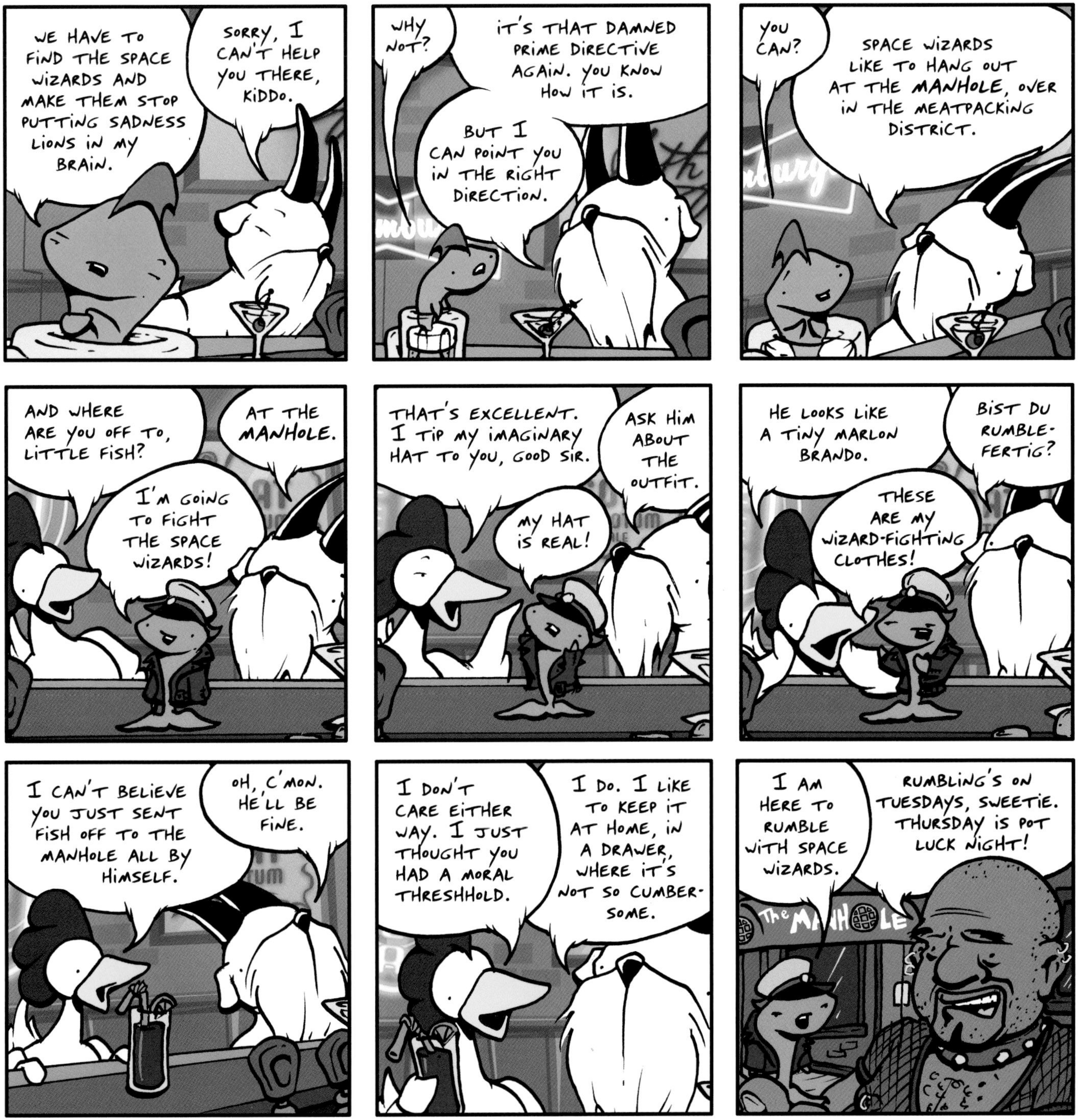
WE HAVE TO FIND THE SPACE WIZARDS AND MAKE THEM STOP PUTTING SADNESS LIONS IN MY BRAIN.
SORRY, I CAN'T HELP YOU THERE, KIDDO.
WHY NOT?
IT'S THAT DAMNED PRIME DIRECTIVE AGAIN. YOU KNOW HOW IT IS.
BUT I CAN POINT YOU IN THE RIGHT DIRECTION.
YOU CAN?
SPACE WIZARDS LIKE TO HANG OUT AT THE MANHOLE, OVER IN THE MEATPACKING DISTRICT.
AND WHERE ARE YOU OFF TO, LITTLE FISH?
AT THE MANHOLE.
I'M GOING TO FIGHT THE SPACE WIZARDS!
THAT'S EXCELLENT. I TIP MY IMAGINARY HAT TO YOU, GOOD SIR.
ASK HIM ABOUT THE OUTFIT.
MY HAT IS REAL!
HE LOOKS LIKE A TINY MARLON BRANDO.
BIST DU RUMBLE-FERTIG?
THESE ARE MY WIZARD-FIGHTING CLOTHES!
I CAN'T BELIEVE YOU JUST SENT FISH OFF TO THE MANHOLE ALL BY HIMSELF.
OH, C'MON. HE'LL BE FINE.
I DON'T CARE EITHER WAY. I JUST THOUGHT YOU HAD A MORAL THRESHHOLD.
I DO. I LIKE TO KEEP IT AT HOME, IN A DRAWER, WHERE IT'S NOT SO CUMBER-SOME.
I AM HERE TO RUMBLE WITH SPACE WIZARDS.
RUMBLING'S ON TUESDAYS, SWEETIE. THURSDAY IS POT LUCK NIGHT!
The MANHOLE

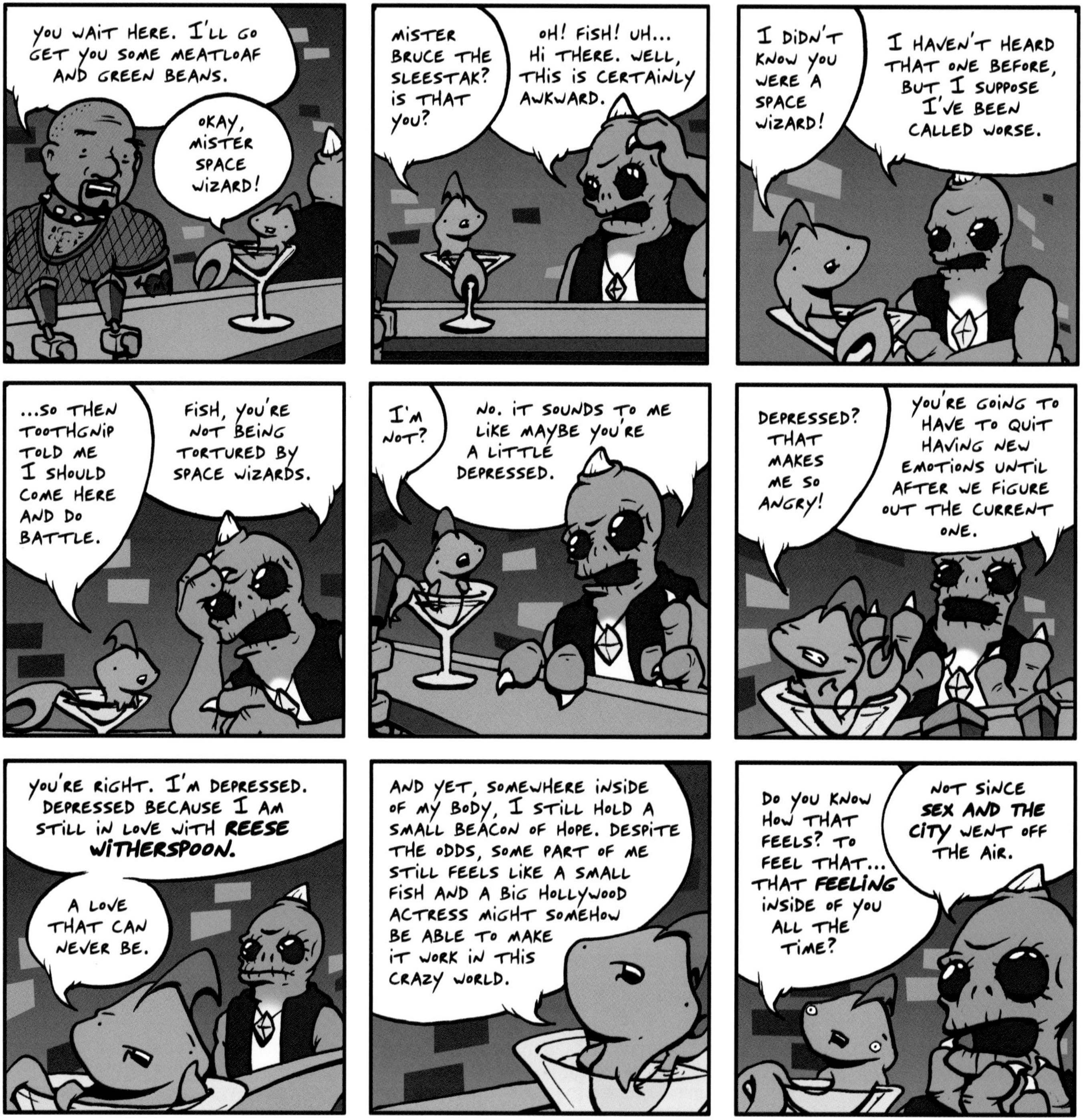
YOU WAIT HERE. I'LL GO GET YOU SOME MEATLOAF AND GREEN BEANS.
OKAY, MISTER SPACE WIZARD!
MISTER BRUCE THE SLEESTAK? IS THAT YOU?
OH! FISH! UH... HI THERE. WELL, THIS IS CERTAINLY AWKWARD.
I DIDN'T KNOW YOU WERE A SPACE WIZARD!
I HAVEN'T HEARD THAT ONE BEFORE, BUT I SUPPOSE I'VE BEEN CALLED WORSE.
...SO THEN TOOTHGNIP TOLD ME I SHOULD COME HERE AND DO BATTLE.
FISH, YOU'RE NOT BEING TORTURED BY SPACE WIZARDS.
I'M NOT?
NO. IT SOUNDS TO ME LIKE MAYBE YOU'RE A LITTLE DEPRESSED.
DEPRESSED? THAT MAKES ME SO ANGRY!
YOU'RE GOING TO HAVE TO QUIT HAVING NEW EMOTIONS UNTIL AFTER WE FIGURE OUT THE CURRENT ONE.
YOU'RE RIGHT. I'M DEPRESSED. DEPRESSED BECAUSE I AM STILL IN LOVE WITH **REESE WITHERSPOON.**
A LOVE THAT CAN NEVER BE.
AND YET, SOMEWHERE INSIDE OF MY BODY, I STILL HOLD A SMALL BEACON OF HOPE. DESPITE THE ODDS, SOME PART OF ME STILL FEELS LIKE A SMALL FISH AND A BIG HOLLYWOOD ACTRESS MIGHT SOMEHOW BE ABLE TO MAKE IT WORK IN THIS CRAZY WORLD.
DO YOU KNOW HOW THAT FEELS? TO FEEL THAT... THAT **FEELING** INSIDE OF YOU ALL THE TIME?
NOT SINCE ***SEX AND THE CITY*** WENT OFF THE AIR.

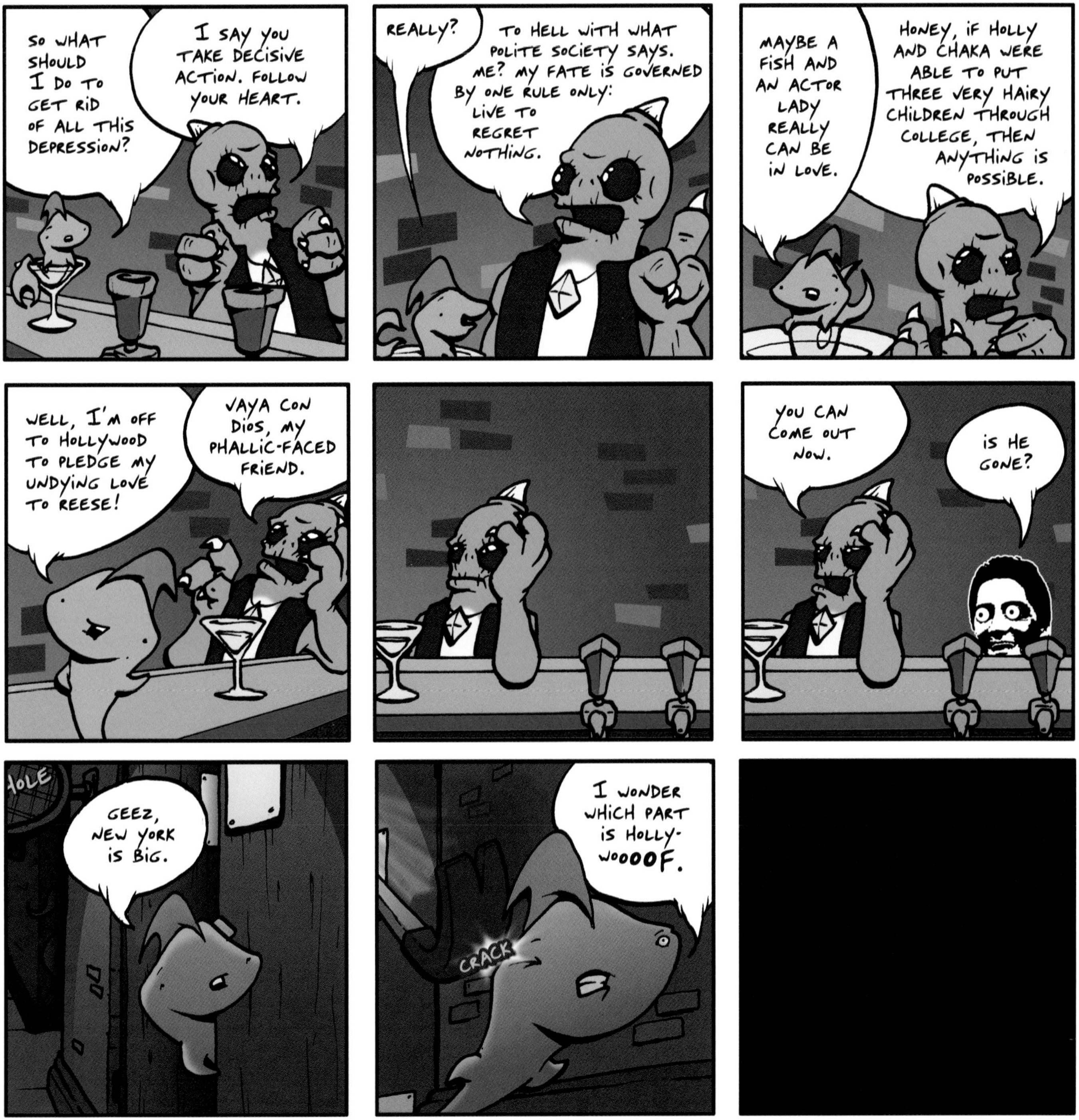
SO WHAT SHOULD I DO TO GET RID OF ALL THIS DEPRESSION?
I SAY YOU TAKE DECISIVE ACTION. FOLLOW YOUR HEART.
REALLY?
TO HELL WITH WHAT POLITE SOCIETY SAYS. ME? MY FATE IS GOVERNED BY ONE RULE ONLY: LIVE TO REGRET NOTHING.
MAYBE A FISH AND AN ACTOR LADY REALLY CAN BE IN LOVE.
HONEY, IF HOLLY AND CHAKA WERE ABLE TO PUT THREE VERY HAIRY CHILDREN THROUGH COLLEGE, THEN ANYTHING IS POSSIBLE.
WELL, I'M OFF TO HOLLYWOOD TO PLEDGE MY UNDYING LOVE TO REESE!
VAYA CON DIOS, MY PHALLIC-FACED FRIEND.
YOU CAN COME OUT NOW.
IS HE GONE?
HOLE
GEEZ, NEW YORK IS BIG.
I WONDER WHICH PART IS HOLLY-WOOOOF.
CRACK

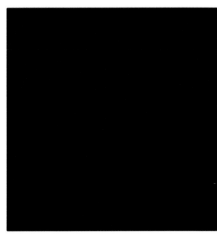

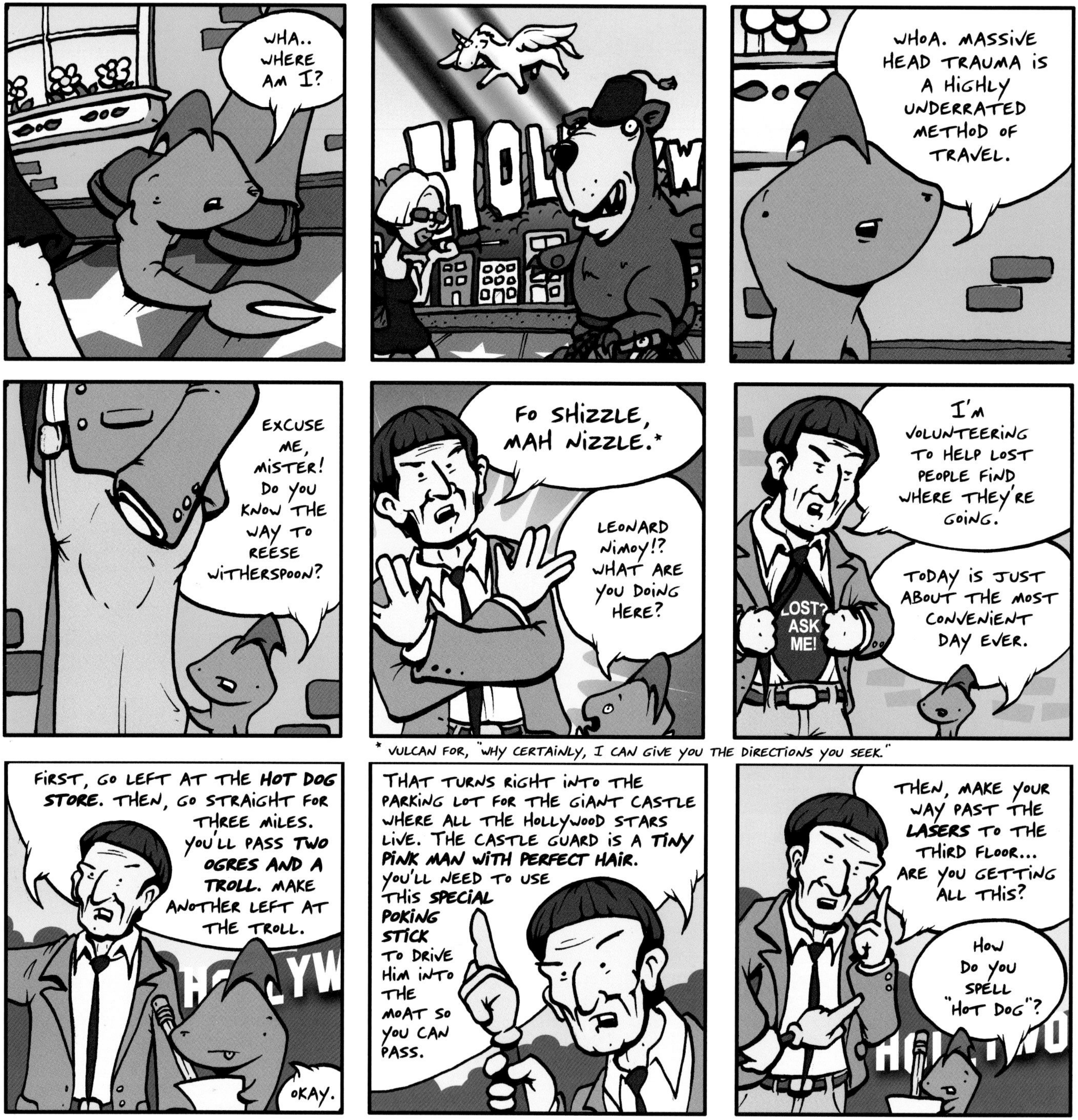
WHA.. WHERE AM I?
WHOA. MASSIVE HEAD TRAUMA IS A HIGHLY UNDERRATED METHOD OF TRAVEL.
EXCUSE ME, MISTER! DO YOU KNOW THE WAY TO REESE WITHERSPOON?
FO SHIZZLE, MAH NIZZLE.*
LEONARD NIMOY!? WHAT ARE YOU DOING HERE?
I'M VOLUNTEERING TO HELP LOST PEOPLE FIND WHERE THEY'RE GOING.
LOST? ASK ME!
TODAY IS JUST ABOUT THE MOST CONVENIENT DAY EVER.
* VULCAN FOR, "WHY CERTAINLY, I CAN GIVE YOU THE DIRECTIONS YOU SEEK."
FIRST, GO LEFT AT THE **HOT DOG STORE**. THEN, GO STRAIGHT FOR THREE MILES. YOU'LL PASS **TWO OGRES AND A TROLL**. MAKE ANOTHER LEFT AT THE TROLL.
OKAY.
THAT TURNS RIGHT INTO THE PARKING LOT FOR THE GIANT CASTLE WHERE ALL THE HOLLYWOOD STARS LIVE. THE CASTLE GUARD IS A **TINY PINK MAN WITH PERFECT HAIR**. YOU'LL NEED TO USE THIS **SPECIAL POKING STICK** TO DRIVE HIM INTO THE MOAT SO YOU CAN PASS.
THEN, MAKE YOUR WAY PAST THE **LASERS** TO THE THIRD FLOOR... ARE YOU GETTING ALL THIS?
HOW DO YOU SPELL "HOT DOG"?

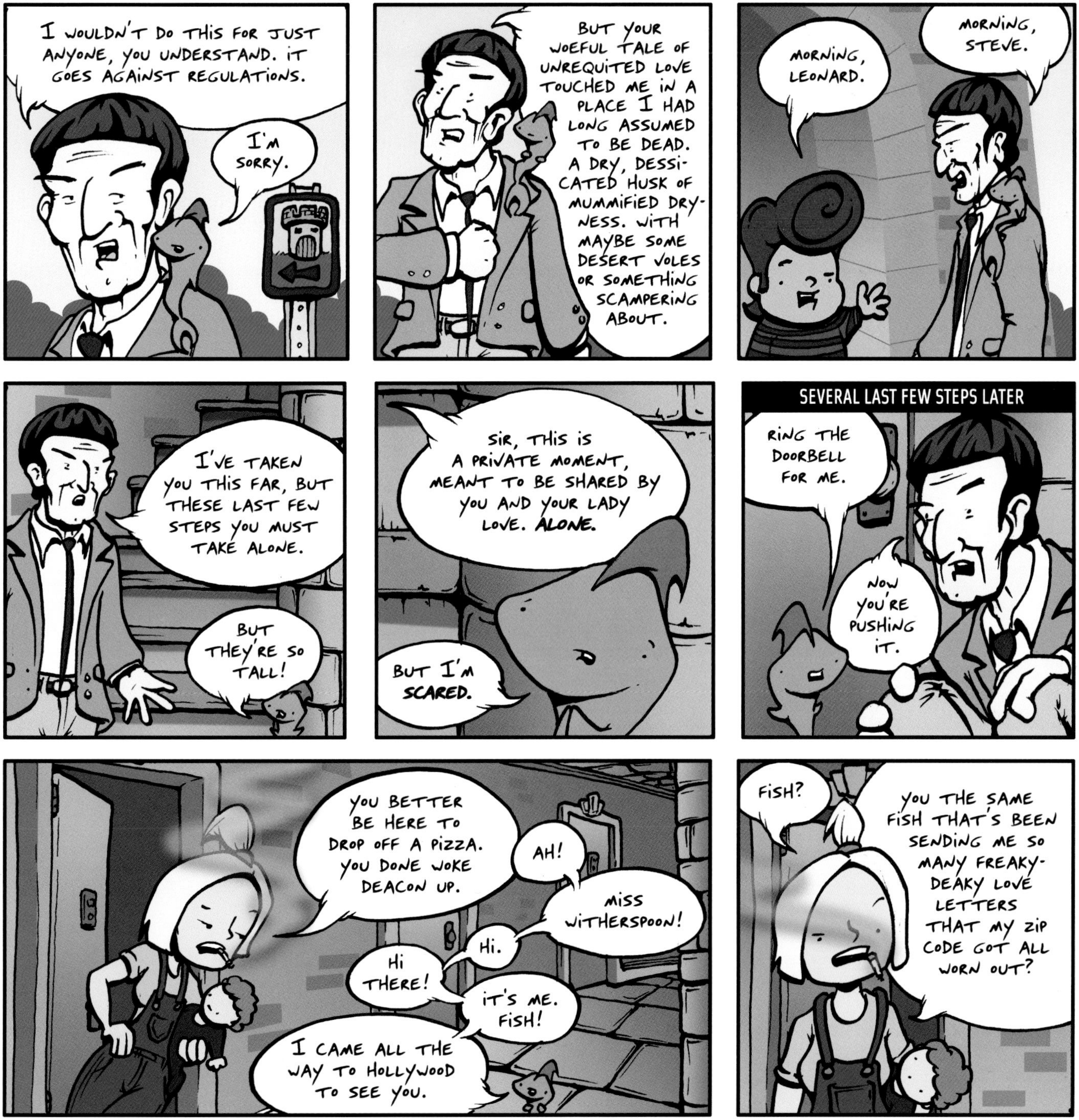
I WOULDN'T DO THIS FOR JUST ANYONE, YOU UNDERSTAND. IT GOES AGAINST REGULATIONS.
I'M SORRY.
BUT YOUR WOEFUL TALE OF UNREQUITED LOVE TOUCHED ME IN A PLACE I HAD LONG ASSUMED TO BE DEAD. A DRY, DESSI-CATED HUSK OF MUMMIFIED DRY-NESS. WITH MAYBE SOME DESERT VOLES OR SOMETHING SCAMPERING ABOUT.
MORNING, LEONARD.
MORNING, STEVE.
I'VE TAKEN YOU THIS FAR, BUT THESE LAST FEW STEPS YOU MUST TAKE ALONE.
BUT THEY'RE SO TALL!
SIR, THIS IS A PRIVATE MOMENT, MEANT TO BE SHARED BY YOU AND YOUR LADY LOVE. **ALONE.**
BUT I'M **SCARED.**
SEVERAL LAST FEW STEPS LATER
RING THE DOORBELL FOR ME.
NOW YOU'RE PUSHING IT.
YOU BETTER BE HERE TO DROP OFF A PIZZA. YOU DONE WOKE DEACON UP.
AH!
MISS WITHERSPOON!
HI.
HI THERE!
IT'S ME. FISH!
I CAME ALL THE WAY TO HOLLYWOOD TO SEE YOU.
FISH?
YOU THE SAME FISH THAT'S BEEN SENDING ME SO MANY FREAKY-DEAKY LOVE LETTERS THAT MY ZIP CODE GOT ALL WORN OUT?

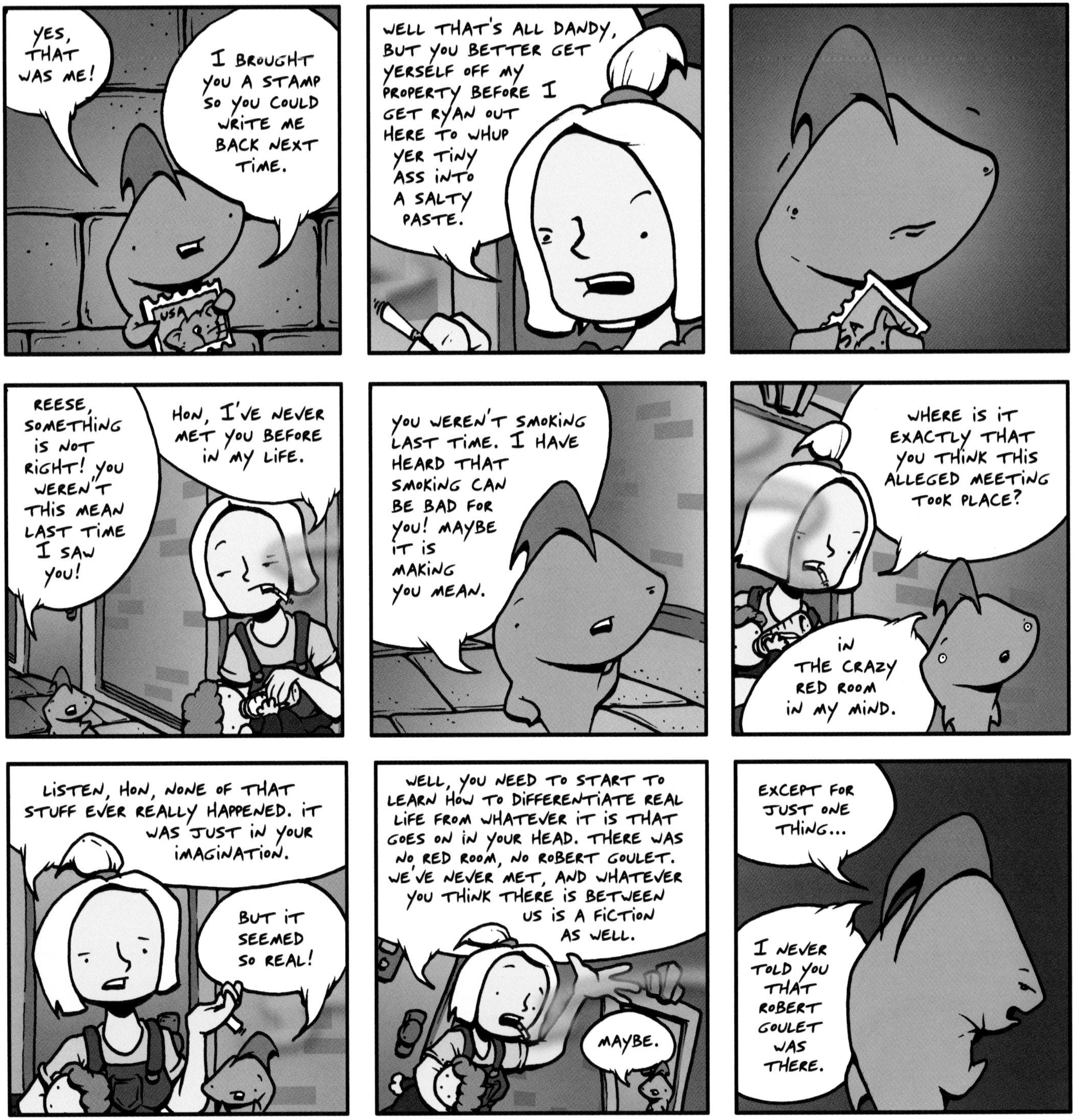
YES, THAT WAS ME!
I BROUGHT YOU A STAMP SO YOU COULD WRITE ME BACK NEXT TIME.
USA
WELL THAT'S ALL DANDY, BUT YOU BETTER GET YERSELF OFF MY PROPERTY BEFORE I GET RYAN OUT HERE TO WHUP YER TINY ASS INTO A SALTY PASTE.
REESE, SOMETHING IS NOT RIGHT! YOU WEREN'T THIS MEAN LAST TIME I SAW YOU!
HON, I'VE NEVER MET YOU BEFORE IN MY LIFE.
YOU WEREN'T SMOKING LAST TIME. I HAVE HEARD THAT SMOKING CAN BE BAD FOR YOU! MAYBE IT IS MAKING YOU MEAN.
WHERE IS IT EXACTLY THAT YOU THINK THIS ALLEGED MEETING TOOK PLACE?
IN THE CRAZY RED ROOM IN MY MIND.
LISTEN, HON, NONE OF THAT STUFF EVER REALLY HAPPENED. IT WAS JUST IN YOUR IMAGINATION.
BUT IT SEEMED SO REAL!
WELL, YOU NEED TO START TO LEARN HOW TO DIFFERENTIATE REAL LIFE FROM WHATEVER IT IS THAT GOES ON IN YOUR HEAD. THERE WAS NO RED ROOM, NO ROBERT GOULET. WE'VE NEVER MET, AND WHATEVER YOU THINK THERE IS BETWEEN US IS A FICTION AS WELL.
MAYBE.
EXCEPT FOR JUST ONE THING...
I NEVER TOLD YOU THAT ROBERT GOULET WAS THERE.

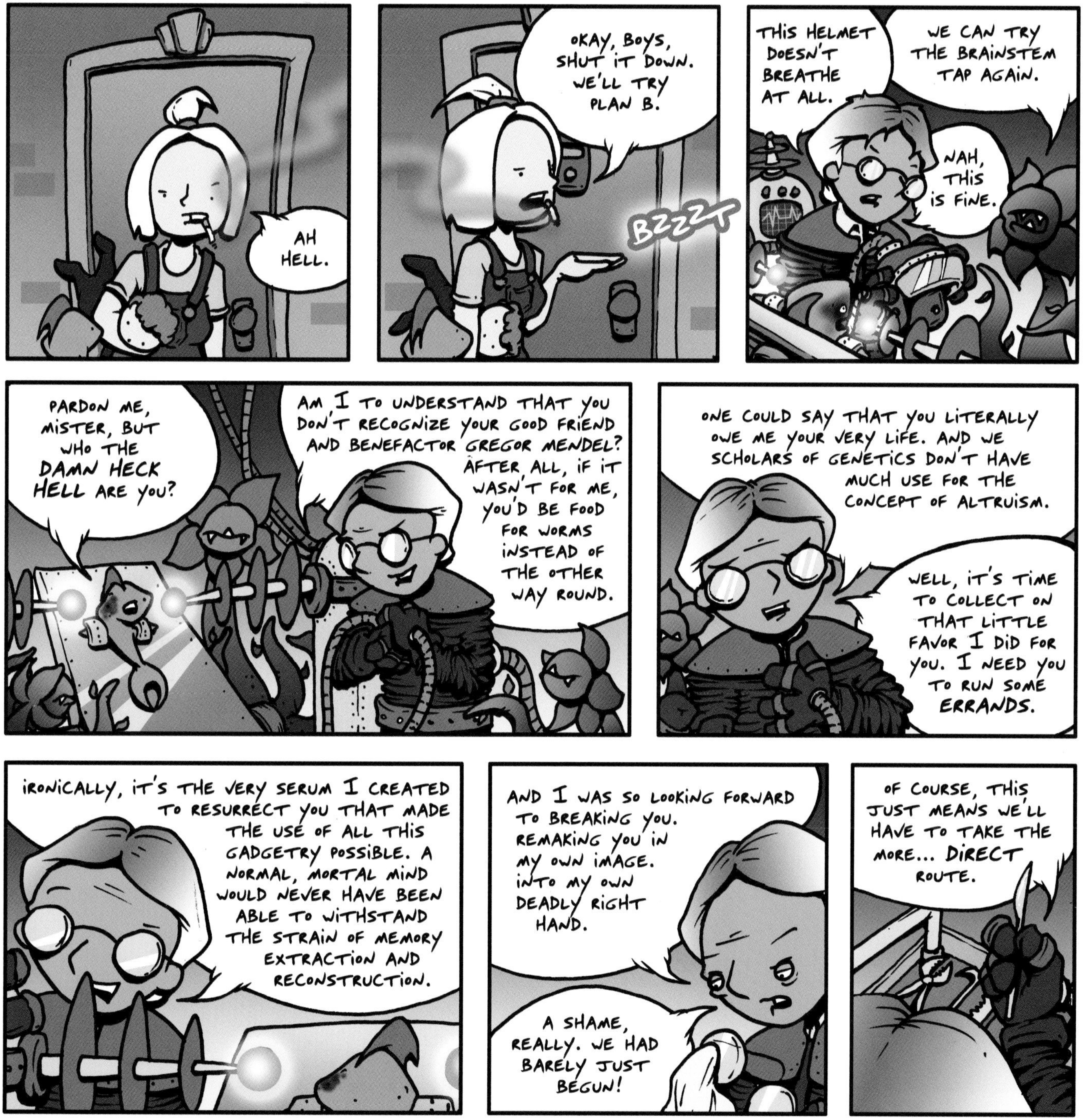

AH HELL.
OKAY, BOYS, SHUT IT DOWN. WE'LL TRY PLAN B.
BZZZT
THIS HELMET DOESN'T BREATHE AT ALL.
WE CAN TRY THE BRAINSTEM TAP AGAIN.
NAH, THIS IS FINE.
PARDON ME, MISTER, BUT WHO THE DAMN HECK HELL ARE YOU?
AM I TO UNDERSTAND THAT YOU DON'T RECOGNIZE YOUR GOOD FRIEND AND BENEFACTOR GREGOR MENDEL? AFTER ALL, IF IT WASN'T FOR ME, YOU'D BE FOOD FOR WORMS INSTEAD OF THE OTHER WAY ROUND.
ONE COULD SAY THAT YOU LITERALLY OWE ME YOUR VERY LIFE. AND WE SCHOLARS OF GENETICS DON'T HAVE MUCH USE FOR THE CONCEPT OF ALTRUISM.
WELL, IT'S TIME TO COLLECT ON THAT LITTLE FAVOR I DID FOR YOU. I NEED YOU TO RUN SOME ERRANDS.
IRONICALLY, IT'S THE VERY SERUM I CREATED TO RESURRECT YOU THAT MADE THE USE OF ALL THIS GADGETRY POSSIBLE. A NORMAL, MORTAL MIND WOULD NEVER HAVE BEEN ABLE TO WITHSTAND THE STRAIN OF MEMORY EXTRACTION AND RECONSTRUCTION.
AND I WAS SO LOOKING FORWARD TO BREAKING YOU. REMAKING YOU IN MY OWN IMAGE. INTO MY OWN DEADLY RIGHT HAND.
A SHAME, REALLY. WE HAD BARELY JUST BEGUN!
OF COURSE, THIS JUST MEANS WE'LL HAVE TO TAKE THE MORE... DIRECT ROUTE.

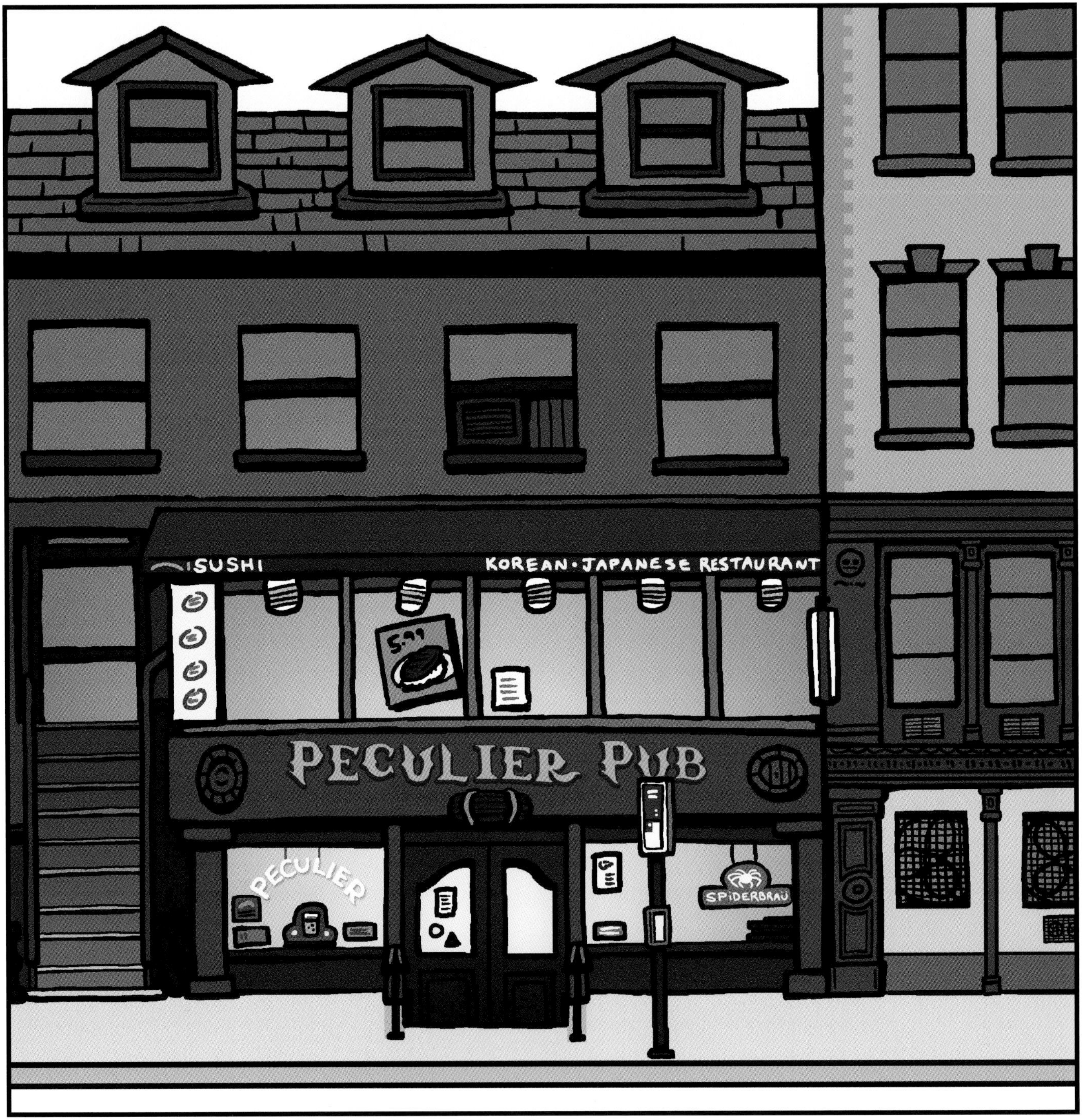
SUSHI
KOREAN·JAPANESE RESTAURANT
5.99
PECULIER PUB
PECULIER
SPIDERBRAU

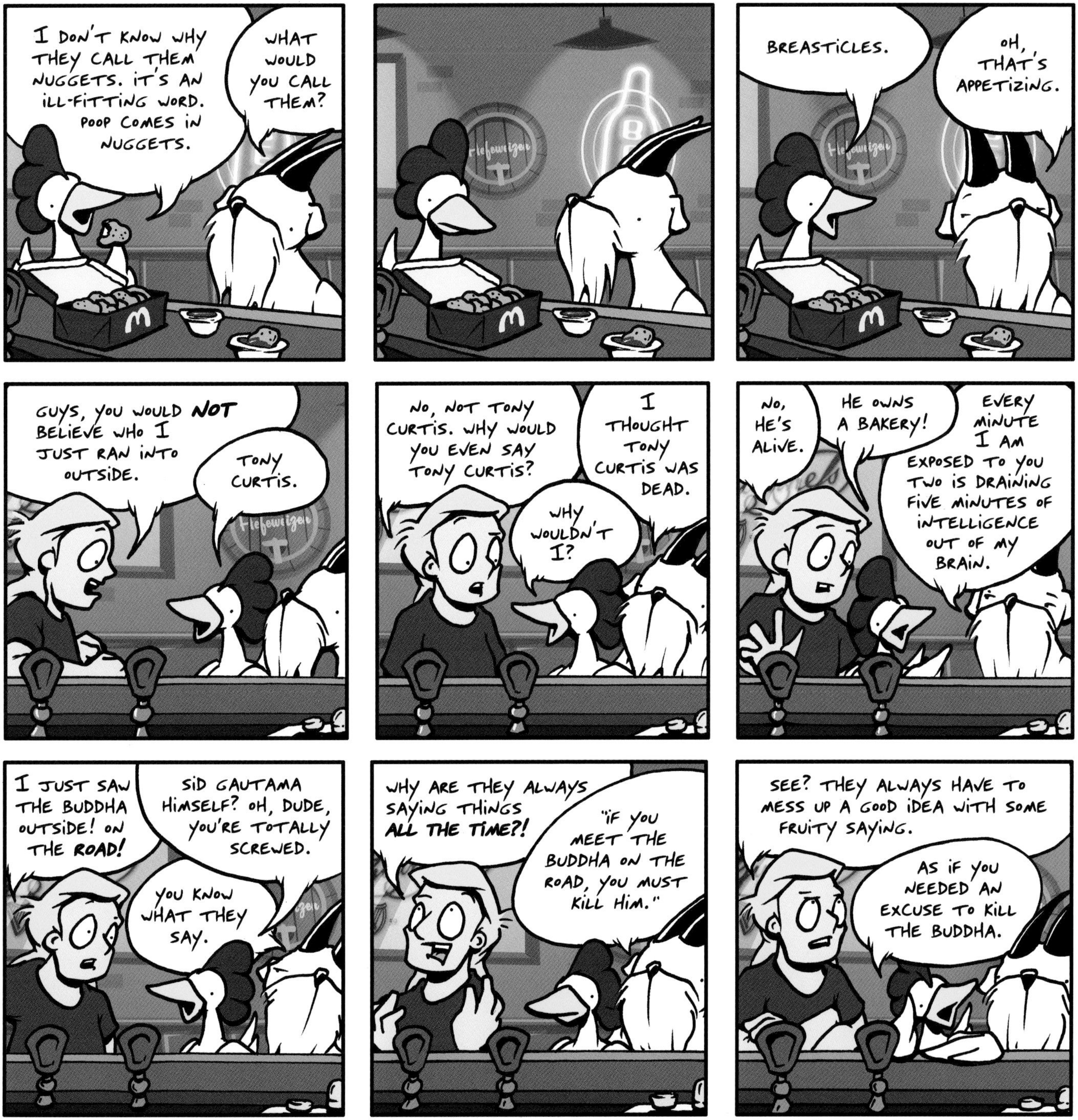
I DON'T KNOW WHY THEY CALL THEM NUGGETS. IT'S AN ILL-FITTING WORD. POOP COMES IN NUGGETS.
WHAT WOULD YOU CALL THEM?
BREASTICLES.
OH, THAT'S APPETIZING.
GUYS, YOU WOULD **NOT** BELIEVE WHO I JUST RAN INTO OUTSIDE.
TONY CURTIS.
NO, NOT TONY CURTIS. WHY WOULD YOU EVEN SAY TONY CURTIS?
I THOUGHT TONY CURTIS WAS DEAD.
WHY WOULDN'T I?
NO, HE'S ALIVE.
HE OWNS A BAKERY!
EVERY MINUTE I AM EXPOSED TO YOU TWO IS DRAINING FIVE MINUTES OF INTELLIGENCE OUT OF MY BRAIN.
I JUST SAW THE BUDDHA OUTSIDE! ON THE **ROAD!**
SID GAUTAMA HIMSELF? OH, DUDE, YOU'RE TOTALLY SCREWED.
YOU KNOW WHAT THEY SAY.
WHY ARE THEY ALWAYS SAYING THINGS **ALL THE TIME?!**
"IF YOU MEET THE BUDDHA ON THE ROAD, YOU MUST KILL HIM."
SEE? THEY ALWAYS HAVE TO MESS UP A GOOD IDEA WITH SOME FRUITY SAYING.
AS IF YOU NEEDED AN EXCUSE TO KILL THE BUDDHA.

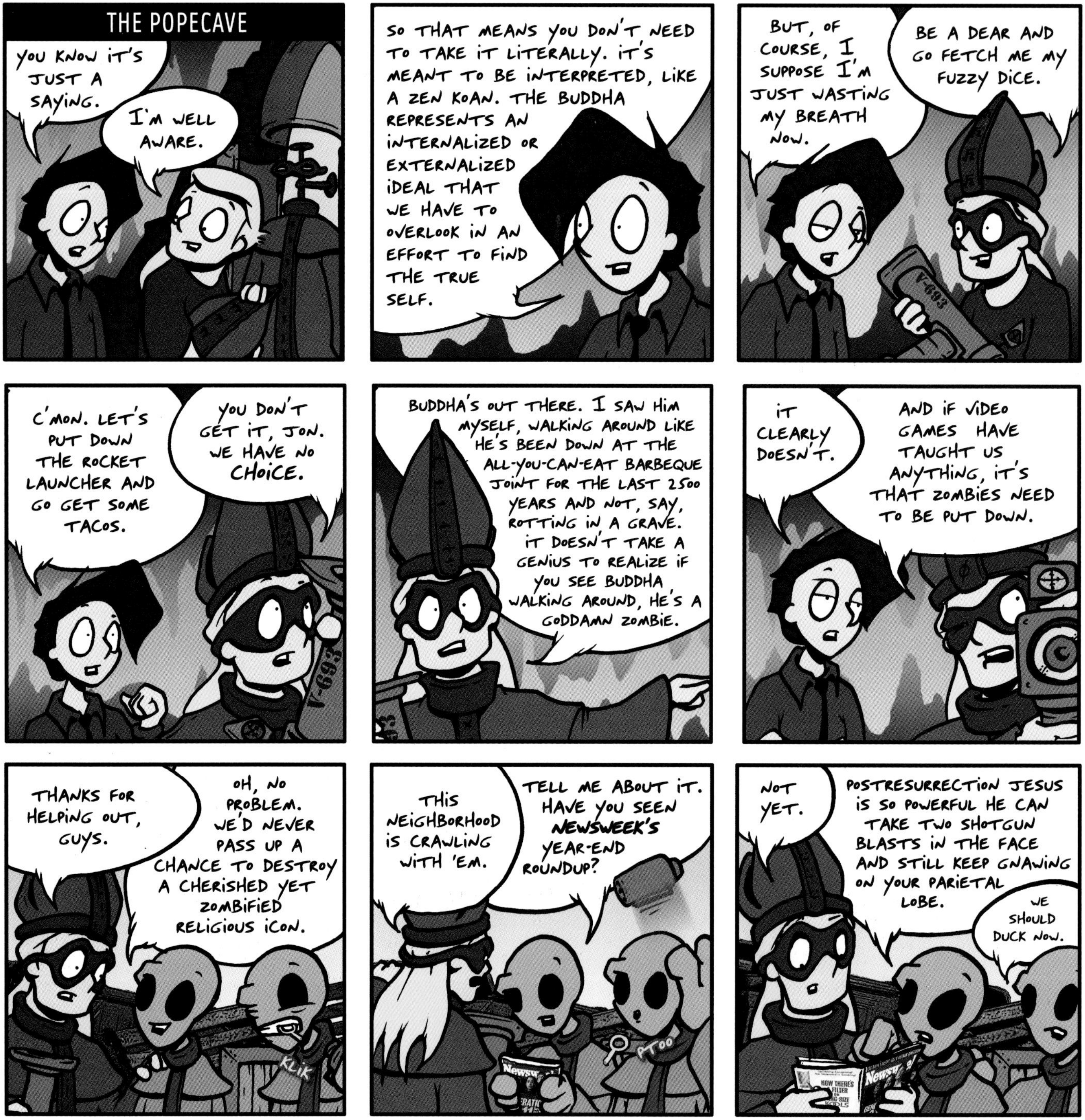
THE POPECAVE
YOU KNOW IT'S JUST A SAYING.
I'M WELL AWARE.
SO THAT MEANS YOU DON'T NEED TO TAKE IT LITERALLY. IT'S MEANT TO BE INTERPRETED, LIKE A ZEN KOAN. THE BUDDHA REPRESENTS AN INTERNALIZED OR EXTERNALIZED IDEAL THAT WE HAVE TO OVERLOOK IN AN EFFORT TO FIND THE TRUE SELF.
BUT, OF COURSE, I SUPPOSE I'M JUST WASTING MY BREATH NOW.
BE A DEAR AND GO FETCH ME MY FUZZY DICE.
V-693
C'MON. LET'S PUT DOWN THE ROCKET LAUNCHER AND GO GET SOME TACOS.
YOU DON'T GET IT, JON. WE HAVE NO CHOICE.
BUDDHA'S OUT THERE. I SAW HIM MYSELF, WALKING AROUND LIKE HE'S BEEN DOWN AT THE ALL-YOU-CAN-EAT BARBEQUE JOINT FOR THE LAST 2500 YEARS AND NOT, SAY, ROTTING IN A GRAVE. IT DOESN'T TAKE A GENIUS TO REALIZE IF YOU SEE BUDDHA WALKING AROUND, HE'S A GODDAMN ZOMBIE.
IT CLEARLY DOESN'T.
AND IF VIDEO GAMES HAVE TAUGHT US ANYTHING, IT'S THAT ZOMBIES NEED TO BE PUT DOWN.
THANKS FOR HELPING OUT, GUYS.
OH, NO PROBLEM. WE'D NEVER PASS UP A CHANCE TO DESTROY A CHERISHED YET ZOMBIFIED RELIGIOUS ICON.
KLIK
THIS NEIGHBORHOOD IS CRAWLING WITH 'EM.
TELL ME ABOUT IT. HAVE YOU SEEN NEWSWEEK'S YEAR-END ROUNDUP?
PTOO
NOT YET.
POSTRESURRECTION JESUS IS SO POWERFUL HE CAN TAKE TWO SHOTGUN BLASTS IN THE FACE AND STILL KEEP GNAWING ON YOUR PARIETAL LOBE.
WE SHOULD DUCK NOW.
NOW THERE'S FILTER ON KING-SIZE KOOLS

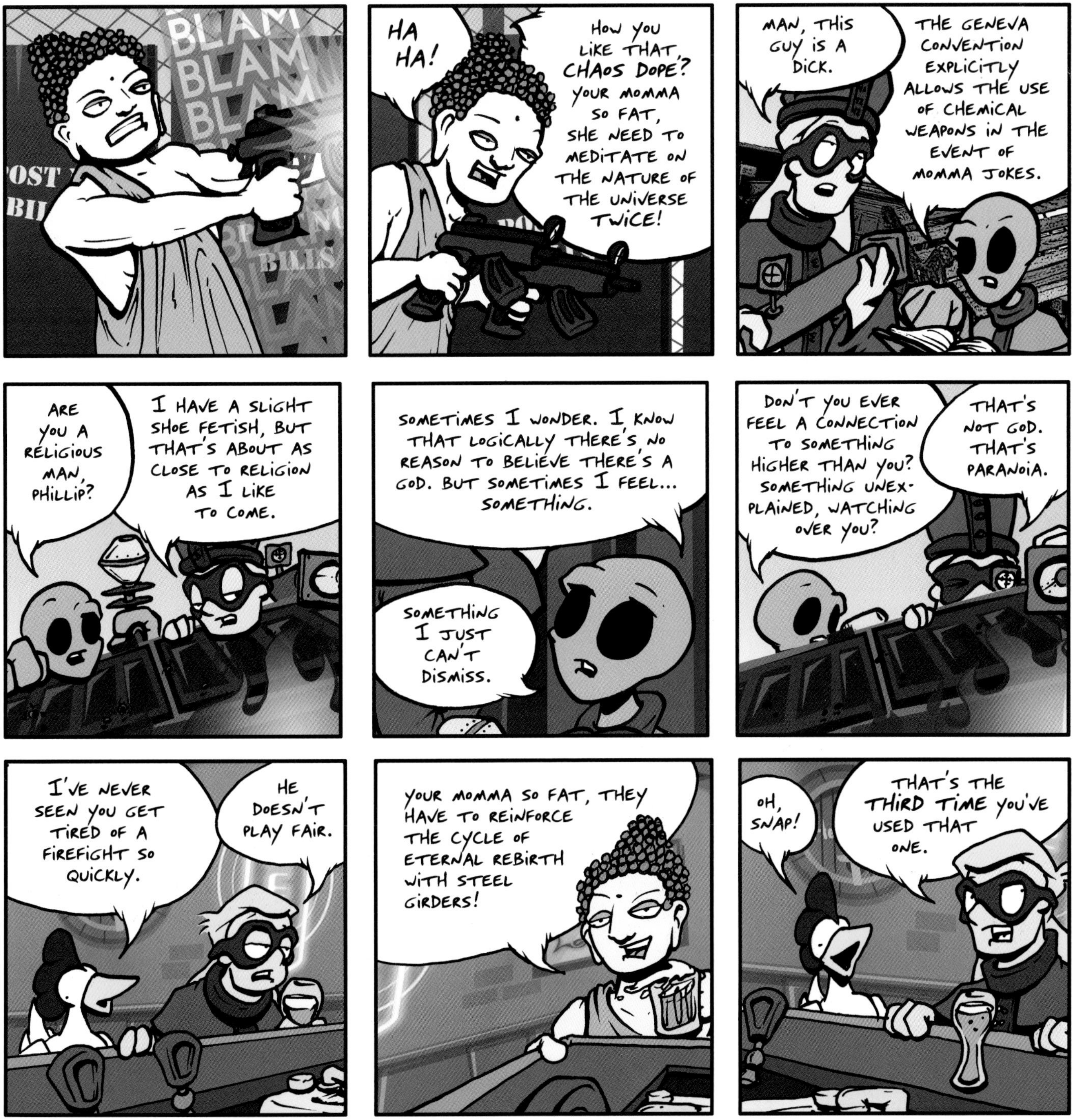
BLAM
BLAM
BLAM
BILLS
HA HA!
HOW YOU LIKE THAT, CHAOS DOPE? YOUR MOMMA SO FAT, SHE NEED TO MEDITATE ON THE NATURE OF THE UNIVERSE TWICE!
MAN, THIS GUY IS A DICK.
THE GENEVA CONVENTION EXPLICITLY ALLOWS THE USE OF CHEMICAL WEAPONS IN THE EVENT OF MOMMA JOKES.
ARE YOU A RELIGIOUS MAN, PHILLIP?
I HAVE A SLIGHT SHOE FETISH, BUT THAT'S ABOUT AS CLOSE TO RELIGION AS I LIKE TO COME.
SOMETIMES I WONDER. I KNOW THAT LOGICALLY THERE'S NO REASON TO BELIEVE THERE'S A GOD. BUT SOMETIMES I FEEL... SOMETHING.
SOMETHING I JUST CAN'T DISMISS.
DON'T YOU EVER FEEL A CONNECTION TO SOMETHING HIGHER THAN YOU? SOMETHING UNEX-PLAINED, WATCHING OVER YOU?
THAT'S NOT GOD. THAT'S PARANOIA.
I'VE NEVER SEEN YOU GET TIRED OF A FIREFIGHT SO QUICKLY.
HE DOESN'T PLAY FAIR.
YOUR MOMMA SO FAT, THEY HAVE TO REINFORCE THE CYCLE OF ETERNAL REBIRTH WITH STEEL GIRDERS!
OH, SNAP!
THAT'S THE THIRD TIME YOU'VE USED THAT ONE.

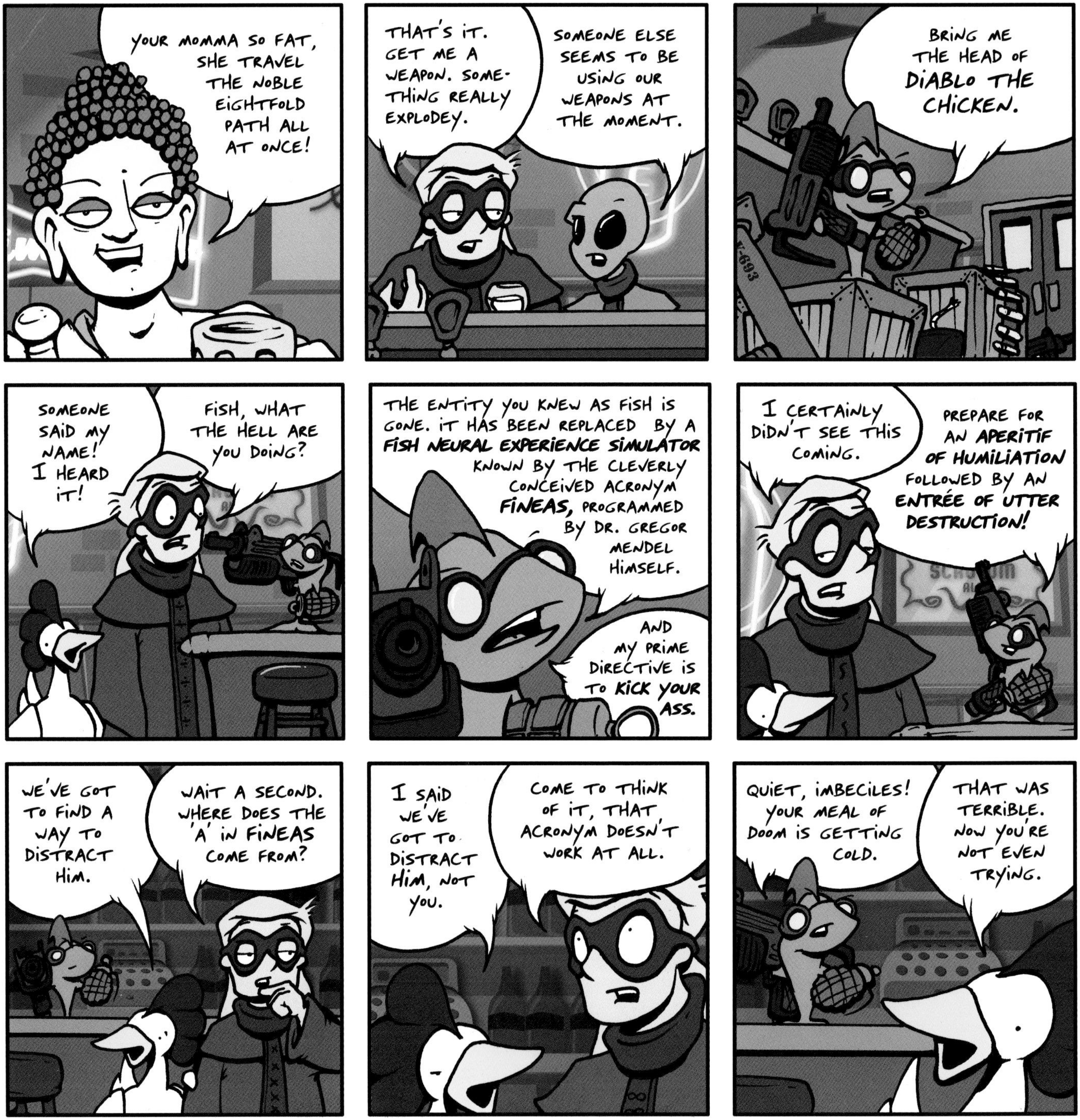
YOUR MOMMA SO FAT, SHE TRAVEL THE NOBLE EIGHTFOLD PATH ALL AT ONCE!
THAT'S IT. GET ME A WEAPON. SOMETHING REALLY EXPLODEY.
SOMEONE ELSE SEEMS TO BE USING OUR WEAPONS AT THE MOMENT.
BRING ME THE HEAD OF DIABLO THE CHICKEN.
SOMEONE SAID MY NAME! I HEARD IT!
FISH, WHAT THE HELL ARE YOU DOING?
THE ENTITY YOU KNEW AS FISH IS GONE. IT HAS BEEN REPLACED BY A FISH NEURAL EXPERIENCE SIMULATOR KNOWN BY THE CLEVERLY CONCEIVED ACRONYM FINEAS, PROGRAMMED BY DR. GREGOR MENDEL HIMSELF.
AND MY PRIME DIRECTIVE IS TO KICK YOUR ASS.
I CERTAINLY DIDN'T SEE THIS COMING.
PREPARE FOR AN APERITIF OF HUMILIATION FOLLOWED BY AN ENTRÉE OF UTTER DESTRUCTION!
WE'VE GOT TO FIND A WAY TO DISTRACT HIM.
WAIT A SECOND. WHERE DOES THE 'A' IN FINEAS COME FROM?
I SAID WE'VE GOT TO DISTRACT HIM, NOT YOU.
COME TO THINK OF IT, THAT ACRONYM DOESN'T WORK AT ALL.
QUIET, IMBECILES! YOUR MEAL OF DOOM IS GETTING COLD.
THAT WAS TERRIBLE. NOW YOU'RE NOT EVEN TRYING.

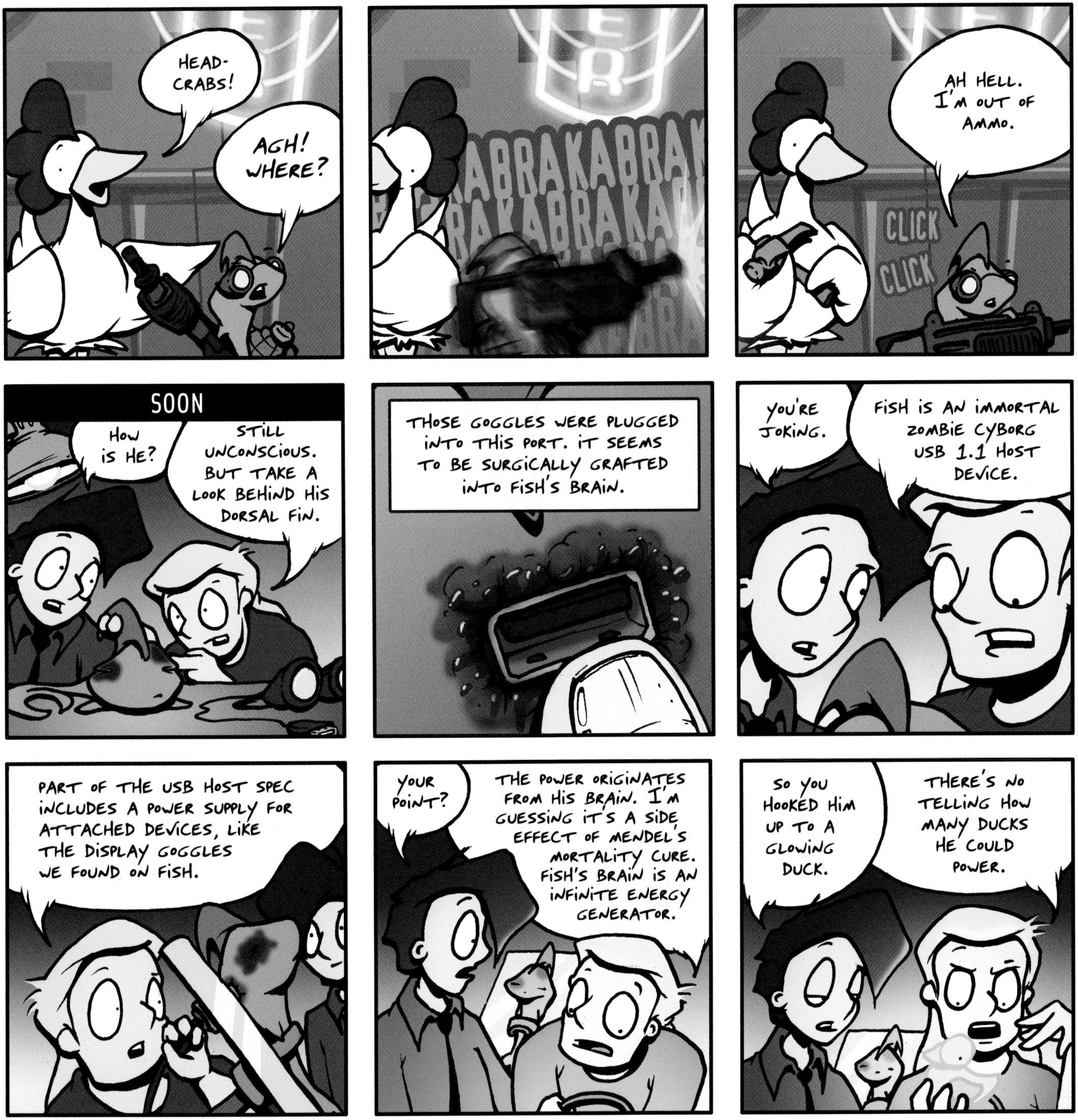
HEAD-CRABS!
AGH! WHERE?
ABRAKABRAKABRAKA
AH HELL. I'M OUT OF AMMO.
CLICK
CLICK
SOON
HOW IS HE?
STILL UNCONSCIOUS. BUT TAKE A LOOK BEHIND HIS DORSAL FIN.
THOSE GOGGLES WERE PLUGGED INTO THIS PORT. IT SEEMS TO BE SURGICALLY GRAFTED INTO FISH'S BRAIN.
YOU'RE JOKING.
FISH IS AN IMMORTAL ZOMBIE CYBORG USB 1.1 HOST DEVICE.
PART OF THE USB HOST SPEC INCLUDES A POWER SUPPLY FOR ATTACHED DEVICES, LIKE THE DISPLAY GOGGLES WE FOUND ON FISH.
YOUR POINT?
THE POWER ORIGINATES FROM HIS BRAIN. I'M GUESSING IT'S A SIDE EFFECT OF MENDEL'S MORTALITY CURE. FISH'S BRAIN IS AN INFINITE ENERGY GENERATOR.
SO YOU HOOKED HIM UP TO A GLOWING DUCK.
THERE'S NO TELLING HOW MANY DUCKS HE COULD POWER.

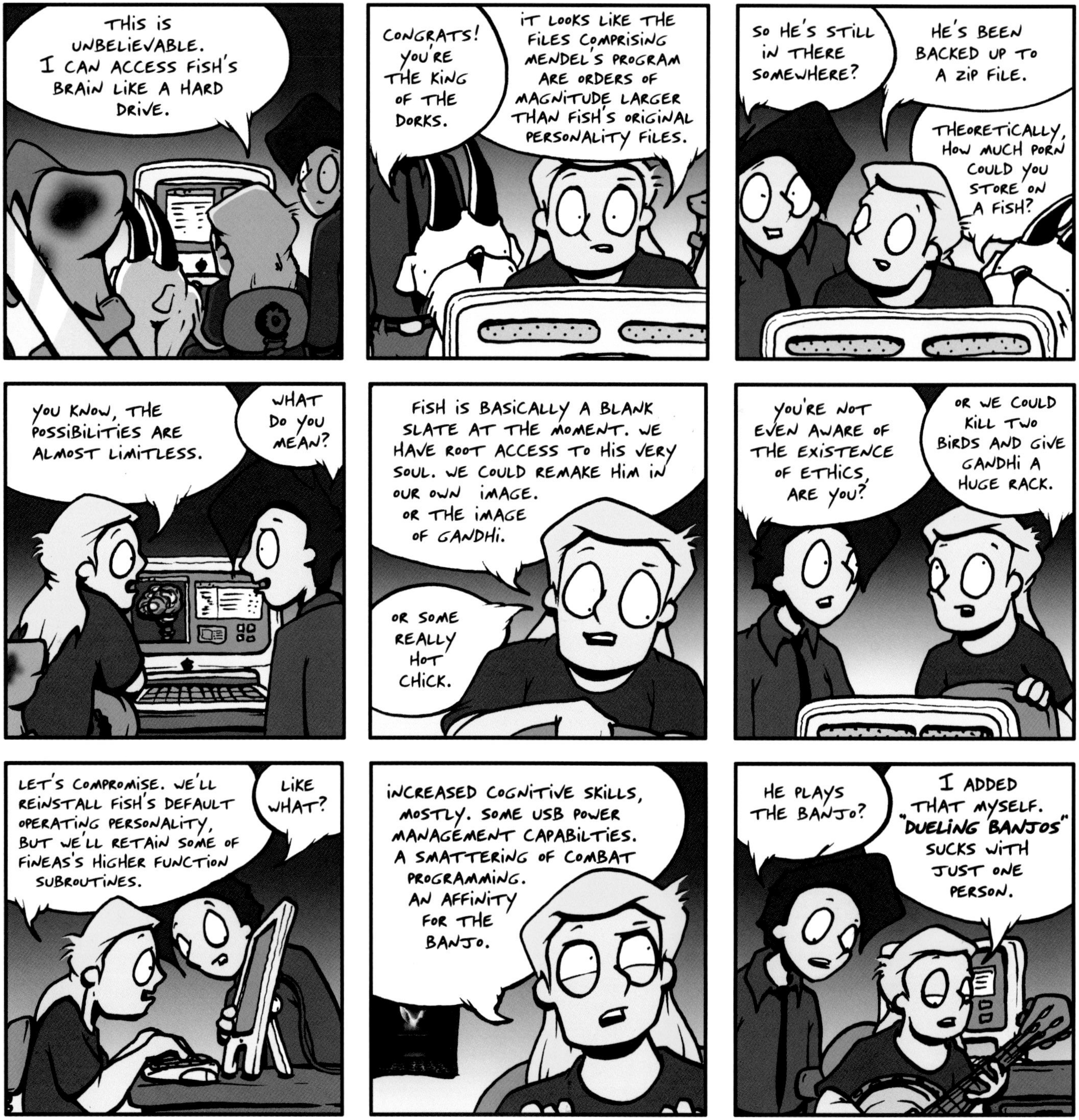
THIS IS UNBELIEVABLE. I CAN ACCESS FISH'S BRAIN LIKE A HARD DRIVE.
CONGRATS! YOU'RE THE KING OF THE DORKS.
IT LOOKS LIKE THE FILES COMPRISING MENDEL'S PROGRAM ARE ORDERS OF MAGNITUDE LARGER THAN FISH'S ORIGINAL PERSONALITY FILES.
SO HE'S STILL IN THERE SOMEWHERE?
HE'S BEEN BACKED UP TO A ZIP FILE.
THEORETICALLY, HOW MUCH PORN COULD YOU STORE ON A FISH?
YOU KNOW, THE POSSIBILITIES ARE ALMOST LIMITLESS.
WHAT DO YOU MEAN?
FISH IS BASICALLY A BLANK SLATE AT THE MOMENT. WE HAVE ROOT ACCESS TO HIS VERY SOUL. WE COULD REMAKE HIM IN OUR OWN IMAGE. OR THE IMAGE OF GANDHI.
OR SOME REALLY HOT CHICK.
YOU'RE NOT EVEN AWARE OF THE EXISTENCE OF ETHICS, ARE YOU?
OR WE COULD KILL TWO BIRDS AND GIVE GANDHI A HUGE RACK.
LET'S COMPROMISE. WE'LL REINSTALL FISH'S DEFAULT OPERATING PERSONALITY, BUT WE'LL RETAIN SOME OF FINEAS'S HIGHER FUNCTION SUBROUTINES.
LIKE WHAT?
INCREASED COGNITIVE SKILLS, MOSTLY. SOME USB POWER MANAGEMENT CAPABILTIES. A SMATTERING OF COMBAT PROGRAMMING. AN AFFINITY FOR THE BANJO.
HE PLAYS THE BANJO?
I ADDED THAT MYSELF. "DUELING BANJOS" SUCKS WITH JUST ONE PERSON.

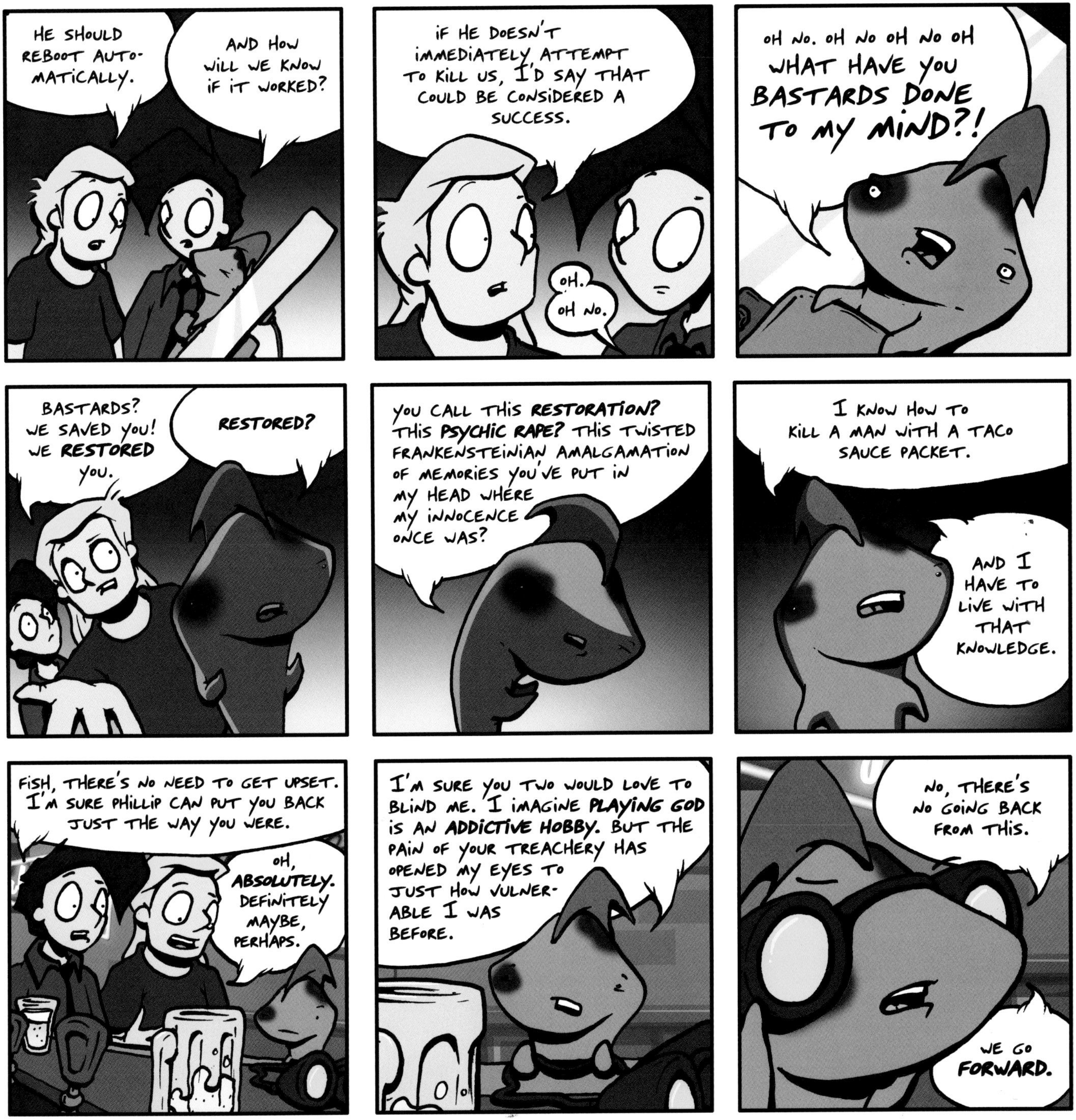
HE SHOULD REBOOT AUTO-MATICALLY.
AND HOW WILL WE KNOW IF IT WORKED?
IF HE DOESN'T IMMEDIATELY ATTEMPT TO KILL US, I'D SAY THAT COULD BE CONSIDERED A SUCCESS.
OH. OH NO.
OH NO. OH NO OH NO OH WHAT HAVE YOU BASTARDS DONE TO MY MIND?!
BASTARDS? WE SAVED YOU! WE RESTORED YOU.
RESTORED?
YOU CALL THIS RESTORATION? THIS PSYCHIC RAPE? THIS TWISTED FRANKENSTEINIAN AMALGAMATION OF MEMORIES YOU'VE PUT IN MY HEAD WHERE MY INNOCENCE ONCE WAS?
I KNOW HOW TO KILL A MAN WITH A TACO SAUCE PACKET.
AND I HAVE TO LIVE WITH THAT KNOWLEDGE.
FISH, THERE'S NO NEED TO GET UPSET. I'M SURE PHILLIP CAN PUT YOU BACK JUST THE WAY YOU WERE.
OH, ABSOLUTELY. DEFINITELY MAYBE, PERHAPS.
I'M SURE YOU TWO WOULD LOVE TO BLIND ME. I IMAGINE PLAYING GOD IS AN ADDICTIVE HOBBY. BUT THE PAIN OF YOUR TREACHERY HAS OPENED MY EYES TO JUST HOW VULNER-ABLE I WAS BEFORE.
NO, THERE'S NO GOING BACK FROM THIS.
WE GO FORWARD.

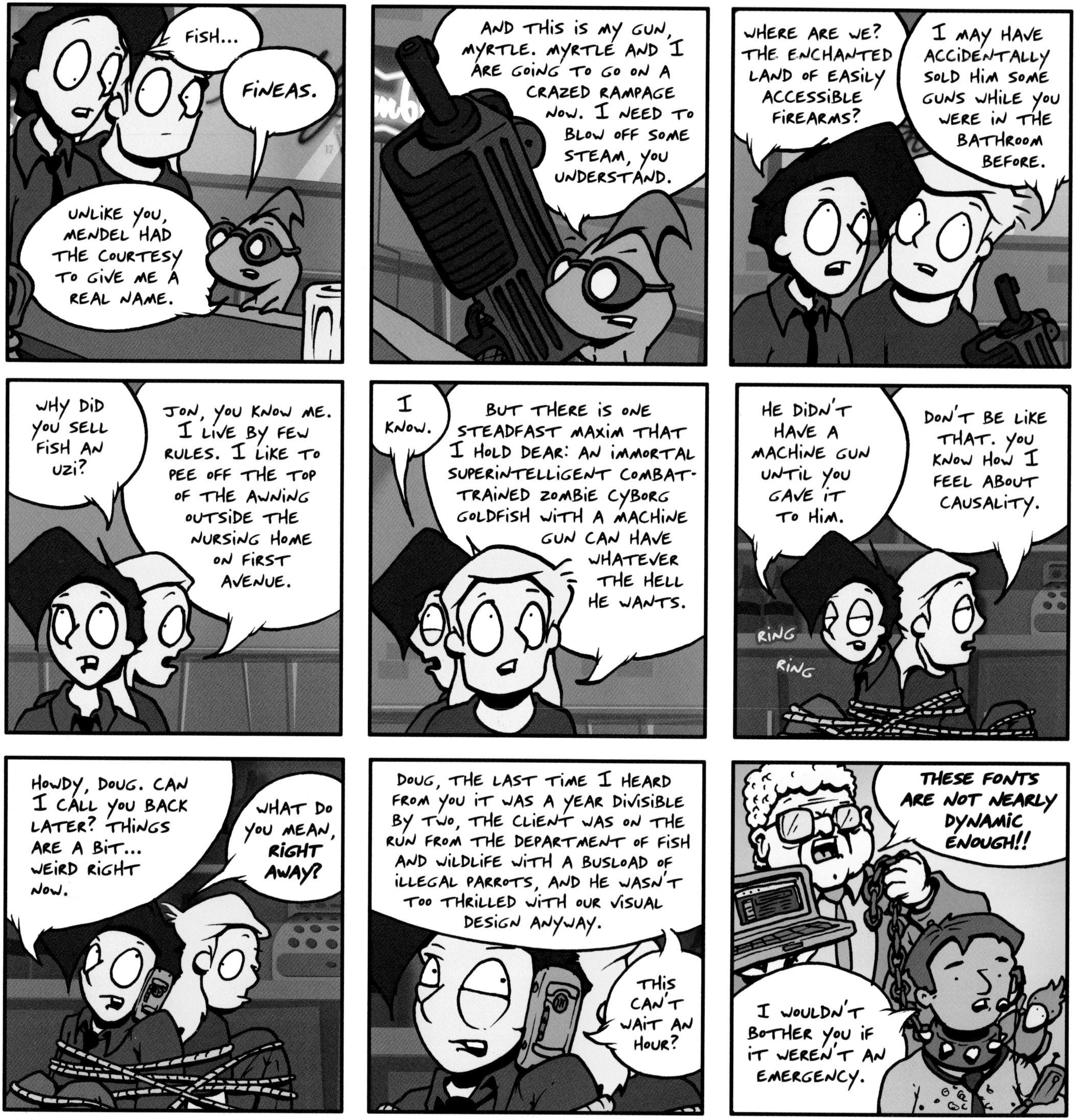
FISH...
FINEAS.
UNLIKE YOU, MENDEL HAD THE COURTESY TO GIVE ME A REAL NAME.
AND THIS IS MY GUN, MYRTLE. MYRTLE AND I ARE GOING TO GO ON A CRAZED RAMPAGE NOW. I NEED TO BLOW OFF SOME STEAM, YOU UNDERSTAND.
WHERE ARE WE? THE ENCHANTED LAND OF EASILY ACCESSIBLE FIREARMS?
I MAY HAVE ACCIDENTALLY SOLD HIM SOME GUNS WHILE YOU WERE IN THE BATHROOM BEFORE.
WHY DID YOU SELL FISH AN UZI?
JON, YOU KNOW ME. I LIVE BY FEW RULES. I LIKE TO PEE OFF THE TOP OF THE AWNING OUTSIDE THE NURSING HOME ON FIRST AVENUE.
I KNOW.
BUT THERE IS ONE STEADFAST MAXIM THAT I HOLD DEAR: AN IMMORTAL SUPERINTELLIGENT COMBAT-TRAINED ZOMBIE CYBORG GOLDFISH WITH A MACHINE GUN CAN HAVE WHATEVER THE HELL HE WANTS.
HE DIDN'T HAVE A MACHINE GUN UNTIL YOU GAVE IT TO HIM.
DON'T BE LIKE THAT. YOU KNOW HOW I FEEL ABOUT CAUSALITY.
RING
RING
HOWDY, DOUG. CAN I CALL YOU BACK LATER? THINGS ARE A BIT... WEIRD RIGHT NOW.
WHAT DO YOU MEAN, **RIGHT AWAY?**
DOUG, THE LAST TIME I HEARD FROM YOU IT WAS A YEAR DIVISIBLE BY TWO, THE CLIENT WAS ON THE RUN FROM THE DEPARTMENT OF FISH AND WILDLIFE WITH A BUSLOAD OF ILLEGAL PARROTS, AND HE WASN'T TOO THRILLED WITH OUR VISUAL DESIGN ANYWAY.
THIS CAN'T WAIT AN HOUR?
THESE FONTS ARE NOT NEARLY DYNAMIC ENOUGH!!
I WOULDN'T BOTHER YOU IF IT WEREN'T AN EMERGENCY.

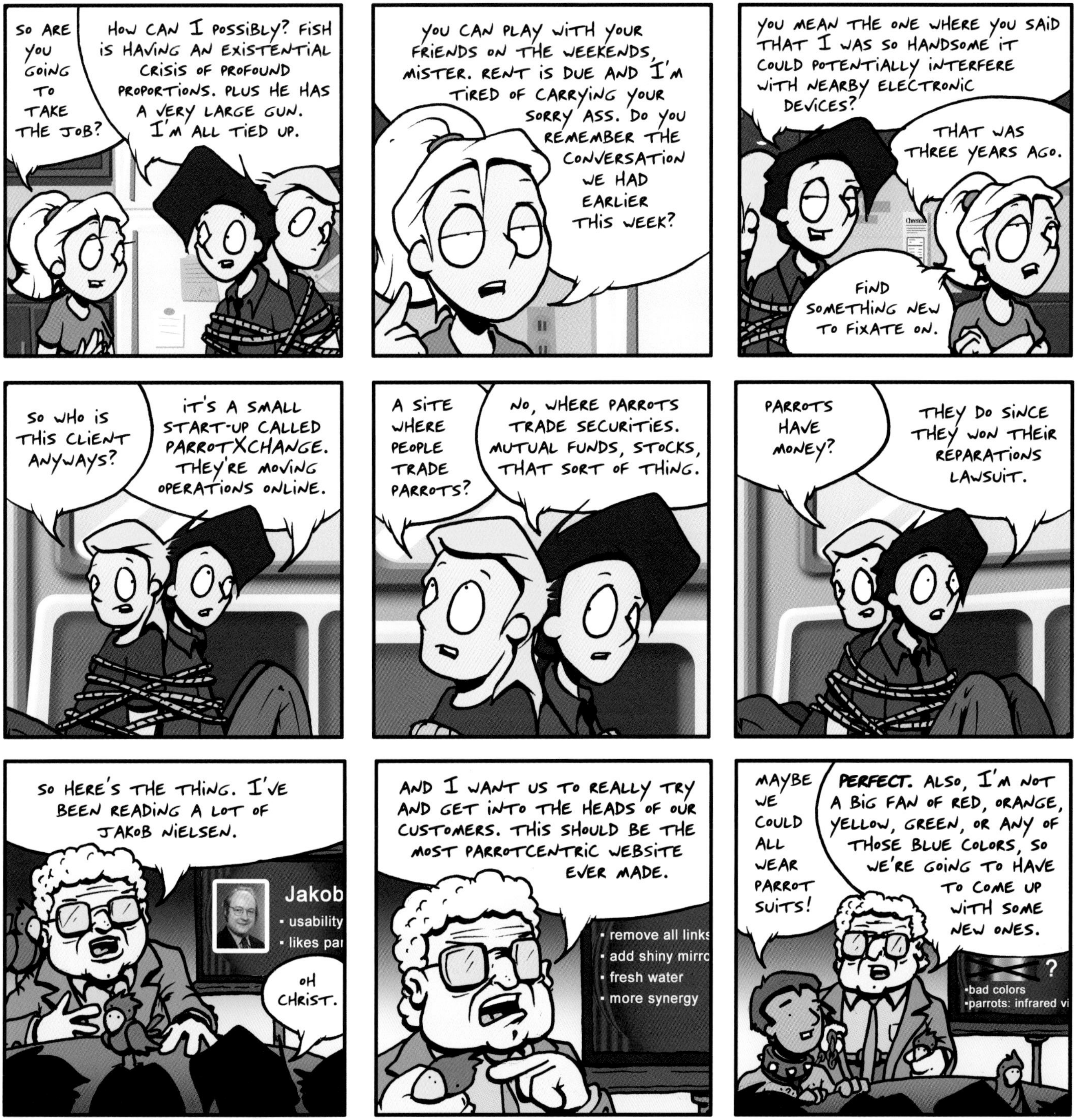

SO ARE YOU GOING TO TAKE THE JOB?
HOW CAN I POSSIBLY? FISH IS HAVING AN EXISTENTIAL CRISIS OF PROFOUND PROPORTIONS. PLUS HE HAS A VERY LARGE GUN. I'M ALL TIED UP.
YOU CAN PLAY WITH YOUR FRIENDS ON THE WEEKENDS, MISTER. RENT IS DUE AND I'M TIRED OF CARRYING YOUR SORRY ASS. DO YOU REMEMBER THE CONVERSATION WE HAD EARLIER THIS WEEK?
YOU MEAN THE ONE WHERE YOU SAID THAT I WAS SO HANDSOME IT COULD POTENTIALLY INTERFERE WITH NEARBY ELECTRONIC DEVICES?
THAT WAS THREE YEARS AGO.
FIND SOMETHING NEW TO FIXATE ON.
SO WHO IS THIS CLIENT ANYWAYS?
IT'S A SMALL START-UP CALLED PARROTXCHANGE. THEY'RE MOVING OPERATIONS ONLINE.
A SITE WHERE PEOPLE TRADE PARROTS?
NO, WHERE PARROTS TRADE SECURITIES. MUTUAL FUNDS, STOCKS, THAT SORT OF THING.
PARROTS HAVE MONEY?
THEY DO SINCE THEY WON THEIR REPARATIONS LAWSUIT.
SO HERE'S THE THING. I'VE BEEN READING A LOT OF JAKOB NIELSEN.
Jakob
▪ usability
▪ likes par
OH CHRIST.
AND I WANT US TO REALLY TRY AND GET INTO THE HEADS OF OUR CUSTOMERS. THIS SHOULD BE THE MOST PARROTCENTRIC WEBSITE EVER MADE.
▪ remove all links
▪ add shiny mirro
▪ fresh water
▪ more synergy
MAYBE WE COULD ALL WEAR PARROT SUITS!
PERFECT. ALSO, I'M NOT A BIG FAN OF RED, ORANGE, YELLOW, GREEN, OR ANY OF THOSE BLUE COLORS, SO WE'RE GOING TO HAVE TO COME UP WITH SOME NEW ONES.
?
▪bad colors
▪parrots: infrared vi

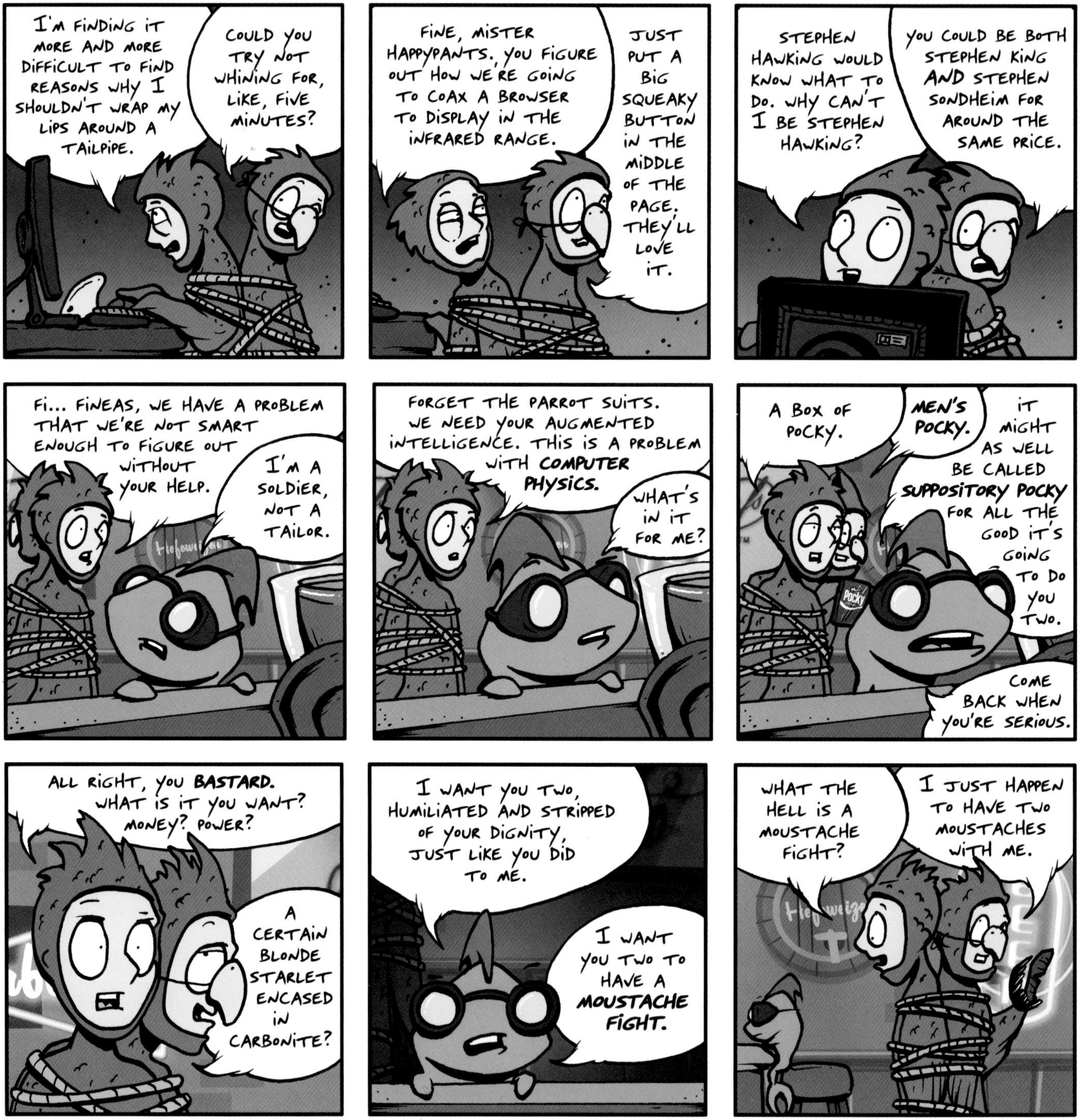
I'M FINDING IT MORE AND MORE DIFFICULT TO FIND REASONS WHY I SHOULDN'T WRAP MY LIPS AROUND A TAILPIPE.
COULD YOU TRY NOT WHINING FOR, LIKE, FIVE MINUTES?
FINE, MISTER HAPPYPANTS. YOU FIGURE OUT HOW WE'RE GOING TO COAX A BROWSER TO DISPLAY IN THE INFRARED RANGE.
JUST PUT A BIG SQUEAKY BUTTON IN THE MIDDLE OF THE PAGE. THEY'LL LOVE IT.
STEPHEN HAWKING WOULD KNOW WHAT TO DO. WHY CAN'T I BE STEPHEN HAWKING?
YOU COULD BE BOTH STEPHEN KING AND STEPHEN SONDHEIM FOR AROUND THE SAME PRICE.
FI... FINEAS, WE HAVE A PROBLEM THAT WE'RE NOT SMART ENOUGH TO FIGURE OUT WITHOUT YOUR HELP.
I'M A SOLDIER, NOT A TAILOR.
FORGET THE PARROT SUITS. WE NEED YOUR AUGMENTED INTELLIGENCE. THIS IS A PROBLEM WITH **COMPUTER PHYSICS.**
WHAT'S IN IT FOR ME?
A BOX OF POCKY.
MEN'S POCKY.
IT MIGHT AS WELL BE CALLED **SUPPOSITORY POCKY** FOR ALL THE GOOD IT'S GOING TO DO YOU TWO.
Pocky
COME BACK WHEN YOU'RE SERIOUS.
ALL RIGHT, YOU **BASTARD.** WHAT IS IT YOU WANT? MONEY? POWER?
A CERTAIN BLONDE STARLET ENCASED IN CARBONITE?
I WANT YOU TWO, HUMILIATED AND STRIPPED OF YOUR DIGNITY, JUST LIKE YOU DID TO ME.
I WANT YOU TWO TO HAVE A **MOUSTACHE FIGHT.**
WHAT THE HELL IS A MOUSTACHE FIGHT?
I JUST HAPPEN TO HAVE TWO MOUSTACHES WITH ME.

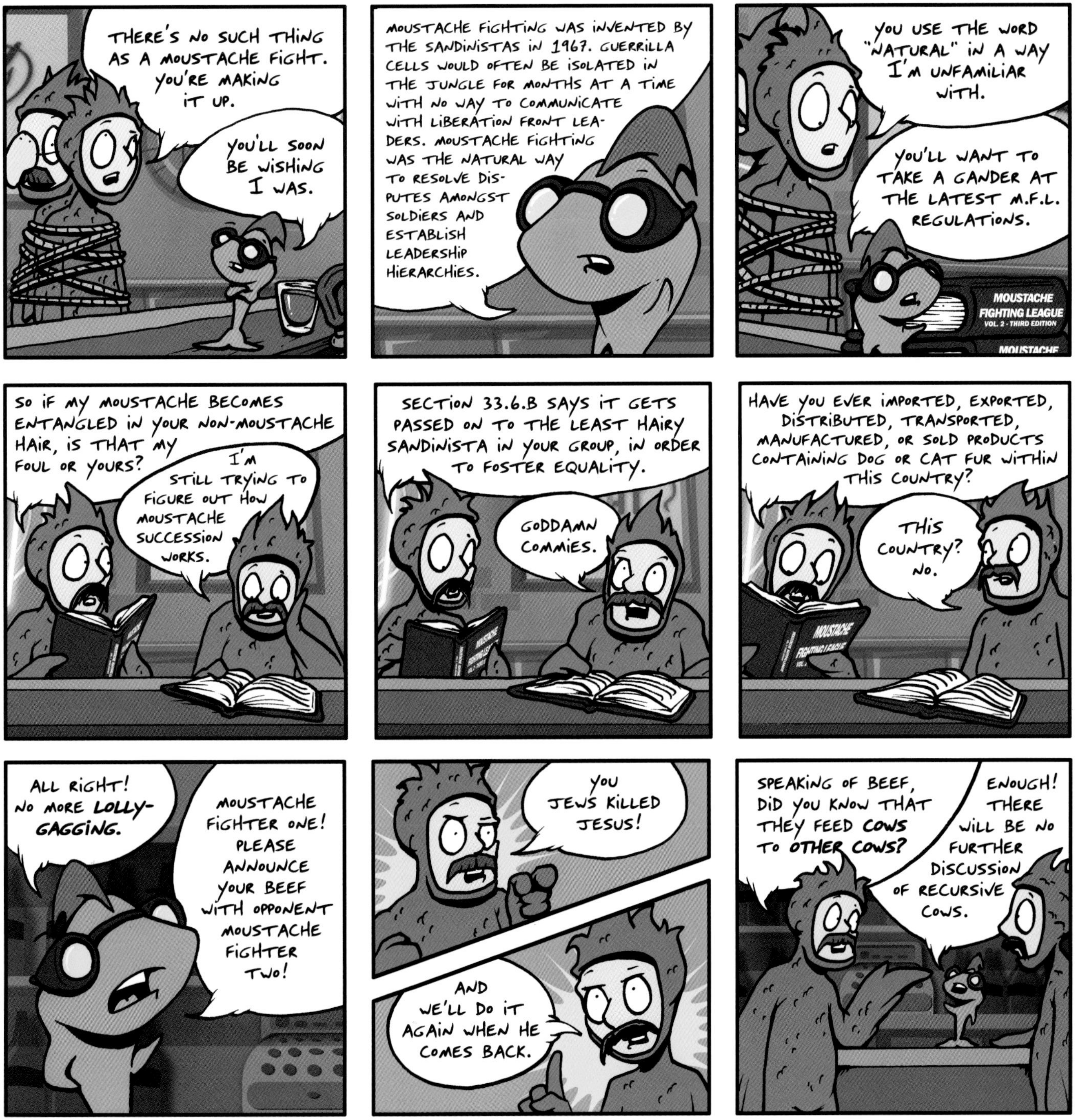
THERE'S NO SUCH THING AS A MOUSTACHE FIGHT. YOU'RE MAKING IT UP.
YOU'LL SOON BE WISHING I WAS.
MOUSTACHE FIGHTING WAS INVENTED BY THE SANDINISTAS IN 1967. GUERRILLA CELLS WOULD OFTEN BE ISOLATED IN THE JUNGLE FOR MONTHS AT A TIME WITH NO WAY TO COMMUNICATE WITH LIBERATION FRONT LEADERS. MOUSTACHE FIGHTING WAS THE NATURAL WAY TO RESOLVE DISPUTES AMONGST SOLDIERS AND ESTABLISH LEADERSHIP HIERARCHIES.
YOU USE THE WORD "NATURAL" IN A WAY I'M UNFAMILIAR WITH.
YOU'LL WANT TO TAKE A GANDER AT THE LATEST M.F.L. REGULATIONS.
MOUSTACHE FIGHTING LEAGUE VOL. 2 - THIRD EDITION
MOUSTACHE
SO IF MY MOUSTACHE BECOMES ENTANGLED IN YOUR NON-MOUSTACHE HAIR, IS THAT MY FOUL OR YOURS?
I'M STILL TRYING TO FIGURE OUT HOW MOUSTACHE SUCCESSION WORKS.
SECTION 33.6.B SAYS IT GETS PASSED ON TO THE LEAST HAIRY SANDINISTA IN YOUR GROUP, IN ORDER TO FOSTER EQUALITY.
GODDAMN COMMIES.
HAVE YOU EVER IMPORTED, EXPORTED, DISTRIBUTED, TRANSPORTED, MANUFACTURED, OR SOLD PRODUCTS CONTAINING DOG OR CAT FUR WITHIN THIS COUNTRY?
THIS COUNTRY? NO.
ALL RIGHT! NO MORE LOLLYGAGGING.
MOUSTACHE FIGHTER ONE! PLEASE ANNOUNCE YOUR BEEF WITH OPPONENT MOUSTACHE FIGHTER TWO!
YOU JEWS KILLED JESUS!
AND WE'LL DO IT AGAIN WHEN HE COMES BACK.
SPEAKING OF BEEF, DID YOU KNOW THAT THEY FEED COWS TO OTHER COWS?
ENOUGH! THERE WILL BE NO FURTHER DISCUSSION OF RECURSIVE COWS.

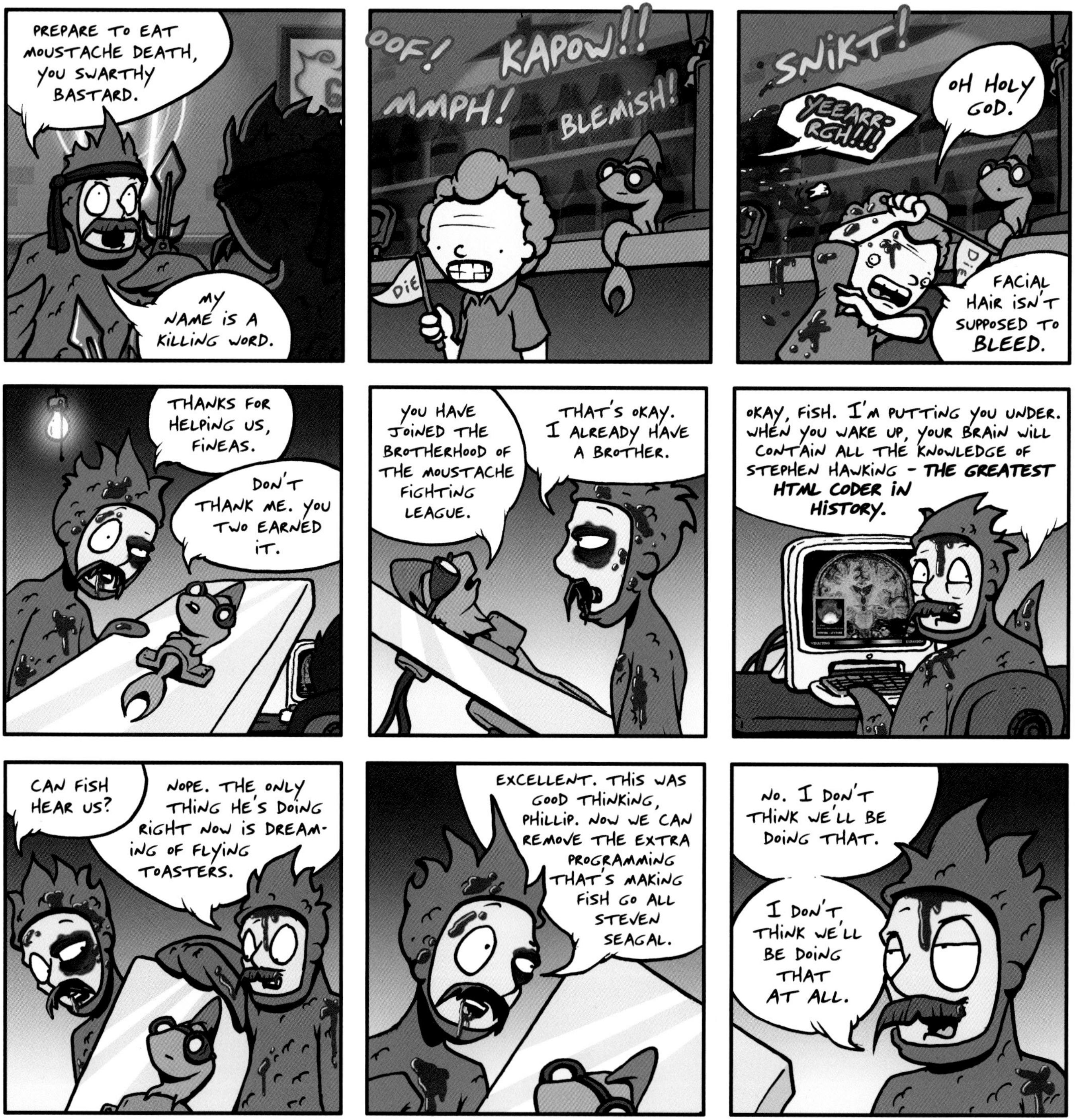
PREPARE TO EAT MOUSTACHE DEATH, YOU SWARTHY BASTARD.
MY NAME IS A KILLING WORD.
OOF!
KAPOW!!
MMPH!
BLEMISH!
DIE
SNIKT!
YEEARR-RGH!!!
OH HOLY GOD.
DIE
FACIAL HAIR ISN'T SUPPOSED TO BLEED.
THANKS FOR HELPING US, FINEAS.
DON'T THANK ME. YOU TWO EARNED IT.
YOU HAVE JOINED THE BROTHERHOOD OF THE MOUSTACHE FIGHTING LEAGUE.
THAT'S OKAY. I ALREADY HAVE A BROTHER.
OKAY, FISH. I'M PUTTING YOU UNDER. WHEN YOU WAKE UP, YOUR BRAIN WILL CONTAIN ALL THE KNOWLEDGE OF STEPHEN HAWKING - THE GREATEST HTML CODER IN HISTORY.
CAN FISH HEAR US?
NOPE. THE ONLY THING HE'S DOING RIGHT NOW IS DREAMING OF FLYING TOASTERS.
EXCELLENT. THIS WAS GOOD THINKING, PHILLIP. NOW WE CAN REMOVE THE EXTRA PROGRAMMING THAT'S MAKING FISH GO ALL STEVEN SEAGAL.
NO. I DON'T THINK WE'LL BE DOING THAT.
I DON'T THINK WE'LL BE DOING THAT AT ALL.

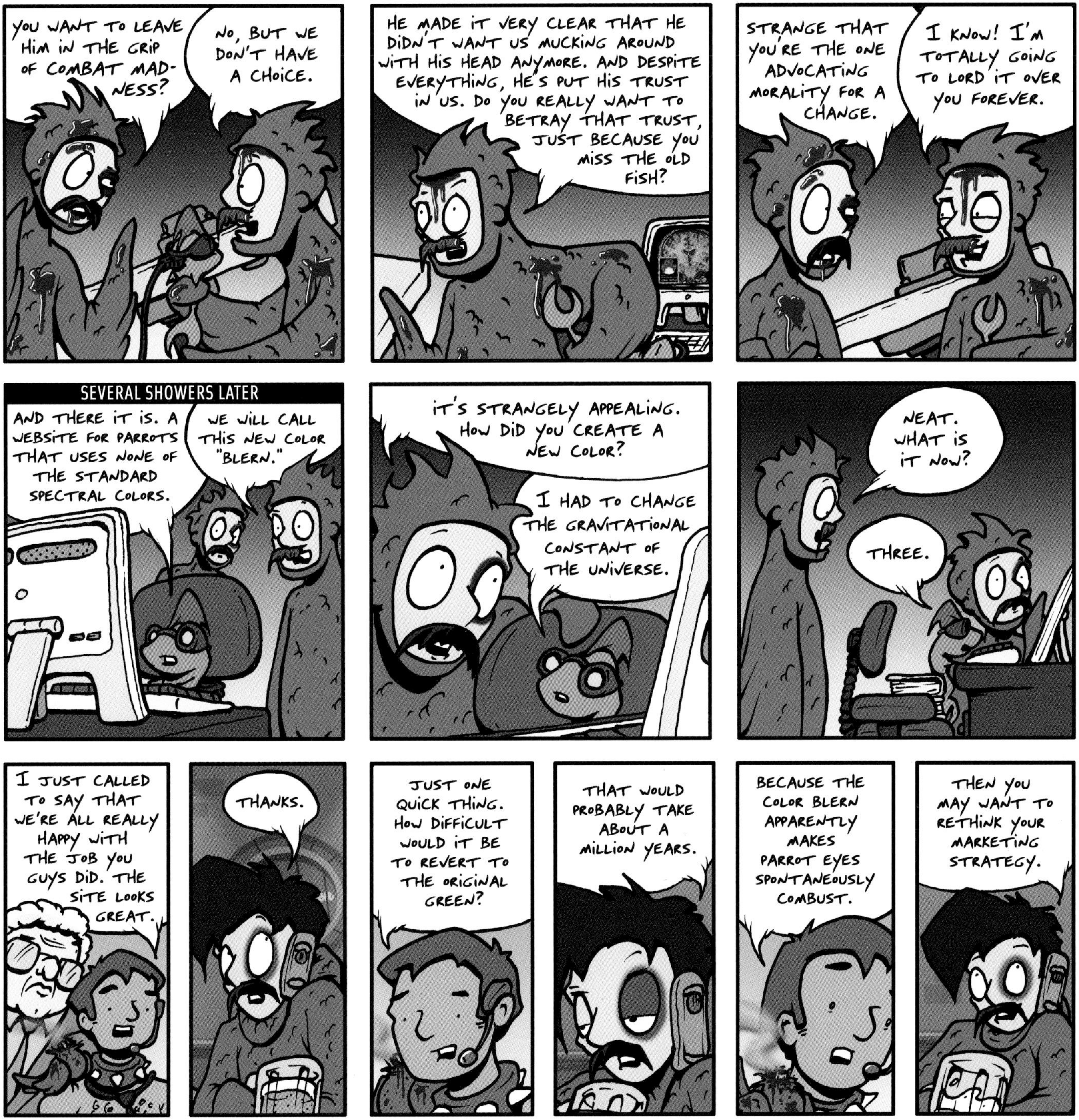
YOU WANT TO LEAVE HIM IN THE GRIP OF COMBAT MADNESS?
NO, BUT WE DON'T HAVE A CHOICE.
HE MADE IT VERY CLEAR THAT HE DIDN'T WANT US MUCKING AROUND WITH HIS HEAD ANYMORE. AND DESPITE EVERYTHING, HE'S PUT HIS TRUST IN US. DO YOU REALLY WANT TO BETRAY THAT TRUST, JUST BECAUSE YOU MISS THE OLD FISH?
STRANGE THAT YOU'RE THE ONE ADVOCATING MORALITY FOR A CHANGE.
I KNOW! I'M TOTALLY GOING TO LORD IT OVER YOU FOREVER.
SEVERAL SHOWERS LATER
AND THERE IT IS. A WEBSITE FOR PARROTS THAT USES NONE OF THE STANDARD SPECTRAL COLORS.
WE WILL CALL THIS NEW COLOR "BLERN."
IT'S STRANGELY APPEALING. HOW DID YOU CREATE A NEW COLOR?
I HAD TO CHANGE THE GRAVITATIONAL CONSTANT OF THE UNIVERSE.
NEAT. WHAT IS IT NOW?
THREE.
I JUST CALLED TO SAY THAT WE'RE ALL REALLY HAPPY WITH THE JOB YOU GUYS DID. THE SITE LOOKS GREAT.
THANKS.
JUST ONE QUICK THING. HOW DIFFICULT WOULD IT BE TO REVERT TO THE ORIGINAL GREEN?
THAT WOULD PROBABLY TAKE ABOUT A MILLION YEARS.
BECAUSE THE COLOR BLERN APPARENTLY MAKES PARROT EYES SPONTANEOUSLY COMBUST.
THEN YOU MAY WANT TO RETHINK YOUR MARKETING STRATEGY.

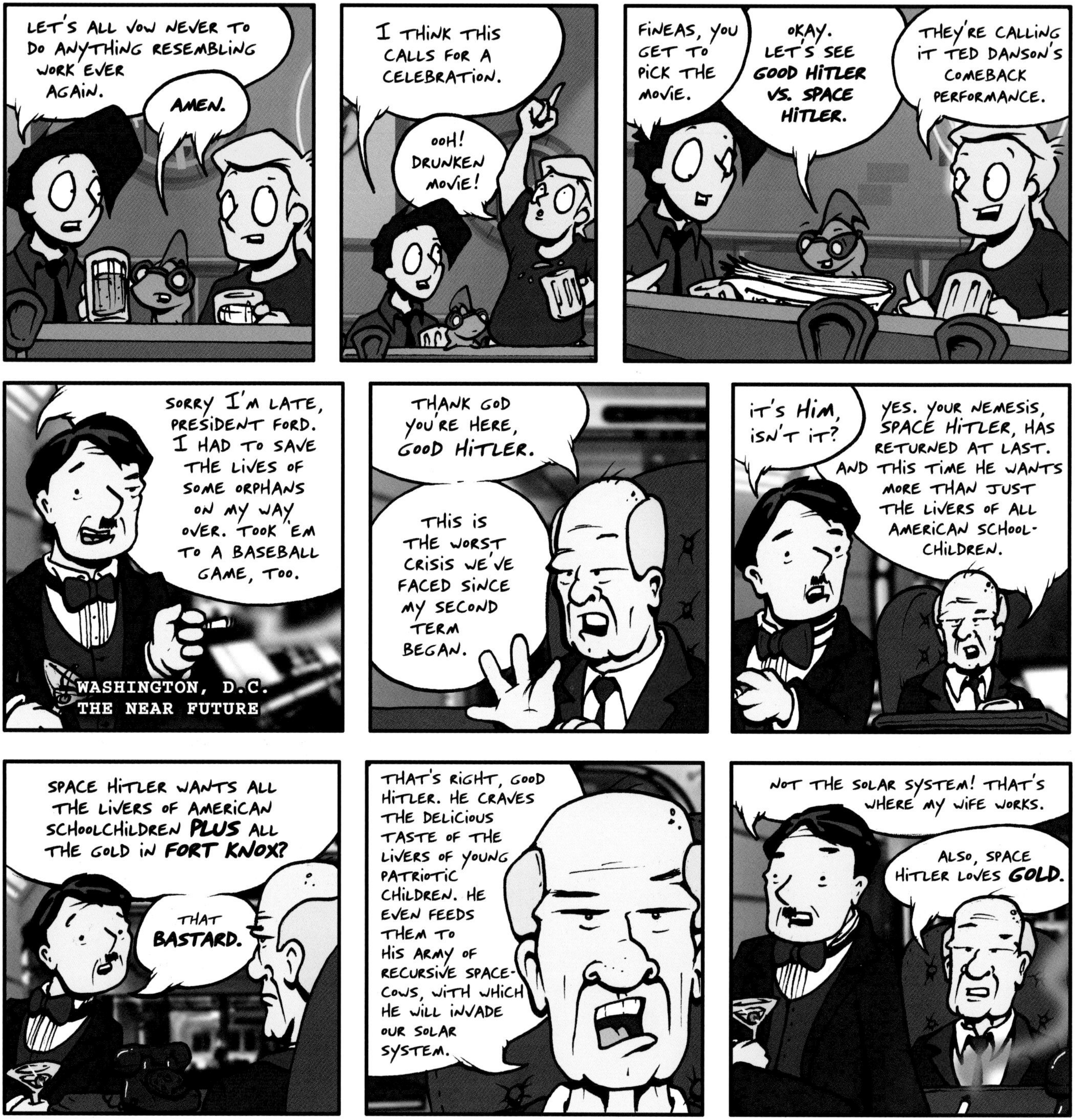
LET'S ALL VOW NEVER TO DO ANYTHING RESEMBLING WORK EVER AGAIN.
AMEN.
I THINK THIS CALLS FOR A CELEBRATION.
OOH! DRUNKEN MOVIE!
FINEAS, YOU GET TO PICK THE MOVIE.
OKAY. LET'S SEE GOOD HITLER VS. SPACE HITLER.
THEY'RE CALLING IT TED DANSON'S COMEBACK PERFORMANCE.
SORRY I'M LATE, PRESIDENT FORD. I HAD TO SAVE THE LIVES OF SOME ORPHANS ON MY WAY OVER. TOOK 'EM TO A BASEBALL GAME, TOO.
WASHINGTON, D.C. THE NEAR FUTURE
THANK GOD YOU'RE HERE, GOOD HITLER.
THIS IS THE WORST CRISIS WE'VE FACED SINCE MY SECOND TERM BEGAN.
IT'S HIM, ISN'T IT?
YES. YOUR NEMESIS, SPACE HITLER, HAS RETURNED AT LAST. AND THIS TIME HE WANTS MORE THAN JUST THE LIVERS OF ALL AMERICAN SCHOOL-CHILDREN.
SPACE HITLER WANTS ALL THE LIVERS OF AMERICAN SCHOOLCHILDREN PLUS ALL THE GOLD IN FORT KNOX?
THAT BASTARD.
THAT'S RIGHT, GOOD HITLER. HE CRAVES THE DELICIOUS TASTE OF THE LIVERS OF YOUNG PATRIOTIC CHILDREN. HE EVEN FEEDS THEM TO HIS ARMY OF RECURSIVE SPACE-COWS, WITH WHICH HE WILL INVADE OUR SOLAR SYSTEM.
NOT THE SOLAR SYSTEM! THAT'S WHERE MY WIFE WORKS.
ALSO, SPACE HITLER LOVES GOLD.

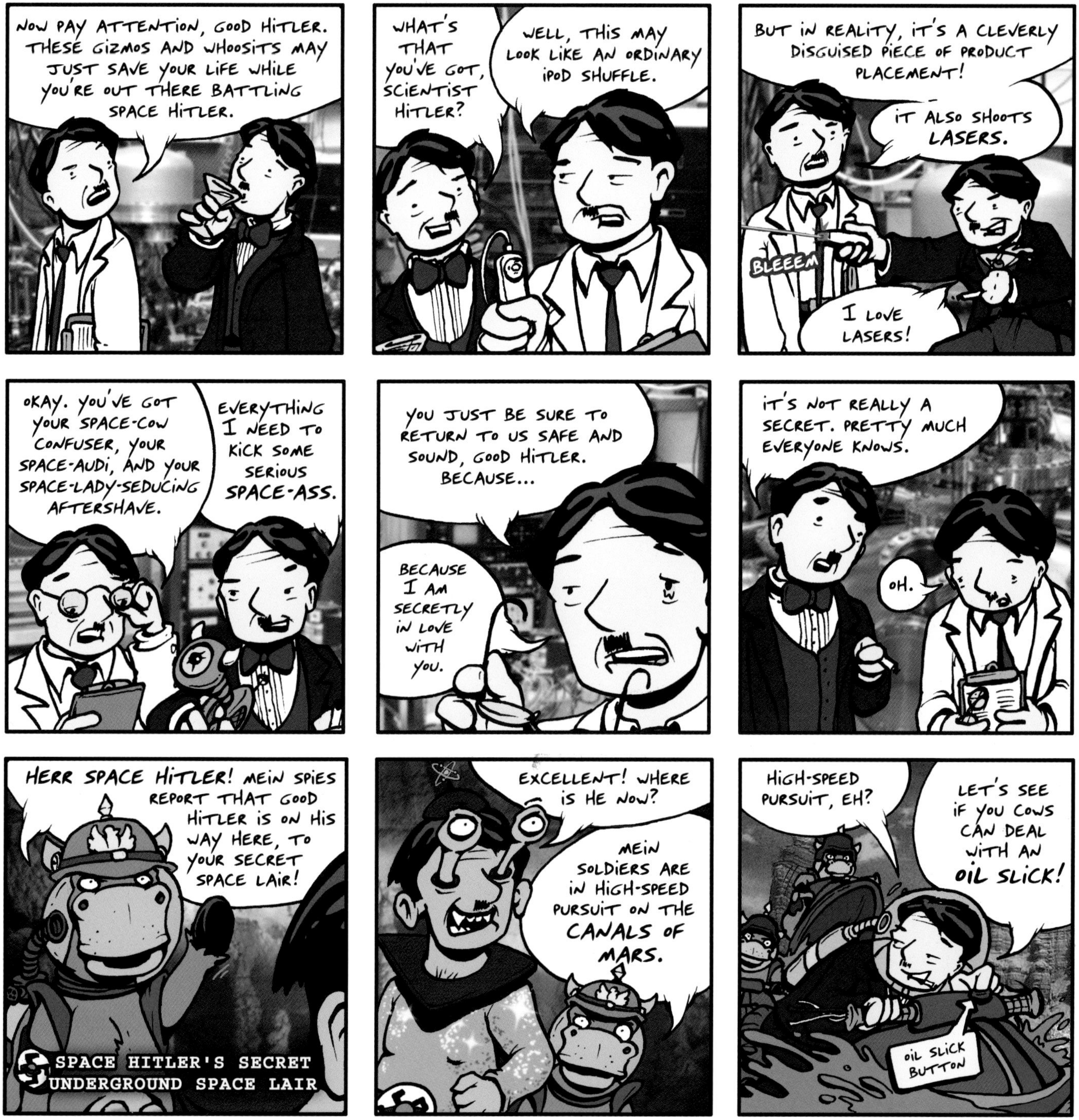
NOW PAY ATTENTION, GOOD HITLER. THESE GIZMOS AND WHOOSITS MAY JUST SAVE YOUR LIFE WHILE YOU'RE OUT THERE BATTLING SPACE HITLER.
WHAT'S THAT YOU'VE GOT, SCIENTIST HITLER?
WELL, THIS MAY LOOK LIKE AN ORDINARY iPOD SHUFFLE.
BUT IN REALITY, IT'S A CLEVERLY DISGUISED PIECE OF PRODUCT PLACEMENT!
IT ALSO SHOOTS LASERS.
BLEEEM
I LOVE LASERS!
OKAY. YOU'VE GOT YOUR SPACE-COW CONFUSER, YOUR SPACE-AUDI, AND YOUR SPACE-LADY-SEDUCING AFTERSHAVE.
EVERYTHING I NEED TO KICK SOME SERIOUS SPACE-ASS.
YOU JUST BE SURE TO RETURN TO US SAFE AND SOUND, GOOD HITLER. BECAUSE...
BECAUSE I AM SECRETLY IN LOVE WITH YOU.
IT'S NOT REALLY A SECRET. PRETTY MUCH EVERYONE KNOWS.
OH.
HERR SPACE HITLER! MEIN SPIES REPORT THAT GOOD HITLER IS ON HIS WAY HERE, TO YOUR SECRET SPACE LAIR!
SPACE HITLER'S SECRET UNDERGROUND SPACE LAIR
EXCELLENT! WHERE IS HE NOW?
MEIN SOLDIERS ARE IN HIGH-SPEED PURSUIT ON THE CANALS OF MARS.
HIGH-SPEED PURSUIT, EH?
LET'S SEE IF YOU COWS CAN DEAL WITH AN OIL SLICK!
OIL SLICK BUTTON

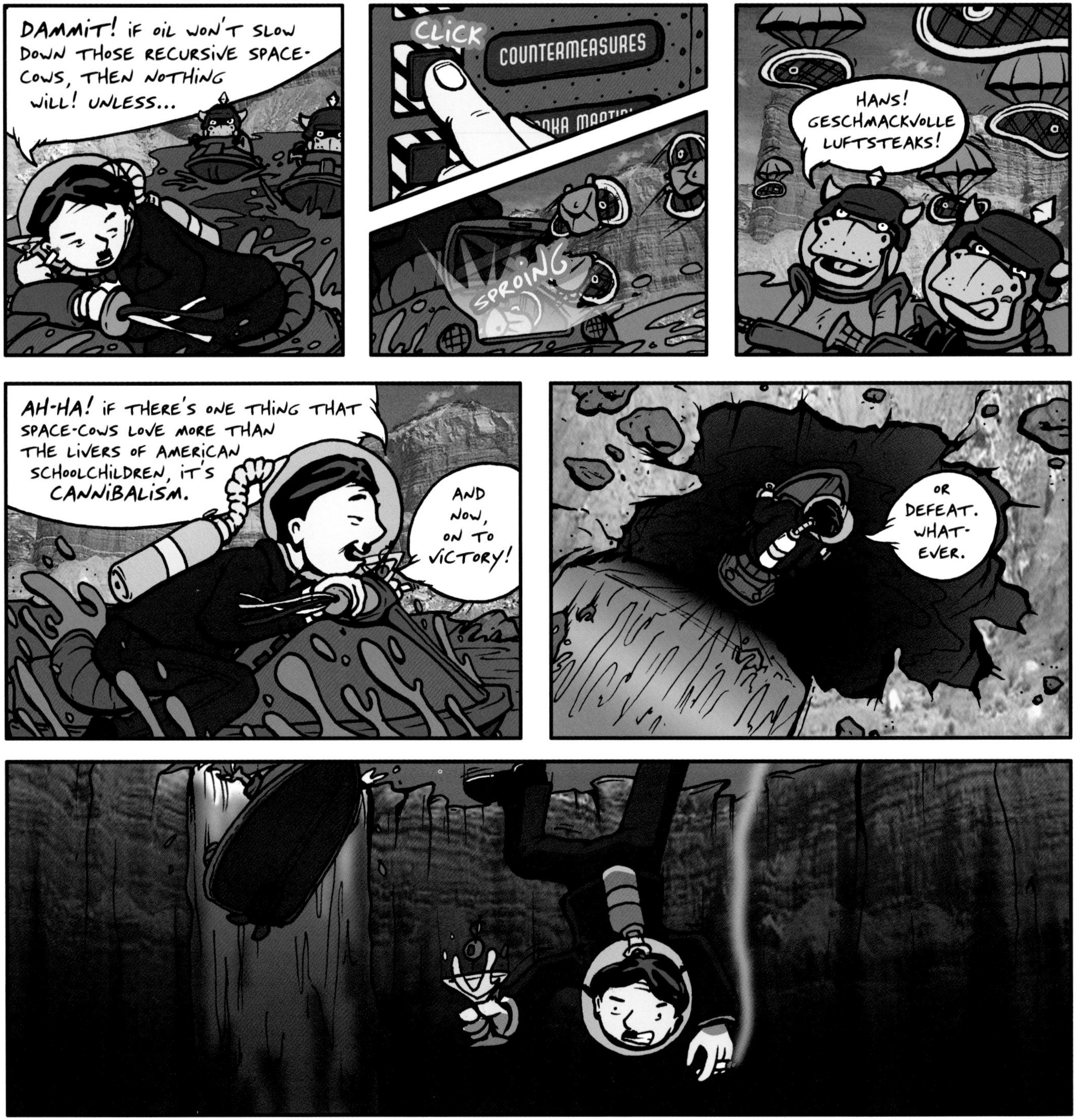
DAMMIT! IF OIL WON'T SLOW DOWN THOSE RECURSIVE SPACE-COWS, THEN NOTHING WILL! UNLESS...
CLICK
COUNTERMEASURES
SPROING
HANS! GESCHMACKVOLLE LUFTSTEAKS!
AH-HA! IF THERE'S ONE THING THAT SPACE-COWS LOVE MORE THAN THE LIVERS OF AMERICAN SCHOOLCHILDREN, IT'S CANNIBALISM.
AND NOW, ON TO VICTORY!
OR DEFEAT. WHAT-EVER.

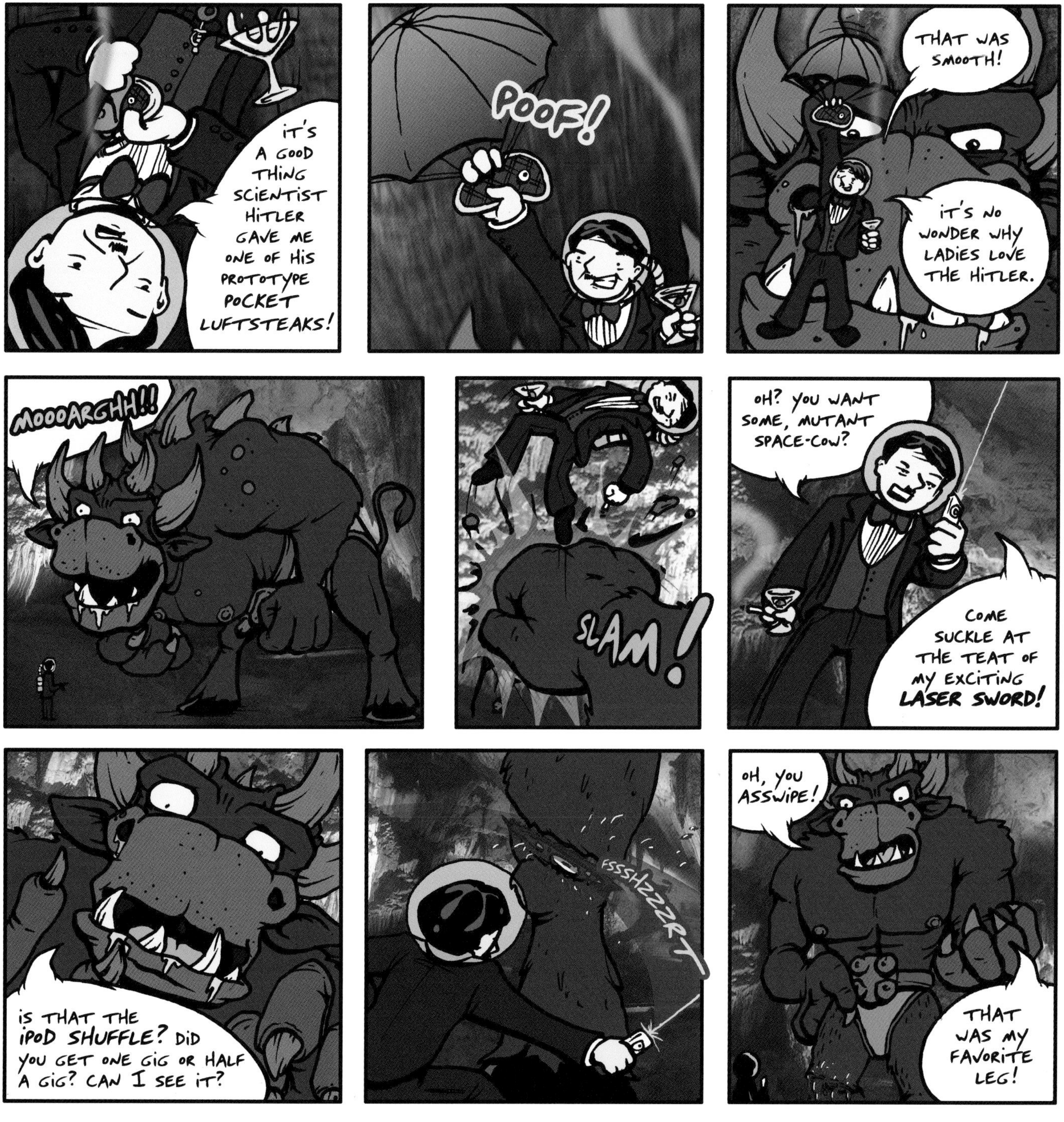
IT'S A GOOD THING SCIENTIST HITLER GAVE ME ONE OF HIS PROTOTYPE POCKET LUFTSTEAKS!
POOF!
THAT WAS SMOOTH!
IT'S NO WONDER WHY LADIES LOVE THE HITLER.
MOOOARGHH!!
SLAM!
OH? YOU WANT SOME, MUTANT SPACE-COW?
COME SUCKLE AT THE TEAT OF MY EXCITING LASER SWORD!
IS THAT THE IPOD SHUFFLE? DID YOU GET ONE GIG OR HALF A GIG? CAN I SEE IT?
FSSSHZZZRT
OH, YOU ASSWIPE!
THAT WAS MY FAVORITE LEG!

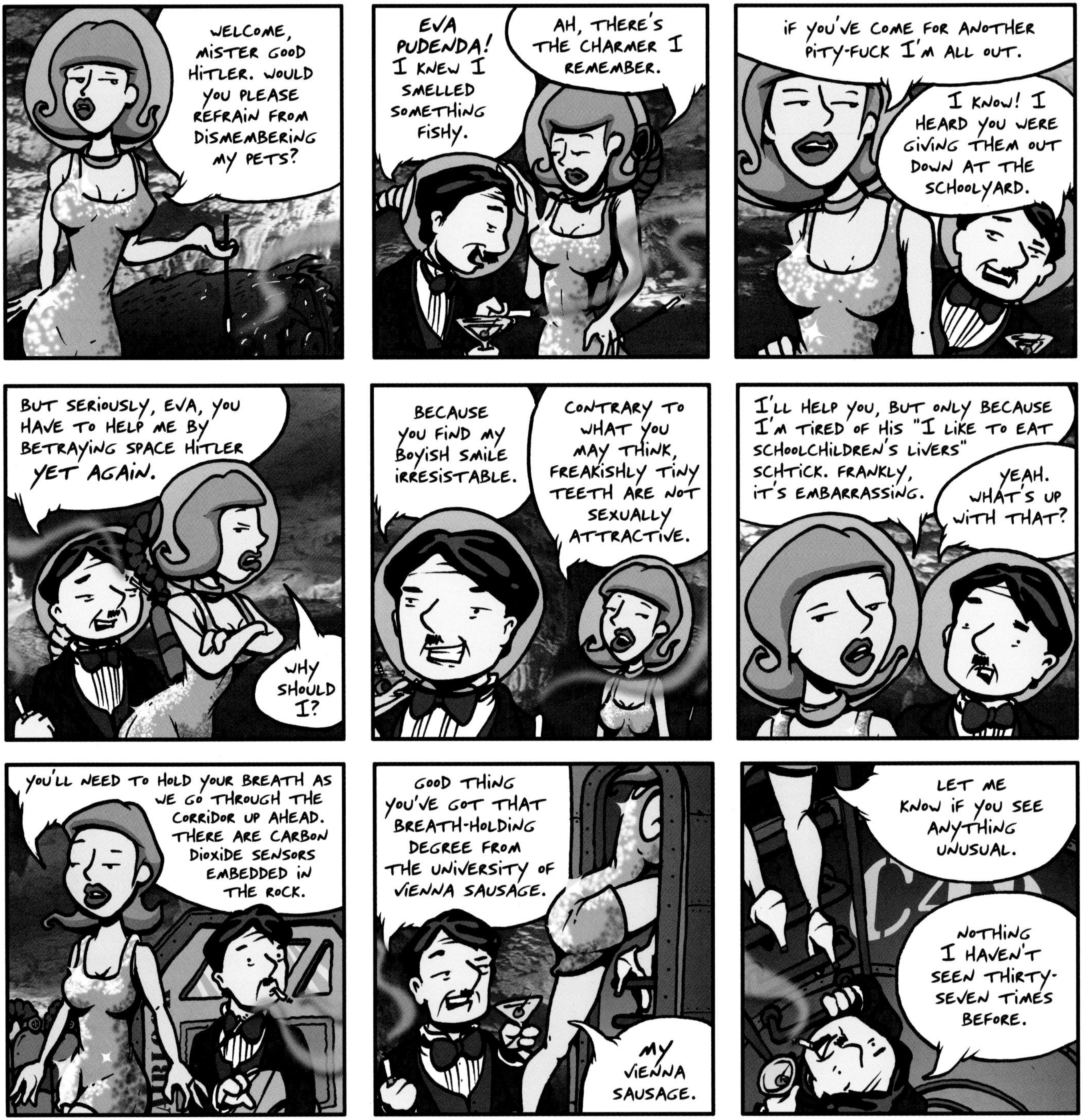

WELCOME, MISTER GOOD HITLER. WOULD YOU PLEASE REFRAIN FROM DISMEMBERING MY PETS?
EVA PUDENDA! I KNEW I SMELLED SOMETHING FISHY.
AH, THERE'S THE CHARMER I REMEMBER.
IF YOU'VE COME FOR ANOTHER PITY-FUCK I'M ALL OUT.
I KNOW! I HEARD YOU WERE GIVING THEM OUT DOWN AT THE SCHOOLYARD.
BUT SERIOUSLY, EVA, YOU HAVE TO HELP ME BY BETRAYING SPACE HITLER YET AGAIN.
WHY SHOULD I?
BECAUSE YOU FIND MY BOYISH SMILE IRRESISTABLE.
CONTRARY TO WHAT YOU MAY THINK, FREAKISHLY TINY TEETH ARE NOT SEXUALLY ATTRACTIVE.
I'LL HELP YOU, BUT ONLY BECAUSE I'M TIRED OF HIS "I LIKE TO EAT SCHOOLCHILDREN'S LIVERS" SCHTICK. FRANKLY, IT'S EMBARRASSING.
YEAH. WHAT'S UP WITH THAT?
YOU'LL NEED TO HOLD YOUR BREATH AS WE GO THROUGH THE CORRIDOR UP AHEAD. THERE ARE CARBON DIOXIDE SENSORS EMBEDDED IN THE ROCK.
GOOD THING YOU'VE GOT THAT BREATH-HOLDING DEGREE FROM THE UNIVERSITY OF VIENNA SAUSAGE.
MY VIENNA SAUSAGE.
LET ME KNOW IF YOU SEE ANYTHING UNUSUAL.
NOTHING I HAVEN'T SEEN THIRTY-SEVEN TIMES BEFORE.

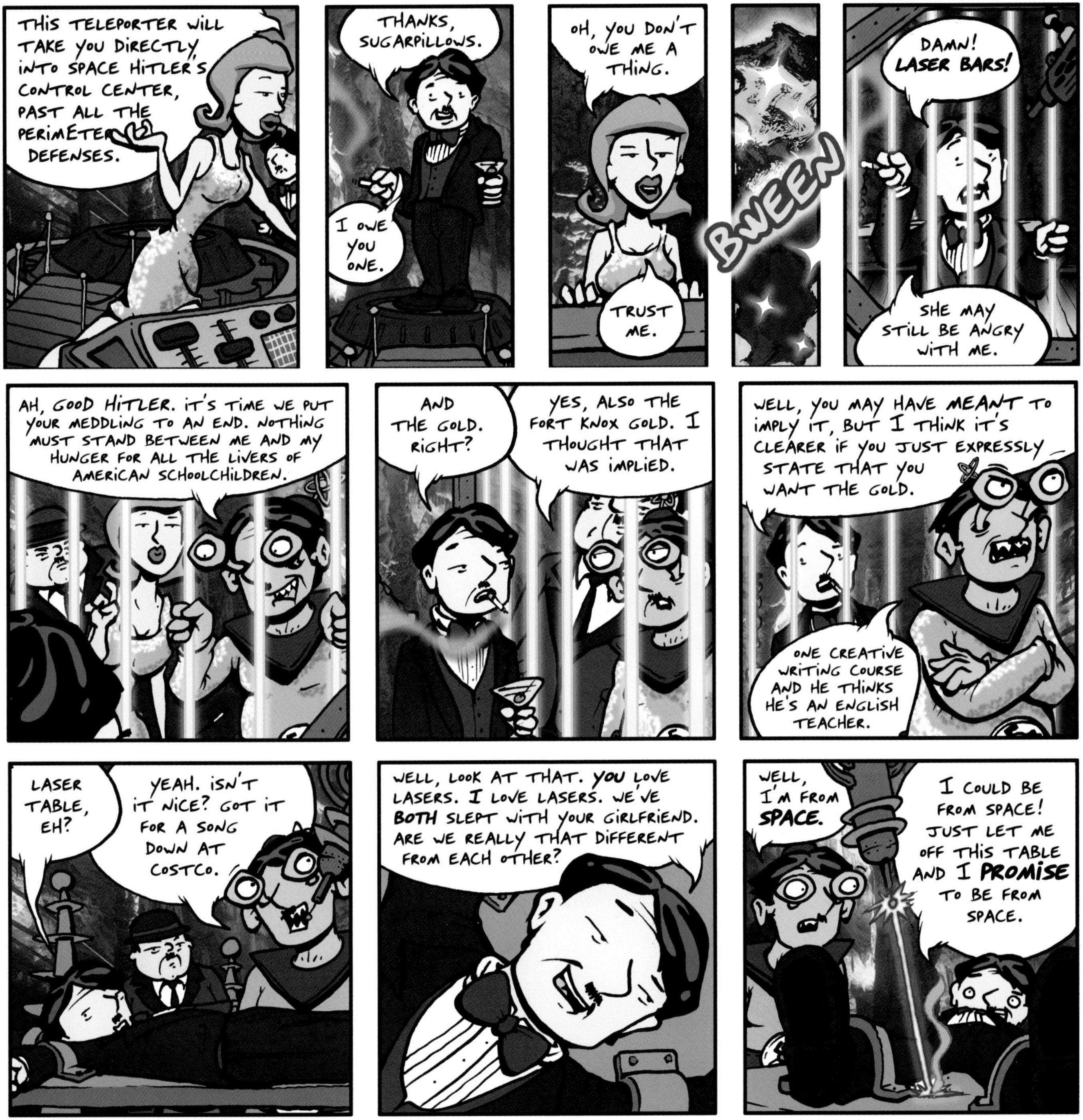
THIS TELEPORTER WILL TAKE YOU DIRECTLY INTO SPACE HITLER'S CONTROL CENTER, PAST ALL THE PERIMETER DEFENSES.
THANKS, SUGARPILLOWS.
I OWE YOU ONE.
OH, YOU DON'T OWE ME A THING.
TRUST ME.
BWEEN
DAMN! LASER BARS!
SHE MAY STILL BE ANGRY WITH ME.
AH, GOOD HITLER. IT'S TIME WE PUT YOUR MEDDLING TO AN END. NOTHING MUST STAND BETWEEN ME AND MY HUNGER FOR ALL THE LIVERS OF AMERICAN SCHOOLCHILDREN.
AND THE GOLD. RIGHT?
YES, ALSO THE FORT KNOX GOLD. I THOUGHT THAT WAS IMPLIED.
WELL, YOU MAY HAVE MEANT TO IMPLY IT, BUT I THINK IT'S CLEARER IF YOU JUST EXPRESSLY STATE THAT YOU WANT THE GOLD.
ONE CREATIVE WRITING COURSE AND HE THINKS HE'S AN ENGLISH TEACHER.
LASER TABLE, EH?
YEAH. ISN'T IT NICE? GOT IT FOR A SONG DOWN AT COSTCO.
WELL, LOOK AT THAT. YOU LOVE LASERS. I LOVE LASERS. WE'VE BOTH SLEPT WITH YOUR GIRLFRIEND. ARE WE REALLY THAT DIFFERENT FROM EACH OTHER?
WELL, I'M FROM SPACE.
I COULD BE FROM SPACE! JUST LET ME OFF THIS TABLE AND I PROMISE TO BE FROM SPACE.

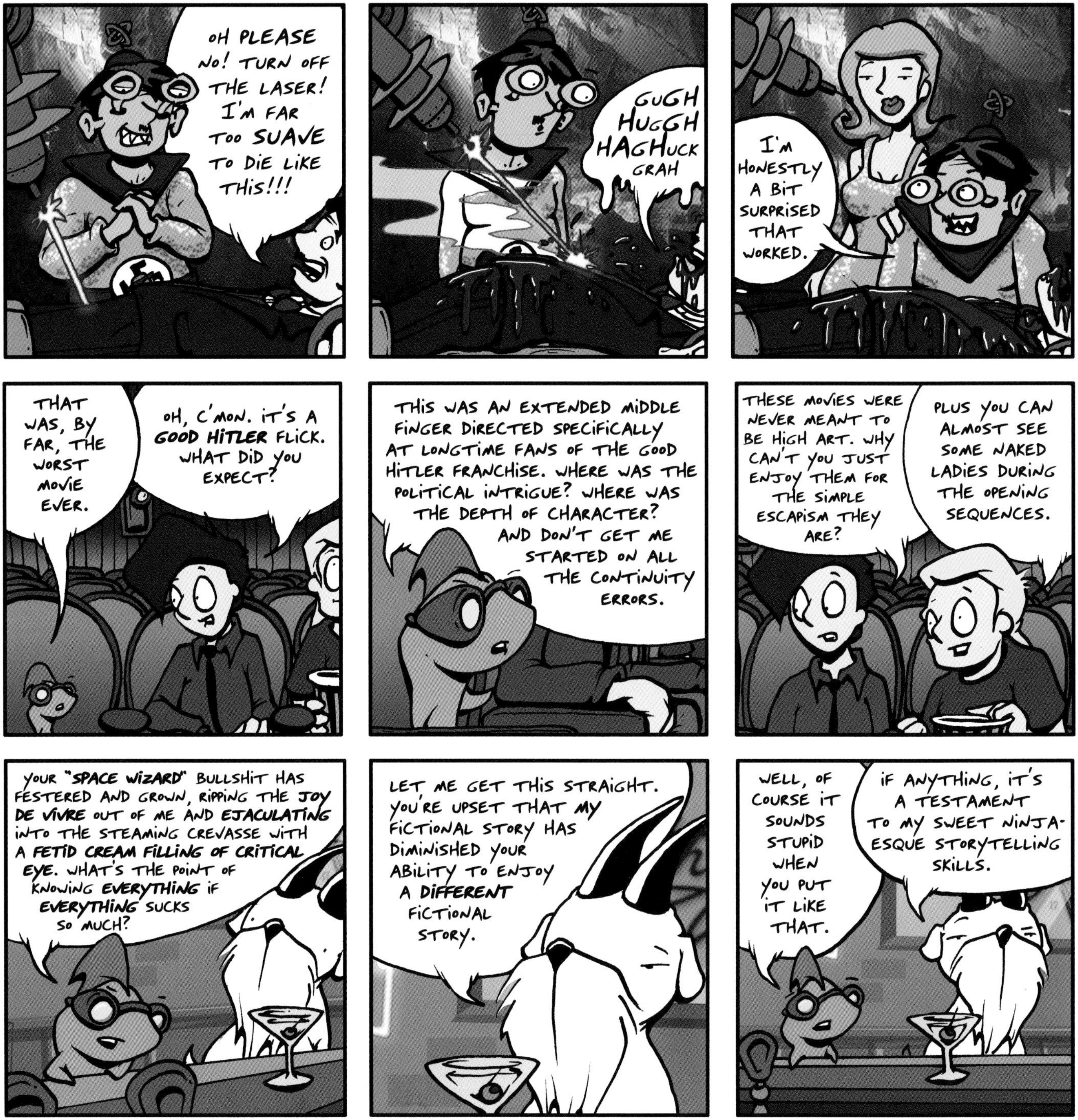
OH PLEASE NO! TURN OFF THE LASER! I'M FAR TOO SUAVE TO DIE LIKE THIS!!!
GUGH HUGGH HAGHUCK GRAH
I'M HONESTLY A BIT SURPRISED THAT WORKED.
THAT WAS, BY FAR, THE WORST MOVIE EVER.
OH, C'MON. IT'S A GOOD HITLER FLICK. WHAT DID YOU EXPECT?
THIS WAS AN EXTENDED MIDDLE FINGER DIRECTED SPECIFICALLY AT LONGTIME FANS OF THE GOOD HITLER FRANCHISE. WHERE WAS THE POLITICAL INTRIGUE? WHERE WAS THE DEPTH OF CHARACTER? AND DON'T GET ME STARTED ON ALL THE CONTINUITY ERRORS.
THESE MOVIES WERE NEVER MEANT TO BE HIGH ART. WHY CAN'T YOU JUST ENJOY THEM FOR THE SIMPLE ESCAPISM THEY ARE?
PLUS YOU CAN ALMOST SEE SOME NAKED LADIES DURING THE OPENING SEQUENCES.
YOUR "SPACE WIZARD" BULLSHIT HAS FESTERED AND GROWN, RIPPING THE JOY DE VIVRE OUT OF ME AND EJACULATING INTO THE STEAMING CREVASSE WITH A FETID CREAM FILLING OF CRITICAL EYE. WHAT'S THE POINT OF KNOWING EVERYTHING IF EVERYTHING SUCKS SO MUCH?
LET ME GET THIS STRAIGHT. YOU'RE UPSET THAT MY FICTIONAL STORY HAS DIMINISHED YOUR ABILITY TO ENJOY A DIFFERENT FICTIONAL STORY.
WELL, OF COURSE IT SOUNDS STUPID WHEN YOU PUT IT LIKE THAT.
IF ANYTHING, IT'S A TESTAMENT TO MY SWEET NINJA-ESQUE STORYTELLING SKILLS.

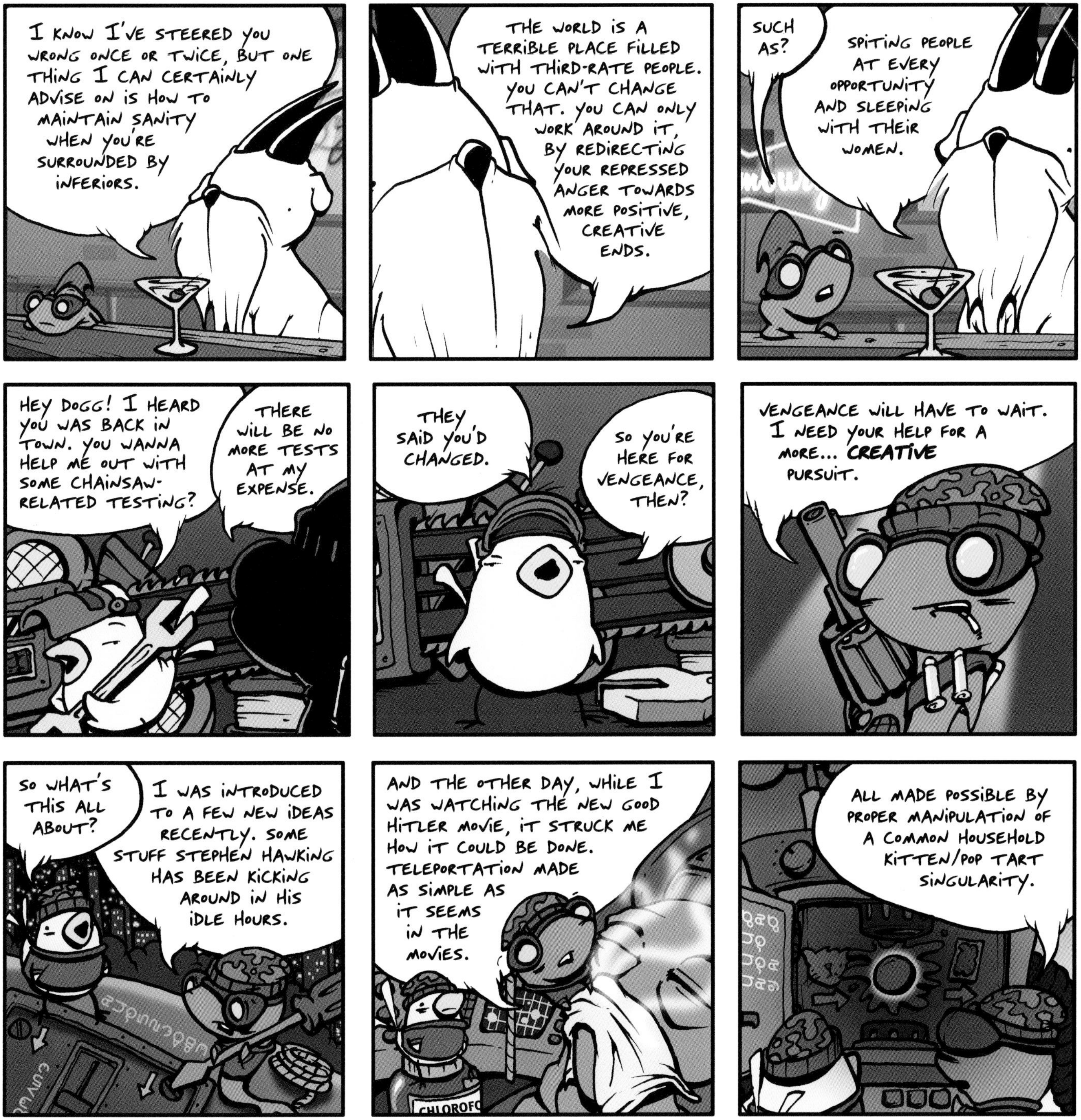
I KNOW I'VE STEERED YOU WRONG ONCE OR TWICE, BUT ONE THING I CAN CERTAINLY ADVISE ON IS HOW TO MAINTAIN SANITY WHEN YOU'RE SURROUNDED BY INFERIORS.
THE WORLD IS A TERRIBLE PLACE FILLED WITH THIRD-RATE PEOPLE. YOU CAN'T CHANGE THAT. YOU CAN ONLY WORK AROUND IT, BY REDIRECTING YOUR REPRESSED ANGER TOWARDS MORE POSITIVE, CREATIVE ENDS.
SUCH AS?
SPITING PEOPLE AT EVERY OPPORTUNITY AND SLEEPING WITH THEIR WOMEN.
HEY DOGG! I HEARD YOU WAS BACK IN TOWN. YOU WANNA HELP ME OUT WITH SOME CHAINSAW-RELATED TESTING?
THERE WILL BE NO MORE TESTS AT MY EXPENSE.
THEY SAID YOU'D CHANGED.
SO YOU'RE HERE FOR VENGEANCE, THEN?
VENGEANCE WILL HAVE TO WAIT. I NEED YOUR HELP FOR A MORE... **CREATIVE** PURSUIT.
SO WHAT'S THIS ALL ABOUT?
I WAS INTRODUCED TO A FEW NEW IDEAS RECENTLY. SOME STUFF STEPHEN HAWKING HAS BEEN KICKING AROUND IN HIS IDLE HOURS.
AND THE OTHER DAY, WHILE I WAS WATCHING THE NEW GOOD HITLER MOVIE, IT STRUCK ME HOW IT COULD BE DONE. TELEPORTATION MADE AS SIMPLE AS IT SEEMS IN THE MOVIES.
CHLOROFO
ALL MADE POSSIBLE BY PROPER MANIPULATION OF A COMMON HOUSEHOLD KITTEN/POP TART SINGULARITY.

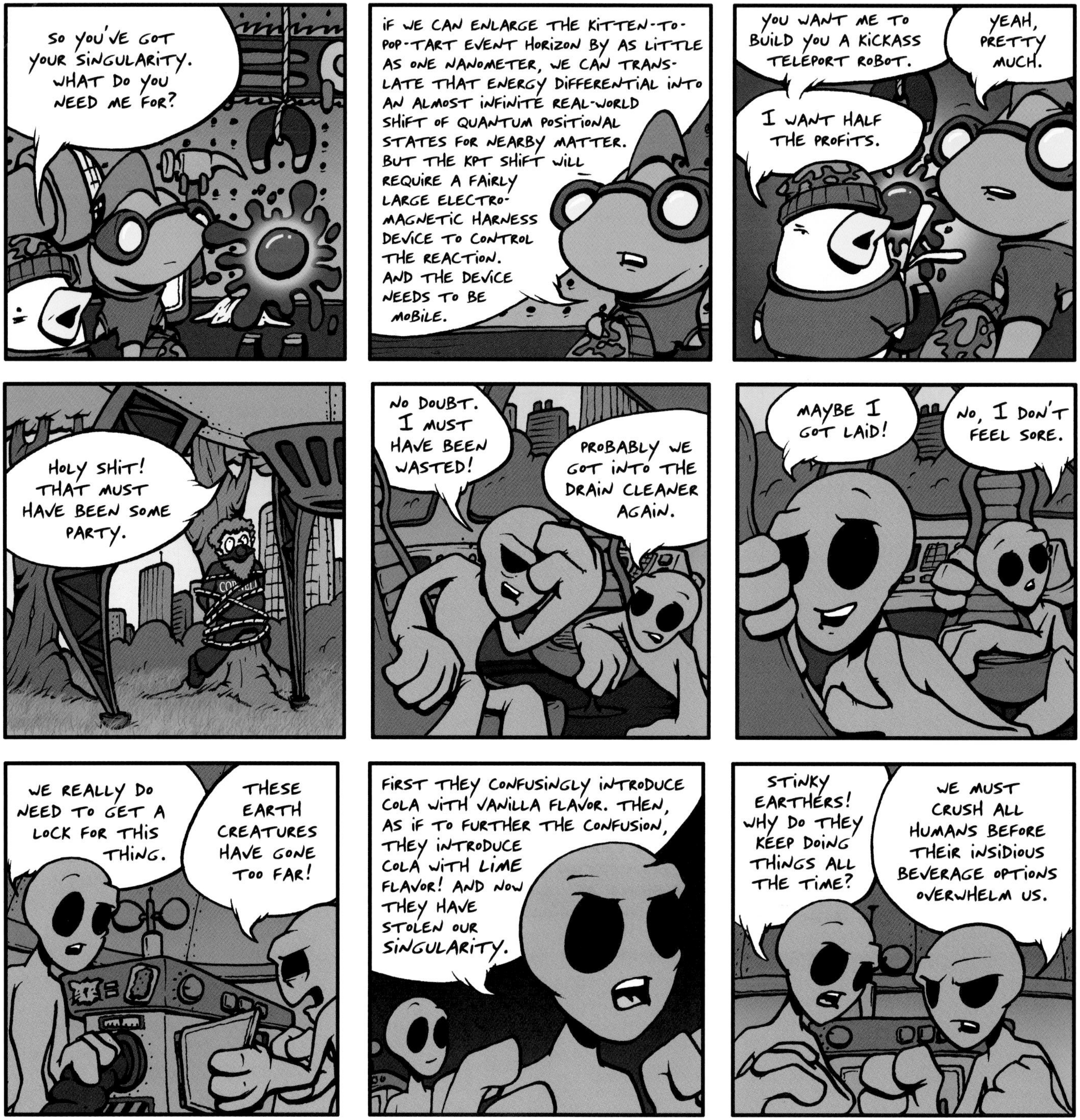
SO YOU'VE GOT YOUR SINGULARITY. WHAT DO YOU NEED ME FOR?
IF WE CAN ENLARGE THE KITTEN-TO-POP-TART EVENT HORIZON BY AS LITTLE AS ONE NANOMETER, WE CAN TRANSLATE THAT ENERGY DIFFERENTIAL INTO AN ALMOST INFINITE REAL-WORLD SHIFT OF QUANTUM POSITIONAL STATES FOR NEARBY MATTER. BUT THE KPT SHIFT WILL REQUIRE A FAIRLY LARGE ELECTROMAGNETIC HARNESS DEVICE TO CONTROL THE REACTION. AND THE DEVICE NEEDS TO BE MOBILE.
YOU WANT ME TO BUILD YOU A KICKASS TELEPORT ROBOT.
YEAH, PRETTY MUCH.
I WANT HALF THE PROFITS.
HOLY SHIT! THAT MUST HAVE BEEN SOME PARTY.
NO DOUBT. I MUST HAVE BEEN WASTED!
PROBABLY WE GOT INTO THE DRAIN CLEANER AGAIN.
MAYBE I GOT LAID!
NO, I DON'T FEEL SORE.
WE REALLY DO NEED TO GET A LOCK FOR THIS THING.
THESE EARTH CREATURES HAVE GONE TOO FAR!
FIRST THEY CONFUSINGLY INTRODUCE COLA WITH VANILLA FLAVOR. THEN, AS IF TO FURTHER THE CONFUSION, THEY INTRODUCE COLA WITH LIME FLAVOR! AND NOW THEY HAVE STOLEN OUR SINGULARITY.
STINKY EARTHERS! WHY DO THEY KEEP DOING THINGS ALL THE TIME?
WE MUST CRUSH ALL HUMANS BEFORE THEIR INSIDIOUS BEVERAGE OPTIONS OVERWHELM US.

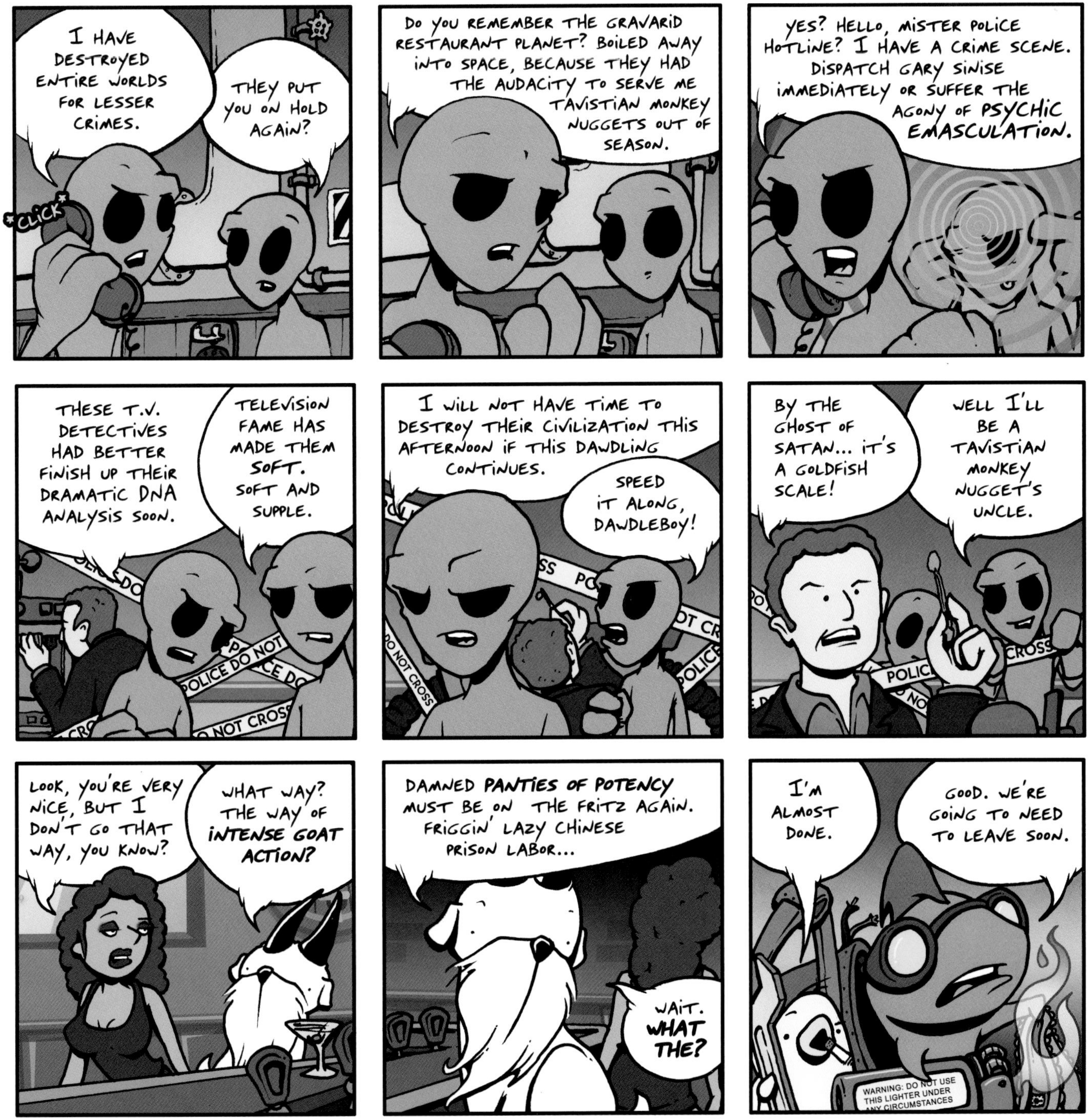

CLICK
I HAVE DESTROYED ENTIRE WORLDS FOR LESSER CRIMES.
THEY PUT YOU ON HOLD AGAIN?
DO YOU REMEMBER THE GRAVARID RESTAURANT PLANET? BOILED AWAY INTO SPACE, BECAUSE THEY HAD THE AUDACITY TO SERVE ME TAVISTIAN MONKEY NUGGETS OUT OF SEASON.
YES? HELLO, MISTER POLICE HOTLINE? I HAVE A CRIME SCENE. DISPATCH GARY SINISE IMMEDIATELY OR SUFFER THE AGONY OF PSYCHIC EMASCULATION.
THESE T.V. DETECTIVES HAD BETTER FINISH UP THEIR DRAMATIC DNA ANALYSIS SOON.
TELEVISION FAME HAS MADE THEM SOFT. SOFT AND SUPPLE.
POLICE DO NOT CROSS
I WILL NOT HAVE TIME TO DESTROY THEIR CIVILIZATION THIS AFTERNOON IF THIS DAWDLING CONTINUES.
SPEED IT ALONG, DAWDLEBOY!
BY THE GHOST OF SATAN... IT'S A GOLDFISH SCALE!
WELL I'LL BE A TAVISTIAN MONKEY NUGGET'S UNCLE.
LOOK, YOU'RE VERY NICE, BUT I DON'T GO THAT WAY, YOU KNOW?
WHAT WAY? THE WAY OF INTENSE GOAT ACTION?
DAMNED PANTIES OF POTENCY MUST BE ON THE FRITZ AGAIN. FRIGGIN' LAZY CHINESE PRISON LABOR...
WAIT. WHAT THE?
I'M ALMOST DONE.
GOOD. WE'RE GOING TO NEED TO LEAVE SOON.
WARNING: DO NOT USE THIS LIGHTER UNDER ANY CIRCUMSTANCES

WHERE IS THAT DAMNED SINGULARITY-STEALING SALAMANDER?
HE'S A FISH.
FISHES AREN'T ALLITERATIVE.
IF YOU'RE LOOKING FOR THAT TWO-TIMING THIEF WITH THE ERECTOR-SET NOGGIN, GET IN LINE.
WHAT LINE?
THE LINE TO BEAT HIS SKULL IN WITH A NAIL-STUDDED BAT.
HOW LONG, EXACTLY, IS THIS LINE?
SO HOW DO WE DE-BONE THE BASTARD IF WE DON'T KNOW WHERE HE IS?
IF YOU'VE GOT A SPACESHIP, I'VE GOT A PLAN.
NOW THIS IS WHAT I CALL A PLAN.
KZZZOK
KZZZOK
OOH! DOUBLE-WIDE STROLLER! TWENTY POINTS!
KZZZOK
SO HOW DOES THE REST OF THIS PLAN GO?
WE KEEP DESTROYING THINGS UNTIL ONE OF THOSE THINGS IS THE FISH.
"THINGS" HAD BETTER NOT INCLUDE ALL THE ICE CREAM, BECAUSE SOMEONE STILL OWES ME A CONE.
KZZZOK
OH, NOT THAT. DON'T BLOW THAT UP.
THEY JUST REBUILT THAT.
KZZZOK

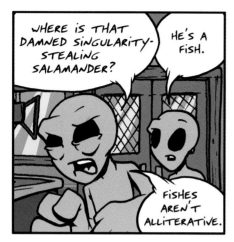

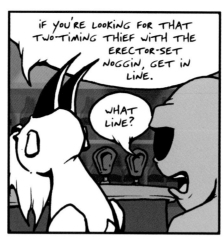

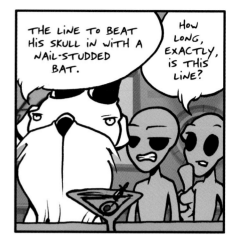

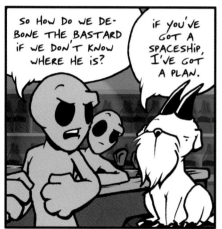

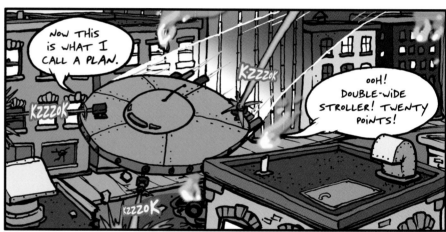

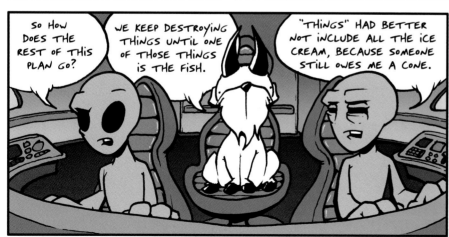

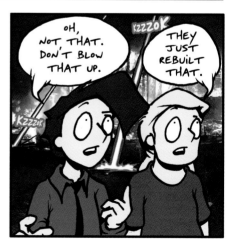

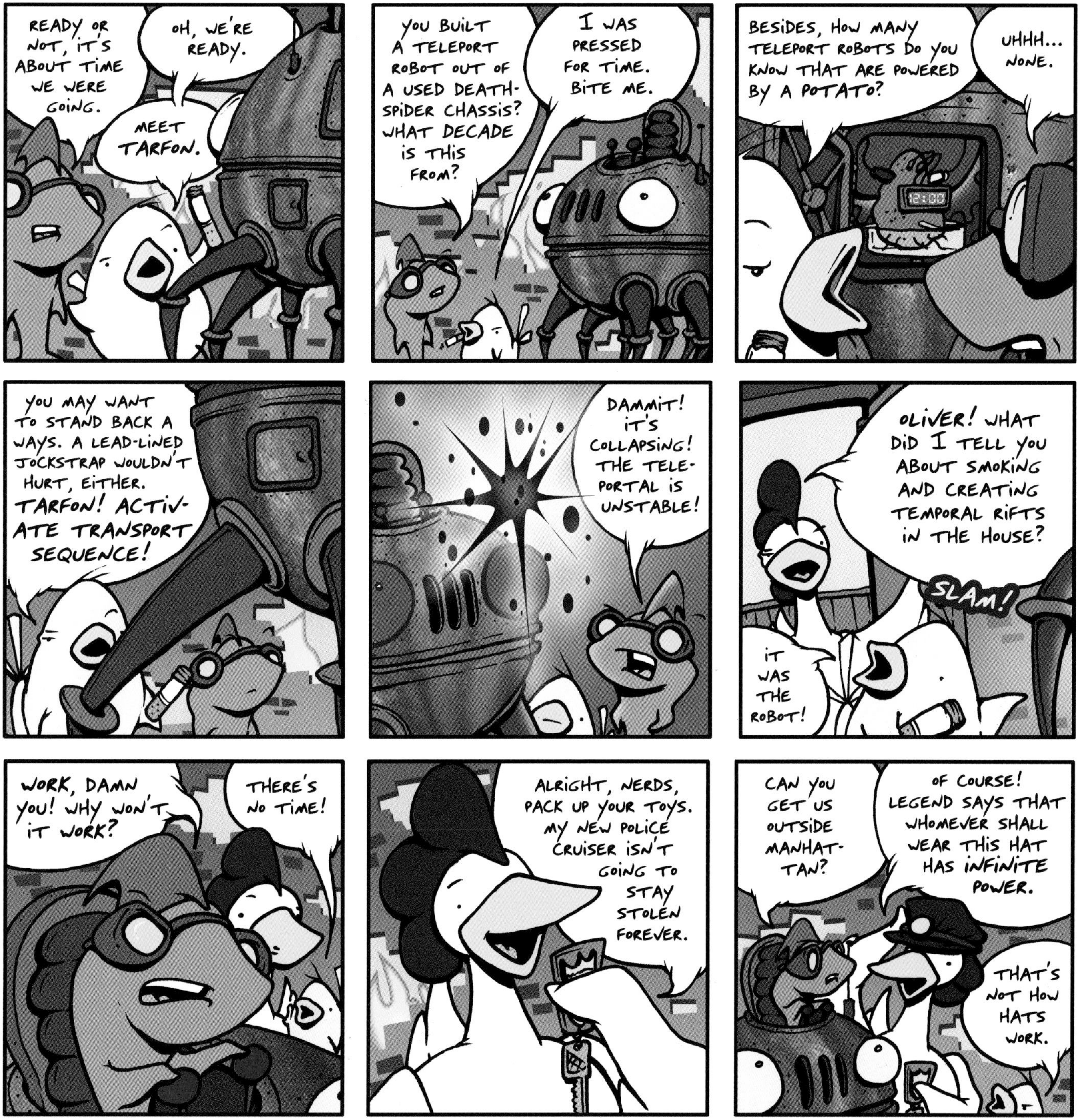
READY OR NOT, IT'S ABOUT TIME WE WERE GOING.
OH, WE'RE READY.
MEET TARFON.
YOU BUILT A TELEPORT ROBOT OUT OF A USED DEATH-SPIDER CHASSIS? WHAT DECADE IS THIS FROM?
I WAS PRESSED FOR TIME. BITE ME.
BESIDES, HOW MANY TELEPORT ROBOTS DO YOU KNOW THAT ARE POWERED BY A POTATO?
UHHH... NONE.
12:00
YOU MAY WANT TO STAND BACK A WAYS. A LEAD-LINED JOCKSTRAP WOULDN'T HURT, EITHER. TARFON! ACTIVATE TRANSPORT SEQUENCE!
DAMMIT! IT'S COLLAPSING! THE TELE-PORTAL IS UNSTABLE!
OLIVER! WHAT DID I TELL YOU ABOUT SMOKING AND CREATING TEMPORAL RIFTS IN THE HOUSE?
SLAM!
IT WAS THE ROBOT!
WORK, DAMN YOU! WHY WON'T IT WORK?
THERE'S NO TIME!
ALRIGHT, NERDS, PACK UP YOUR TOYS. MY NEW POLICE CRUISER ISN'T GOING TO STAY STOLEN FOREVER.
CAN YOU GET US OUTSIDE MANHAT-TAN?
OF COURSE! LEGEND SAYS THAT WHOMEVER SHALL WEAR THIS HAT HAS INFINITE POWER.
THAT'S NOT HOW HATS WORK.

MAYBE THE MAGNETS AREN'T ALIGNED RIGHT.

THEN WE WOULDN'T SEE ANYTHING AT ALL. IT'S AS IF THE TELEPORT RIFTS ARE HEALING THEMSELVES.

CAN YOU KEEP THE DORK TALK DOWN FOR FIFTEEN MORE MINUTES? WE'RE ALMOST THERE.

NYPD

TP N TURNPIKE J

EXIT 9C

Hell

DIABLO! THIS IS A SURPRISE!

SATAN, I'D LIKE YOU TO MEET MY SON OLIVER, HIS FRIEND FINEAS, AND THEIR TELEPORT ROBOT TARFON.

STAN

THIS AIN'T NO SATAN! SATAN GOT RED SKIN AND 100% LESS PLAID SHIRTS.

YOU'RE RIGHT. I'M NOT REALLY SATAN.

THAT'S EXACTLY THE SORT OF CLEVER MISDIRECTION THAT SATAN WOULD EMPLOY.

I'M TRYING TO THINK OF WAYS IN WHICH THIS IS AN IMPROVEMENT OVER BEING BURNED ALIVE IN THE FLAMING RUINS OF MANHATTAN.

IT'S GOOD TO MEET ALL OF YOU. ESPECIALLY YOU, OLIVER! YOU'RE THE SPITTING IMAGE OF YOUR DAD. SO WHAT BRINGS YOU BY? I DON'T GET MUCH COMPANY SINCE I MOVED OUT TO JERSEY.

STAN

TWO ALIENS AND A GOAT BURNED DOWN OUR CITY BECAUSE WE STOLE THEIR PANTIES AND SINGULARITIES.

SO YOU'LL BE STAYING FOR DINNER.

DINNER? DIDN'T YOU HEAR THE CHICKEN? WE'VE GOT A HOMICIDAL GOAT WITH A LASER-ENCRUSTED FLYING SAUCER AFTER US.

JUST CHEESECAKE, THEN.

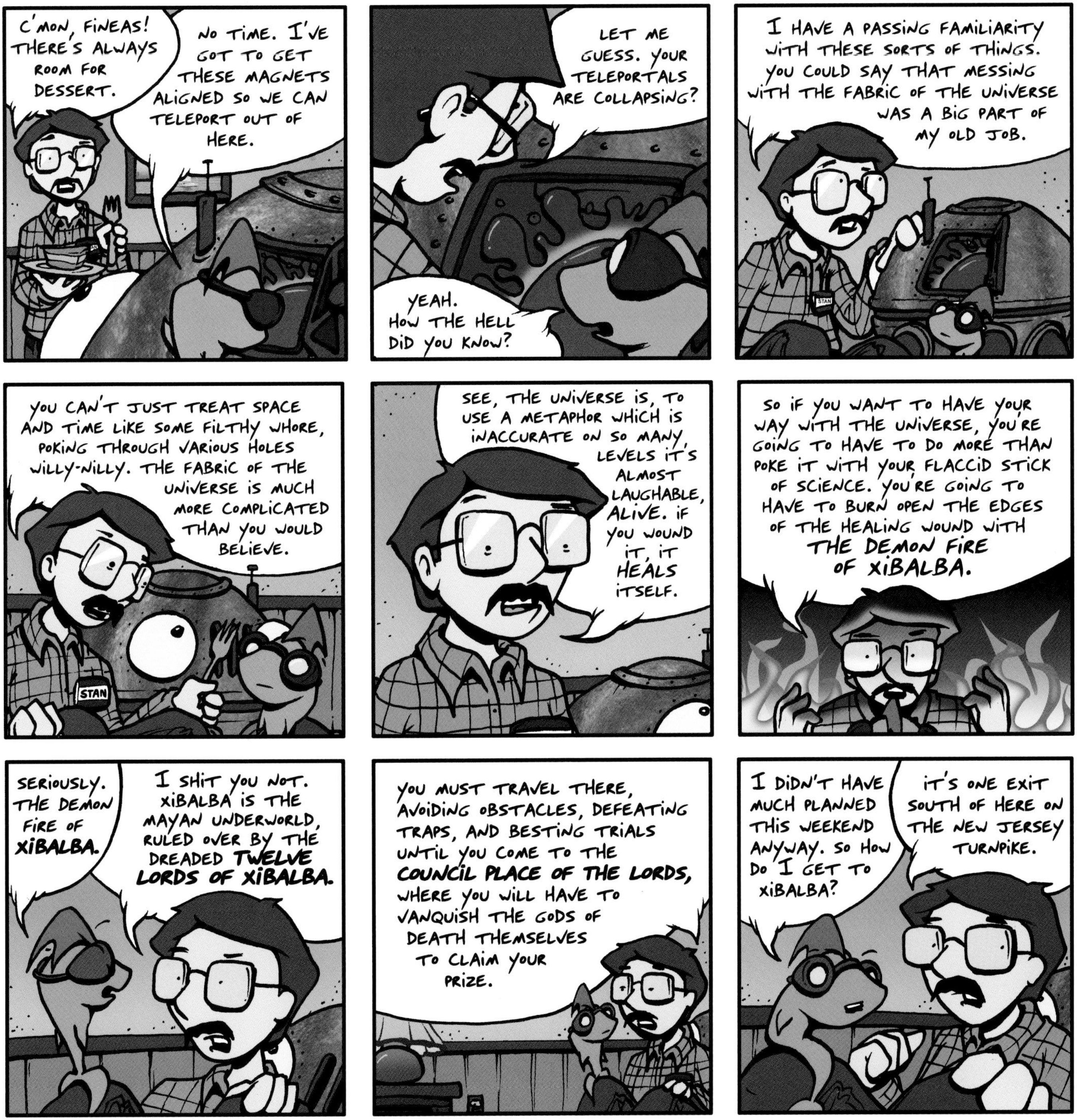
C'MON, FINEAS! THERE'S ALWAYS ROOM FOR DESSERT.
NO TIME. I'VE GOT TO GET THESE MAGNETS ALIGNED SO WE CAN TELEPORT OUT OF HERE.
LET ME GUESS. YOUR TELEPORTALS ARE COLLAPSING?
YEAH. HOW THE HELL DID YOU KNOW?
I HAVE A PASSING FAMILIARITY WITH THESE SORTS OF THINGS. YOU COULD SAY THAT MESSING WITH THE FABRIC OF THE UNIVERSE WAS A BIG PART OF MY OLD JOB.
STAN
YOU CAN'T JUST TREAT SPACE AND TIME LIKE SOME FILTHY WHORE, POKING THROUGH VARIOUS HOLES WILLY-NILLY. THE FABRIC OF THE UNIVERSE IS MUCH MORE COMPLICATED THAN YOU WOULD BELIEVE.
STAN
SEE, THE UNIVERSE IS, TO USE A METAPHOR WHICH IS INACCURATE ON SO MANY LEVELS IT'S ALMOST LAUGHABLE, ALIVE. IF YOU WOUND IT, IT HEALS ITSELF.
SO IF YOU WANT TO HAVE YOUR WAY WITH THE UNIVERSE, YOU'RE GOING TO HAVE TO DO MORE THAN POKE IT WITH YOUR FLACCID STICK OF SCIENCE. YOU'RE GOING TO HAVE TO BURN OPEN THE EDGES OF THE HEALING WOUND WITH **THE DEMON FIRE OF XIBALBA.**
SERIOUSLY. THE DEMON FIRE OF **XIBALBA.**
I SHIT YOU NOT. XIBALBA IS THE MAYAN UNDERWORLD, RULED OVER BY THE DREADED **TWELVE LORDS OF XIBALBA.**
YOU MUST TRAVEL THERE, AVOIDING OBSTACLES, DEFEATING TRAPS, AND BESTING TRIALS UNTIL YOU COME TO THE **COUNCIL PLACE OF THE LORDS,** WHERE YOU WILL HAVE TO VANQUISH THE GODS OF DEATH THEMSELVES TO CLAIM YOUR PRIZE.
I DIDN'T HAVE MUCH PLANNED THIS WEEKEND ANYWAY. SO HOW DO I GET TO XIBALBA?
IT'S ONE EXIT SOUTH OF HERE ON THE NEW JERSEY TURNPIKE.

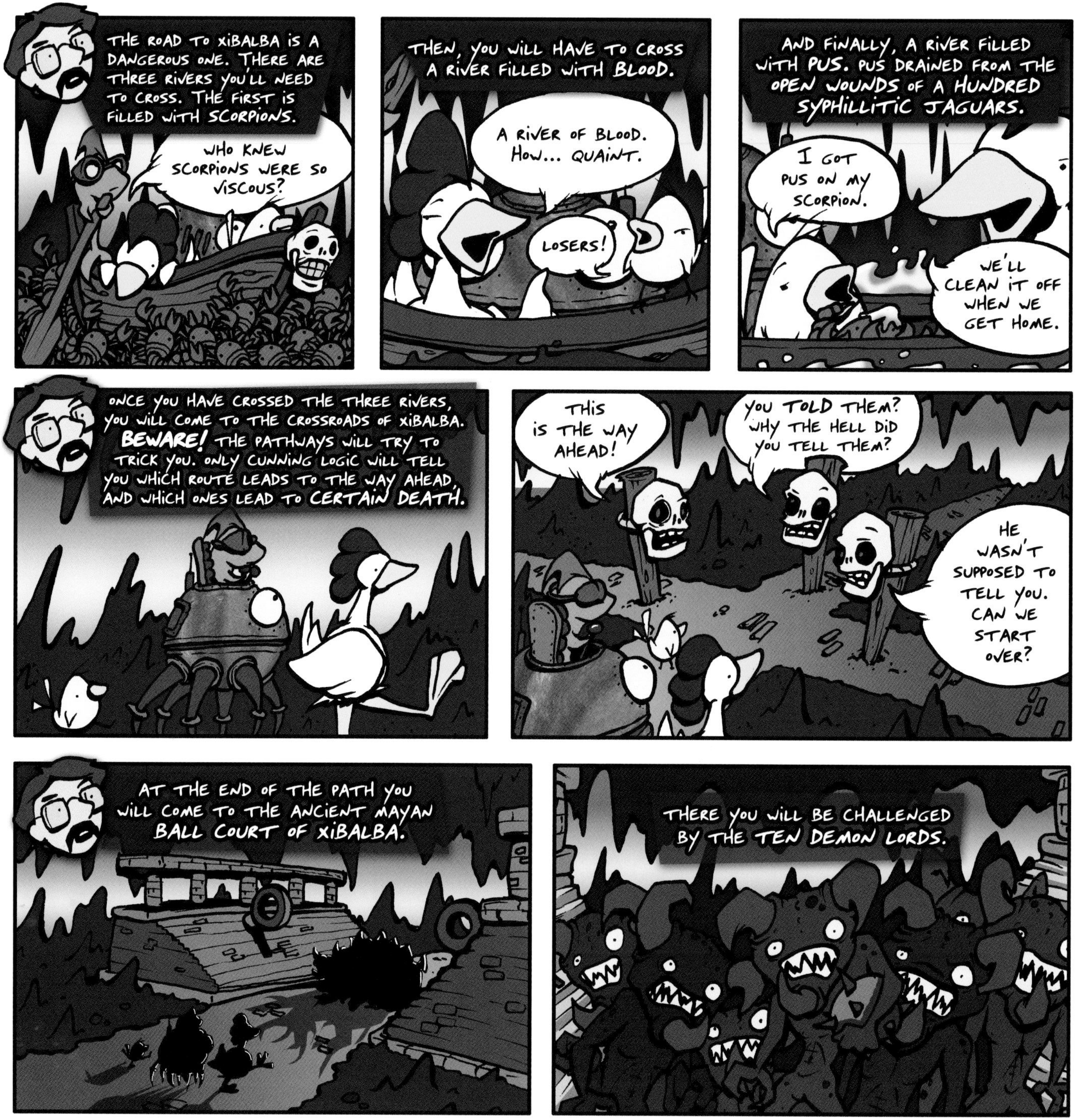
THE ROAD TO XIBALBA IS A DANGEROUS ONE. THERE ARE THREE RIVERS YOU'LL NEED TO CROSS. THE FIRST IS FILLED WITH SCORPIONS.
WHO KNEW SCORPIONS WERE SO VISCOUS?
THEN, YOU WILL HAVE TO CROSS A RIVER FILLED WITH BLOOD.
A RIVER OF BLOOD. HOW... QUAINT.
LOSERS!
AND FINALLY, A RIVER FILLED WITH PUS. PUS DRAINED FROM THE OPEN WOUNDS OF A HUNDRED SYPHILLITIC JAGUARS.
I GOT PUS ON MY SCORPION.
WE'LL CLEAN IT OFF WHEN WE GET HOME.
ONCE YOU HAVE CROSSED THE THREE RIVERS, YOU WILL COME TO THE CROSSROADS OF XIBALBA. BEWARE! THE PATHWAYS WILL TRY TO TRICK YOU. ONLY CUNNING LOGIC WILL TELL YOU WHICH ROUTE LEADS TO THE WAY AHEAD, AND WHICH ONES LEAD TO CERTAIN DEATH.
THIS IS THE WAY AHEAD!
YOU TOLD THEM? WHY THE HELL DID YOU TELL THEM?
HE WASN'T SUPPOSED TO TELL YOU. CAN WE START OVER?
AT THE END OF THE PATH YOU WILL COME TO THE ANCIENT MAYAN BALL COURT OF XIBALBA.
THERE YOU WILL BE CHALLENGED BY THE TEN DEMON LORDS.

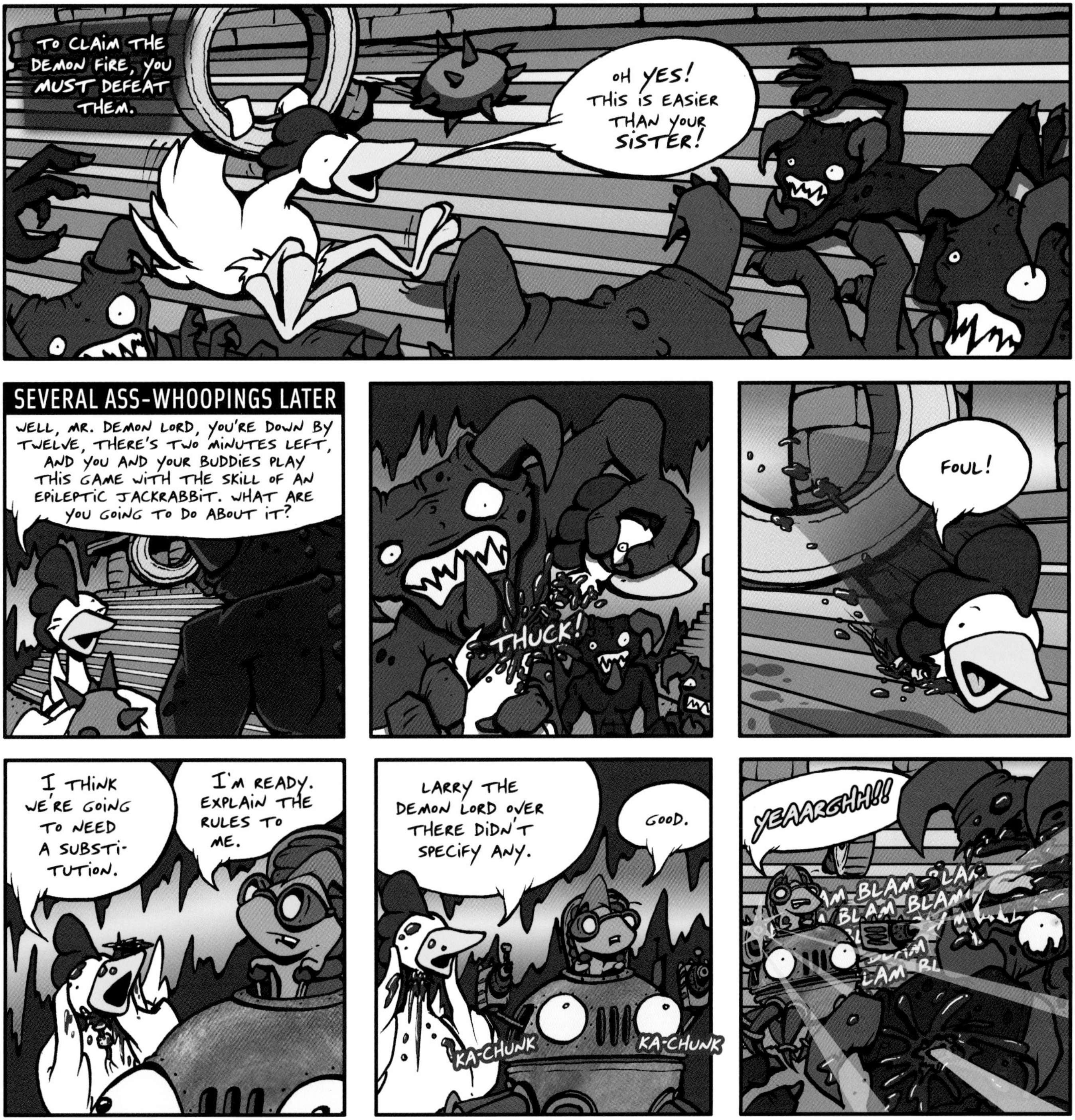
TO CLAIM THE DEMON FIRE, YOU MUST DEFEAT THEM.
OH YES! THIS IS EASIER THAN YOUR SISTER!
SEVERAL ASS-WHOOPINGS LATER
WELL, MR. DEMON LORD, YOU'RE DOWN BY TWELVE, THERE'S TWO MINUTES LEFT, AND YOU AND YOUR BUDDIES PLAY THIS GAME WITH THE SKILL OF AN EPILEPTIC JACKRABBIT. WHAT ARE YOU GOING TO DO ABOUT IT?
THUCK!
FOUL!
I THINK WE'RE GOING TO NEED A SUBSTI-TUTION.
I'M READY. EXPLAIN THE RULES TO ME.
LARRY THE DEMON LORD OVER THERE DIDN'T SPECIFY ANY.
GOOD.
KA-CHUNK
KA-CHUNK
YEAARGHH!!
BLAM BLAM BLAM

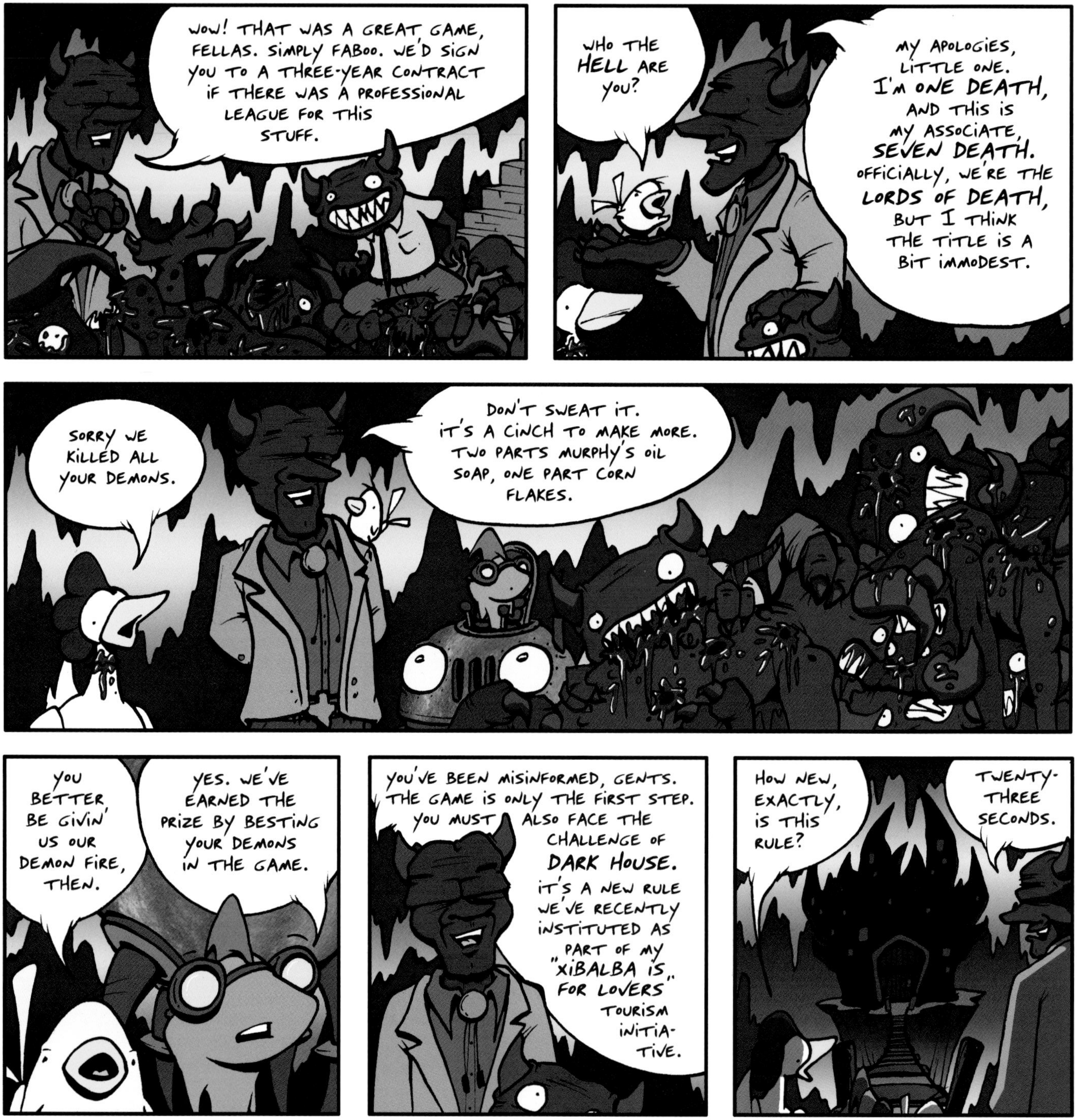
WOW! THAT WAS A GREAT GAME, FELLAS. SIMPLY FABOO. WE'D SIGN YOU TO A THREE-YEAR CONTRACT IF THERE WAS A PROFESSIONAL LEAGUE FOR THIS STUFF.
WHO THE HELL ARE YOU?
MY APOLOGIES, LITTLE ONE. I'M ONE DEATH, AND THIS IS MY ASSOCIATE, SEVEN DEATH. OFFICIALLY, WE'RE THE LORDS OF DEATH, BUT I THINK THE TITLE IS A BIT IMMODEST.
SORRY WE KILLED ALL YOUR DEMONS.
DON'T SWEAT IT. IT'S A CINCH TO MAKE MORE. TWO PARTS MURPHY'S OIL SOAP, ONE PART CORN FLAKES.
YOU BETTER BE GIVIN' US OUR DEMON FIRE, THEN.
YES. WE'VE EARNED THE PRIZE BY BESTING YOUR DEMONS IN THE GAME.
YOU'VE BEEN MISINFORMED, GENTS. THE GAME IS ONLY THE FIRST STEP. YOU MUST ALSO FACE THE CHALLENGE OF DARK HOUSE. IT'S A NEW RULE WE'VE RECENTLY INSTITUTED AS PART OF MY "XIBALBA IS FOR LOVERS" TOURISM INITIA-TIVE.
HOW NEW, EXACTLY, IS THIS RULE?
TWENTY-THREE SECONDS.

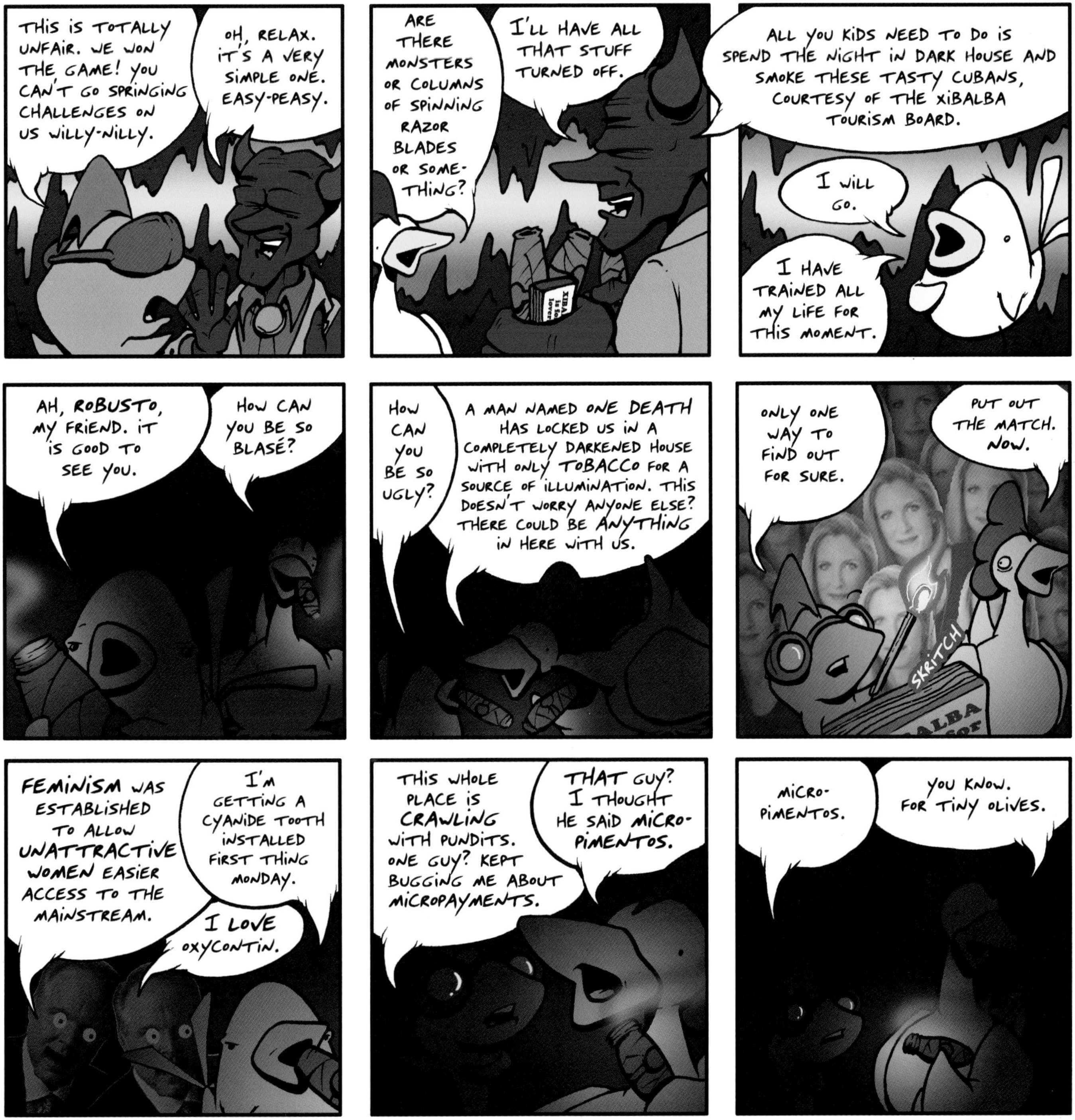
THIS IS TOTALLY UNFAIR. WE WON THE GAME! YOU CAN'T GO SPRINGING CHALLENGES ON US WILLY-NILLY.
OH, RELAX. IT'S A VERY SIMPLE ONE. EASY-PEASY.
ARE THERE MONSTERS OR COLUMNS OF SPINNING RAZOR BLADES OR SOME-THING?
I'LL HAVE ALL THAT STUFF TURNED OFF.
XIBALBA is for lovers
ALL YOU KIDS NEED TO DO IS SPEND THE NIGHT IN DARK HOUSE AND SMOKE THESE TASTY CUBANS, COURTESY OF THE XIBALBA TOURISM BOARD.
I WILL GO.
I HAVE TRAINED ALL MY LIFE FOR THIS MOMENT.
AH, ROBUSTO, MY FRIEND. IT IS GOOD TO SEE YOU.
HOW CAN YOU BE SO BLASÉ?
HOW CAN YOU BE SO UGLY?
A MAN NAMED ONE DEATH HAS LOCKED US IN A COMPLETELY DARKENED HOUSE WITH ONLY TOBACCO FOR A SOURCE OF ILLUMINATION. THIS DOESN'T WORRY ANYONE ELSE? THERE COULD BE ANYTHING IN HERE WITH US.
ONLY ONE WAY TO FIND OUT FOR SURE.
PUT OUT THE MATCH. NOW.
SKRITCH
FEMINISM WAS ESTABLISHED TO ALLOW UNATTRACTIVE WOMEN EASIER ACCESS TO THE MAINSTREAM.
I'M GETTING A CYANIDE TOOTH INSTALLED FIRST THING MONDAY.
I LOVE OXYCONTIN.
THIS WHOLE PLACE IS CRAWLING WITH PUNDITS. ONE GUY? KEPT BUGGING ME ABOUT MICROPAYMENTS.
THAT GUY? I THOUGHT HE SAID MICRO-PIMENTOS.
MICRO-PIMENTOS.
YOU KNOW. FOR TINY OLIVES.

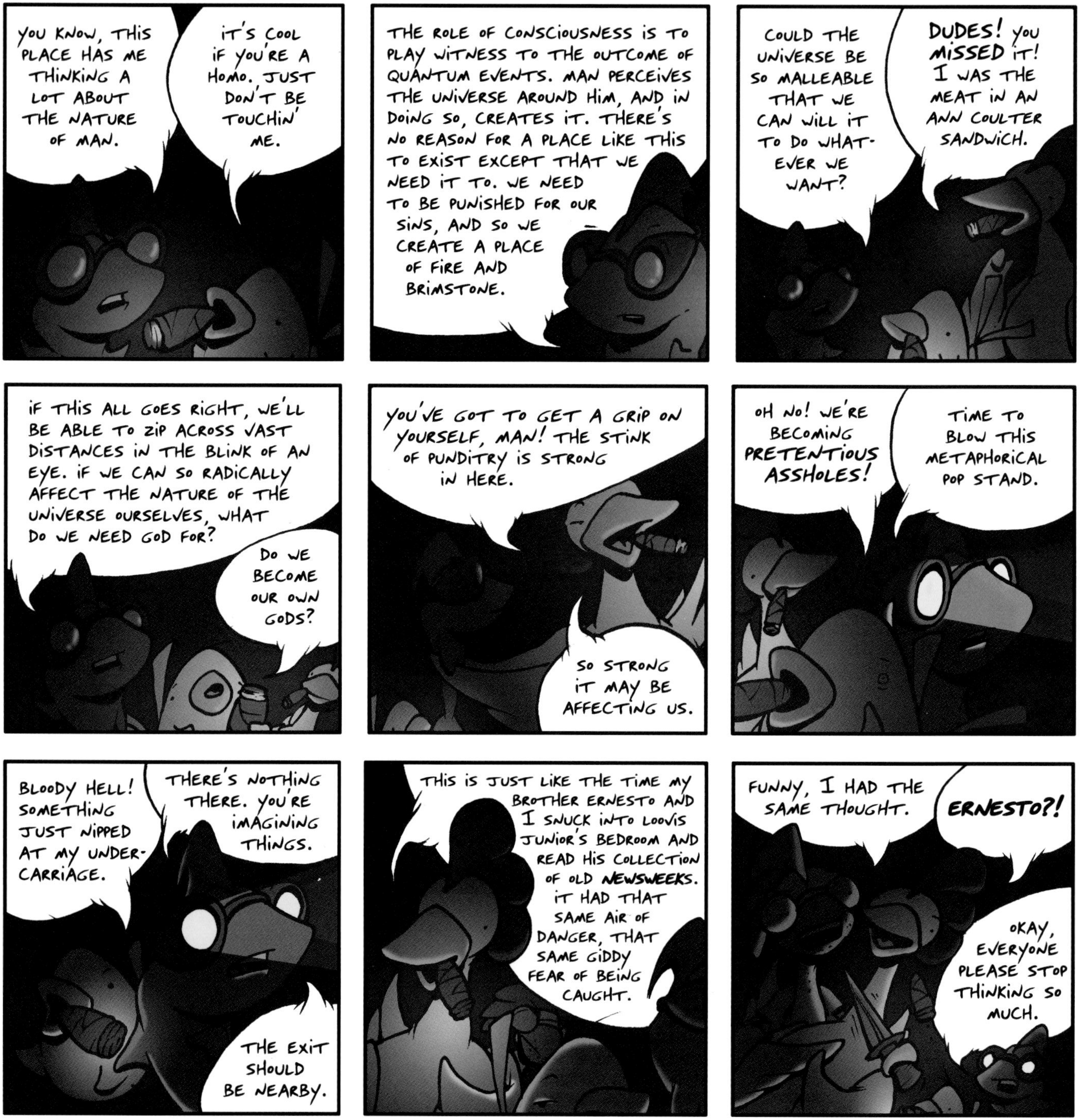

YOU KNOW, THIS PLACE HAS ME THINKING A LOT ABOUT THE NATURE OF MAN.
IT'S COOL IF YOU'RE A HOMO. JUST DON'T BE TOUCHIN' ME.
THE ROLE OF CONSCIOUSNESS IS TO PLAY WITNESS TO THE OUTCOME OF QUANTUM EVENTS. MAN PERCEIVES THE UNIVERSE AROUND HIM, AND IN DOING SO, CREATES IT. THERE'S NO REASON FOR A PLACE LIKE THIS TO EXIST EXCEPT THAT WE NEED IT TO. WE NEED TO BE PUNISHED FOR OUR SINS, AND SO WE CREATE A PLACE OF FIRE AND BRIMSTONE.
COULD THE UNIVERSE BE SO MALLEABLE THAT WE CAN WILL IT TO DO WHATEVER WE WANT?
DUDES! YOU **MISSED** IT! I WAS THE MEAT IN AN ANN COULTER SANDWICH.
IF THIS ALL GOES RIGHT, WE'LL BE ABLE TO ZIP ACROSS VAST DISTANCES IN THE BLINK OF AN EYE. IF WE CAN SO RADICALLY AFFECT THE NATURE OF THE UNIVERSE OURSELVES, WHAT DO WE NEED GOD FOR?
DO WE BECOME OUR OWN GODS?
YOU'VE GOT TO GET A GRIP ON YOURSELF, MAN! THE STINK OF PUNDITRY IS STRONG IN HERE.
SO STRONG IT MAY BE AFFECTING US.
OH NO! WE'RE BECOMING **PRETENTIOUS ASSHOLES!**
TIME TO BLOW THIS METAPHORICAL POP STAND.
BLOODY HELL! SOMETHING JUST NIPPED AT MY UNDERCARRIAGE.
THERE'S NOTHING THERE. YOU'RE IMAGINING THINGS.
THE EXIT SHOULD BE NEARBY.
THIS IS JUST LIKE THE TIME MY BROTHER ERNESTO AND I SNUCK INTO LOOVIS JUNIOR'S BEDROOM AND READ HIS COLLECTION OF OLD **NEWSWEEKS**. IT HAD THAT SAME AIR OF DANGER, THAT SAME GIDDY FEAR OF BEING CAUGHT.
FUNNY, I HAD THE SAME THOUGHT.
ERNESTO?!
OKAY, EVERYONE PLEASE STOP THINKING SO MUCH.

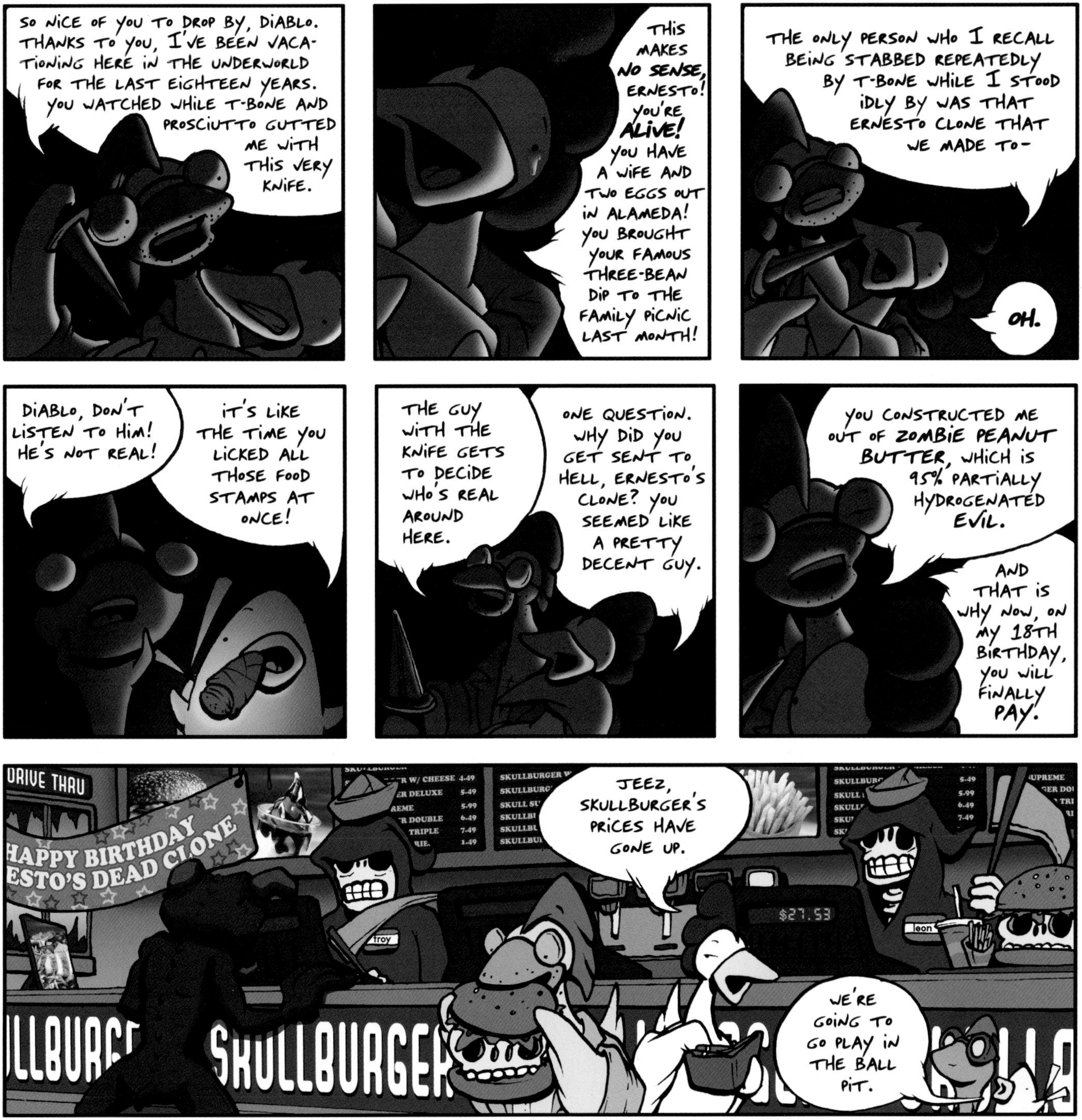
SO NICE OF YOU TO DROP BY, DIABLO. THANKS TO YOU, I'VE BEEN VACATIONING HERE IN THE UNDERWORLD FOR THE LAST EIGHTEEN YEARS. YOU WATCHED WHILE T-BONE AND PROSCIUTTO GUTTED ME WITH THIS VERY KNIFE.
THIS MAKES NO SENSE, ERNESTO! YOU'RE ALIVE! YOU HAVE A WIFE AND TWO EGGS OUT IN ALAMEDA! YOU BROUGHT YOUR FAMOUS THREE-BEAN DIP TO THE FAMILY PICNIC LAST MONTH!
THE ONLY PERSON WHO I RECALL BEING STABBED REPEATEDLY BY T-BONE WHILE I STOOD IDLY BY WAS THAT ERNESTO CLONE THAT WE MADE TO–
OH.
DIABLO, DON'T LISTEN TO HIM! HE'S NOT REAL!
IT'S LIKE THE TIME YOU LICKED ALL THOSE FOOD STAMPS AT ONCE!
THE GUY WITH THE KNIFE GETS TO DECIDE WHO'S REAL AROUND HERE.
ONE QUESTION. WHY DID YOU GET SENT TO HELL, ERNESTO'S CLONE? YOU SEEMED LIKE A PRETTY DECENT GUY.
YOU CONSTRUCTED ME OUT OF ZOMBIE PEANUT BUTTER, WHICH IS 95% PARTIALLY HYDROGENATED EVIL.
AND THAT IS WHY NOW, ON MY 18TH BIRTHDAY, YOU WILL FINALLY PAY.
DRIVE THRU
HAPPY BIRTHDAY
ESTO'S DEAD CLONE
JEEZ, SKULLBURGER'S PRICES HAVE GONE UP.
troy
$27.53
leon
SKULLBURGER
WE'RE GOING TO GO PLAY IN THE BALL PIT.

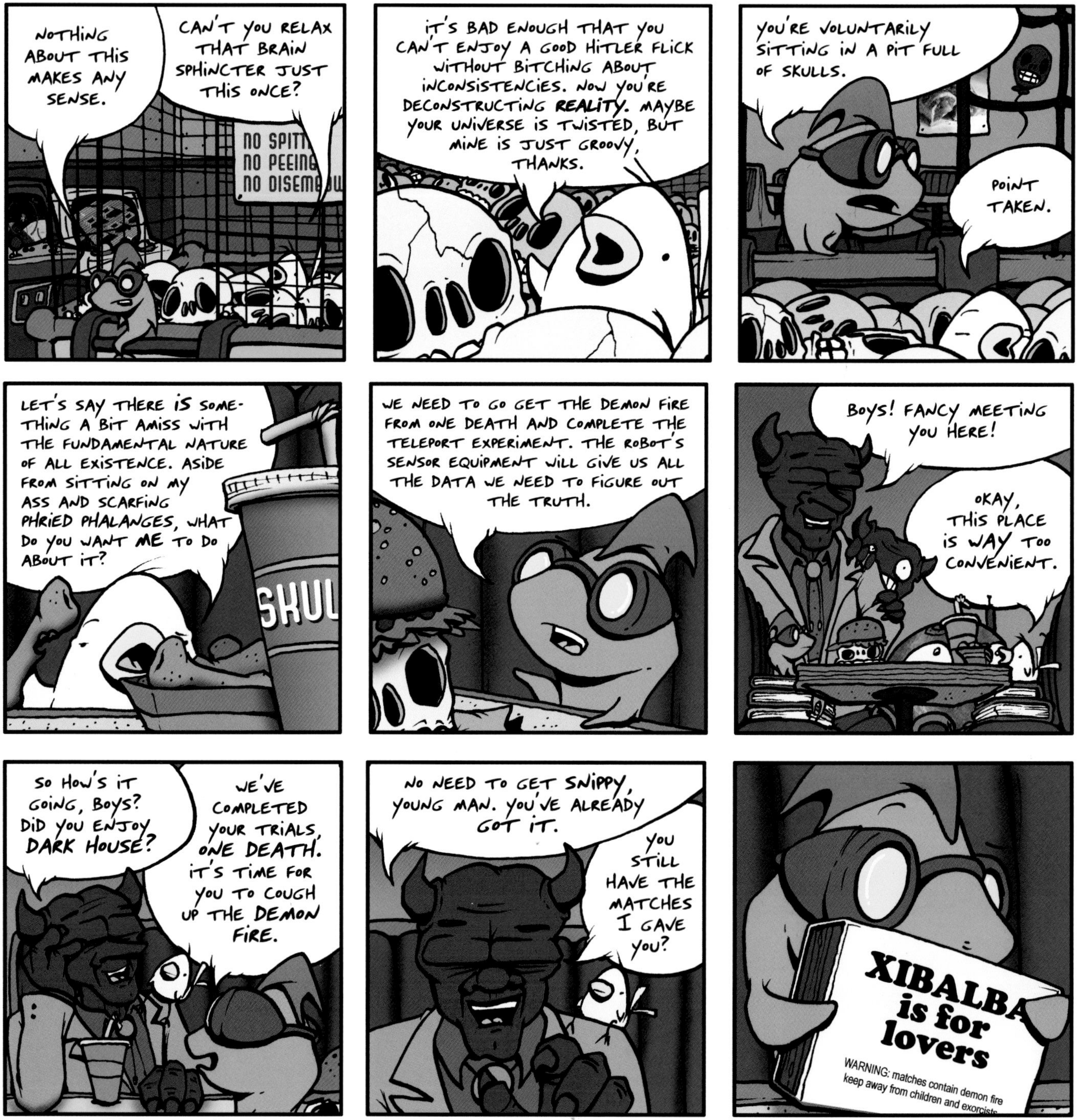
NOTHING ABOUT THIS MAKES ANY SENSE.
CAN'T YOU RELAX THAT BRAIN SPHINCTER JUST THIS ONCE?
NO SPITTI
NO PEEING
NO DISEMB
IT'S BAD ENOUGH THAT YOU CAN'T ENJOY A GOOD HITLER FLICK WITHOUT BITCHING ABOUT INCONSISTENCIES. NOW YOU'RE DECONSTRUCTING REALITY. MAYBE YOUR UNIVERSE IS TWISTED, BUT MINE IS JUST GROOVY, THANKS.
YOU'RE VOLUNTARILY SITTING IN A PIT FULL OF SKULLS.
POINT TAKEN.
LET'S SAY THERE IS SOMETHING A BIT AMISS WITH THE FUNDAMENTAL NATURE OF ALL EXISTENCE. ASIDE FROM SITTING ON MY ASS AND SCARFING PHRIED PHALANGES, WHAT DO YOU WANT ME TO DO ABOUT IT?
SKUL
WE NEED TO GO GET THE DEMON FIRE FROM ONE DEATH AND COMPLETE THE TELEPORT EXPERIMENT. THE ROBOT'S SENSOR EQUIPMENT WILL GIVE US ALL THE DATA WE NEED TO FIGURE OUT THE TRUTH.
BOYS! FANCY MEETING YOU HERE!
OKAY, THIS PLACE IS WAY TOO CONVENIENT.
SO HOW'S IT GOING, BOYS? DID YOU ENJOY DARK HOUSE?
WE'VE COMPLETED YOUR TRIALS, ONE DEATH. IT'S TIME FOR YOU TO COUGH UP THE DEMON FIRE.
NO NEED TO GET SNIPPY, YOUNG MAN. YOU'VE ALREADY GOT IT.
YOU STILL HAVE THE MATCHES I GAVE YOU?
XIBALBA is for lovers
WARNING: matches contain demon fire
keep away from children and exorcists

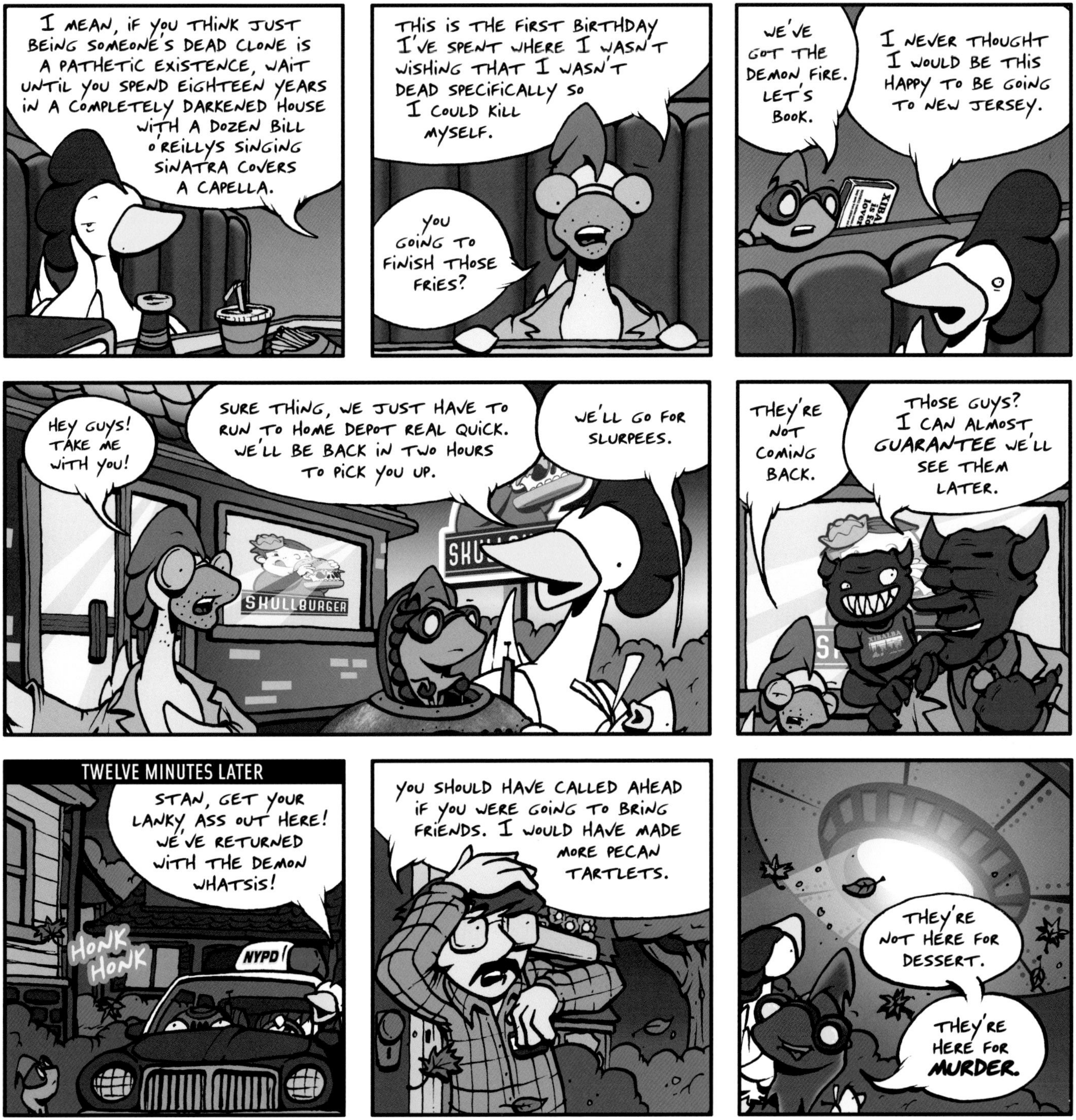
I MEAN, IF YOU THINK JUST BEING SOMEONE'S DEAD CLONE IS A PATHETIC EXISTENCE, WAIT UNTIL YOU SPEND EIGHTEEN YEARS IN A COMPLETELY DARKENED HOUSE WITH A DOZEN BILL O'REILLYS SINGING SINATRA COVERS A CAPELLA.
THIS IS THE FIRST BIRTHDAY I'VE SPENT WHERE I WASN'T WISHING THAT I WASN'T DEAD SPECIFICALLY SO I COULD KILL MYSELF.
YOU GOING TO FINISH THOSE FRIES?
WE'VE GOT THE DEMON FIRE. LET'S BOOK.
I NEVER THOUGHT I WOULD BE THIS HAPPY TO BE GOING TO NEW JERSEY.
HEY GUYS! TAKE ME WITH YOU!
SURE THING, WE JUST HAVE TO RUN TO HOME DEPOT REAL QUICK. WE'LL BE BACK IN TWO HOURS TO PICK YOU UP.
WE'LL GO FOR SLURPEES.
SKULLBURGER
THEY'RE NOT COMING BACK.
THOSE GUYS? I CAN ALMOST GUARANTEE WE'LL SEE THEM LATER.
XIBALBA
TWELVE MINUTES LATER
STAN, GET YOUR LANKY ASS OUT HERE! WE'VE RETURNED WITH THE DEMON WHATSIS!
HONK HONK
NYPD
YOU SHOULD HAVE CALLED AHEAD IF YOU WERE GOING TO BRING FRIENDS. I WOULD HAVE MADE MORE PECAN TARTLETS.
THEY'RE NOT HERE FOR DESSERT.
THEY'RE HERE FOR **MURDER.**

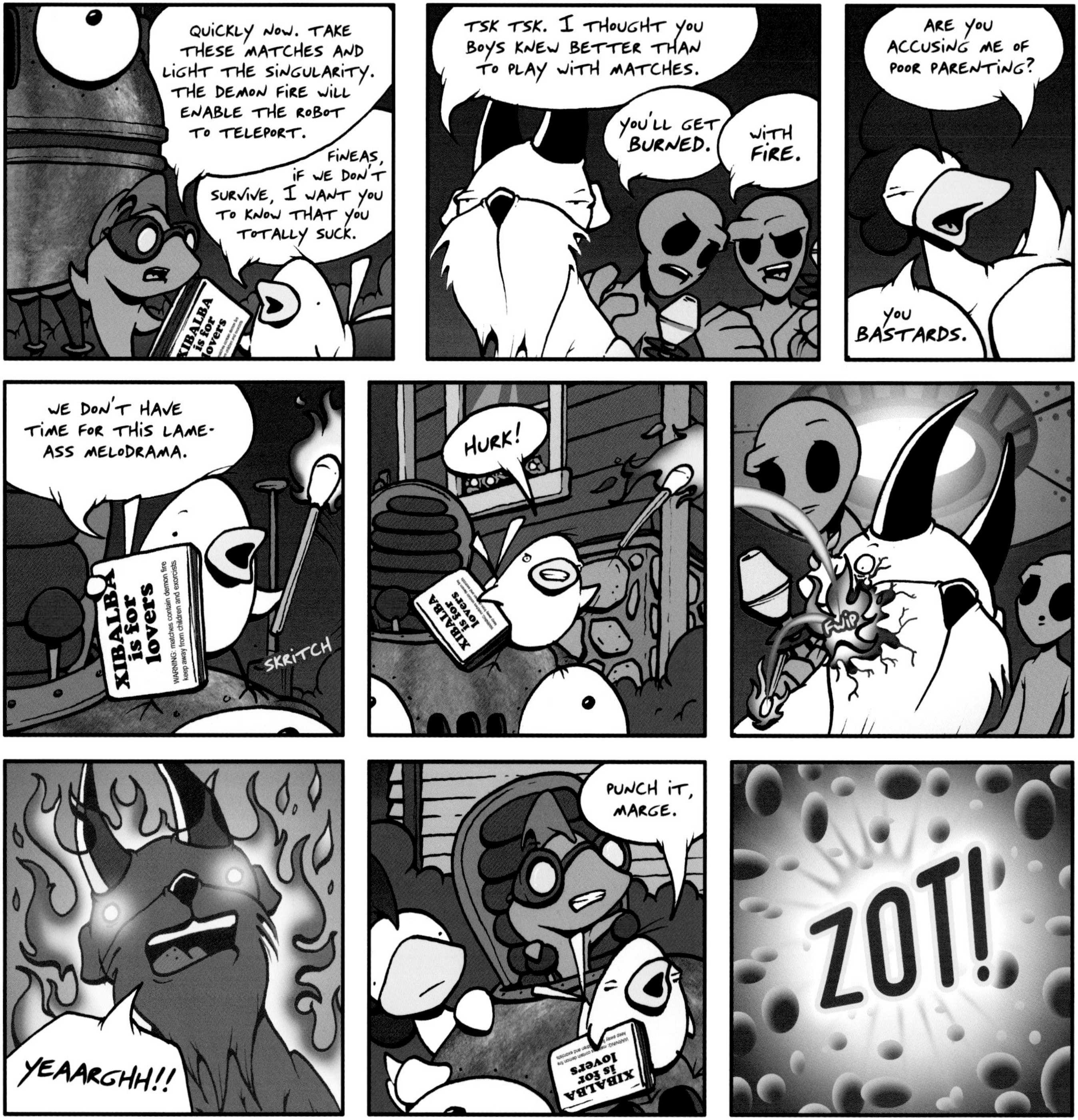
QUICKLY NOW. TAKE THESE MATCHES AND LIGHT THE SINGULARITY. THE DEMON FIRE WILL ENABLE THE ROBOT TO TELEPORT.
FINEAS, IF WE DON'T SURVIVE, I WANT YOU TO KNOW THAT YOU TOTALLY SUCK.
TSK TSK. I THOUGHT YOU BOYS KNEW BETTER THAN TO PLAY WITH MATCHES.
YOU'LL GET BURNED.
WITH FIRE.
ARE YOU ACCUSING ME OF POOR PARENTING?
YOU BASTARDS.
WE DON'T HAVE TIME FOR THIS LAME-ASS MELODRAMA.
XIBALBA is for lovers
WARNING: matches contain demon fire keep away from children and exorcists
SKRITCH
HURK!
FWIP
YEAARGHH!!
PUNCH IT, MARGE.
ZOT!

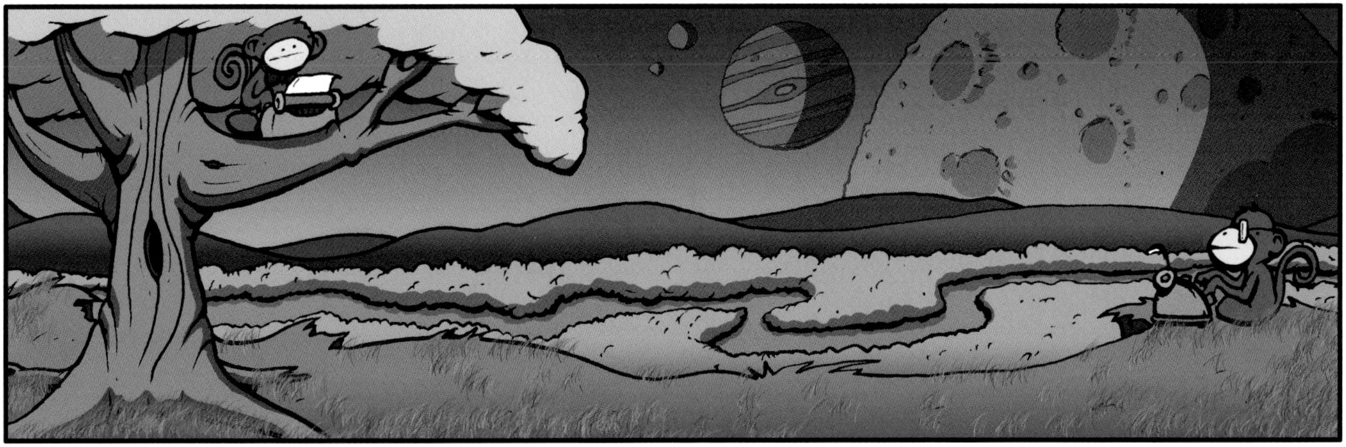
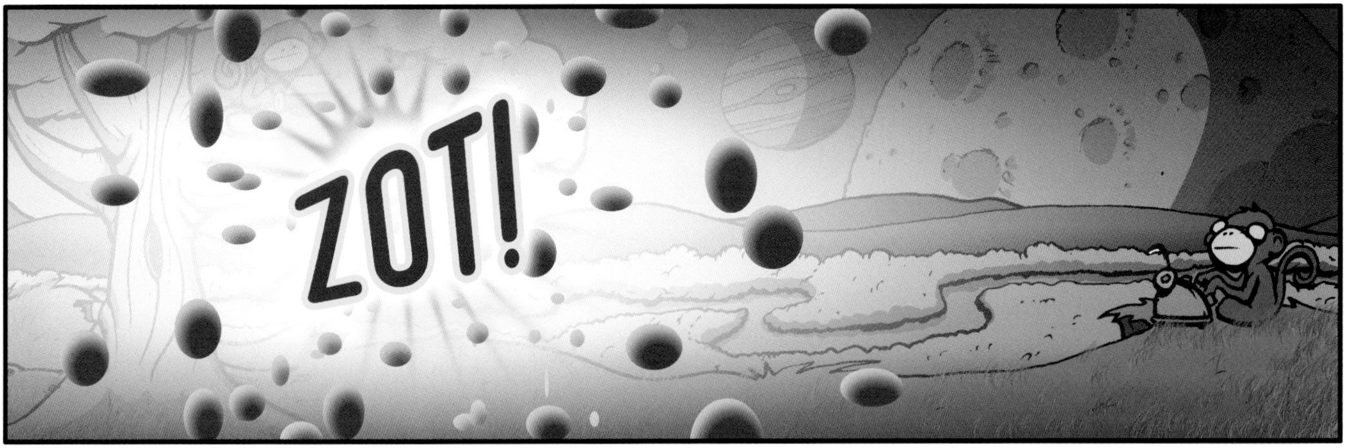
ZOT!
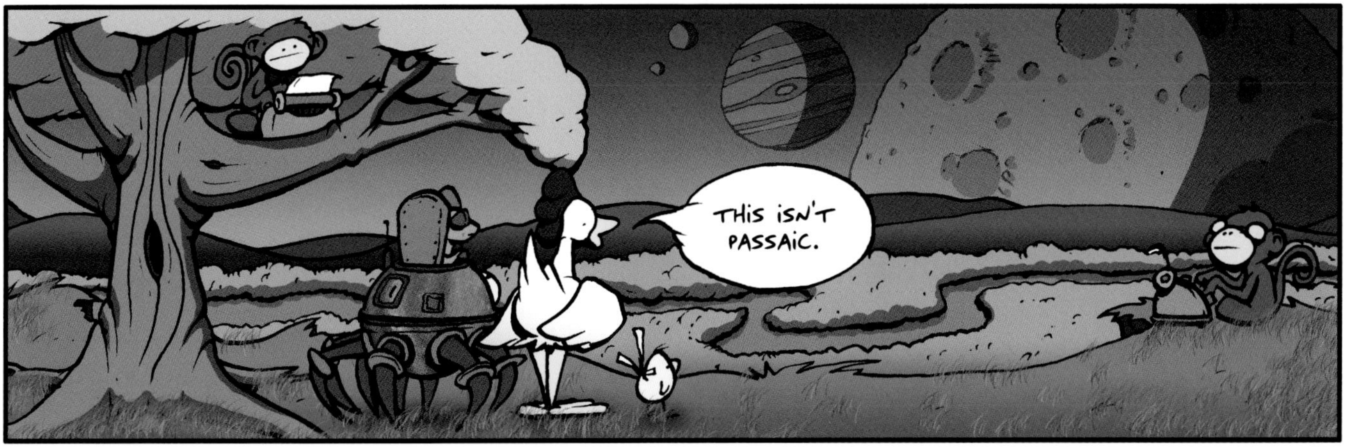
THIS ISN'T PASSAIC.

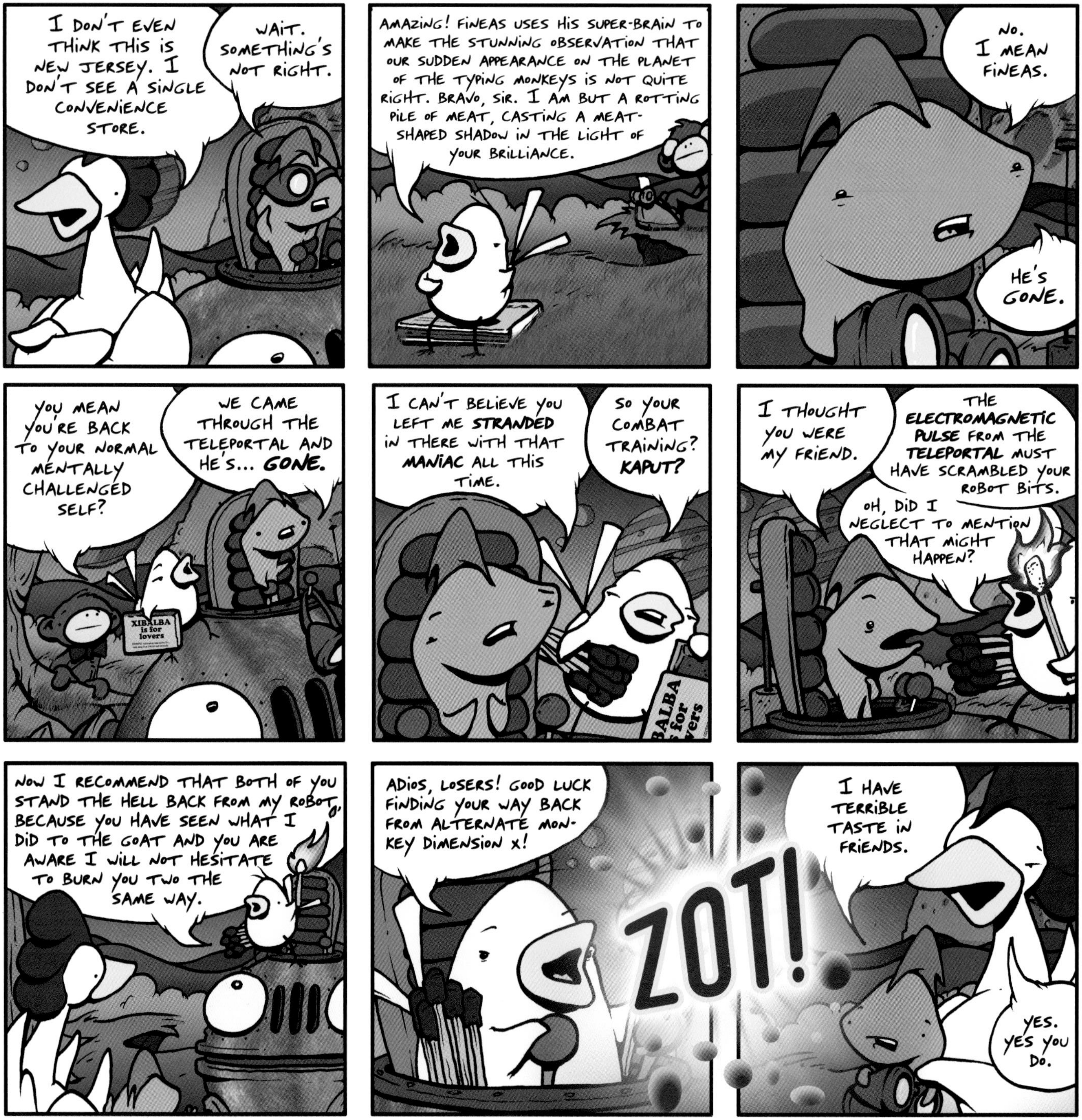
I DON'T EVEN THINK THIS IS NEW JERSEY. I DON'T SEE A SINGLE CONVENIENCE STORE.
WAIT. SOMETHING'S NOT RIGHT.
AMAZING! FINEAS USES HIS SUPER-BRAIN TO MAKE THE STUNNING OBSERVATION THAT OUR SUDDEN APPEARANCE ON THE PLANET OF THE TYPING MONKEYS IS NOT QUITE RIGHT. BRAVO, SIR. I AM BUT A ROTTING PILE OF MEAT, CASTING A MEAT-SHAPED SHADOW IN THE LIGHT OF YOUR BRILLIANCE.
NO. I MEAN FINEAS.
HE'S GONE.
YOU MEAN YOU'RE BACK TO YOUR NORMAL MENTALLY CHALLENGED SELF?
WE CAME THROUGH THE TELEPORTAL AND HE'S... **GONE.**
XIBALBA is for lovers
I CAN'T BELIEVE YOU LEFT ME **STRANDED** IN THERE WITH THAT **MANIAC** ALL THIS TIME.
SO YOUR COMBAT TRAINING? **KAPUT?**
I THOUGHT YOU WERE MY FRIEND.
THE **ELECTROMAGNETIC PULSE** FROM THE **TELEPORTAL** MUST HAVE SCRAMBLED YOUR ROBOT BITS.
OH, DID I NEGLECT TO MENTION THAT MIGHT HAPPEN?
NOW I RECOMMEND THAT BOTH OF YOU STAND THE HELL BACK FROM MY ROBOT, BECAUSE YOU HAVE SEEN WHAT I DID TO THE GOAT AND YOU ARE AWARE I WILL NOT HESITATE TO BURN YOU TWO THE SAME WAY.
ADIOS, LOSERS! GOOD LUCK FINDING YOUR WAY BACK FROM ALTERNATE MONKEY DIMENSION X!
ZOT!
I HAVE TERRIBLE TASTE IN FRIENDS.
YES. YES YOU DO.

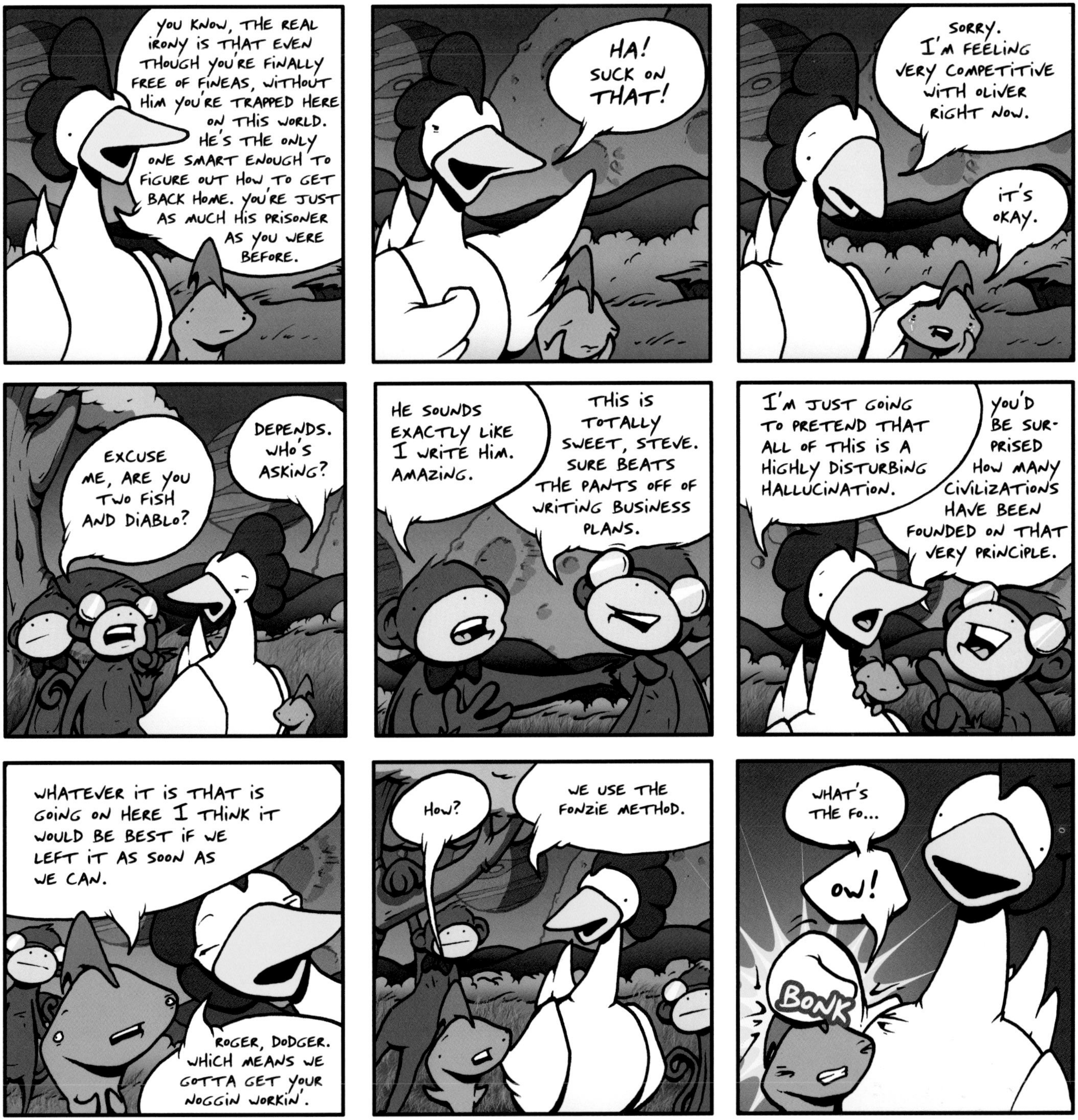
YOU KNOW, THE REAL IRONY IS THAT EVEN THOUGH YOU'RE FINALLY FREE OF FINEAS, WITHOUT HIM YOU'RE TRAPPED HERE ON THIS WORLD. HE'S THE ONLY ONE SMART ENOUGH TO FIGURE OUT HOW TO GET BACK HOME. YOU'RE JUST AS MUCH HIS PRISONER AS YOU WERE BEFORE.
HA! SUCK ON THAT!
SORRY. I'M FEELING VERY COMPETITIVE WITH OLIVER RIGHT NOW.
IT'S OKAY.
EXCUSE ME, ARE YOU TWO FISH AND DIABLO?
DEPENDS. WHO'S ASKING?
HE SOUNDS EXACTLY LIKE I WRITE HIM. AMAZING.
THIS IS TOTALLY SWEET, STEVE. SURE BEATS THE PANTS OFF OF WRITING BUSINESS PLANS.
I'M JUST GOING TO PRETEND THAT ALL OF THIS IS A HIGHLY DISTURBING HALLUCINATION.
YOU'D BE SURPRISED HOW MANY CIVILIZATIONS HAVE BEEN FOUNDED ON THAT VERY PRINCIPLE.
WHATEVER IT IS THAT IS GOING ON HERE I THINK IT WOULD BE BEST IF WE LEFT IT AS SOON AS WE CAN.
ROGER, DODGER. WHICH MEANS WE GOTTA GET YOUR NOGGIN WORKIN'.
HOW?
WE USE THE FONZIE METHOD.
WHAT'S THE FO...
OW!
BONK

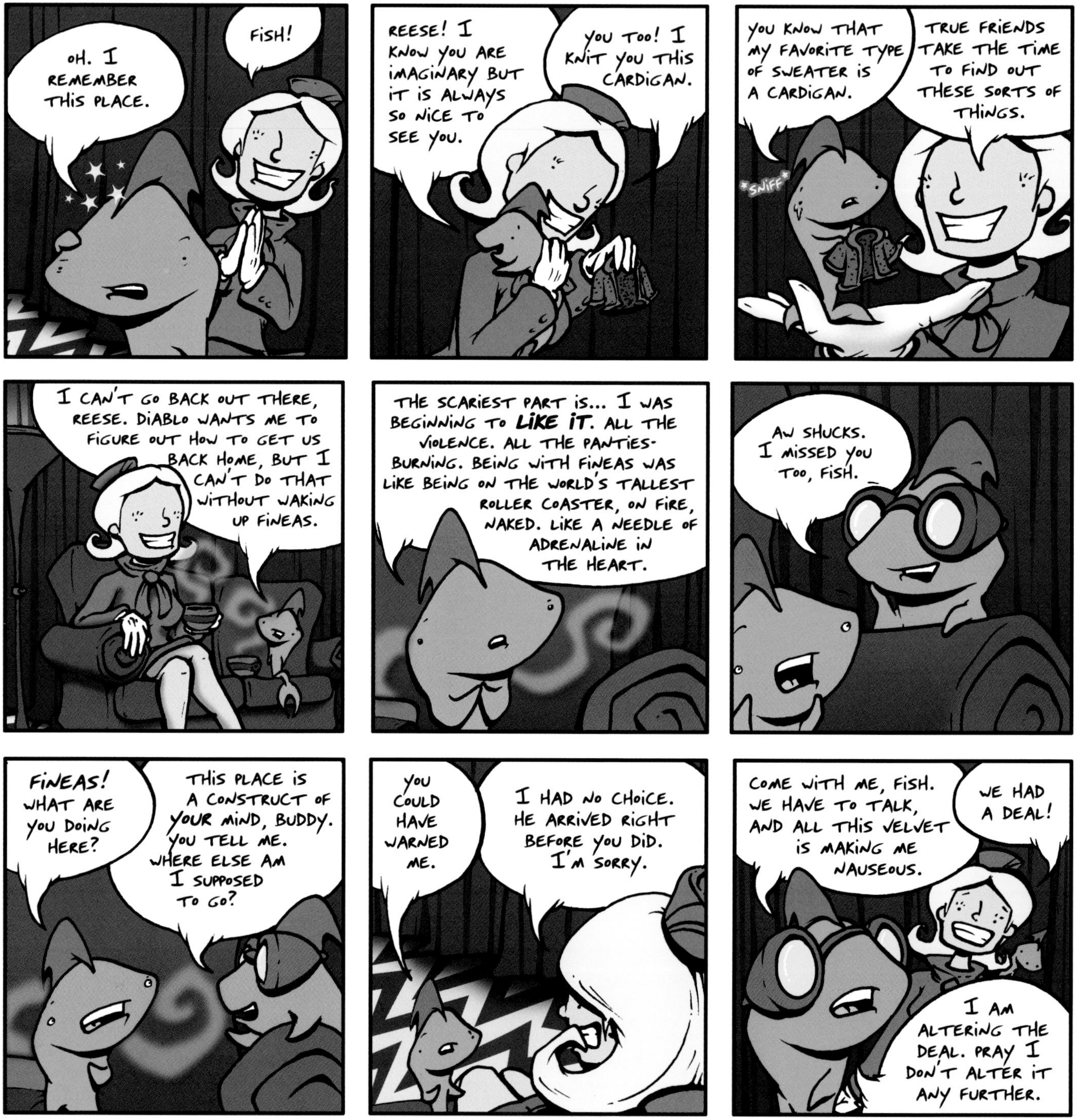
OH. I REMEMBER THIS PLACE.
FISH!
REESE! I KNOW YOU ARE IMAGINARY BUT IT IS ALWAYS SO NICE TO SEE YOU.
YOU TOO! I KNIT YOU THIS CARDIGAN.
YOU KNOW THAT MY FAVORITE TYPE OF SWEATER IS A CARDIGAN.
TRUE FRIENDS TAKE THE TIME TO FIND OUT THESE SORTS OF THINGS.
SNIFF
I CAN'T GO BACK OUT THERE, REESE. DIABLO WANTS ME TO FIGURE OUT HOW TO GET US BACK HOME, BUT I CAN'T DO THAT WITHOUT WAKING UP FINEAS.
THE SCARIEST PART IS... I WAS BEGINNING TO LIKE IT. ALL THE VIOLENCE. ALL THE PANTIES-BURNING. BEING WITH FINEAS WAS LIKE BEING ON THE WORLD'S TALLEST ROLLER COASTER, ON FIRE, NAKED. LIKE A NEEDLE OF ADRENALINE IN THE HEART.
AW SHUCKS. I MISSED YOU TOO, FISH.
FINEAS! WHAT ARE YOU DOING HERE?
THIS PLACE IS A CONSTRUCT OF YOUR MIND, BUDDY. YOU TELL ME. WHERE ELSE AM I SUPPOSED TO GO?
YOU COULD HAVE WARNED ME.
I HAD NO CHOICE. HE ARRIVED RIGHT BEFORE YOU DID. I'M SORRY.
COME WITH ME, FISH. WE HAVE TO TALK, AND ALL THIS VELVET IS MAKING ME NAUSEOUS.
WE HAD A DEAL!
I AM ALTERING THE DEAL. PRAY I DON'T ALTER IT ANY FURTHER.

REESE IS QUITE THE IMAGINARY DISH. I CAN SEE WHY YOU GROOVE ON HER SO MUCH.

DON'T YOU **DARE** TALK ABOUT REESE WITH YOUR **MURDERER'S MOUTH.**

SHE IS THE STAR OF COUNTLESS ROMANTIC COMEDIES AND HAS EARNED THE RESPECT OF THE WORLD. ALL **YOU** HAVE DONE IS INFLICT PAIN AND CAUSE SADNESS AND TERROR WHEREVER YOU HAVE GONE.

A KILLER LIKE YOU ISN'T WORTHY OF THE UNPOPPED KERNELS OF CORN ON THE STICKY FLOOR OF A MOVIE THEATER SHOWING REESE'S NEW MOVIE **JUST LIKE HEAVEN,** IN WHICH SHE IS THE SPIRIT OF A COMA LADY WHO FALLS IN LOVE WITH MARK RUFFALO.

WAIT, THIS IS PRECIOUS. YOU THINK **I'M** THE MALEFACTOR?

WELL, YES, WHAT WITH ALL THE **MALEFACTORING** YOU TEND TO DO.

FISH, ALL **I** AM IS A FEW COMBAT SUBROUTINES AND A DATABASE OF WEAPONS SPECIFICATIONS WRAPPED UP IN A TORTILLA SHELL OF PERSONALITY. I'M NOT CAPABLE OF MOTIVE. ALL THOSE AWFUL THINGS WE DID CAME FROM YOUR SIDE OF THE CORPUS CALLOSUM.

THAT IS NOT POSSIBLE. I AM AN INNOCENT FLOWER.

I KNOW A RON HOWARD, A HENRY KISSINGER, AND A TINY DOG THAT WOULD DISAGREE.

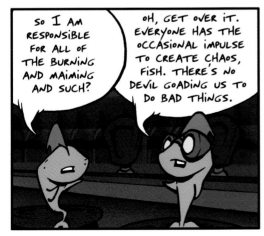

SO I AM RESPONSIBLE FOR ALL OF THE BURNING AND MAIMING AND SUCH?

OH, GET OVER IT. EVERYONE HAS THE OCCASIONAL IMPULSE TO CREATE CHAOS, FISH. THERE'S NO DEVIL GOADING US TO DO BAD THINGS.

EXCEPT DIABLO'S FRIEND STAN.

YES, EXCEPT STAN.

AND ONE DEATH! THAT GUY FROM XIBALBA.

YEAH, HIM TOO.

AND KARL ROVE.

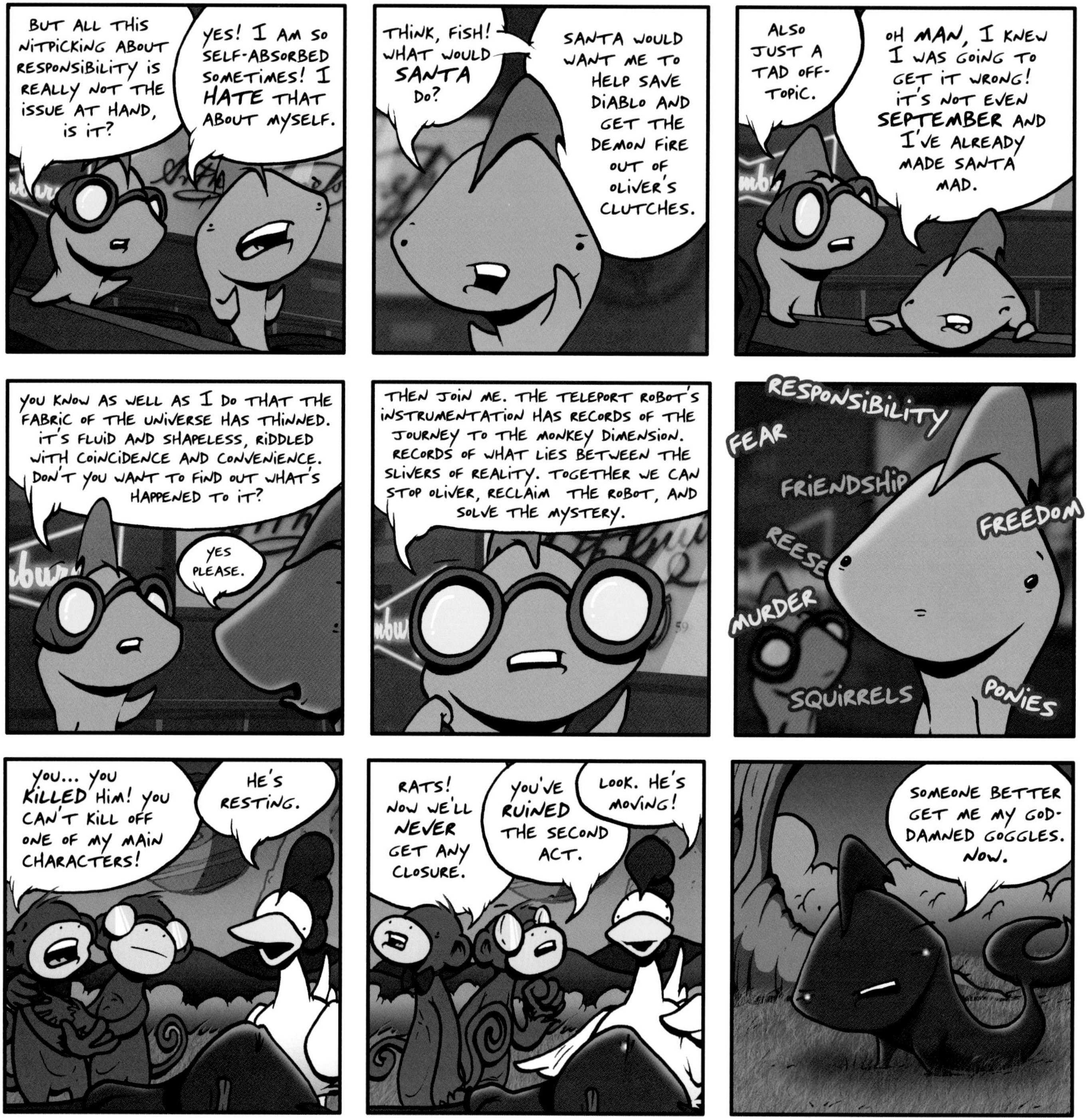
BUT ALL THIS NITPICKING ABOUT RESPONSIBILITY IS REALLY NOT THE ISSUE AT HAND, IS IT?
YES! I AM SO SELF-ABSORBED SOMETIMES! I HATE THAT ABOUT MYSELF.
THINK, FISH! WHAT WOULD SANTA DO?
SANTA WOULD WANT ME TO HELP SAVE DIABLO AND GET THE DEMON FIRE OUT OF OLIVER'S CLUTCHES.
ALSO JUST A TAD OFF-TOPIC.
OH MAN, I KNEW I WAS GOING TO GET IT WRONG! IT'S NOT EVEN SEPTEMBER AND I'VE ALREADY MADE SANTA MAD.
YOU KNOW AS WELL AS I DO THAT THE FABRIC OF THE UNIVERSE HAS THINNED. IT'S FLUID AND SHAPELESS, RIDDLED WITH COINCIDENCE AND CONVENIENCE. DON'T YOU WANT TO FIND OUT WHAT'S HAPPENED TO IT?
YES PLEASE.
THEN JOIN ME. THE TELEPORT ROBOT'S INSTRUMENTATION HAS RECORDS OF THE JOURNEY TO THE MONKEY DIMENSION. RECORDS OF WHAT LIES BETWEEN THE SLIVERS OF REALITY. TOGETHER WE CAN STOP OLIVER, RECLAIM THE ROBOT, AND SOLVE THE MYSTERY.
RESPONSIBILITY
FEAR
FRIENDSHIP
FREEDOM
REESE
MURDER
SQUIRRELS
PONIES
YOU... YOU KILLED HIM! YOU CAN'T KILL OFF ONE OF MY MAIN CHARACTERS!
HE'S RESTING.
RATS! NOW WE'LL NEVER GET ANY CLOSURE.
YOU'VE RUINED THE SECOND ACT.
LOOK. HE'S MOVING!
SOMEONE BETTER GET ME MY GOD-DAMNED GOGGLES. NOW.

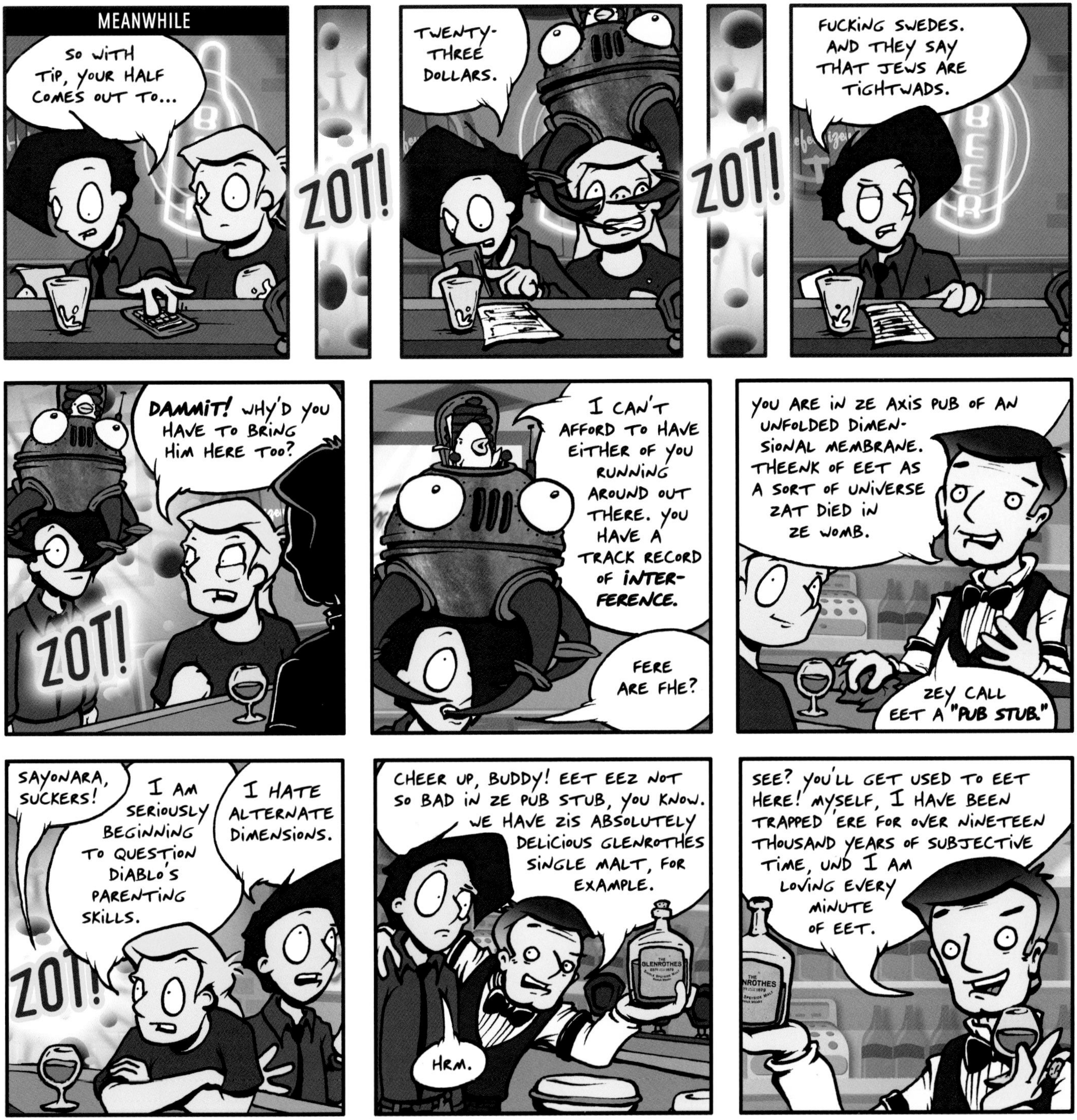
MEANWHILE
SO WITH TIP, YOUR HALF COMES OUT TO...
ZOT!
TWENTY-THREE DOLLARS.
ZOT!
FUCKING SWEDES. AND THEY SAY THAT JEWS ARE TIGHTWADS.
DAMMIT! WHY'D YOU HAVE TO BRING HIM HERE TOO?
ZOT!
I CAN'T AFFORD TO HAVE EITHER OF YOU RUNNING AROUND OUT THERE. YOU HAVE A TRACK RECORD OF INTERFERENCE.
FERE ARE FHE?
YOU ARE IN ZE AXIS PUB OF AN UNFOLDED DIMENSIONAL MEMBRANE. THEENK OF EET AS A SORT OF UNIVERSE ZAT DIED IN ZE WOMB.
ZEY CALL EET A "PUB STUB."
SAYONARA, SUCKERS!
ZOT!
I AM SERIOUSLY BEGINNING TO QUESTION DIABLO'S PARENTING SKILLS.
I HATE ALTERNATE DIMENSIONS.
CHEER UP, BUDDY! EET EEZ NOT SO BAD IN ZE PUB STUB, YOU KNOW. WE HAVE ZIS ABSOLUTELY DELICIOUS GLENROTHES SINGLE MALT, FOR EXAMPLE.
HRM.
SEE? YOU'LL GET USED TO EET HERE! MYSELF, I HAVE BEEN TRAPPED 'ERE FOR OVER NINETEEN THOUSAND YEARS OF SUBJECTIVE TIME, UND I AM LOVING EVERY MINUTE OF EET.

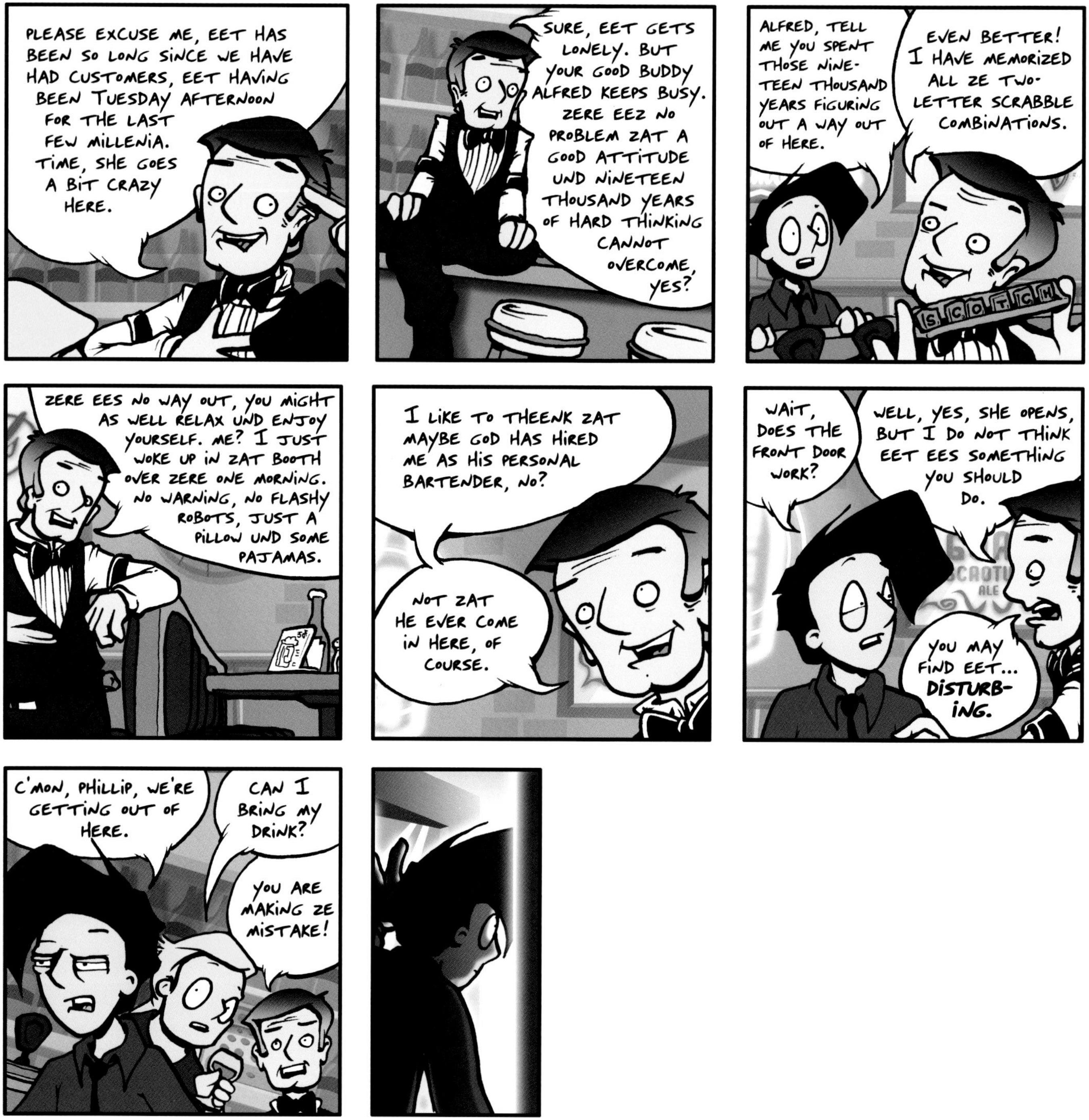
PLEASE EXCUSE ME, EET HAS BEEN SO LONG SINCE WE HAVE HAD CUSTOMERS, EET HAVING BEEN TUESDAY AFTERNOON FOR THE LAST FEW MILLENIA. TIME, SHE GOES A BIT CRAZY HERE.
SURE, EET GETS LONELY. BUT YOUR GOOD BUDDY ALFRED KEEPS BUSY. ZERE EEZ NO PROBLEM ZAT A GOOD ATTITUDE UND NINETEEN THOUSAND YEARS OF HARD THINKING CANNOT OVERCOME, YES?
ALFRED, TELL ME YOU SPENT THOSE NINETEEN THOUSAND YEARS FIGURING OUT A WAY OUT OF HERE.
EVEN BETTER! I HAVE MEMORIZED ALL ZE TWO-LETTER SCRABBLE COMBINATIONS.
SCOTCH
ZERE EES NO WAY OUT, YOU MIGHT AS WELL RELAX UND ENJOY YOURSELF. ME? I JUST WOKE UP IN ZAT BOOTH OVER ZERE ONE MORNING. NO WARNING, NO FLASHY ROBOTS, JUST A PILLOW UND SOME PAJAMAS.
I LIKE TO THEENK ZAT MAYBE GOD HAS HIRED ME AS HIS PERSONAL BARTENDER, NO?
NOT ZAT HE EVER COME IN HERE, OF COURSE.
WAIT, DOES THE FRONT DOOR WORK?
WELL, YES, SHE OPENS, BUT I DO NOT THINK EET EES SOMETHING YOU SHOULD DO.
YOU MAY FIND EET... **DISTURBING.**
C'MON, PHILLIP, WE'RE GETTING OUT OF HERE.
CAN I BRING MY DRINK?
YOU ARE MAKING ZE MISTAKE!

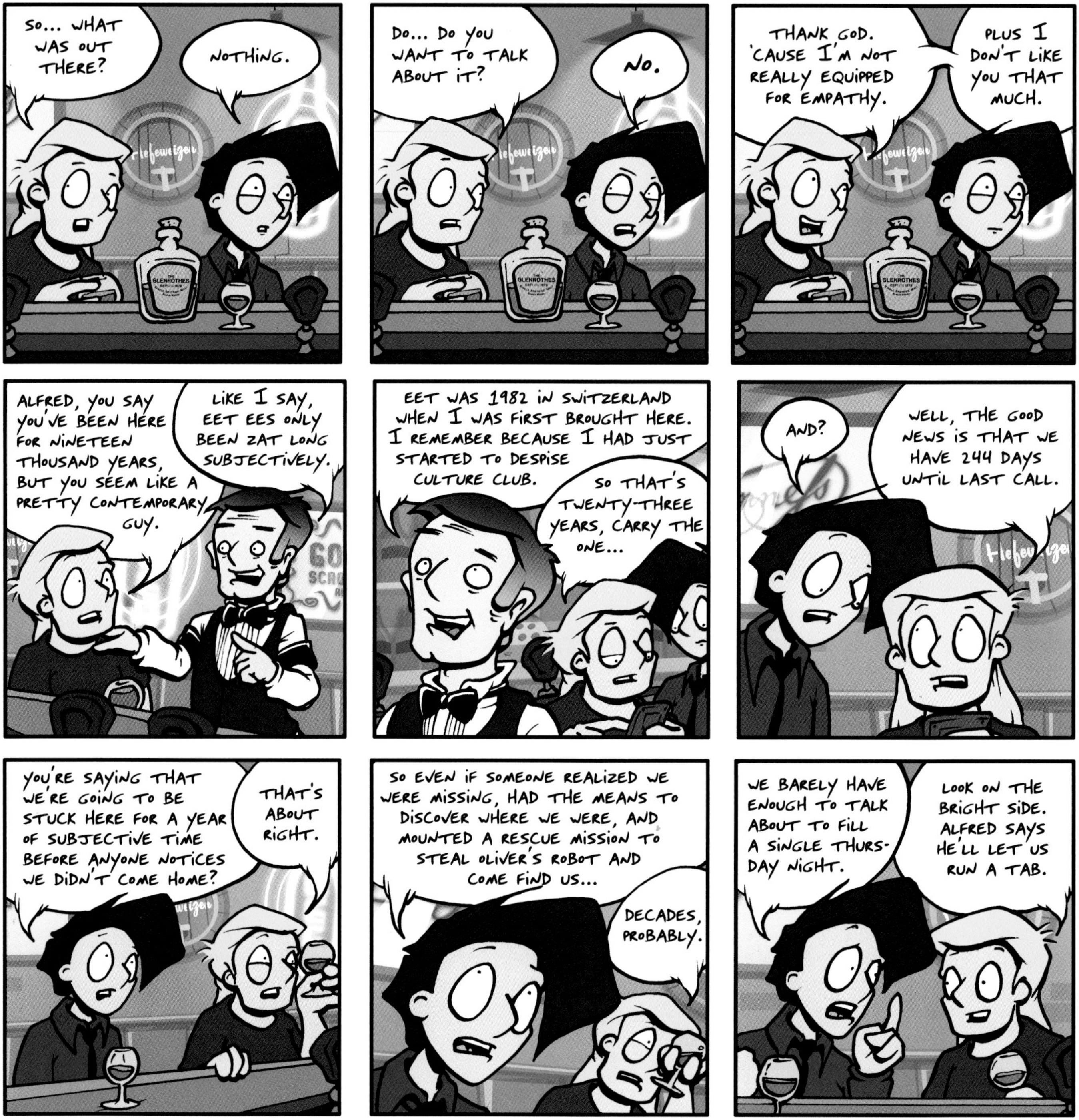
SO... WHAT WAS OUT THERE?
NOTHING.
DO... DO YOU WANT TO TALK ABOUT IT?
NO.
THANK GOD. 'CAUSE I'M NOT REALLY EQUIPPED FOR EMPATHY.
PLUS I DON'T LIKE YOU THAT MUCH.
ALFRED, YOU SAY YOU'VE BEEN HERE FOR NINETEEN THOUSAND YEARS, BUT YOU SEEM LIKE A PRETTY CONTEMPORARY GUY.
LIKE I SAY, EET EES ONLY BEEN ZAT LONG SUBJECTIVELY.
EET WAS 1982 IN SWITZERLAND WHEN I WAS FIRST BROUGHT HERE. I REMEMBER BECAUSE I HAD JUST STARTED TO DESPISE CULTURE CLUB.
SO THAT'S TWENTY-THREE YEARS, CARRY THE ONE...
AND?
WELL, THE GOOD NEWS IS THAT WE HAVE 244 DAYS UNTIL LAST CALL.
YOU'RE SAYING THAT WE'RE GOING TO BE STUCK HERE FOR A YEAR OF SUBJECTIVE TIME BEFORE ANYONE NOTICES WE DIDN'T COME HOME?
THAT'S ABOUT RIGHT.
SO EVEN IF SOMEONE REALIZED WE WERE MISSING, HAD THE MEANS TO DISCOVER WHERE WE WERE, AND MOUNTED A RESCUE MISSION TO STEAL OLIVER'S ROBOT AND COME FIND US...
DECADES, PROBABLY.
WE BARELY HAVE ENOUGH TO TALK ABOUT TO FILL A SINGLE THURS-DAY NIGHT.
LOOK ON THE BRIGHT SIDE. ALFRED SAYS HE'LL LET US RUN A TAB.

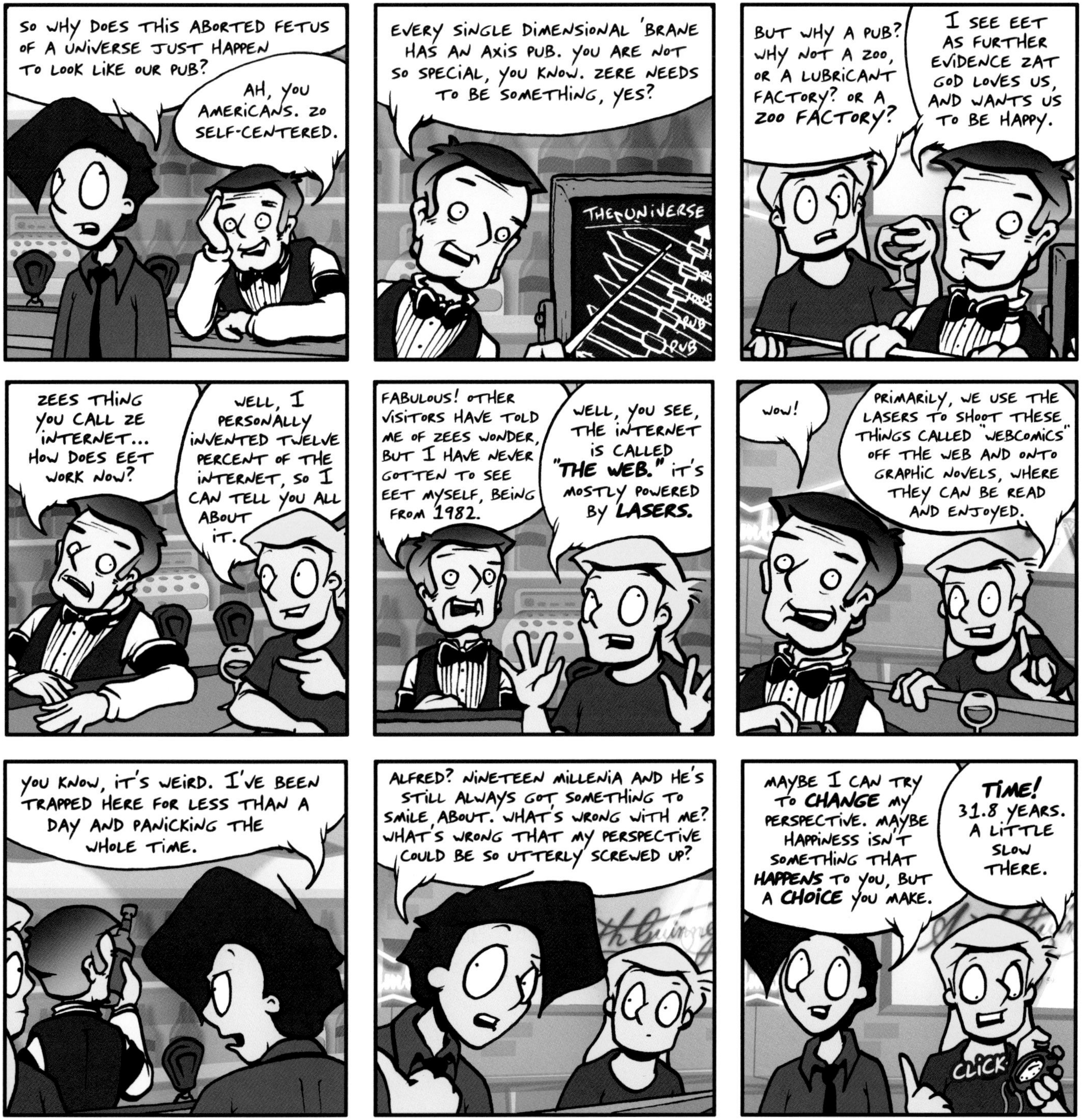
SO WHY DOES THIS ABORTED FETUS OF A UNIVERSE JUST HAPPEN TO LOOK LIKE OUR PUB?
AH, YOU AMERICANS. ZO SELF-CENTERED.
EVERY SINGLE DIMENSIONAL 'BRANE HAS AN AXIS PUB. YOU ARE NOT SO SPECIAL, YOU KNOW. ZERE NEEDS TO BE SOMETHING, YES?
THE UNIVERSE
PUB
PUB
BUT WHY A PUB? WHY NOT A ZOO, OR A LUBRICANT FACTORY? OR A ZOO FACTORY?
I SEE EET AS FURTHER EVIDENCE ZAT GOD LOVES US, AND WANTS US TO BE HAPPY.
ZEES THING YOU CALL ZE INTERNET... HOW DOES EET WORK NOW?
WELL, I PERSONALLY INVENTED TWELVE PERCENT OF THE INTERNET, SO I CAN TELL YOU ALL ABOUT IT.
FABULOUS! OTHER VISITORS HAVE TOLD ME OF ZEES WONDER, BUT I HAVE NEVER GOTTEN TO SEE EET MYSELF, BEING FROM 1982.
WELL, YOU SEE, THE INTERNET IS CALLED "THE WEB." IT'S MOSTLY POWERED BY LASERS.
WOW!
PRIMARILY, WE USE THE LASERS TO SHOOT THESE THINGS CALLED "WEBCOMICS" OFF THE WEB AND ONTO GRAPHIC NOVELS, WHERE THEY CAN BE READ AND ENJOYED.
YOU KNOW, IT'S WEIRD. I'VE BEEN TRAPPED HERE FOR LESS THAN A DAY AND PANICKING THE WHOLE TIME.
ALFRED? NINETEEN MILLENIA AND HE'S STILL ALWAYS GOT SOMETHING TO SMILE ABOUT. WHAT'S WRONG WITH ME? WHAT'S WRONG THAT MY PERSPECTIVE COULD BE SO UTTERLY SCREWED UP?
MAYBE I CAN TRY TO CHANGE MY PERSPECTIVE. MAYBE HAPPINESS ISN'T SOMETHING THAT HAPPENS TO YOU, BUT A CHOICE YOU MAKE.
TIME! 31.8 YEARS. A LITTLE SLOW THERE.
CLICK

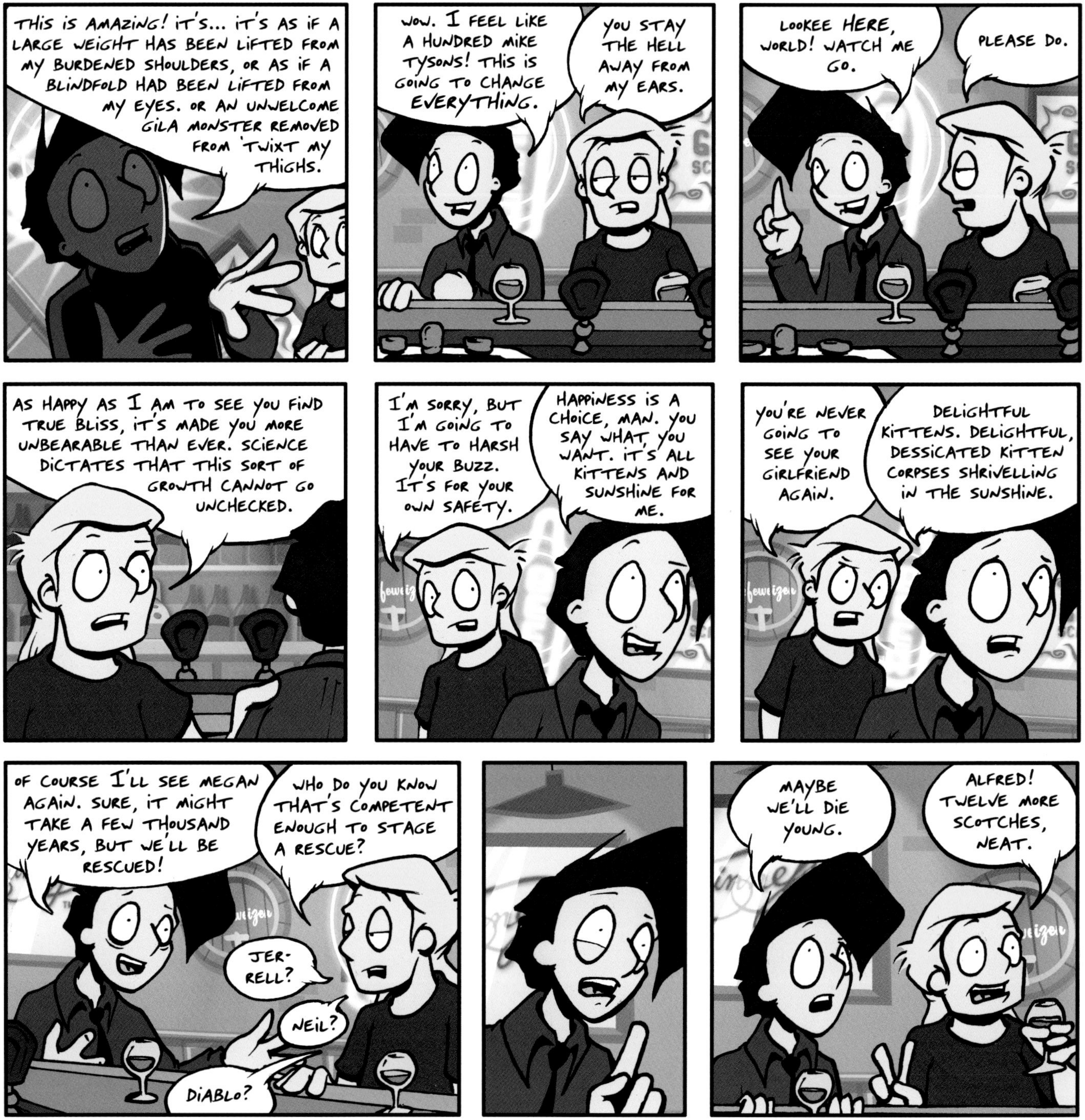
THIS IS AMAZING! IT'S... IT'S AS IF A LARGE WEIGHT HAS BEEN LIFTED FROM MY BURDENED SHOULDERS, OR AS IF A BLINDFOLD HAD BEEN LIFTED FROM MY EYES. OR AN UNWELCOME GILA MONSTER REMOVED FROM 'TWIXT MY THIGHS.
WOW. I FEEL LIKE A HUNDRED MIKE TYSONS! THIS IS GOING TO CHANGE EVERYTHING.
YOU STAY THE HELL AWAY FROM MY EARS.
LOOKEE HERE, WORLD! WATCH ME GO.
PLEASE DO.
AS HAPPY AS I AM TO SEE YOU FIND TRUE BLISS, IT'S MADE YOU MORE UNBEARABLE THAN EVER. SCIENCE DICTATES THAT THIS SORT OF GROWTH CANNOT GO UNCHECKED.
I'M SORRY, BUT I'M GOING TO HAVE TO HARSH YOUR BUZZ. IT'S FOR YOUR OWN SAFETY.
HAPPINESS IS A CHOICE, MAN. YOU SAY WHAT YOU WANT. IT'S ALL KITTENS AND SUNSHINE FOR ME.
YOU'RE NEVER GOING TO SEE YOUR GIRLFRIEND AGAIN.
DELIGHTFUL KITTENS. DELIGHTFUL, DESSICATED KITTEN CORPSES SHRIVELLING IN THE SUNSHINE.
OF COURSE I'LL SEE MEGAN AGAIN. SURE, IT MIGHT TAKE A FEW THOUSAND YEARS, BUT WE'LL BE RESCUED!
WHO DO YOU KNOW THAT'S COMPETENT ENOUGH TO STAGE A RESCUE?
JER-RELL?
NEIL?
DIABLO?
MAYBE WE'LL DIE YOUNG.
ALFRED! TWELVE MORE SCOTCHES, NEAT.

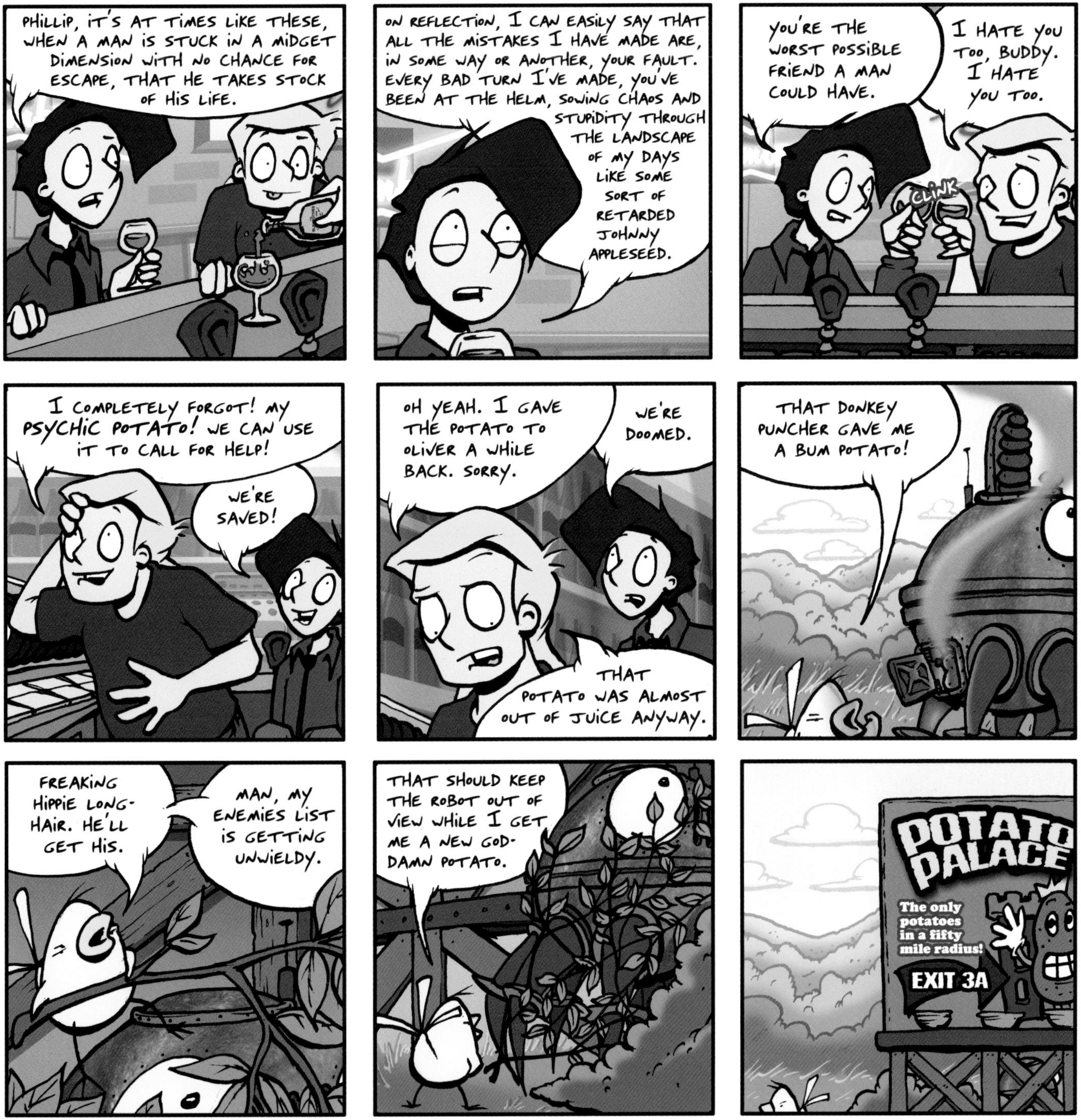
PHILLIP, IT'S AT TIMES LIKE THESE, WHEN A MAN IS STUCK IN A MIDGET DIMENSION WITH NO CHANCE FOR ESCAPE, THAT HE TAKES STOCK OF HIS LIFE.
ON REFLECTION, I CAN EASILY SAY THAT ALL THE MISTAKES I HAVE MADE ARE, IN SOME WAY OR ANOTHER, YOUR FAULT. EVERY BAD TURN I'VE MADE, YOU'VE BEEN AT THE HELM, SOWING CHAOS AND STUPIDITY THROUGH THE LANDSCAPE OF MY DAYS LIKE SOME SORT OF RETARDED JOHNNY APPLESEED.
YOU'RE THE WORST POSSIBLE FRIEND A MAN COULD HAVE.
I HATE YOU TOO, BUDDY. I HATE YOU TOO.
CLINK
I COMPLETELY FORGOT! MY PSYCHIC POTATO! WE CAN USE IT TO CALL FOR HELP!
WE'RE SAVED!
OH YEAH. I GAVE THE POTATO TO OLIVER A WHILE BACK. SORRY.
WE'RE DOOMED.
THAT POTATO WAS ALMOST OUT OF JUICE ANYWAY.
THAT DONKEY PUNCHER GAVE ME A BUM POTATO!
FREAKING HIPPIE LONG-HAIR. HE'LL GET HIS.
MAN, MY ENEMIES LIST IS GETTING UNWIELDY.
THAT SHOULD KEEP THE ROBOT OUT OF VIEW WHILE I GET ME A NEW GOD-DAMN POTATO.
POTATO PALACE
The only potatoes in a fifty mile radius!
EXIT 3A

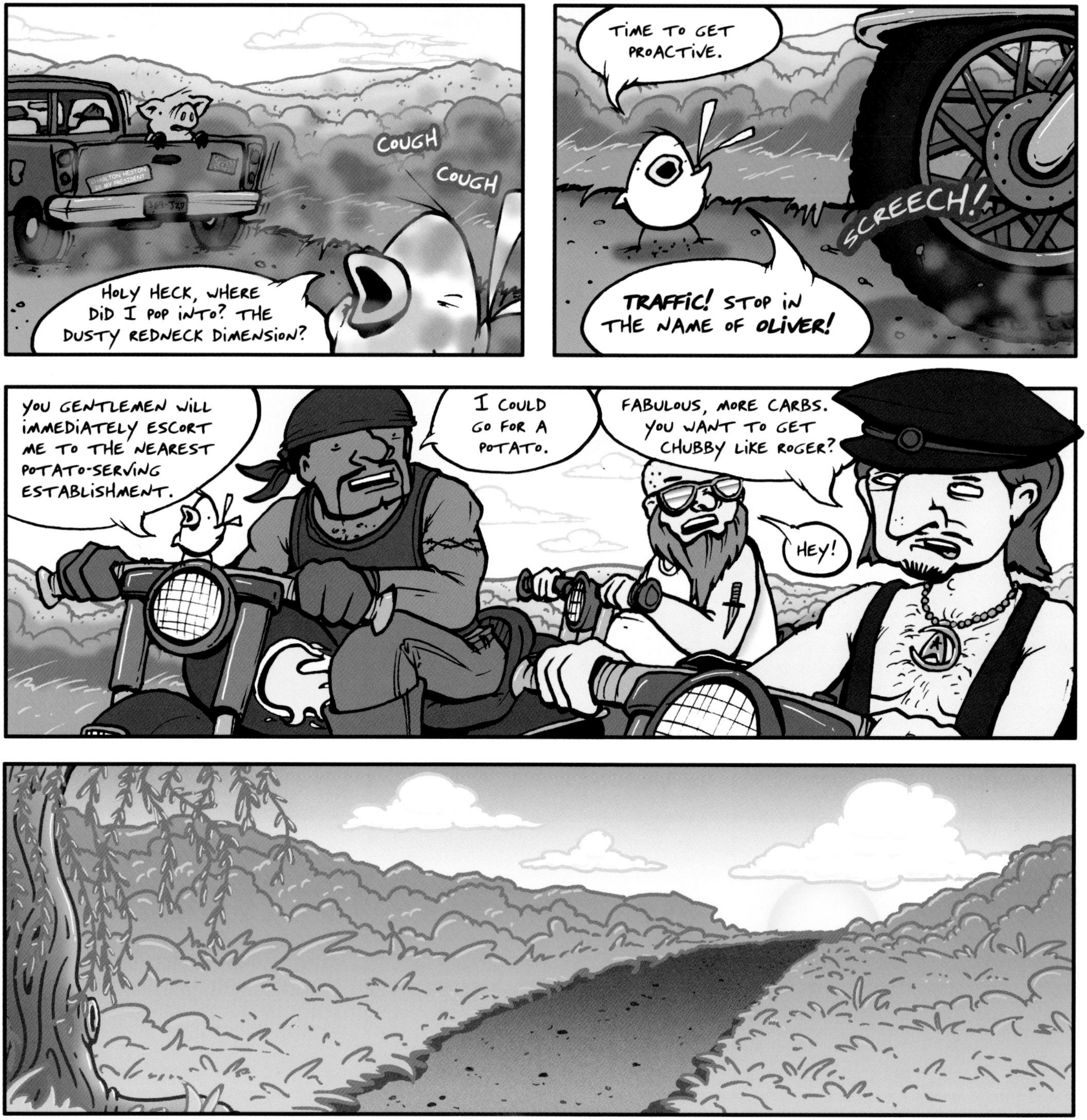

COUGH
COUGH
CHARLTON HESTON IS MY PRESIDENT
HOLY HECK, WHERE DID I POP INTO? THE DUSTY REDNECK DIMENSION?
TIME TO GET PROACTIVE.
SCREECH!
TRAFFIC! STOP IN THE NAME OF OLIVER!
YOU GENTLEMEN WILL IMMEDIATELY ESCORT ME TO THE NEAREST POTATO-SERVING ESTABLISHMENT.
I COULD GO FOR A POTATO.
FABULOUS, MORE CARBS. YOU WANT TO GET CHUBBY LIKE ROGER?
HEY!

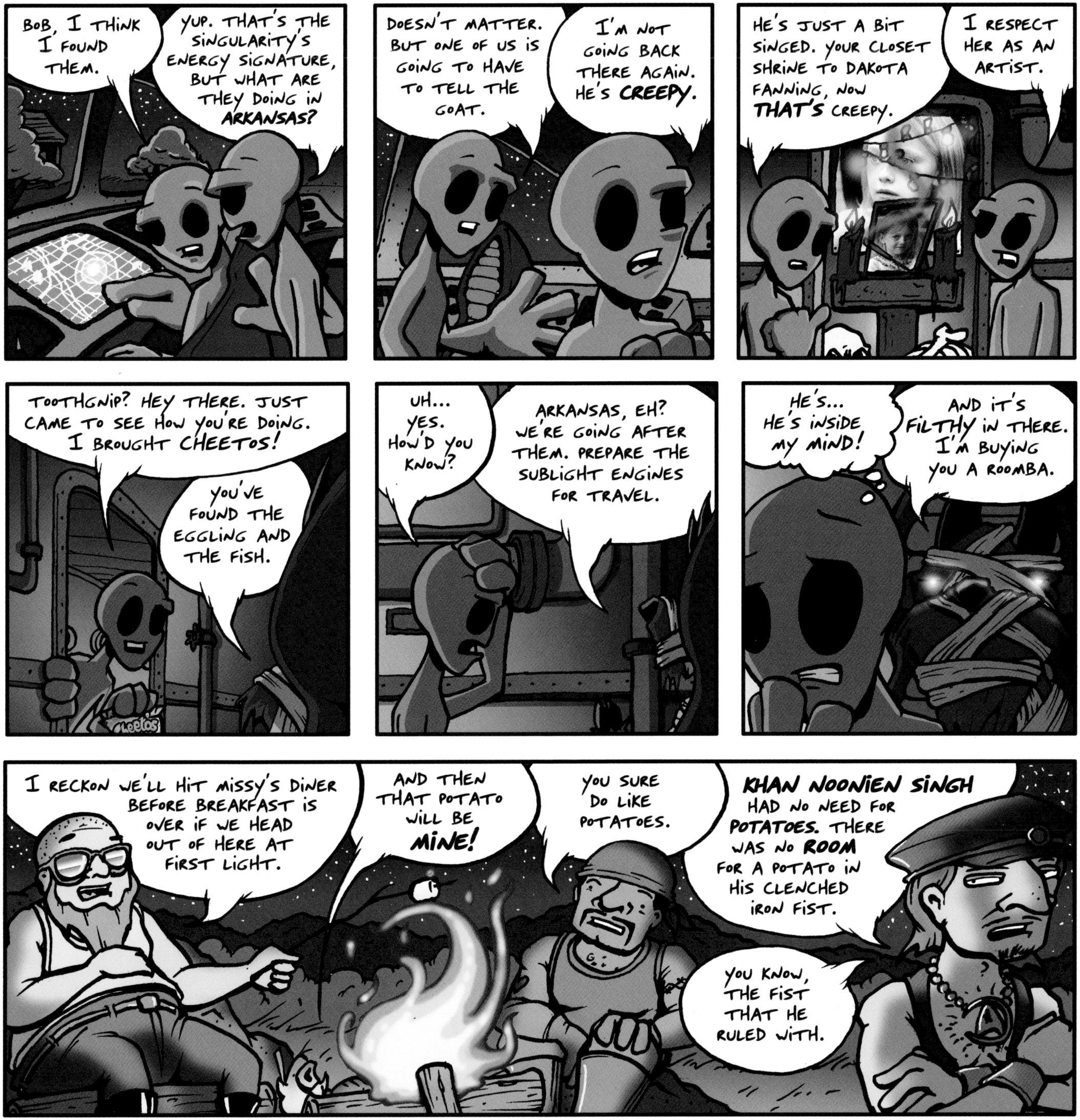
BOB, I THINK I FOUND THEM.
YUP. THAT'S THE SINGULARITY'S ENERGY SIGNATURE, BUT WHAT ARE THEY DOING IN ARKANSAS?
DOESN'T MATTER. BUT ONE OF US IS GOING TO HAVE TO TELL THE GOAT.
I'M NOT GOING BACK THERE AGAIN. HE'S CREEPY.
HE'S JUST A BIT SINGED. YOUR CLOSET SHRINE TO DAKOTA FANNING, NOW THAT'S CREEPY.
I RESPECT HER AS AN ARTIST.
TOOTHGNIP? HEY THERE. JUST CAME TO SEE HOW YOU'RE DOING. I BROUGHT CHEETOS!
YOU'VE FOUND THE EGGLING AND THE FISH.
Cheetos
UH... YES. HOW'D YOU KNOW?
ARKANSAS, EH? WE'RE GOING AFTER THEM. PREPARE THE SUBLIGHT ENGINES FOR TRAVEL.
HE'S... HE'S INSIDE MY MIND!
AND IT'S FILTHY IN THERE. I'M BUYING YOU A ROOMBA.
I RECKON WE'LL HIT MISSY'S DINER BEFORE BREAKFAST IS OVER IF WE HEAD OUT OF HERE AT FIRST LIGHT.
AND THEN THAT POTATO WILL BE MINE!
YOU SURE DO LIKE POTATOES.
KHAN NOONIEN SINGH HAD NO NEED FOR POTATOES. THERE WAS NO ROOM FOR A POTATO IN HIS CLENCHED IRON FIST.
YOU KNOW, THE FIST THAT HE RULED WITH.

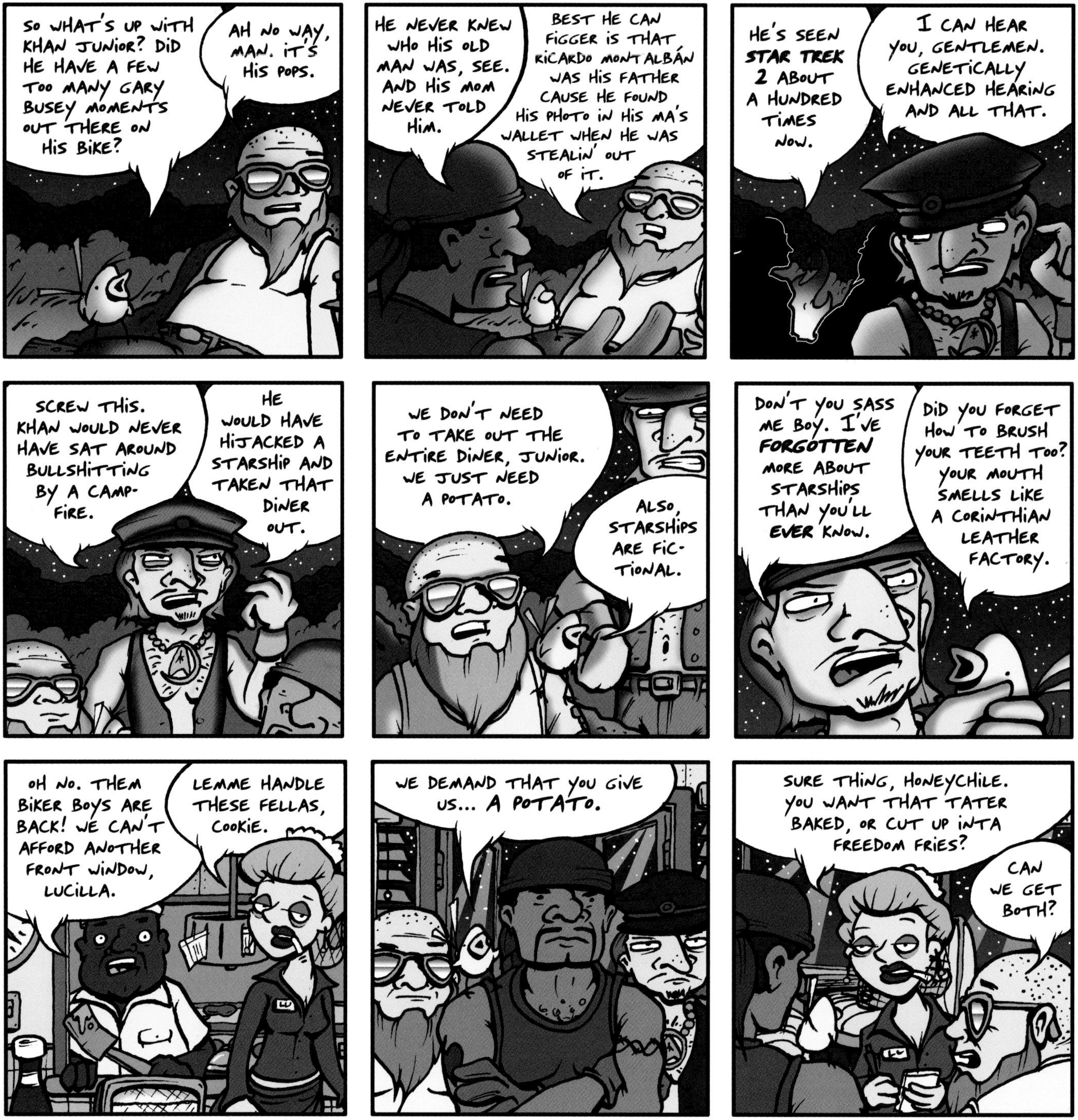
SO WHAT'S UP WITH KHAN JUNIOR? DID HE HAVE A FEW TOO MANY GARY BUSEY MOMENTS OUT THERE ON HIS BIKE?
AH NO WAY, MAN. IT'S HIS POPS.
HE NEVER KNEW WHO HIS OLD MAN WAS, SEE. AND HIS MOM NEVER TOLD HIM.
BEST HE CAN FIGGER IS THAT RICARDO MONTALBÁN WAS HIS FATHER CAUSE HE FOUND HIS PHOTO IN HIS MA'S WALLET WHEN HE WAS STEALIN' OUT OF IT.
HE'S SEEN STAR TREK 2 ABOUT A HUNDRED TIMES NOW.
I CAN HEAR YOU, GENTLEMEN. GENETICALLY ENHANCED HEARING AND ALL THAT.
SCREW THIS. KHAN WOULD NEVER HAVE SAT AROUND BULLSHITTING BY A CAMP-FIRE.
HE WOULD HAVE HIJACKED A STARSHIP AND TAKEN THAT DINER OUT.
WE DON'T NEED TO TAKE OUT THE ENTIRE DINER, JUNIOR. WE JUST NEED A POTATO.
ALSO, STARSHIPS ARE FIC-TIONAL.
DON'T YOU SASS ME BOY. I'VE FORGOTTEN MORE ABOUT STARSHIPS THAN YOU'LL EVER KNOW.
DID YOU FORGET HOW TO BRUSH YOUR TEETH TOO? YOUR MOUTH SMELLS LIKE A CORINTHIAN LEATHER FACTORY.
OH NO. THEM BIKER BOYS ARE BACK! WE CAN'T AFFORD ANOTHER FRONT WINDOW, LUCILLA.
LEMME HANDLE THESE FELLAS, COOKIE.
WE DEMAND THAT YOU GIVE US... A POTATO.
SURE THING, HONEYCHILE. YOU WANT THAT TATER BAKED, OR CUT UP INTA FREEDOM FRIES?
CAN WE GET BOTH?

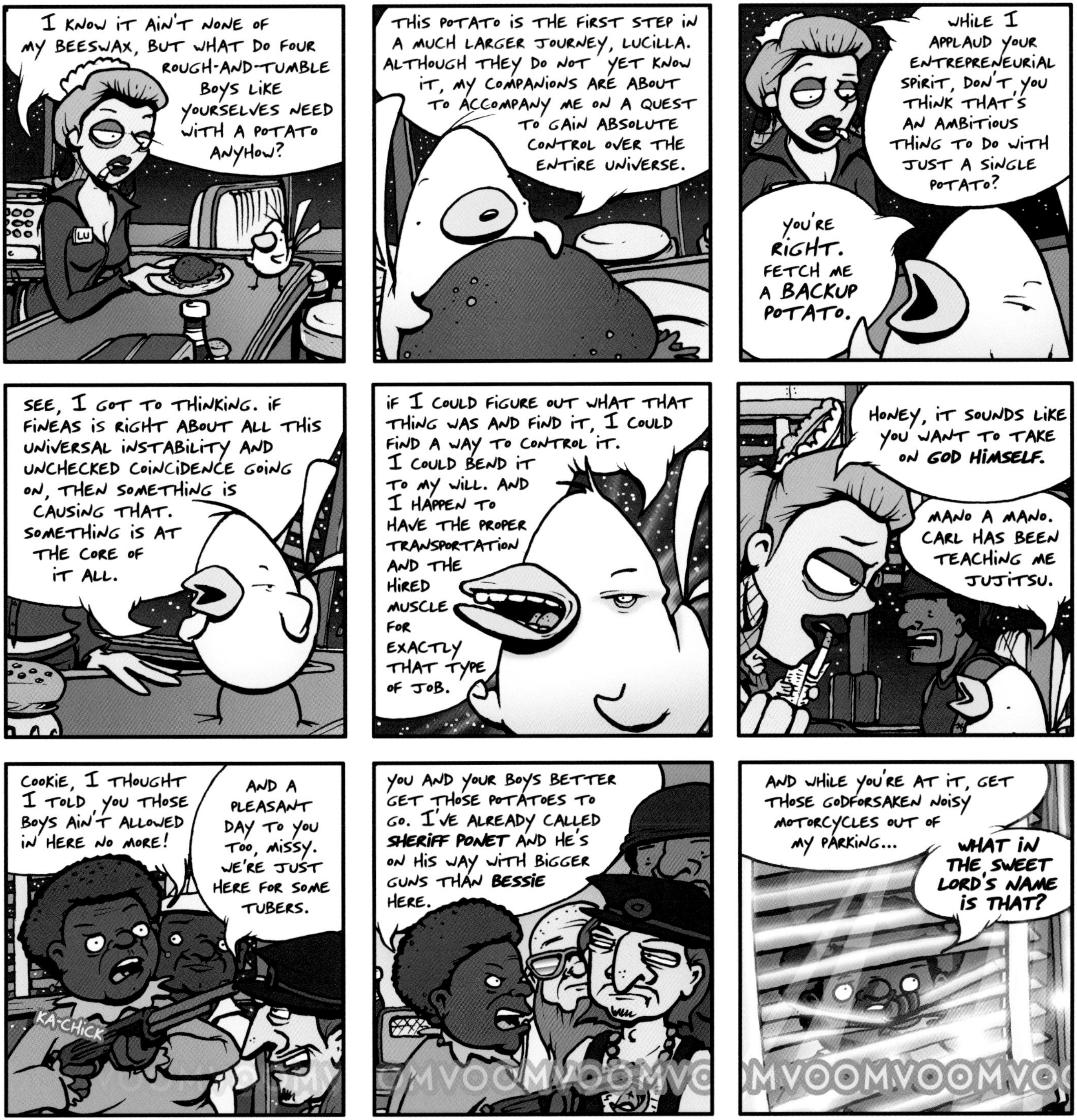
I KNOW IT AIN'T NONE OF MY BEESWAX, BUT WHAT DO FOUR ROUGH-AND-TUMBLE BOYS LIKE YOURSELVES NEED WITH A POTATO ANYHOW?
LU
THIS POTATO IS THE FIRST STEP IN A MUCH LARGER JOURNEY, LUCILLA. ALTHOUGH THEY DO NOT YET KNOW IT, MY COMPANIONS ARE ABOUT TO ACCOMPANY ME ON A QUEST TO GAIN ABSOLUTE CONTROL OVER THE ENTIRE UNIVERSE.
WHILE I APPLAUD YOUR ENTREPRENEURIAL SPIRIT, DON'T YOU THINK THAT'S AN AMBITIOUS THING TO DO WITH JUST A SINGLE POTATO?
YOU'RE RIGHT. FETCH ME A BACKUP POTATO.
SEE, I GOT TO THINKING. IF FINEAS IS RIGHT ABOUT ALL THIS UNIVERSAL INSTABILITY AND UNCHECKED COINCIDENCE GOING ON, THEN SOMETHING IS CAUSING THAT. SOMETHING IS AT THE CORE OF IT ALL.
IF I COULD FIGURE OUT WHAT THAT THING WAS AND FIND IT, I COULD FIND A WAY TO CONTROL IT. I COULD BEND IT TO MY WILL. AND I HAPPEN TO HAVE THE PROPER TRANSPORTATION AND THE HIRED MUSCLE FOR EXACTLY THAT TYPE OF JOB.
HONEY, IT SOUNDS LIKE YOU WANT TO TAKE ON GOD HIMSELF.
MANO A MANO. CARL HAS BEEN TEACHING ME JUJITSU.
COOKIE, I THOUGHT I TOLD YOU THOSE BOYS AIN'T ALLOWED IN HERE NO MORE!
AND A PLEASANT DAY TO YOU TOO, MISSY. WE'RE JUST HERE FOR SOME TUBERS.
KA-CHICK
YOU AND YOUR BOYS BETTER GET THOSE POTATOES TO GO. I'VE ALREADY CALLED SHERIFF PONET AND HE'S ON HIS WAY WITH BIGGER GUNS THAN BESSIE HERE.
AND WHILE YOU'RE AT IT, GET THOSE GODFORSAKEN NOISY MOTORCYCLES OUT OF MY PARKING...
WHAT IN THE SWEET LORD'S NAME IS THAT?
VOOMVOOMVOOMVOOMVOOMVOOMVOOMVOOMVOOMVO

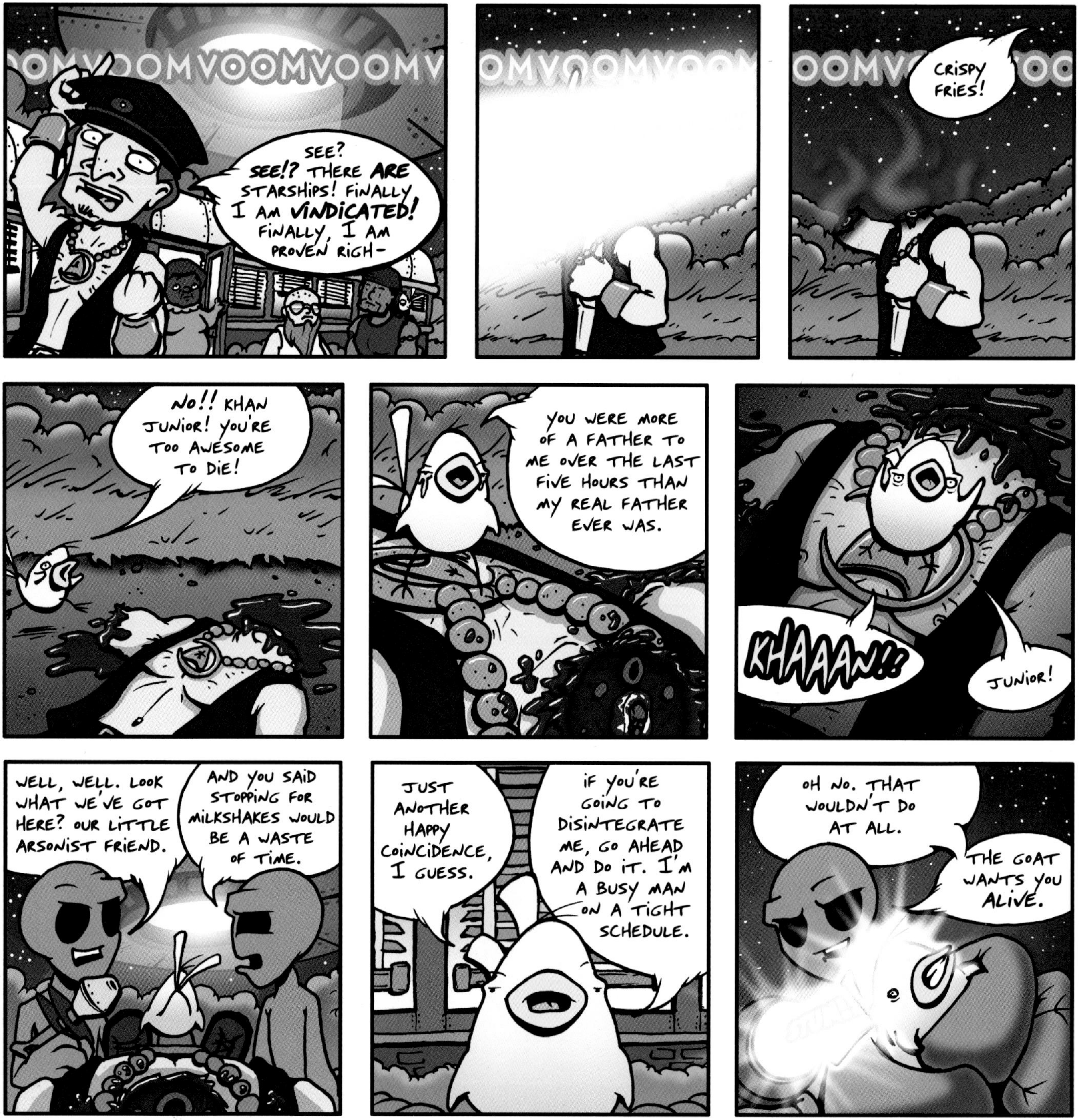
VOOMVOOMVOOMV
SEE? SEE!? THERE ARE STARSHIPS! FINALLY I AM VINDICATED! FINALLY, I AM PROVEN RIGH-
OMVOOMVOOM
OOMV OO
CRISPY FRIES!
NO!! KHAN JUNIOR! YOU'RE TOO AWESOME TO DIE!
YOU WERE MORE OF A FATHER TO ME OVER THE LAST FIVE HOURS THAN MY REAL FATHER EVER WAS.
KHAAAN!!
JUNIOR!
WELL, WELL. LOOK WHAT WE'VE GOT HERE? OUR LITTLE ARSONIST FRIEND.
AND YOU SAID STOPPING FOR MILKSHAKES WOULD BE A WASTE OF TIME.
JUST ANOTHER HAPPY COINCIDENCE, I GUESS.
IF YOU'RE GOING TO DISINTEGRATE ME, GO AHEAD AND DO IT. I'M A BUSY MAN ON A TIGHT SCHEDULE.
OH NO. THAT WOULDN'T DO AT ALL.
THE GOAT WANTS YOU ALIVE.

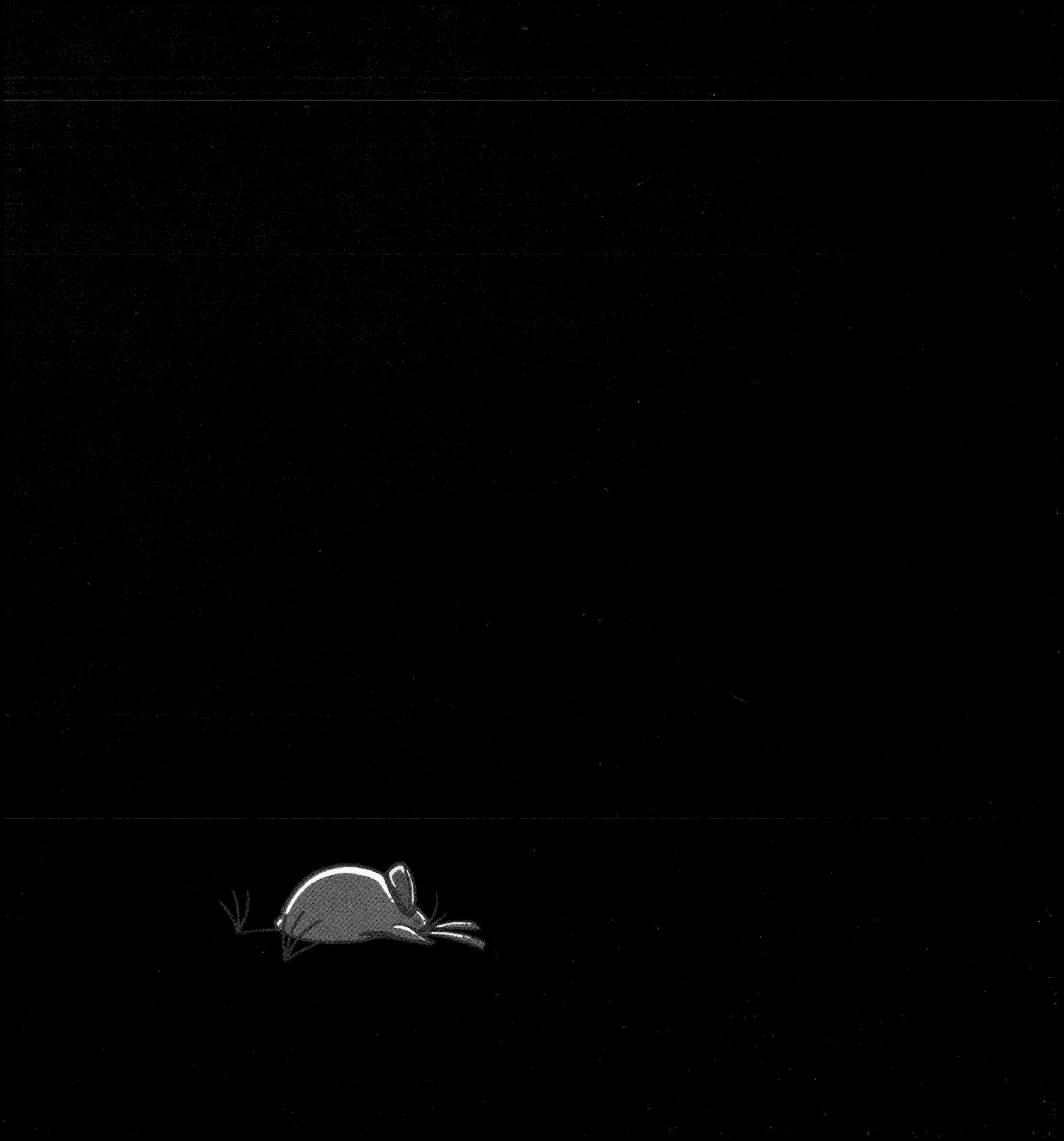

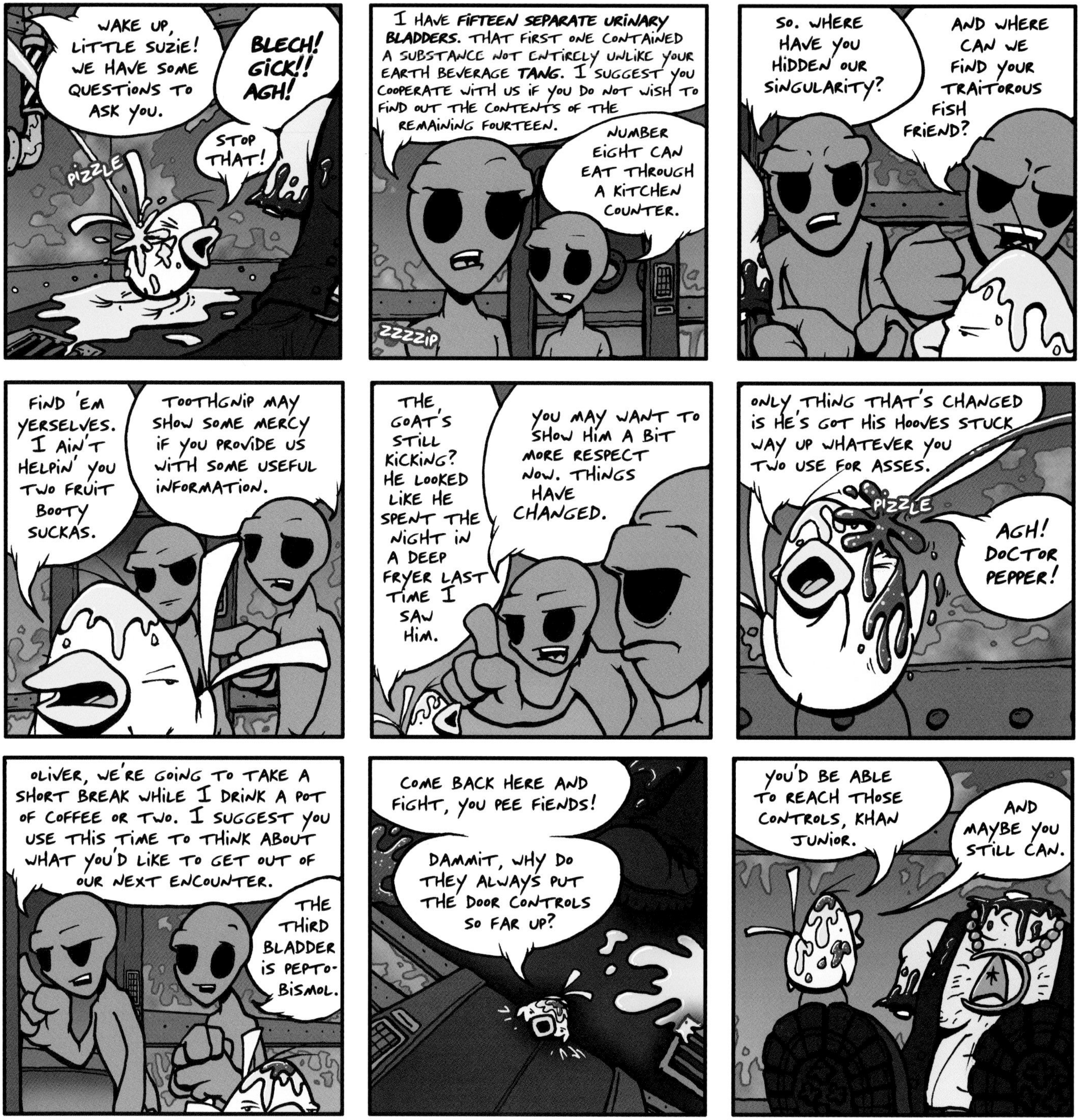
WAKE UP, LITTLE SUZIE! WE HAVE SOME QUESTIONS TO ASK YOU.
BLECH! GICK!! AGH!
PIZZLE
STOP THAT!
I HAVE **FIFTEEN SEPARATE URINARY BLADDERS.** THAT FIRST ONE CONTAINED A SUBSTANCE NOT ENTIRELY UNLIKE YOUR EARTH BEVERAGE **TANG.** I SUGGEST YOU COOPERATE WITH US IF YOU DO NOT WISH TO FIND OUT THE CONTENTS OF THE REMAINING FOURTEEN.
NUMBER EIGHT CAN EAT THROUGH A KITCHEN COUNTER.
ZZZZIP
SO. WHERE HAVE YOU HIDDEN OUR SINGULARITY?
AND WHERE CAN WE FIND YOUR TRAITOROUS FISH FRIEND?
FIND 'EM YERSELVES. I AIN'T HELPIN' YOU TWO FRUIT BOOTY SUCKAS.
TOOTHGNIP MAY SHOW SOME MERCY IF YOU PROVIDE US WITH SOME USEFUL INFORMATION.
THE GOAT'S STILL KICKING? HE LOOKED LIKE HE SPENT THE NIGHT IN A DEEP FRYER LAST TIME I SAW HIM.
YOU MAY WANT TO SHOW HIM A BIT MORE RESPECT NOW. THINGS HAVE CHANGED.
ONLY THING THAT'S CHANGED IS HE'S GOT HIS HOOVES STUCK WAY UP WHATEVER YOU TWO USE FOR ASSES.
PIZZLE
AGH! DOCTOR PEPPER!
OLIVER, WE'RE GOING TO TAKE A SHORT BREAK WHILE I DRINK A POT OF COFFEE OR TWO. I SUGGEST YOU USE THIS TIME TO THINK ABOUT WHAT YOU'D LIKE TO GET OUT OF OUR NEXT ENCOUNTER.
THE THIRD BLADDER IS PEPTO-BISMOL.
COME BACK HERE AND FIGHT, YOU PEE FIENDS!
DAMMIT, WHY DO THEY ALWAYS PUT THE DOOR CONTROLS SO FAR UP?
YOU'D BE ABLE TO REACH THOSE CONTROLS, KHAN JUNIOR.
AND MAYBE YOU STILL CAN.

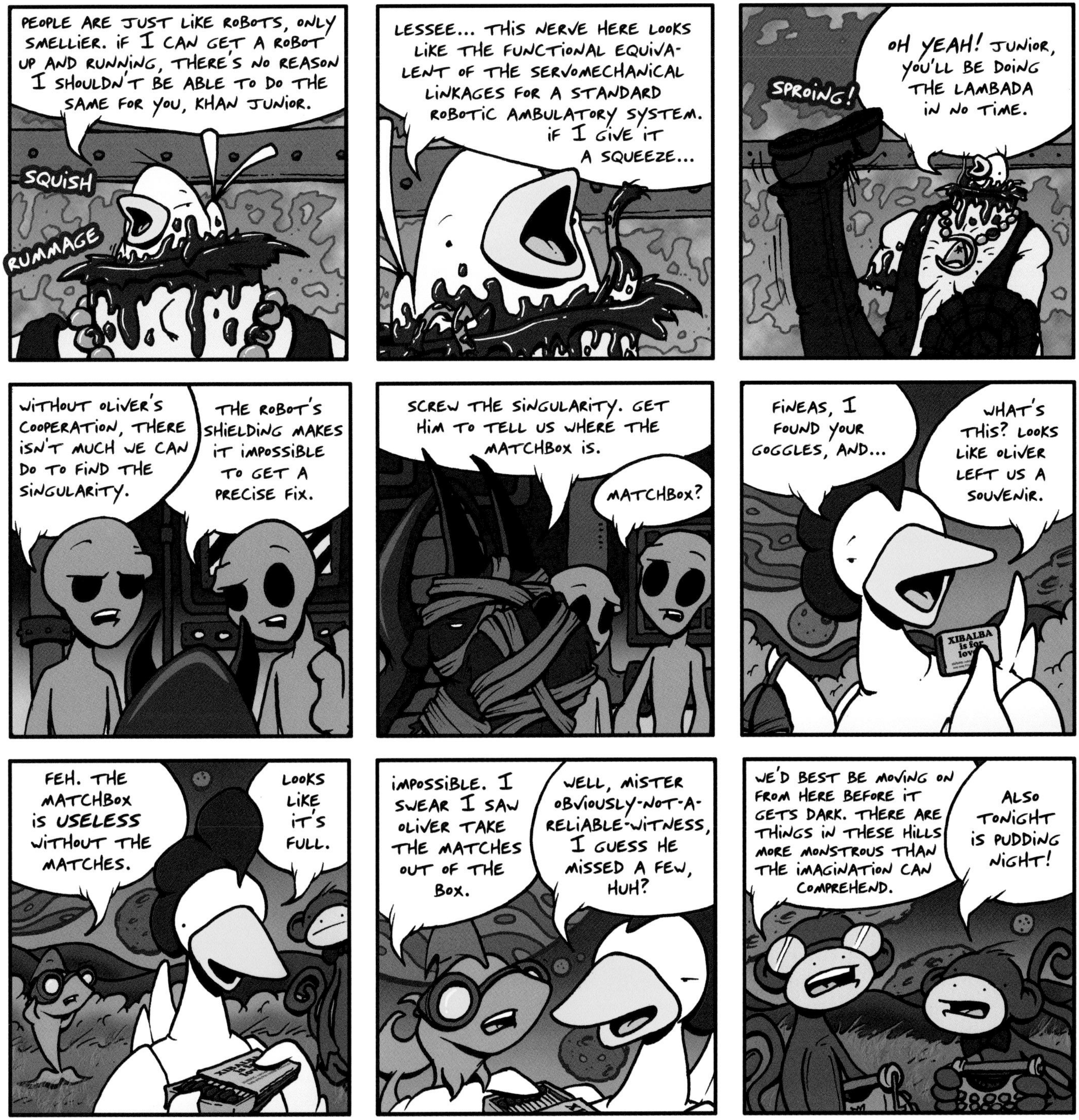
PEOPLE ARE JUST LIKE ROBOTS, ONLY SMELLIER. IF I CAN GET A ROBOT UP AND RUNNING, THERE'S NO REASON I SHOULDN'T BE ABLE TO DO THE SAME FOR YOU, KHAN JUNIOR.
SQUISH
RUMMAGE
LESSEE... THIS NERVE HERE LOOKS LIKE THE FUNCTIONAL EQUIVALENT OF THE SERVOMECHANICAL LINKAGES FOR A STANDARD ROBOTIC AMBULATORY SYSTEM. IF I GIVE IT A SQUEEZE...
SPROING!
OH YEAH! JUNIOR, YOU'LL BE DOING THE LAMBADA IN NO TIME.
WITHOUT OLIVER'S COOPERATION, THERE ISN'T MUCH WE CAN DO TO FIND THE SINGULARITY.
THE ROBOT'S SHIELDING MAKES IT IMPOSSIBLE TO GET A PRECISE FIX.
SCREW THE SINGULARITY. GET HIM TO TELL US WHERE THE MATCHBOX IS.
MATCHBOX?
FINEAS, I FOUND YOUR GOGGLES, AND...
WHAT'S THIS? LOOKS LIKE OLIVER LEFT US A SOUVENIR.
XIBALBA is for lovers
FEH. THE MATCHBOX IS USELESS WITHOUT THE MATCHES.
LOOKS LIKE IT'S FULL.
IMPOSSIBLE. I SWEAR I SAW OLIVER TAKE THE MATCHES OUT OF THE BOX.
WELL, MISTER OBVIOUSLY-NOT-A-RELIABLE-WITNESS, I GUESS HE MISSED A FEW, HUH?
WE'D BEST BE MOVING ON FROM HERE BEFORE IT GETS DARK. THERE ARE THINGS IN THESE HILLS MORE MONSTROUS THAN THE IMAGINATION CAN COMPREHEND.
ALSO TONIGHT IS PUDDING NIGHT!

DOES EVERY ALTERNATE DIMENSION HAVE A PUDDING NIGHT?

COULDN'T TELL YOU. WE'RE ONLY ASSISTANT EDITORS FOR MANHATTAN 3.

WE DON'T HAVE ACCESS TO MAKE CHANGES TO ANY OTHER LEVELS.

HOW MANY LEVELS ARE THERE?

THERE'S AN INFINITE NUMBER OF LEVELS, AND A TEAM OF ASSITANT EDITORS FOR EACH.

WHICH IS WHY IT'S VITALLY IMPORTANT WE GET TO PUDDING NIGHT AS SOON AS POSSIBLE. THE LINES GET RIDICULOUS.

I GOTTA TELL YOU, WE HAD TO GO THROUGH QUITE SOME TROUBLE TO GET YOU HERE FROM MANHATTAN 3.

WE GOT HERE OURSELVES LAST I CHECKED.

YOU DIDN'T THINK A CONFLUENCE OF BIZARRE EVENTS LIKE YOU GUYS HAVE BEEN GOING THROUGH JUST HAPPENS NATURALLY, DID YOU?

THERE WAS SOME MEDDLING INVOLVED.

MEDDLING? WE'VE BEEN THROUGH TWO SEPARATE INCARNATIONS OF HELL. ALIENS ARE CHASING US. HALF OF NEW YORK IS IN FLAMES.

WE'RE PROFESSIONALS.

SO YOU GUYS ARE OUR... CREATORS?

OH, NO. ASSISTANT EDITORS DON'T HAVE PERMISSION TO CREATE ANYTHING LARGER THAN A POTATO, REALLY.

WE DON'T CREATE THE UNIVERSES. WE JUST MAKE TWEAKS, TRIM THEM HERE AND THERE, KEEP THINGS NEAT. THINK OF US AS GOD'S GARDENERS.

SO THERE IS A GOD?

NOT LIKE HE'S TRADITIONALLY THOUGHT OF ON YOUR LEVEL, WHAT WITH THE BEARD AND THE FLOWING ROBES AND THE GOOD COP/BAD COP ROUTINE.

HE'S ONLY GOT A MOUSTACHE.

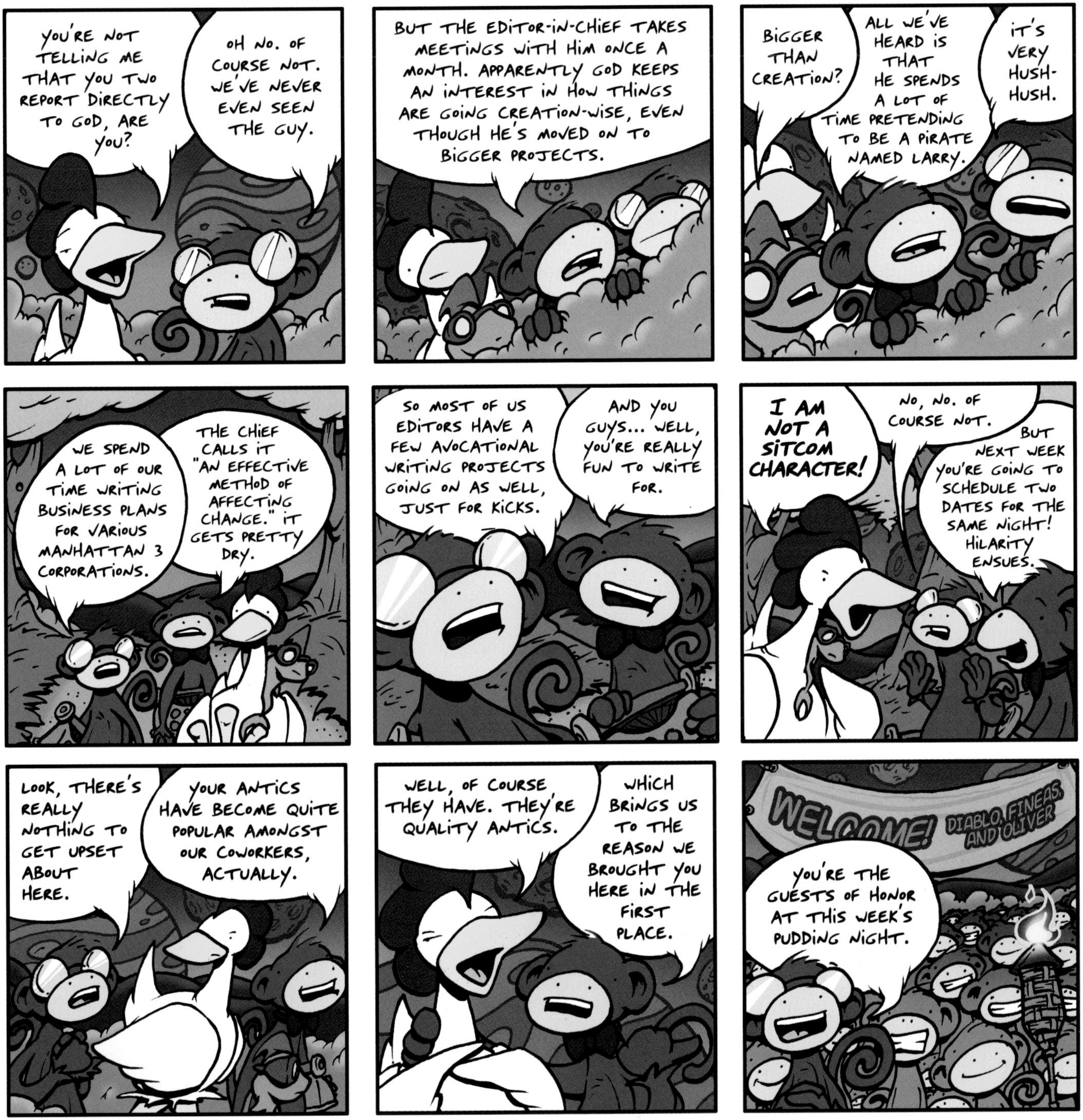
YOU'RE NOT TELLING ME THAT YOU TWO REPORT DIRECTLY TO GOD, ARE YOU?
OH NO. OF COURSE NOT. WE'VE NEVER EVEN SEEN THE GUY.
BUT THE EDITOR-IN-CHIEF TAKES MEETINGS WITH HIM ONCE A MONTH. APPARENTLY GOD KEEPS AN INTEREST IN HOW THINGS ARE GOING CREATION-WISE, EVEN THOUGH HE'S MOVED ON TO BIGGER PROJECTS.
BIGGER THAN CREATION?
ALL WE'VE HEARD IS THAT HE SPENDS A LOT OF TIME PRETENDING TO BE A PIRATE NAMED LARRY.
IT'S VERY HUSH-HUSH.
WE SPEND A LOT OF OUR TIME WRITING BUSINESS PLANS FOR VARIOUS MANHATTAN 3 CORPORATIONS.
THE CHIEF CALLS IT "AN EFFECTIVE METHOD OF AFFECTING CHANGE." IT GETS PRETTY DRY.
SO MOST OF US EDITORS HAVE A FEW AVOCATIONAL WRITING PROJECTS GOING ON AS WELL, JUST FOR KICKS.
AND YOU GUYS... WELL, YOU'RE REALLY FUN TO WRITE FOR.
I AM NOT A SITCOM CHARACTER!
NO, NO. OF COURSE NOT.
BUT NEXT WEEK YOU'RE GOING TO SCHEDULE TWO DATES FOR THE SAME NIGHT! HILARITY ENSUES.
LOOK, THERE'S REALLY NOTHING TO GET UPSET ABOUT HERE.
YOUR ANTICS HAVE BECOME QUITE POPULAR AMONGST OUR COWORKERS, ACTUALLY.
WELL, OF COURSE THEY HAVE. THEY'RE QUALITY ANTICS.
WHICH BRINGS US TO THE REASON WE BROUGHT YOU HERE IN THE FIRST PLACE.
WELCOME! DIABLO, FINEAS, AND OLIVER
YOU'RE THE GUESTS OF HONOR AT THIS WEEK'S PUDDING NIGHT.

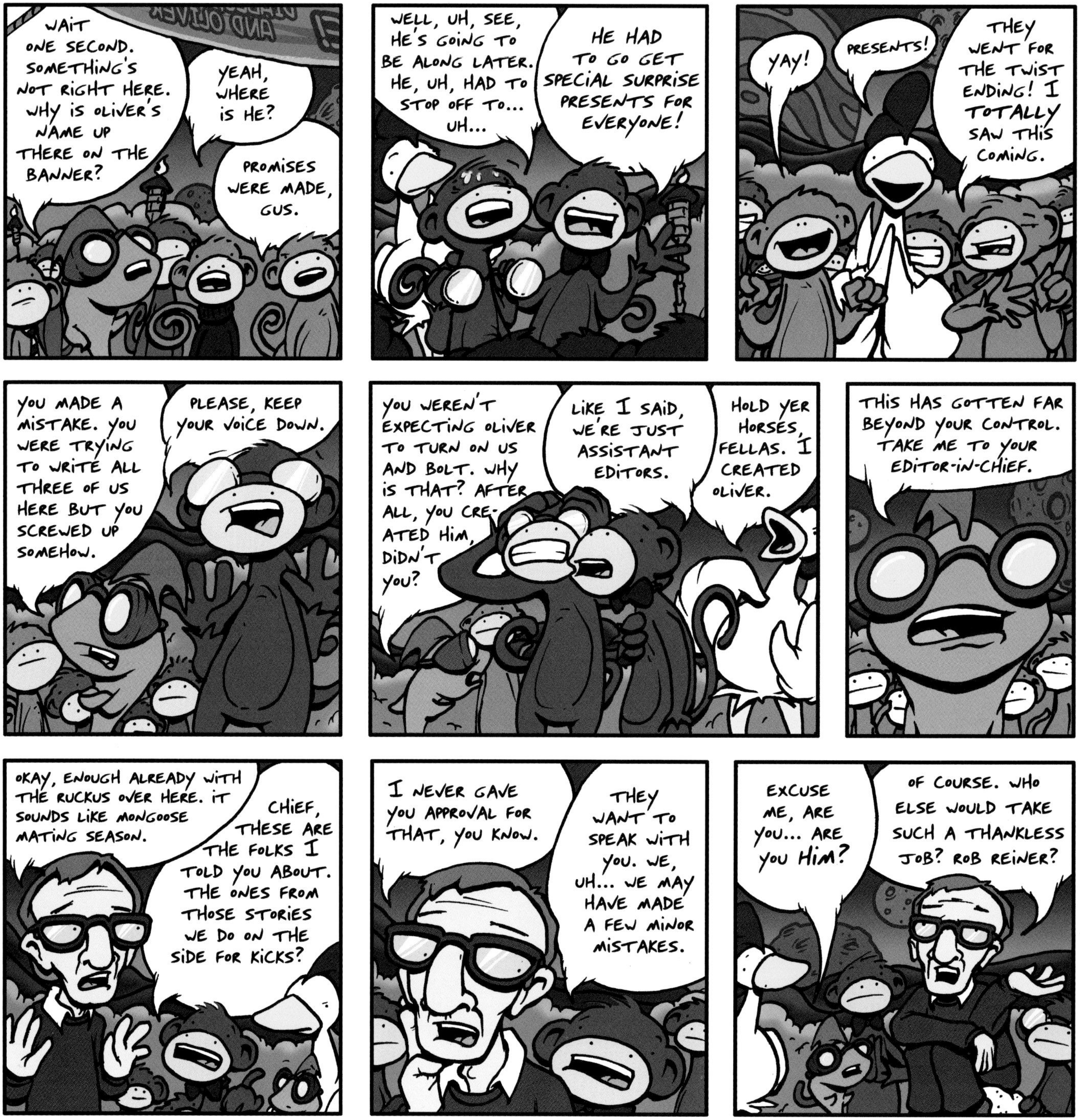
WAIT ONE SECOND. SOMETHING'S NOT RIGHT HERE. WHY IS OLIVER'S NAME UP THERE ON THE BANNER?
YEAH, WHERE IS HE?
PROMISES WERE MADE, GUS.
WELL, UH, SEE, HE'S GOING TO BE ALONG LATER. HE, UH, HAD TO STOP OFF TO... UH...
HE HAD TO GO GET SPECIAL SURPRISE PRESENTS FOR EVERYONE!
YAY!
PRESENTS!
THEY WENT FOR THE TWIST ENDING! I TOTALLY SAW THIS COMING.
YOU MADE A MISTAKE. YOU WERE TRYING TO WRITE ALL THREE OF US HERE BUT YOU SCREWED UP SOMEHOW.
PLEASE, KEEP YOUR VOICE DOWN.
YOU WEREN'T EXPECTING OLIVER TO TURN ON US AND BOLT. WHY IS THAT? AFTER ALL, YOU CRE-ATED HIM, DIDN'T YOU?
LIKE I SAID, WE'RE JUST ASSISTANT EDITORS.
HOLD YER HORSES, FELLAS. I CREATED OLIVER.
THIS HAS GOTTEN FAR BEYOND YOUR CONTROL. TAKE ME TO YOUR EDITOR-IN-CHIEF.
OKAY, ENOUGH ALREADY WITH THE RUCKUS OVER HERE. IT SOUNDS LIKE MONGOOSE MATING SEASON.
CHIEF, THESE ARE THE FOLKS I TOLD YOU ABOUT. THE ONES FROM THOSE STORIES WE DO ON THE SIDE FOR KICKS?
I NEVER GAVE YOU APPROVAL FOR THAT, YOU KNOW.
THEY WANT TO SPEAK WITH YOU. WE, UH... WE MAY HAVE MADE A FEW MINOR MISTAKES.
EXCUSE ME, ARE YOU... ARE YOU HIM?
OF COURSE. WHO ELSE WOULD TAKE SUCH A THANKLESS JOB? ROB REINER?

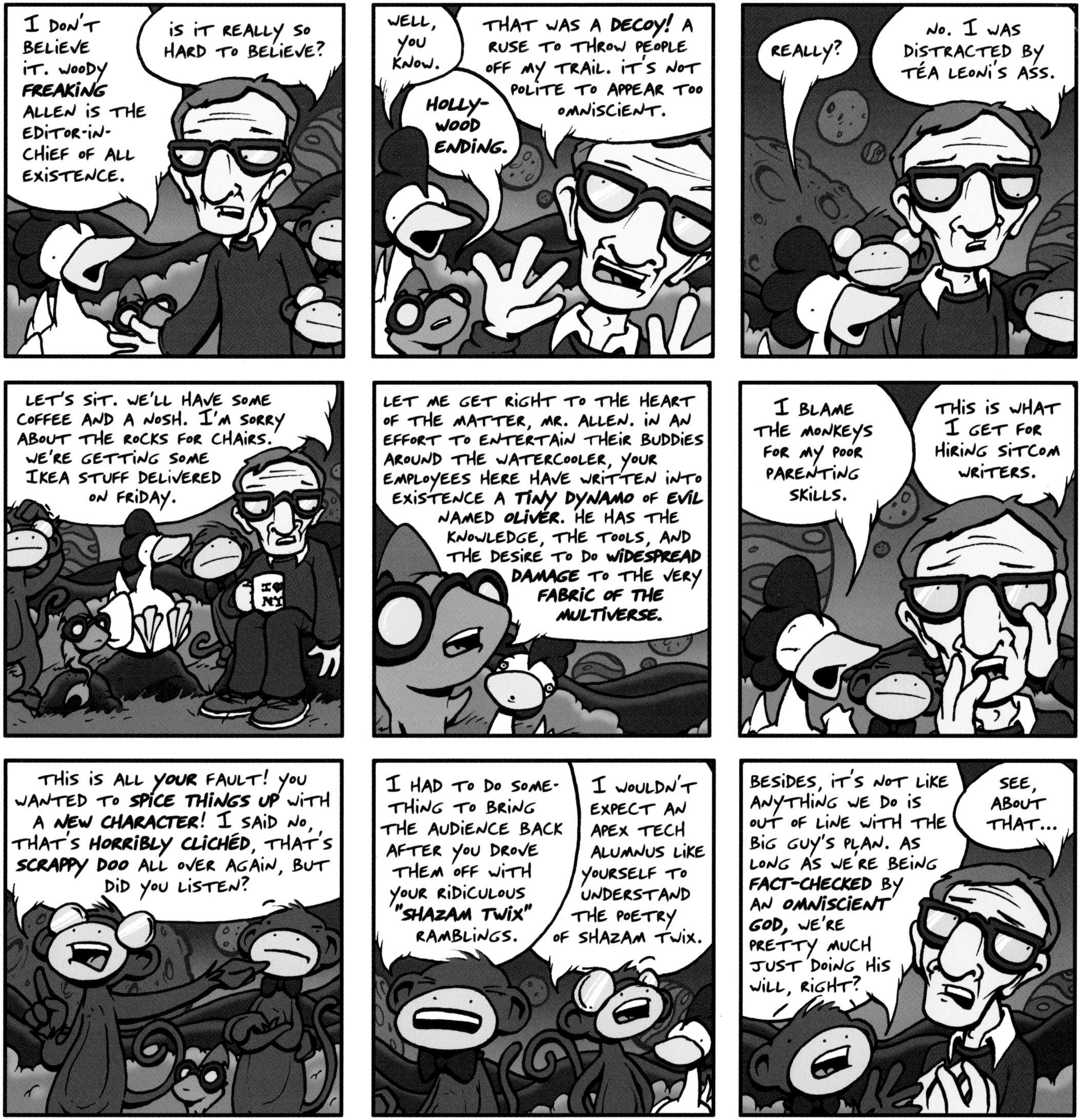
I DON'T BELIEVE IT. WOODY FREAKING ALLEN IS THE EDITOR-IN-CHIEF OF ALL EXISTENCE.
IS IT REALLY SO HARD TO BELIEVE?
WELL, YOU KNOW.
HOLLY-WOOD ENDING.
THAT WAS A DECOY! A RUSE TO THROW PEOPLE OFF MY TRAIL. IT'S NOT POLITE TO APPEAR TOO OMNISCIENT.
REALLY?
NO. I WAS DISTRACTED BY TÉA LEONI'S ASS.
LET'S SIT. WE'LL HAVE SOME COFFEE AND A NOSH. I'M SORRY ABOUT THE ROCKS FOR CHAIRS. WE'RE GETTING SOME IKEA STUFF DELIVERED ON FRIDAY.
I ♥ NY
LET ME GET RIGHT TO THE HEART OF THE MATTER, MR. ALLEN. IN AN EFFORT TO ENTERTAIN THEIR BUDDIES AROUND THE WATERCOOLER, YOUR EMPLOYEES HERE HAVE WRITTEN INTO EXISTENCE A TINY DYNAMO OF EVIL NAMED OLIVER. HE HAS THE KNOWLEDGE, THE TOOLS, AND THE DESIRE TO DO WIDESPREAD DAMAGE TO THE VERY FABRIC OF THE MULTIVERSE.
I BLAME THE MONKEYS FOR MY POOR PARENTING SKILLS.
THIS IS WHAT I GET FOR HIRING SITCOM WRITERS.
THIS IS ALL YOUR FAULT! YOU WANTED TO SPICE THINGS UP WITH A NEW CHARACTER! I SAID NO, THAT'S HORRIBLY CLICHÉD, THAT'S SCRAPPY DOO ALL OVER AGAIN, BUT DID YOU LISTEN?
I HAD TO DO SOME-THING TO BRING THE AUDIENCE BACK AFTER YOU DROVE THEM OFF WITH YOUR RIDICULOUS "SHAZAM TWIX" RAMBLINGS.
I WOULDN'T EXPECT AN APEX TECH ALUMNUS LIKE YOURSELF TO UNDERSTAND THE POETRY OF SHAZAM TWIX.
BESIDES, IT'S NOT LIKE ANYTHING WE DO IS OUT OF LINE WITH THE BIG GUY'S PLAN. AS LONG AS WE'RE BEING FACT-CHECKED BY AN OMNISCIENT GOD, WE'RE PRETTY MUCH JUST DOING HIS WILL, RIGHT?
SEE, ABOUT THAT...

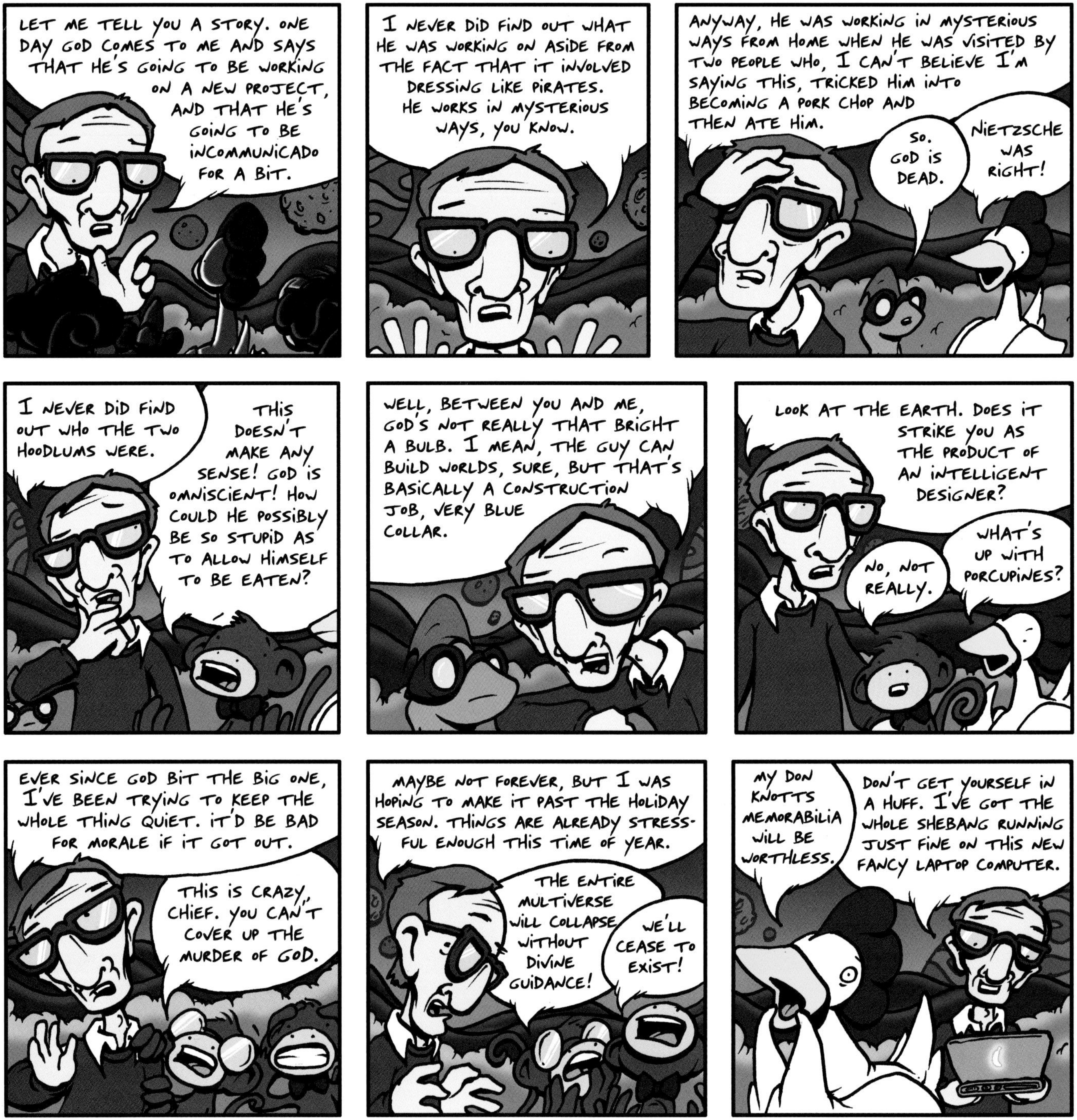
LET ME TELL YOU A STORY. ONE DAY GOD COMES TO ME AND SAYS THAT HE'S GOING TO BE WORKING ON A NEW PROJECT, AND THAT HE'S GOING TO BE INCOMMUNICADO FOR A BIT.
I NEVER DID FIND OUT WHAT HE WAS WORKING ON ASIDE FROM THE FACT THAT IT INVOLVED DRESSING LIKE PIRATES. HE WORKS IN MYSTERIOUS WAYS, YOU KNOW.
ANYWAY, HE WAS WORKING IN MYSTERIOUS WAYS FROM HOME WHEN HE WAS VISITED BY TWO PEOPLE WHO, I CAN'T BELIEVE I'M SAYING THIS, TRICKED HIM INTO BECOMING A PORK CHOP AND THEN ATE HIM.
SO. GOD IS DEAD.
NIETZSCHE WAS RIGHT!
I NEVER DID FIND OUT WHO THE TWO HOODLUMS WERE.
THIS DOESN'T MAKE ANY SENSE! GOD IS OMNISCIENT! HOW COULD HE POSSIBLY BE SO STUPID AS TO ALLOW HIMSELF TO BE EATEN?
WELL, BETWEEN YOU AND ME, GOD'S NOT REALLY THAT BRIGHT A BULB. I MEAN, THE GUY CAN BUILD WORLDS, SURE, BUT THAT'S BASICALLY A CONSTRUCTION JOB, VERY BLUE COLLAR.
LOOK AT THE EARTH. DOES IT STRIKE YOU AS THE PRODUCT OF AN INTELLIGENT DESIGNER?
NO, NOT REALLY.
WHAT'S UP WITH PORCUPINES?
EVER SINCE GOD BIT THE BIG ONE, I'VE BEEN TRYING TO KEEP THE WHOLE THING QUIET. IT'D BE BAD FOR MORALE IF IT GOT OUT.
THIS IS CRAZY, CHIEF. YOU CAN'T COVER UP THE MURDER OF GOD.
MAYBE NOT FOREVER, BUT I WAS HOPING TO MAKE IT PAST THE HOLIDAY SEASON. THINGS ARE ALREADY STRESSFUL ENOUGH THIS TIME OF YEAR.
THE ENTIRE MULTIVERSE WILL COLLAPSE WITHOUT DIVINE GUIDANCE!
WE'LL CEASE TO EXIST!
MY DON KNOTTS MEMORABILIA WILL BE WORTHLESS.
DON'T GET YOURSELF IN A HUFF. I'VE GOT THE WHOLE SHEBANG RUNNING JUST FINE ON THIS NEW FANCY LAPTOP COMPUTER.

WE MAY HAVE BEEN A MOTE IN GOD'S EYE BEFORE, BUT NOW WE'RE RUNNING ON **THIS BABY.** THE STOCK MARKETS OF SEVENTEEN DIFFERENT VERSIONS OF EARTH ARE TIED DIRECTLY TO MY HIGH SCORE IN MINESWEEPER.

YOU'RE RUNNING THE INFINITE MULTIDIMENSIONAL WHOLE OF EXISTENCE ON A NOTEBOOK COMPUTER?

I OUTSOURCED THE WHOLE THING TO THIS VERY NICE RED FELLOW WITH A TEAM OF A DOZEN DEAD ANCIENT MAYAN PROGRAMMERS.

THEN OLIVER MUST BE IN THERE SOMEWHERE. I'M GOING TO NEED YOU TO **JACK ME ON TO THE MULTIVERSE.**

LOOK MISTER, I DON'T KNOW WHAT YOU'VE READ ABOUT ME, BUT I DON'T DO THAT SORT OF THING WITH ANIMALS.

WHAT TIPPED YOU OFF THAT THE MONKEYS CREATED OLIVER?

JUST A HUNCH. NO ONE THAT CLICHÉD COULD EXIST IN REAL LIFE.

I THOUGHT THEY SAID THEY COULDN'T ACTUALLY CREATE ANYTHING, THOUGH.

NOTHING BIGGER THAN A POTATO. OLIVER IS THREE PERCENT SMALLER BY VOLUME THAN YOUR AVERAGE IDAHO TATER.

IF I'M NOT REALLY OLIVER'S FATHER WE'RE GOING TO HAVE TO RECONSIDER HIS ALLOWANCE.

RECONSIDER IT TO **ZERO.** I MAY HAVE TO KILL HIM.

LOOK, I MAY ONLY BE OLIVER'S FATHER BY PROXY, BUT I DON'T WANT TO SEE HIM **MURDERED.** NOT BY SOMEONE BESIDES ME, ANYWAY.

IT'S THE **ONLY** WAY.

THE ASSITANT EDITORS JUICED UP OLIVER WITH **UNNATURAL LEVELS** OF **AMBITION** AND **TECHNICAL EXPERTISE** IN THEIR PURSUIT TO CREATE A SORT OF COMPELLING REAL-LIFE THIRD-SEASON CAST REPLACEMENT. BUT THEY WENT **TOO FAR.**

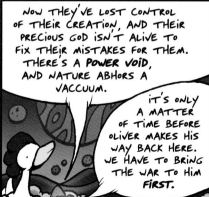

NOW THEY'VE LOST CONTROL OF THEIR CREATION, AND THEIR PRECIOUS GOD ISN'T ALIVE TO FIX THEIR MISTAKES FOR THEM. THERE'S A **POWER VOID,** AND NATURE ABHORS A VACCUUM.

IT'S ONLY A MATTER OF TIME BEFORE OLIVER MAKES HIS WAY BACK HERE. WE HAVE TO BRING THE WAR TO HIM **FIRST.**

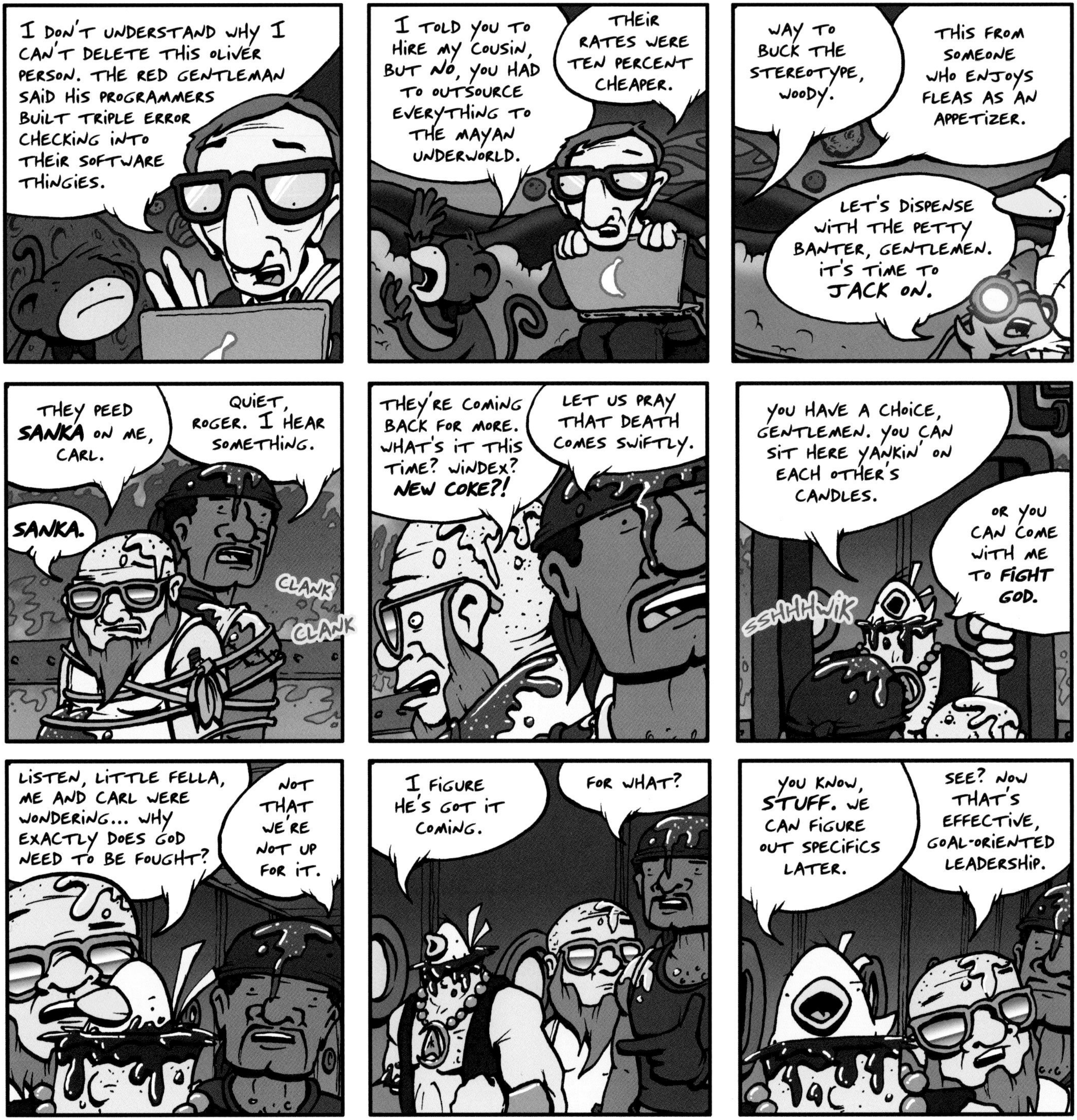

I DON'T UNDERSTAND WHY I CAN'T DELETE THIS OLIVER PERSON. THE RED GENTLEMAN SAID HIS PROGRAMMERS BUILT TRIPLE ERROR CHECKING INTO THEIR SOFTWARE THINGIES.
I TOLD YOU TO HIRE MY COUSIN, BUT NO, YOU HAD TO OUTSOURCE EVERYTHING TO THE MAYAN UNDERWORLD.
THEIR RATES WERE TEN PERCENT CHEAPER.
WAY TO BUCK THE STEREOTYPE, WOODY.
THIS FROM SOMEONE WHO ENJOYS FLEAS AS AN APPETIZER.
LET'S DISPENSE WITH THE PETTY BANTER, GENTLEMEN. IT'S TIME TO JACK ON.
THEY PEED SANKA ON ME, CARL.
QUIET, ROGER. I HEAR SOMETHING.
SANKA.
CLANK
CLANK
THEY'RE COMING BACK FOR MORE. WHAT'S IT THIS TIME? WINDEX? NEW COKE?!
LET US PRAY THAT DEATH COMES SWIFTLY.
YOU HAVE A CHOICE, GENTLEMEN. YOU CAN SIT HERE YANKIN' ON EACH OTHER'S CANDLES.
SSHHHHWIK
OR YOU CAN COME WITH ME TO FIGHT GOD.
LISTEN, LITTLE FELLA, ME AND CARL WERE WONDERING... WHY EXACTLY DOES GOD NEED TO BE FOUGHT?
NOT THAT WE'RE NOT UP FOR IT.
I FIGURE HE'S GOT IT COMING.
FOR WHAT?
YOU KNOW, STUFF. WE CAN FIGURE OUT SPECIFICS LATER.
SEE? NOW THAT'S EFFECTIVE, GOAL-ORIENTED LEADERSHIP.

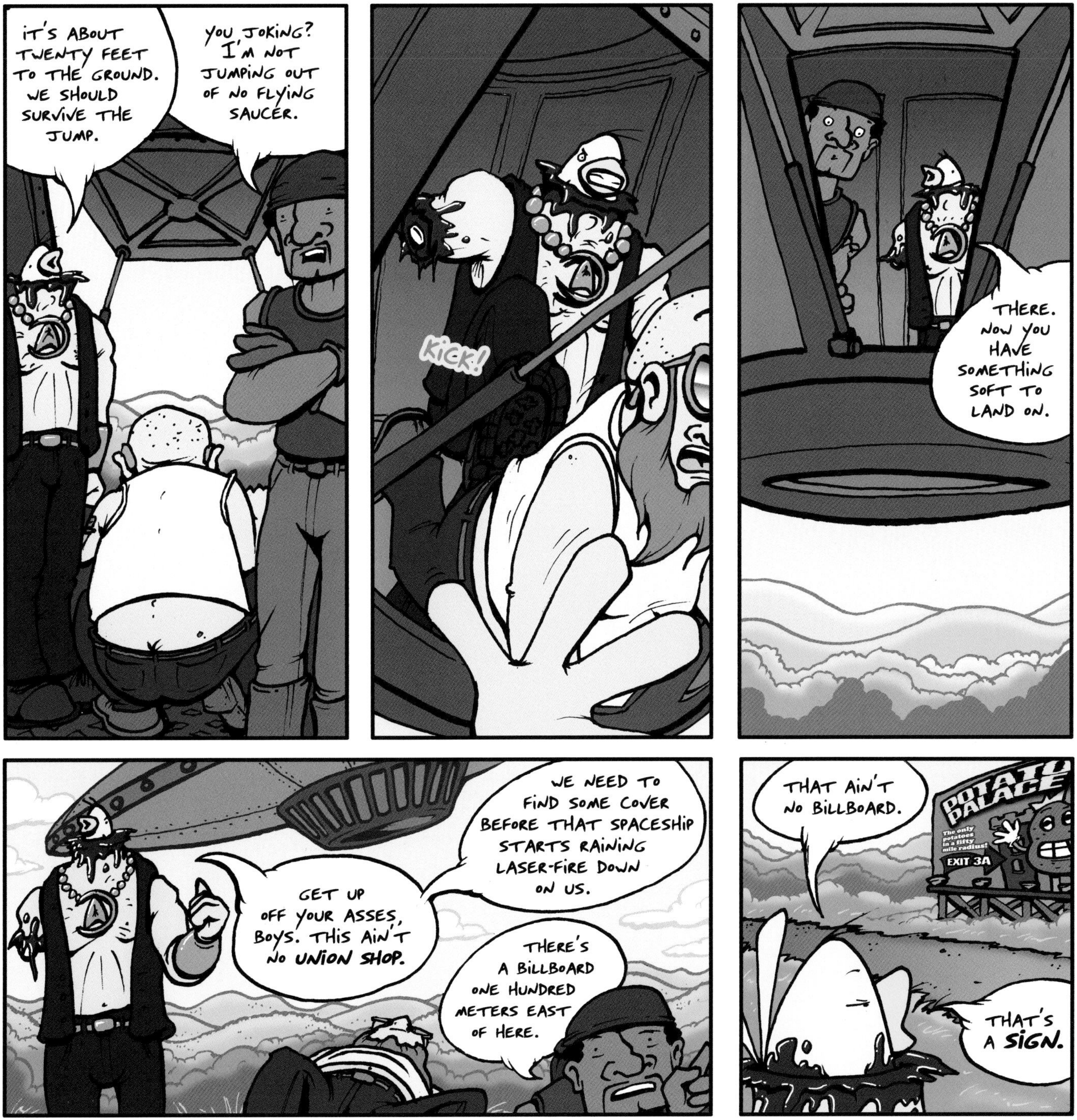
IT'S ABOUT TWENTY FEET TO THE GROUND. WE SHOULD SURVIVE THE JUMP.
YOU JOKING? I'M NOT JUMPING OUT OF NO FLYING SAUCER.
KICK!
THERE. NOW YOU HAVE SOMETHING SOFT TO LAND ON.
GET UP OFF YOUR ASSES, BOYS. THIS AIN'T NO UNION SHOP.
WE NEED TO FIND SOME COVER BEFORE THAT SPACESHIP STARTS RAINING LASER-FIRE DOWN ON US.
THERE'S A BILLBOARD ONE HUNDRED METERS EAST OF HERE.
THAT AIN'T NO BILLBOARD.
POTATO PALACE
The only potatoes in a fifty mile radius!
EXIT 3A
THAT'S A SIGN.

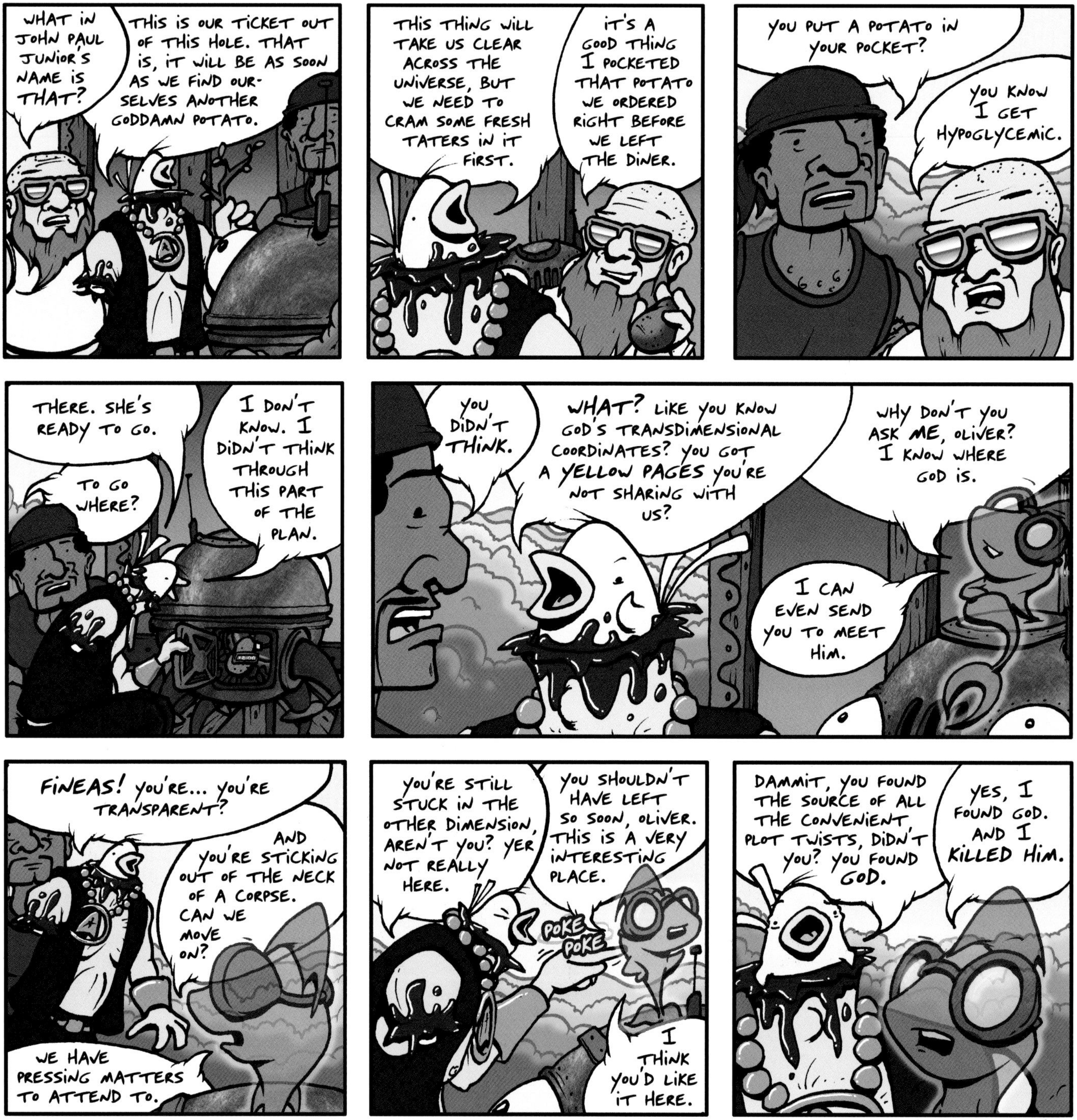
WHAT IN JOHN PAUL JUNIOR'S NAME IS THAT?
THIS IS OUR TICKET OUT OF THIS HOLE. THAT IS, IT WILL BE AS SOON AS WE FIND OURSELVES ANOTHER GODDAMN POTATO.
THIS THING WILL TAKE US CLEAR ACROSS THE UNIVERSE, BUT WE NEED TO CRAM SOME FRESH TATERS IN IT FIRST.
IT'S A GOOD THING I POCKETED THAT POTATO WE ORDERED RIGHT BEFORE WE LEFT THE DINER.
YOU PUT A POTATO IN YOUR POCKET?
YOU KNOW I GET HYPOGLYCEMIC.
THERE. SHE'S READY TO GO.
TO GO WHERE?
I DON'T KNOW. I DIDN'T THINK THROUGH THIS PART OF THE PLAN.
YOU DIDN'T THINK.
WHAT? LIKE YOU KNOW GOD'S TRANSDIMENSIONAL COORDINATES? YOU GOT A YELLOW PAGES YOU'RE NOT SHARING WITH US?
WHY DON'T YOU ASK ME, OLIVER? I KNOW WHERE GOD IS.
I CAN EVEN SEND YOU TO MEET HIM.
FINEAS! YOU'RE... YOU'RE TRANSPARENT?
AND YOU'RE STICKING OUT OF THE NECK OF A CORPSE. CAN WE MOVE ON?
WE HAVE PRESSING MATTERS TO ATTEND TO.
YOU'RE STILL STUCK IN THE OTHER DIMENSION, AREN'T YOU? YER NOT REALLY HERE.
YOU SHOULDN'T HAVE LEFT SO SOON, OLIVER. THIS IS A VERY INTERESTING PLACE.
POKE
POKE
I THINK YOU'D LIKE IT HERE.
DAMMIT, YOU FOUND THE SOURCE OF ALL THE CONVENIENT PLOT TWISTS, DIDN'T YOU? YOU FOUND GOD.
YES, I FOUND GOD. AND I KILLED HIM.

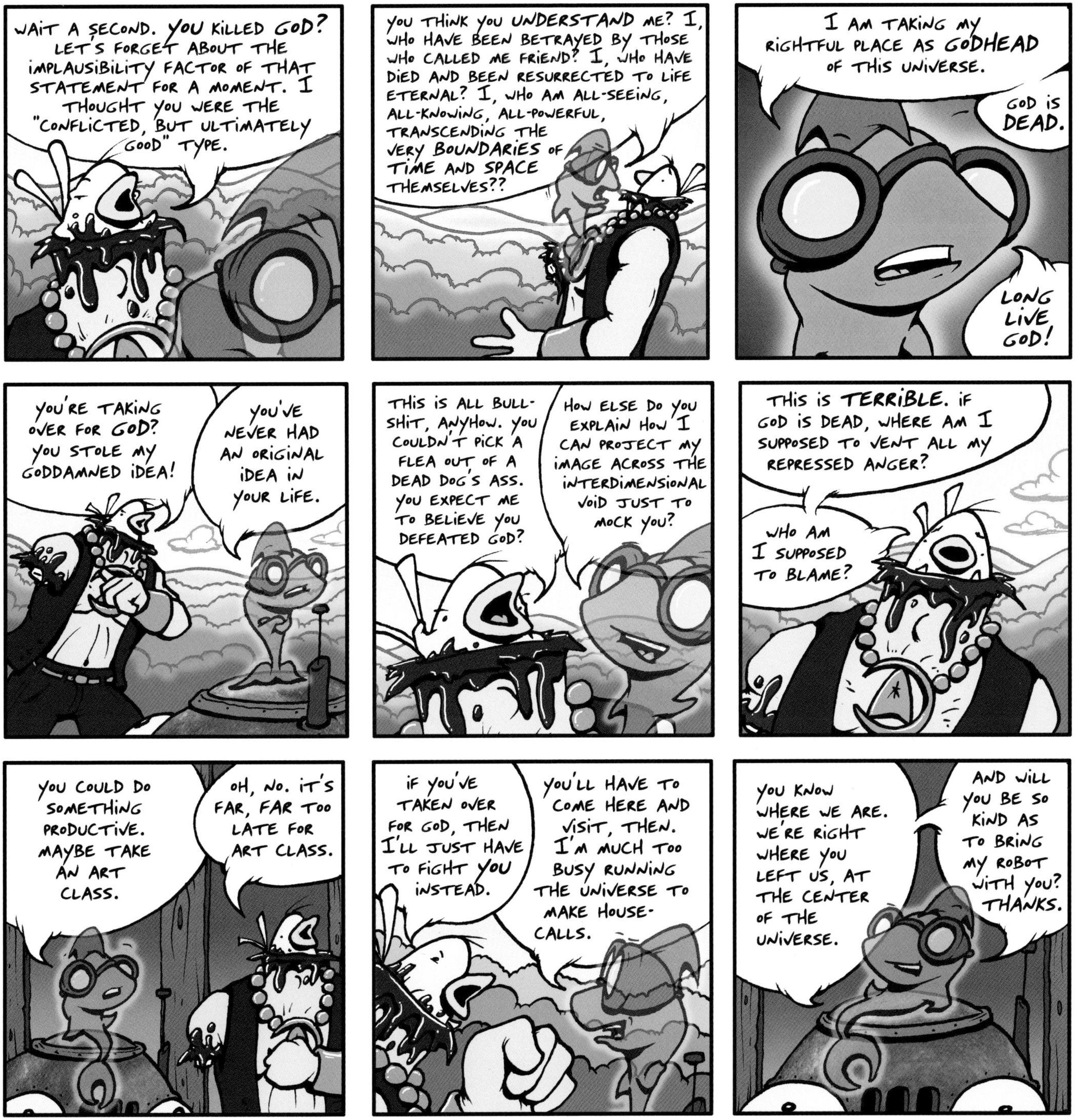
WAIT A SECOND. YOU KILLED GOD? LET'S FORGET ABOUT THE IMPLAUSIBILITY FACTOR OF THAT STATEMENT FOR A MOMENT. I THOUGHT YOU WERE THE "CONFLICTED, BUT ULTIMATELY GOOD" TYPE.
YOU THINK YOU UNDERSTAND ME? I, WHO HAVE BEEN BETRAYED BY THOSE WHO CALLED ME FRIEND? I, WHO HAVE DIED AND BEEN RESURRECTED TO LIFE ETERNAL? I, WHO AM ALL-SEEING, ALL-KNOWING, ALL-POWERFUL, TRANSCENDING THE VERY BOUNDARIES OF TIME AND SPACE THEMSELVES??
I AM TAKING MY RIGHTFUL PLACE AS GODHEAD OF THIS UNIVERSE.
GOD IS DEAD.
LONG LIVE GOD!
YOU'RE TAKING OVER FOR GOD? YOU STOLE MY GODDAMNED IDEA!
YOU'VE NEVER HAD AN ORIGINAL IDEA IN YOUR LIFE.
THIS IS ALL BULLSHIT, ANYHOW. YOU COULDN'T PICK A FLEA OUT OF A DEAD DOG'S ASS. YOU EXPECT ME TO BELIEVE YOU DEFEATED GOD?
HOW ELSE DO YOU EXPLAIN HOW I CAN PROJECT MY IMAGE ACROSS THE INTERDIMENSIONAL VOID JUST TO MOCK YOU?
THIS IS TERRIBLE. IF GOD IS DEAD, WHERE AM I SUPPOSED TO VENT ALL MY REPRESSED ANGER?
WHO AM I SUPPOSED TO BLAME?
YOU COULD DO SOMETHING PRODUCTIVE. MAYBE TAKE AN ART CLASS.
OH, NO. IT'S FAR, FAR TOO LATE FOR ART CLASS.
IF YOU'VE TAKEN OVER FOR GOD, THEN I'LL JUST HAVE TO FIGHT YOU INSTEAD.
YOU'LL HAVE TO COME HERE AND VISIT, THEN. I'M MUCH TOO BUSY RUNNING THE UNIVERSE TO MAKE HOUSE-CALLS.
YOU KNOW WHERE WE ARE. WE'RE RIGHT WHERE YOU LEFT US, AT THE CENTER OF THE UNIVERSE.
AND WILL YOU BE SO KIND AS TO BRING MY ROBOT WITH YOU? THANKS.

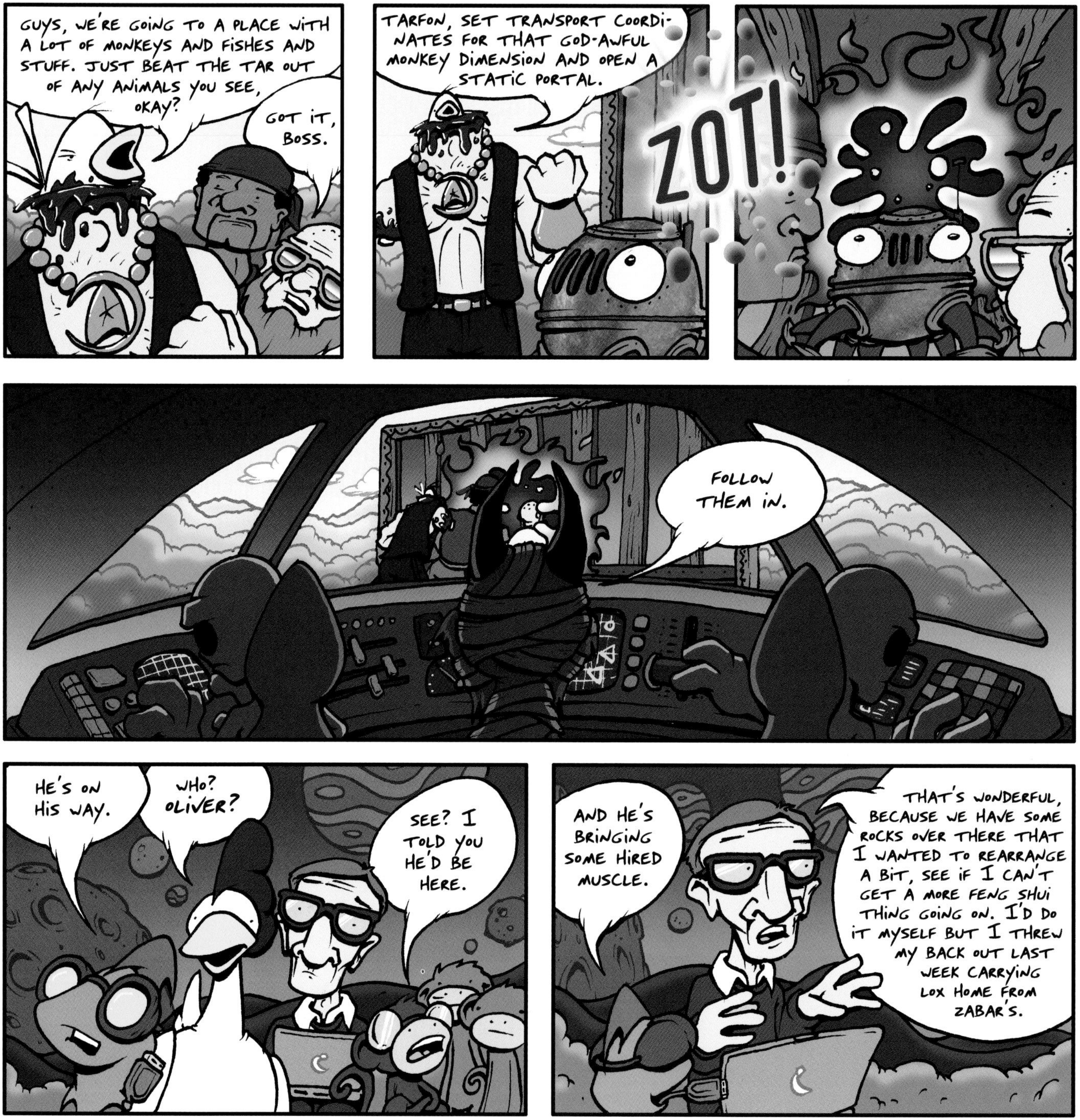
GUYS, WE'RE GOING TO A PLACE WITH A LOT OF MONKEYS AND FISHES AND STUFF. JUST BEAT THE TAR OUT OF ANY ANIMALS YOU SEE, OKAY?
GOT IT, BOSS.
TARFON, SET TRANSPORT COORDINATES FOR THAT GOD-AWFUL MONKEY DIMENSION AND OPEN A STATIC PORTAL.
ZOT!
FOLLOW THEM IN.
HE'S ON HIS WAY.
WHO? OLIVER?
SEE? I TOLD YOU HE'D BE HERE.
AND HE'S BRINGING SOME HIRED MUSCLE.
THAT'S WONDERFUL, BECAUSE WE HAVE SOME ROCKS OVER THERE THAT I WANTED TO REARRANGE A BIT, SEE IF I CAN'T GET A MORE FENG SHUI THING GOING ON. I'D DO IT MYSELF BUT I THREW MY BACK OUT LAST WEEK CARRYING LOX HOME FROM ZABAR'S.

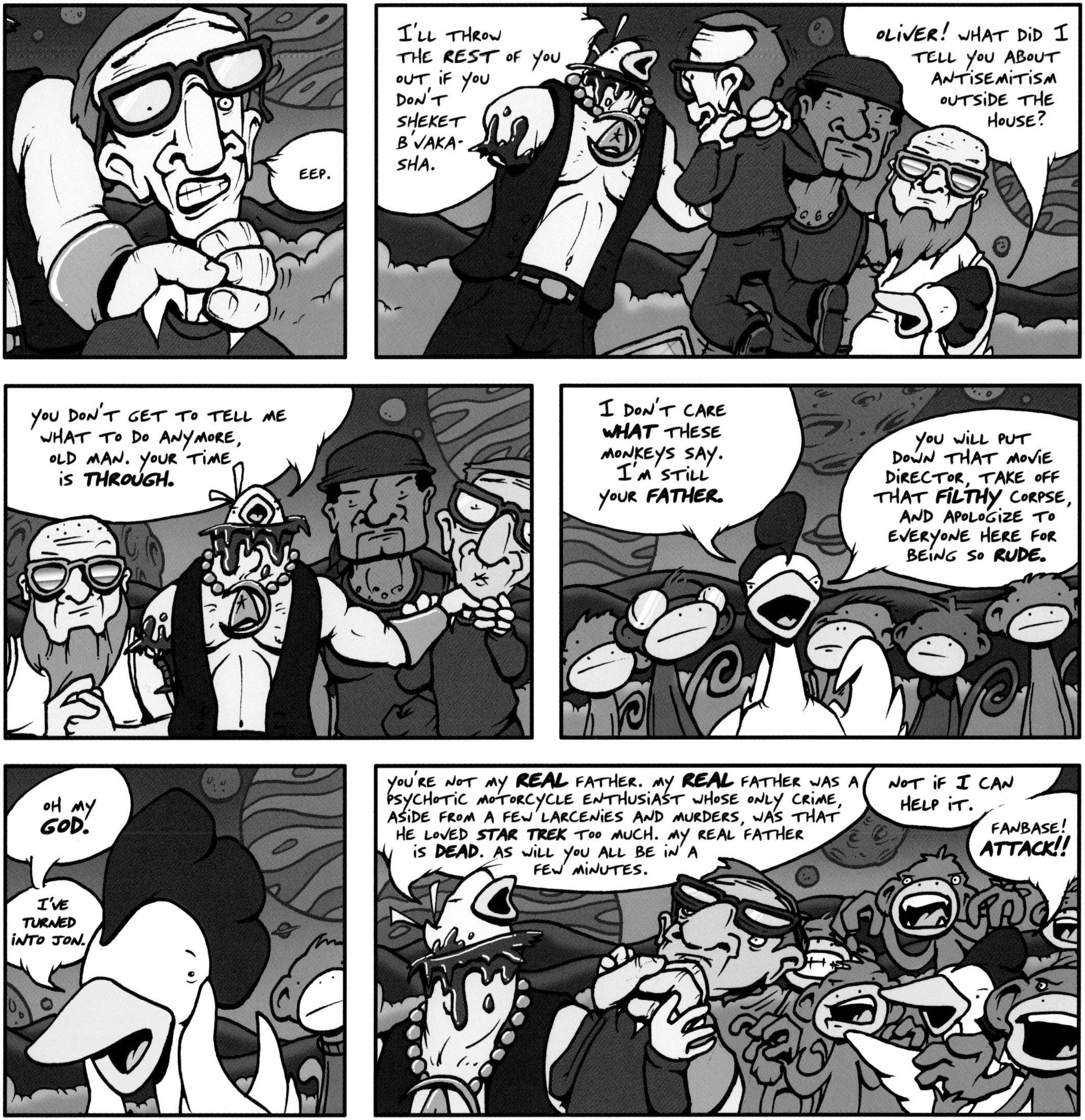
EEP.
I'LL THROW THE REST OF YOU OUT IF YOU DON'T SHEKET B'VAKA-SHA.
OLIVER! WHAT DID I TELL YOU ABOUT ANTISEMITISM OUTSIDE THE HOUSE?
YOU DON'T GET TO TELL ME WHAT TO DO ANYMORE, OLD MAN. YOUR TIME IS THROUGH.
I DON'T CARE WHAT THESE MONKEYS SAY. I'M STILL YOUR FATHER.
YOU WILL PUT DOWN THAT MOVIE DIRECTOR, TAKE OFF THAT FILTHY CORPSE, AND APOLOGIZE TO EVERYONE HERE FOR BEING SO RUDE.
OH MY GOD.
I'VE TURNED INTO JON.
YOU'RE NOT MY REAL FATHER. MY REAL FATHER WAS A PSYCHOTIC MOTORCYCLE ENTHUSIAST WHOSE ONLY CRIME, ASIDE FROM A FEW LARCENIES AND MURDERS, WAS THAT HE LOVED STAR TREK TOO MUCH. MY REAL FATHER IS DEAD. AS WILL YOU ALL BE IN A FEW MINUTES.
NOT IF I CAN HELP IT.
FANBASE! ATTACK!!

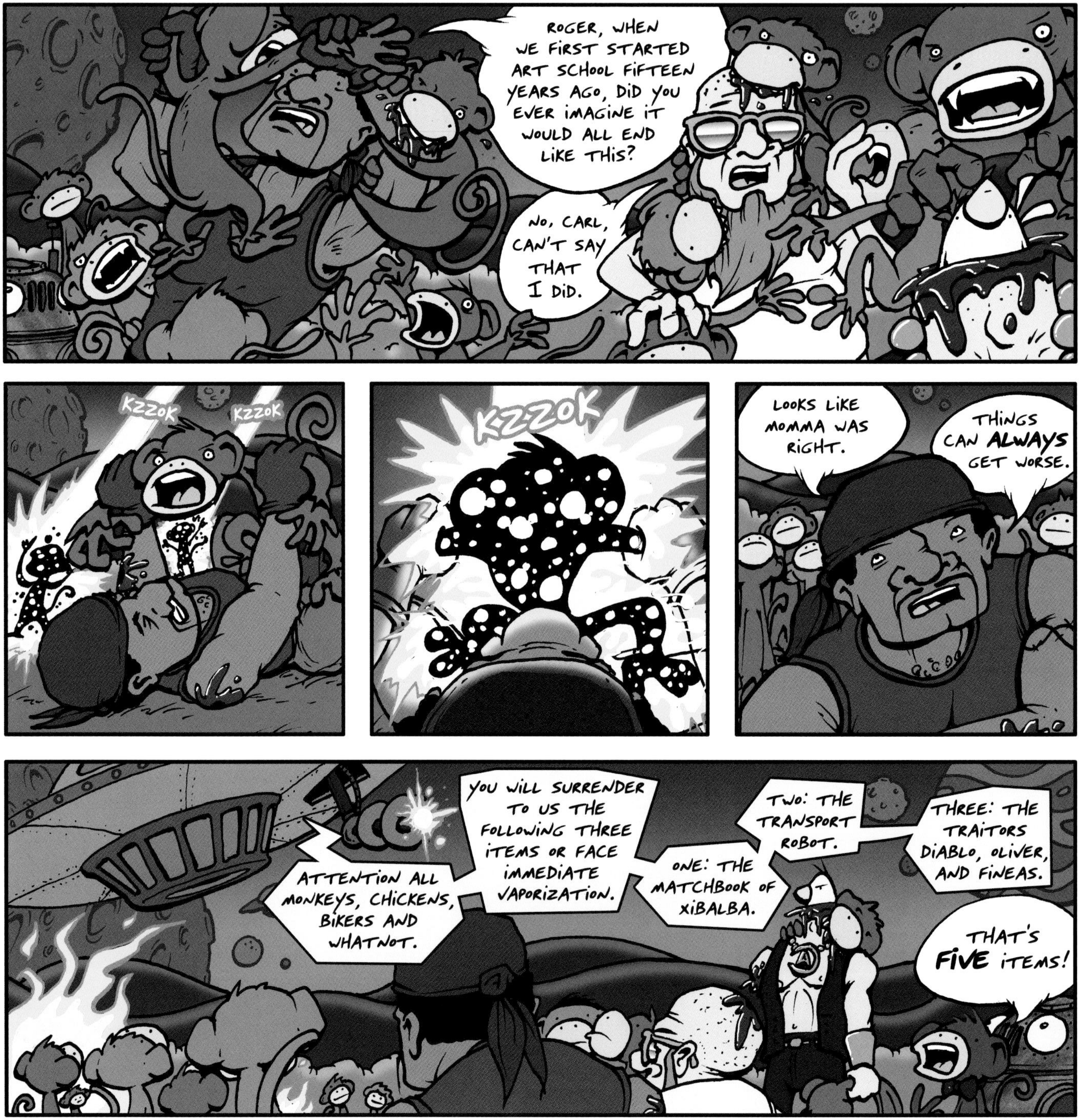
ROGER, WHEN WE FIRST STARTED ART SCHOOL FIFTEEN YEARS AGO, DID YOU EVER IMAGINE IT WOULD ALL END LIKE THIS?
NO, CARL, CAN'T SAY THAT I DID.
KZZOK
KZZOK
KZZOK
LOOKS LIKE MOMMA WAS RIGHT.
THINGS CAN **ALWAYS** GET WORSE.
ATTENTION ALL MONKEYS, CHICKENS, BIKERS AND WHATNOT.
YOU WILL SURRENDER TO US THE FOLLOWING THREE ITEMS OR FACE IMMEDIATE VAPORIZATION.
ONE: THE MATCHBOOK OF XIBALBA.
TWO: THE TRANSPORT ROBOT.
THREE: THE TRAITORS DIABLO, OLIVER, AND FINEAS.
THAT'S **FIVE** ITEMS!

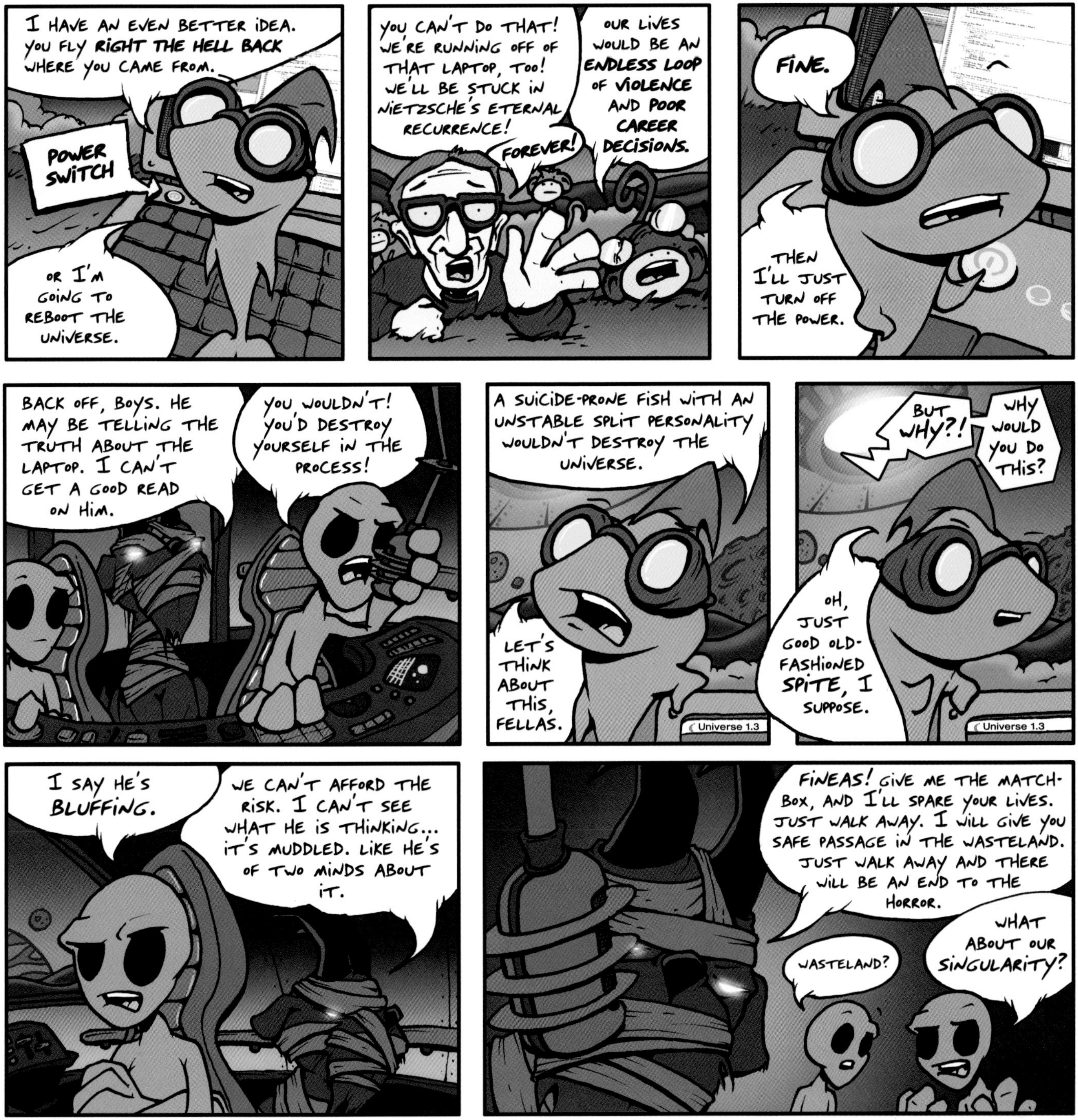
I HAVE AN EVEN BETTER IDEA. YOU FLY RIGHT THE HELL BACK WHERE YOU CAME FROM.
POWER SWITCH
OR I'M GOING TO REBOOT THE UNIVERSE.
YOU CAN'T DO THAT! WE'RE RUNNING OFF OF THAT LAPTOP, TOO! WE'LL BE STUCK IN NIETZSCHE'S ETERNAL RECURRENCE!
FOREVER!
OUR LIVES WOULD BE AN ENDLESS LOOP OF VIOLENCE AND POOR CAREER DECISIONS.
FINE.
THEN I'LL JUST TURN OFF THE POWER.
BACK OFF, BOYS. HE MAY BE TELLING THE TRUTH ABOUT THE LAPTOP. I CAN'T GET A GOOD READ ON HIM.
YOU WOULDN'T! YOU'D DESTROY YOURSELF IN THE PROCESS!
A SUICIDE-PRONE FISH WITH AN UNSTABLE SPLIT PERSONALITY WOULDN'T DESTROY THE UNIVERSE.
LET'S THINK ABOUT THIS, FELLAS.
Universe 1.3
BUT WHY?!
WHY WOULD YOU DO THIS?
OH, JUST GOOD OLD-FASHIONED SPITE, I SUPPOSE.
Universe 1.3
I SAY HE'S BLUFFING.
WE CAN'T AFFORD THE RISK. I CAN'T SEE WHAT HE IS THINKING... IT'S MUDDLED. LIKE HE'S OF TWO MINDS ABOUT IT.
FINEAS! GIVE ME THE MATCH-BOX, AND I'LL SPARE YOUR LIVES. JUST WALK AWAY. I WILL GIVE YOU SAFE PASSAGE IN THE WASTELAND. JUST WALK AWAY AND THERE WILL BE AN END TO THE HORROR.
WASTELAND?
WHAT ABOUT OUR SINGULARITY?

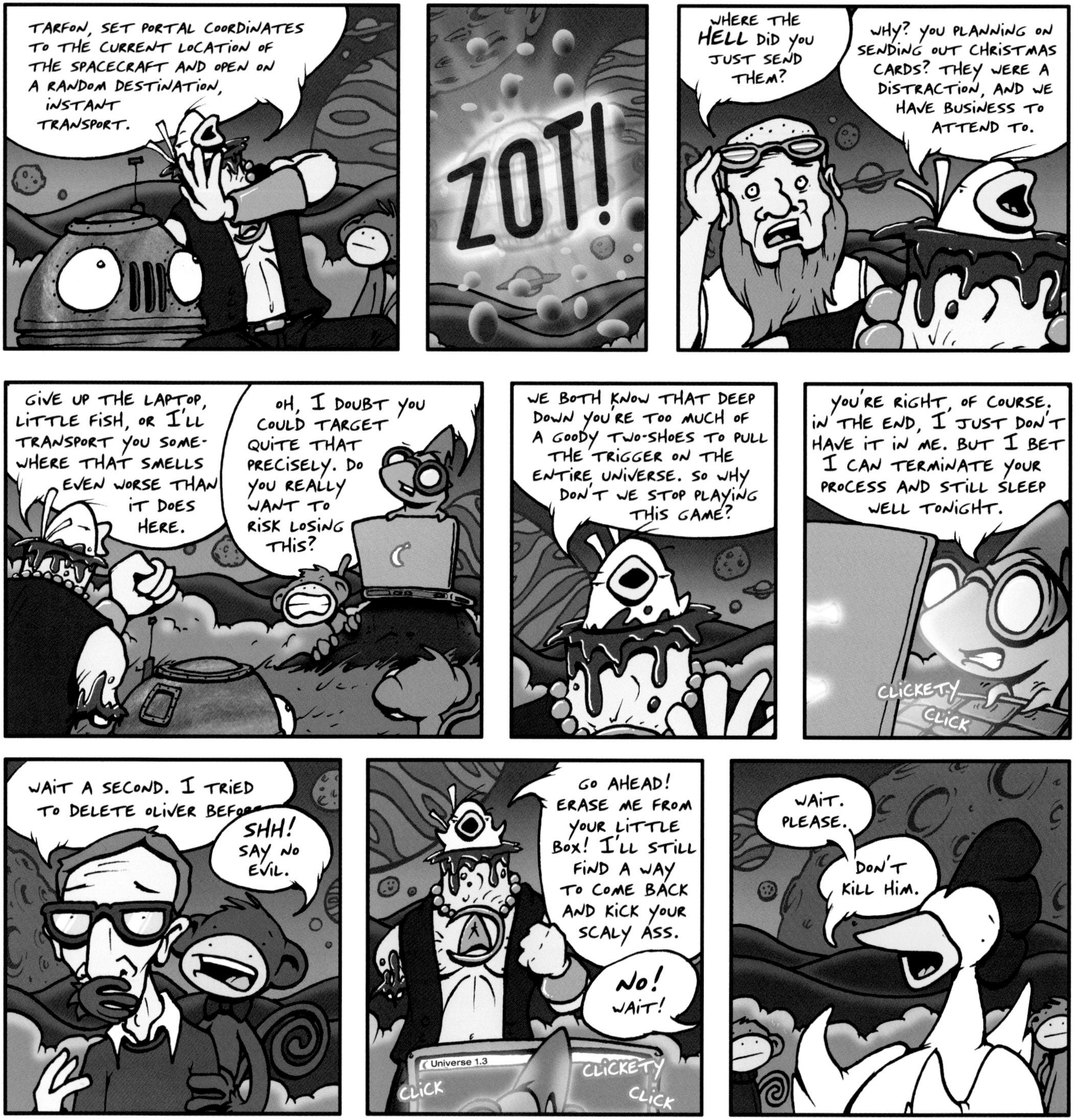
TARFON, SET PORTAL COORDINATES TO THE CURRENT LOCATION OF THE SPACECRAFT AND OPEN ON A RANDOM DESTINATION, INSTANT TRANSPORT.
ZOT!
WHERE THE HELL DID YOU JUST SEND THEM?
WHY? YOU PLANNING ON SENDING OUT CHRISTMAS CARDS? THEY WERE A DISTRACTION, AND WE HAVE BUSINESS TO ATTEND TO.
GIVE UP THE LAPTOP, LITTLE FISH, OR I'LL TRANSPORT YOU SOME-WHERE THAT SMELLS EVEN WORSE THAN IT DOES HERE.
OH, I DOUBT YOU COULD TARGET QUITE THAT PRECISELY. DO YOU REALLY WANT TO RISK LOSING THIS?
WE BOTH KNOW THAT DEEP DOWN YOU'RE TOO MUCH OF A GOODY TWO-SHOES TO PULL THE TRIGGER ON THE ENTIRE UNIVERSE. SO WHY DON'T WE STOP PLAYING THIS GAME?
YOU'RE RIGHT, OF COURSE. IN THE END, I JUST DON'T HAVE IT IN ME. BUT I BET I CAN TERMINATE YOUR PROCESS AND STILL SLEEP WELL TONIGHT.
CLICKETY CLICK
WAIT A SECOND. I TRIED TO DELETE OLIVER BEFO
SHH! SAY NO EVIL.
GO AHEAD! ERASE ME FROM YOUR LITTLE BOX! I'LL STILL FIND A WAY TO COME BACK AND KICK YOUR SCALY ASS.
NO! WAIT!
Universe 1.3
CLICK
CLICKETY CLICK
WAIT. PLEASE.
DON'T KILL HIM.

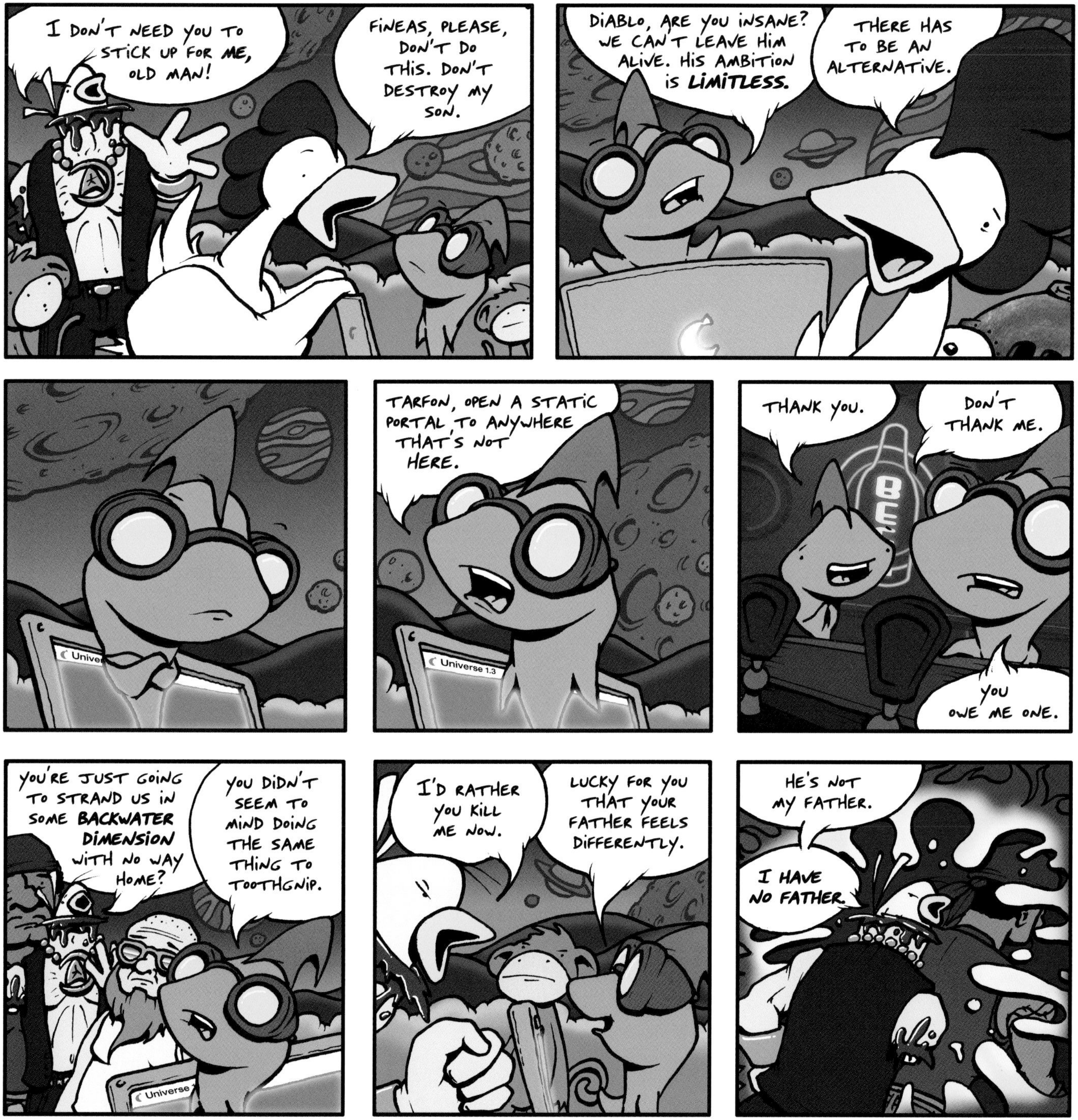
I DON'T NEED YOU TO STICK UP FOR ME, OLD MAN!
FINEAS, PLEASE, DON'T DO THIS. DON'T DESTROY MY SON.
DIABLO, ARE YOU INSANE? WE CAN'T LEAVE HIM ALIVE. HIS AMBITION IS LIMITLESS.
THERE HAS TO BE AN ALTERNATIVE.
Universe
TARFON, OPEN A STATIC PORTAL TO ANYWHERE THAT'S NOT HERE.
Universe 1.3
THANK YOU.
DON'T THANK ME.
YOU OWE ME ONE.
YOU'RE JUST GOING TO STRAND US IN SOME BACKWATER DIMENSION WITH NO WAY HOME?
YOU DIDN'T SEEM TO MIND DOING THE SAME THING TO TOOTHGNIP.
Universe
I'D RATHER YOU KILL ME NOW.
LUCKY FOR YOU THAT YOUR FATHER FEELS DIFFERENTLY.
HE'S NOT MY FATHER.
I HAVE NO FATHER.

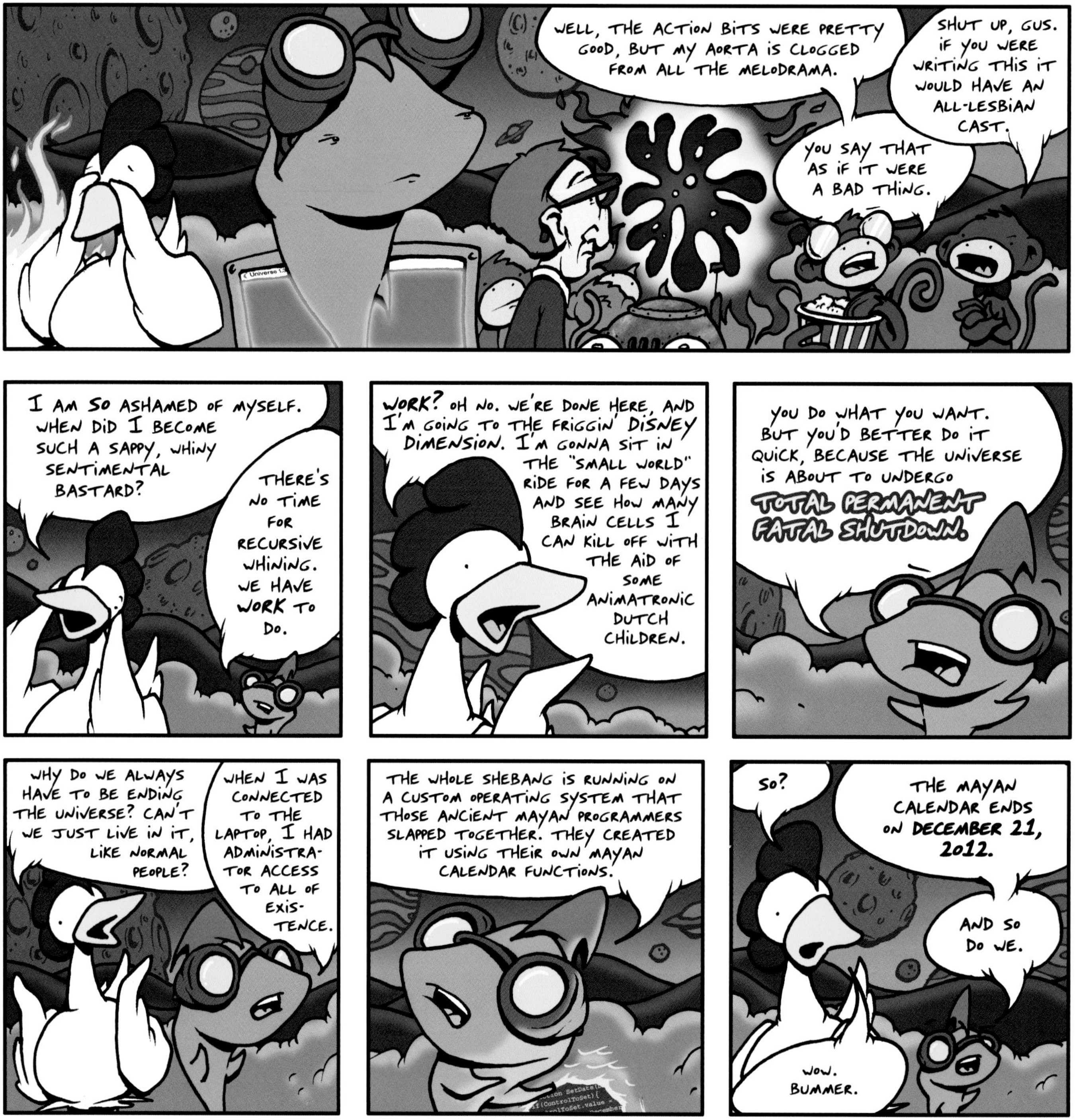
WELL, THE ACTION BITS WERE PRETTY GOOD, BUT MY AORTA IS CLOGGED FROM ALL THE MELODRAMA.
SHUT UP, GUS. IF YOU WERE WRITING THIS IT WOULD HAVE AN ALL-LESBIAN CAST.
YOU SAY THAT AS IF IT WERE A BAD THING.
I AM SO ASHAMED OF MYSELF. WHEN DID I BECOME SUCH A SAPPY, WHINY SENTIMENTAL BASTARD?
THERE'S NO TIME FOR RECURSIVE WHINING. WE HAVE WORK TO DO.
WORK? OH NO. WE'RE DONE HERE, AND I'M GOING TO THE FRIGGIN' DISNEY DIMENSION. I'M GONNA SIT IN THE "SMALL WORLD" RIDE FOR A FEW DAYS AND SEE HOW MANY BRAIN CELLS I CAN KILL OFF WITH THE AID OF SOME ANIMATRONIC DUTCH CHILDREN.
YOU DO WHAT YOU WANT. BUT YOU'D BETTER DO IT QUICK, BECAUSE THE UNIVERSE IS ABOUT TO UNDERGO TOTAL PERMANENT FATAL SHUTDOWN.
WHY DO WE ALWAYS HAVE TO BE ENDING THE UNIVERSE? CAN'T WE JUST LIVE IN IT, LIKE NORMAL PEOPLE?
WHEN I WAS CONNECTED TO THE LAPTOP, I HAD ADMINISTRATOR ACCESS TO ALL OF EXISTENCE.
THE WHOLE SHEBANG IS RUNNING ON A CUSTOM OPERATING SYSTEM THAT THOSE ANCIENT MAYAN PROGRAMMERS SLAPPED TOGETHER. THEY CREATED IT USING THEIR OWN MAYAN CALENDAR FUNCTIONS.
SO?
THE MAYAN CALENDAR ENDS ON DECEMBER 21, 2012.
AND SO DO WE.
WOW. BUMMER.

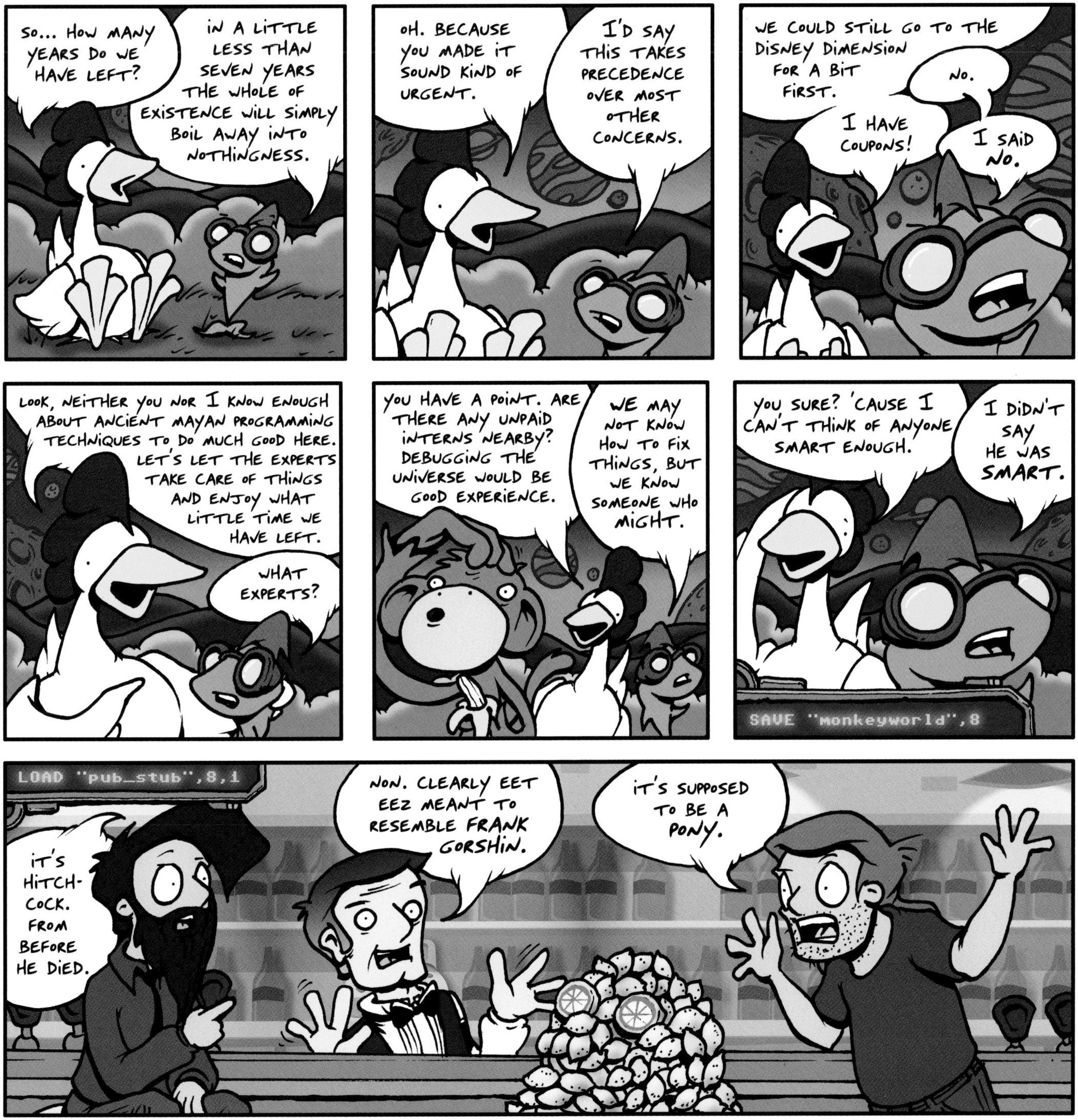
SO... HOW MANY YEARS DO WE HAVE LEFT?
IN A LITTLE LESS THAN SEVEN YEARS THE WHOLE OF EXISTENCE WILL SIMPLY BOIL AWAY INTO NOTHINGNESS.
OH. BECAUSE YOU MADE IT SOUND KIND OF URGENT.
I'D SAY THIS TAKES PRECEDENCE OVER MOST OTHER CONCERNS.
WE COULD STILL GO TO THE DISNEY DIMENSION FOR A BIT FIRST.
NO.
I HAVE COUPONS!
I SAID NO.
LOOK, NEITHER YOU NOR I KNOW ENOUGH ABOUT ANCIENT MAYAN PROGRAMMING TECHNIQUES TO DO MUCH GOOD HERE. LET'S LET THE EXPERTS TAKE CARE OF THINGS AND ENJOY WHAT LITTLE TIME WE HAVE LEFT.
WHAT EXPERTS?
YOU HAVE A POINT. ARE THERE ANY UNPAID INTERNS NEARBY? DEBUGGING THE UNIVERSE WOULD BE GOOD EXPERIENCE.
WE MAY NOT KNOW HOW TO FIX THINGS, BUT WE KNOW SOMEONE WHO MIGHT.
YOU SURE? 'CAUSE I CAN'T THINK OF ANYONE SMART ENOUGH.
I DIDN'T SAY HE WAS SMART.
SAVE "monkeyworld",8
LOAD "pub_stub",8,1
IT'S HITCH-COCK. FROM BEFORE HE DIED.
NON. CLEARLY EET EEZ MEANT TO RESEMBLE FRANK GORSHIN.
IT'S SUPPOSED TO BE A PONY.

Jonathan Rosenberg was born on November 27th, 1973. He tries not to think too much about his childhood. Rosenberg's hobbies include awkward social encounters, drinking, and procrastination.

Professionally, Rosenberg has slung beef at a Burger King, filed dead trees at a super-computing facility, harangued hundreds as a telemarketer, received karmic retribution as Receiver of Complaints for an HVAC repair company, accomplished little of conse-quence as a game designer, and taught himself to draw comics while pretending to excel at several consecutive bullshit internet jobs.

Today Rosenberg lives with his wife and daughter in Westchester, NY, where he is a full-time honest-to-gosh internet cartoonist and founder of TEAM FORCE ALPHA, an elite team-based secret force that answers to no government and kicks ass wherever necessary.

You can see more of Rosenberg's work at goats.com.

and the adventure continues...

goats
the corndog imperative
jonathan rosenberg

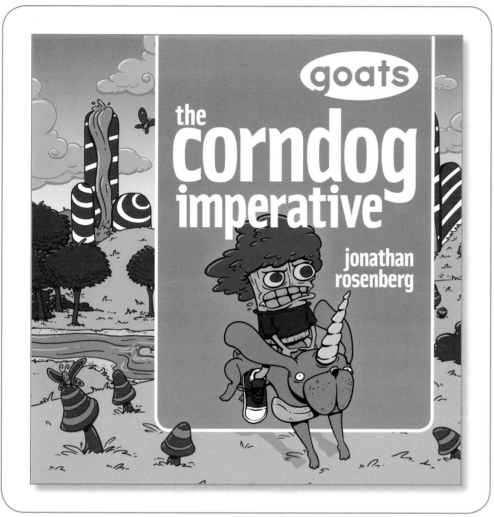